Mass Media
and Elections

Mass Media and Elections

Richard Joslyn
Temple University

Random House New York

Library of Congress Cataloging in Publication Data

Joslyn, Richard A.
  Mass media and elections.

  Includes index.
  1. Advertising, Political.   2. Press and politics.
3. Electioneering.   4. Voting.   1. Title.
JF2112.A4J67   1984   324.7′3′0973   83-26632
ISBN 0-394-34949-0

First Edition

98765

Manufactured in the United States of America

To my parents

Preface

Elections have always had a special place in the United States' political system. From James Madison's claim that frequent elections are the only way to ensure that representatives "have an immediate dependence on, and an intimate sympathy with, the people," to more contemporary assertions that elections provide the populace with a measure of control over public policy decisions, we have expected much of and hoped for much from the electoral process.

Yet it is clear that our electoral process has not remained unchanged throughout our two-hundred-year history. It has been transformed by the invention of a two-party sytem, the extension of the franchise, Reconstruction, changes in the geographical distribution of partisan competition, the Progressive attack on urban political "machines," the "democratization" of the presidential selection process, and the national government's intervention in the area of campaign finance. The recent involvement of the mass media in our election campaigns is only the most recent transformation of our electoral process.

In writing this book about the media's role in our contemporary elections, I have been guided by three main goals. First, I have tried to describe the ways in which candidates for public office and journalists use the media to provide the citizenry with a *mediated* version of an election campaign. This has involved describing how candidates think of their potential constituency; how they devise themes, slogans, and rhetoric to appeal to that constituency; and how they attempt to reach portions of that constituency through the mass media. It has also meant investigating how journalists cover an election campaign, what they tend to see in an election campaign, and what kinds of stories about a campaign they are trained to write.

Second, I have tried to present election campaigns as the result of the interactions among candidates, journalists, and the public. Although the literature on election campaigns has become quite rich regarding the behavior of both journalists and voters (this is less true of candidates), this book is unusual in its attempt to present the perspectives and behavior of all three participants simultaneously, and to deal with the relationships among them. Clearly the behavior of candidates cannot be understood unless we also understand how they anticipate the needs and motives of journalists and the preferences and habits of voters; the behavior of journalists cannot be understood apart from the campaign activities of candidates and the capabilities and interests of media audiences; and the behavior of voters cannot be understood wihout a consideration of the ways in which candidates and journalists delimit popular understandings and electoral choices.

Third, I have tried to write a book that forces—or at least allows—students to *evaluate* the worth of our contemporary electoral process and the effects that the mass media have had on that process. Most studies of elections focus on the candidate choices of the electorate and how the modern campaign shapes those choices—and this book deals with that subject also. An equally, perhaps more, important question, however, deals with the educative effect of elections and the extent to which election campaigns enhance the political awareness of the citizenry. Quite apart from who wins or loses, most theories of self-government presume or hope that the choices made by the electorate will be informed and sensible ones based on a body of more or less accurate beliefs and reasonable preferences. To the extent that our electoral process fails to contribute to the political education of the citizenry, an opportunity for furthering the cause of democracy has been squandered. We often assume that elections have a worthwhile educative effect, but the empirical evidence is a good deal less reassuring. I hope that the material in this book will encourage students to raise such questions as "What does the public learn from election campaigns?" "Who benefits from the electoral process?" and "What is the broader meaning or consequences of elections?" as well as the more obvious and familiar concern with why some candidates win and others lose.

In the process of writing this book, I have benefited from the assistance of many people. Robert Weissberg, Benjamin Ginsberg, and David Danelski all provided gentle yet sagacious counsel while the ideas behind the book were taking shape in graduate school at Cornell University; they have given freely of their advice and insight since then as well. At Temple University, I received considerable data analysis help from Jeffrey Hyman and Ed Blair of the Social Science Data Library; research assistance from Mark Sklarow; cheerful and expert typing help from Gloria Basmajian and Marie Jester; financial assistance from a Summer Research Grant and Grant-In-Aid of Research; and encouragement, criticism, and numerous examples of the media's involvement in election campaigns from my students. I am also indebted to the following people: Stuart Johnson, who showed faith in this project when it was still in its formative stage, and Debra Hunter, whose expert advice and gentle prodding helped me see the book through to completion; and to Scott Keeter, Rutgers University, Doris Graber, University of Illinois, Chicago Circle, Marion R. Just, Wellesley College, Lee Sigelman, University of Kentucky, and Robert Meadow, University of South Carolina, who provided thorough and helpful reviews of the manuscript at a crucial stage in the process. I have also benefited tremendously from the advice and assistance of Tom Sweitzer—student, friend, and practicing media consultant—and from the editorial suggestions of my mother, Stella Joslyn.

Finally, I would like to thank my wife, Kathy, and children, Erin and Andrew, for providing the encouragement, time, motivation, diversion, and affection necessary for an enterprise such as this. Through their touch, smiles, laughter, and tears I have been continuously reminded that there are more important things in daily life than the next impending deadline.

R.J.

Philadelphia, Pennsylvania
December 1983

Contents

Mass Media
and Elections

1
Introduction

American politics and television are now so completely locked together that is it impossible to tell the story of the one without the other.
—Theodore White, *America in Search of Itself*

Consider the following episodes from seven of our last eight presidential election campaigns:

- In 1952 the Republican party nominated Dwight D. Eisenhower as its presidential candidate and Richard M. Nixon as his vice-presidential running mate. Soon after the nominating convention, charges surfaced that Nixon had accepted gifts and money while in office. These accusations placed Nixon's position on the ballot in jeopardy. Nixon responded by purchasing a half hour of television time to answer the charges with an accounting of his expenses, a depiction of the Nixon family's modest means, and a melodramatic presentation of the Nixon family's household pet—a dog named Checkers. This "Checkers" speech apparently persuaded the Republican party to keep Nixon on the ballot, thereby helping to launch the career of a politician who would become the first president to resign from office. Later, during the 1952 general election campaign, the Republicans also made political history by becoming the first presidential candidates to use brief television announcements (spot ads). A series of sixty-second commercials, run under the title "The Man from Abilene," included responses by Eisenhower to questions posed by "ordinary citizens." This form of campaign communication represented a significant departure from the practice of buying half-hour segments of broadcast time.
- In 1960 the Republicans nominated then Vice-President Richard Nixon as their presidential candidate. The Democrats nominated Massachusetts Senator John F. Kennedy. The two candidates agreed to hold a series of four televised debates during the general election campaign, the first such debates between presidential candidates. The television audience for the first debate thought that Kennedy's performance was better than expected—and better than Nixon's (although the radio audience was more impressed with Nixon's performance). Shortly after the first debate, Kennedy picked up noticeable support from the electorate,

1

particularly among undecided Democrats. This debate, then, was probably one of many factors responsible for Kennedy's razor-thin victory margin in November.

- In 1964 the Republican presidential candidate was Arizona Senator Barry M. Goldwater. The Democratic nominee was Lyndon B. Johnson, who had been Kennedy's vice-presidential candidate in 1960 and had assumed the office of president upon Kennedy's death in 1963. Campaign strategists working for the Johnson campaign produced the single most famous television commercial in U.S. electoral history, the so-called Daisy Spot. This commercial began with a young girl picking petals off a daisy while counting (incorrectly) from one to ten, continued with the somber voice of a countdown and film footage of a nuclear explosion, and concluded with Johnson's voice encouraging voters to cast a vote for him because "the stakes are too high for you to stay home." The commercial was shown only once; it caused so much protest that it was promptly withdrawn by the Johnson campaign. Nonetheless, discussion of the commercial has continued, and the spot established the reputation of its creator, Tony Schwartz, still active as a political consultant.

- In 1968 the Democratic party nominated then Vice-President Hubert Humphrey as its presidential candidate. Humphrey was nominated in Chicago at a convention that was accompanied by anti–Vietnam War protests and violent clashes between police and demonstrators. On the night that Humphrey received his party's nomination, the furious street protests and the ensuing violence were captured by television cameras stationed outside convention headquarters. Network news programs juxtaposed pictures of youth chanting "The whole world's watching" while engaged in hand-to-hand combat with Chicago police with the angry face and words of Chicago Mayor Richard Daley inside the convention hall. In this way the Humphrey campaign became firmly associated in the public mind with conflict, divisiveness, and protest. Humphrey was prevented from receiving what ordinarily would have been a large dose of favorable campaign communication, and he narrowly lost the general election three months later.

The 1968 Republican presidential nominee was again Richard Nixon, who had been out of public office since his defeat in the California gubernatorial campaign in 1962. Nixon's presidential campaign was noted for its innovative use of television and for the carefully controlled settings in which Nixon was allowed to appear. The assumptions, tactics, and decisions involved in this advertising campaign were revealed in a book—*The Selling of the President, 1968*—by journalist Joseph McGinniss, who personally observed the inner workings of the Nixon campaign. The book has become a classic account of a staged and carefully contrived political campaign.

• In 1972 the Republicans renominated Richard Nixon as their presidential candidate. The quest for the Democratic nomination involved numerous candidates, including Senators Edmund Muskie and George McGovern, former presidential candidate Hubert Humphrey, and Alabama Governor George Wallace. In the early days of the 1972 nomination campaign, Muskie was generally considered the front-runner for the Democratic nod. During a campaign appearance prior to the New Hampshire primary, however, Muskie was reported to have broken into tears during a speech in which he blasted New Hampshire newspaper publisher William Loeb. Loeb, the owner and editor of the *Manchester Union Leader*, the only daily newspaper with a statewide circulation in New Hampshire, was noted for his conservative political views and for his willingness to express those views openly and aggressively in the pages of his newspaper. In 1972 Loeb triggered Muskie's response by criticizing Muskie's wife and charging that Muskie condoned the use of the word "Canuck" to describe Americans of French-Canadian descent. The episode proved damaging to Muskie because it allowed the press to reflect on Muskie's stability and in particular to speculate about Muskie's violent temper. A less-than-spectacular performance in the New Hampshire primary then helped scuttle what had appeared to be a promising candidacy.

The Democrats ended up nominating South Dakota Senator George McGovern in 1972. Shortly after the Democratic convention, however, McGovern's vice-presidential running mate, Missouri Senator Thomas Eagleton, confessed at what was to be a routine July press conference that he had been admitted to hospitals three times in the 1960s for nervous exhaustion, depression, and fatigue, and had twice undergone electric-shock treatments. The announcement was made to head off the imminent publication by Knight newspapers of the details of these treatments. It was followed two days later by columnist Jack Anderson's charges that Eagleton had also been arrested for drunken and reckless driving. Although Eagleton vehemently denied the Anderson allegations and Anderson later retracted them, so much controversy was aroused that McGovern replaced Eagleton on the ballot with Sargent Shriver. It was an episode from which the McGovern campaign never fully recovered.

• At the beginning of the 1976 presidential campaign, the Democratic party was again looking at an array of presidential hopefuls, including Senators Birch Bayh, Fred Harris, and Henry Jackson; Arizona Congressman Morris Udall; former Georgia Governor Jimmy Carter; former Peace Corps director and vice-presidential candidate Sargent Shriver; George Wallace; and Hubert Humphrey. Attention was once again directed toward the first primary in New Hampshire, in which Carter, Udall, Bayh, Harris, and Shriver were campaigning seriously. A few months before the New Hampshire primary, however, the Carter campaign decided that the Iowa caucuses, to be held on January 19, 1976, would be a fruitful place to begin their campaign in earnest. When it became clear that the nation's journalists would be covering the Iowa caucuses extensively, Morris Udall changed his strategy and split his time and money between Iowa and New Hampshire. His resources were stretched thin in both states, he did poorly in both delegate-selection processes, and the press opined that his nomination campaign had gotten off to a lackluster beginning. Jimmy Carter, on the other hand, had been campaigning in both Iowa and New Hampshire for months. He came in first in both states and was propelled into the forefront of the Democratic race. A subsequent victory in the Florida primary, along with the press's fascination with this political newcomer who was doing so much better than anyone had expected, established Carter as the front-runner for the Democratic nomination.

Jimmy Carter was the Democratic nominee in 1976; incumbent President Gerald Ford won the Republican nod in a tight race with former California Governor Ronald Reagan. Before the general election, campaign blunders by both candidates hurt each of their campaigns. Carter's blunder was his discussion of the meaning of lust and adultery in an interview granted to *Playboy* magazine. Gerald Ford's blunder was his assertion, during a televised debate with his opponent, that Eastern Europe was not dominated by the Soviet Union. In both cases the press highlighted the utterance, pressed for clarification, and forced the candidate to dwell on an issue not of his own choosing. Furthermore, both candidates' pollsters claimed that each blunder hurt their candidate with the electorate.

• In 1980 the Democratic nomination campaign was between incumbent President Jimmy Carter and Massachusetts Senator Edward Kennedy. In the latter part of 1979 Kennedy was winning public opinion polls among Democrats by wide margins. In November 1979, however, Kennedy appeared on a news interview show with CBS correspondent Roger Mudd. The program revealed a hesitant, inarticulate candidate and raised anew public concerns regarding Kennedy's behavior in the 1969 Chappaquiddick incident. Although very few people saw the show, many of those who did were political activists, and journalists commented on Kennedy's desultory performance for weeks afterward. Kennedy's campaign subsequently sputtered, and Carter was able to secure renomination from a reluctant Democratic party.

The preceding episodes illustrate the importance of the mass media in recent presidential election campaigns. Electoral communication has undergone a fundamental change, and the messages transmitted by mass media sources have such a significant influence on the conduct of election campaigns that the electoral process itself is being transformed. In some cases the origins of these campaign messages are the candidates themselves (as in Ford's Eastern European remark, the Muskie crying incident, and Kennedy's interview with Roger Mudd), and widespread familiarity with the messages is the result of the reach of the U.S. news media. In other cases the origins of the messages are journalists (as in the press's fascination with Jimmy Carter in 1976 and Jack Anderson's charge concerning Eagleton in 1972).

The purpose of this book is to explore and analyze the role and influence of the mass media in U.S. election campaigns: how candidates for public office use the media to advance their own campaign goals, how journalists cover election campaigns, how the public responds to the plethora of campaign messages, and how campaign communication has affected the electoral process generally. The focus of this discussion will be on presidential election campaigns, simply because we have more knowledge about that electoral level than any other. The broader implications of recent changes in electoral communication are ones that pertain in both presidential and nonpresidential arenas.

Historical Development in Electoral Communication

This book revolves around three themes. The first is that the mass media have contributed to a radical transformation of election campaigns in the United States. This transformation involves changes in how political candidates communicate with the citizenry, in the information journalists provide about election campaigns, and in the flow of available information to and subsequent behavior of the U.S. electorate. Since a campaign may be thought of as a communication exchange, these changes have altered the meaning of the electoral process.

It is difficult to appreciate fully the significance of the changes in electoral communication that have taken place in the last three decades. Table 1–1 lists some media-related milestones in the electoral process since 1952. There we can see that changes in the behavior of political candidates, public officials, media organizations, and book publishers have all reshaped electoral communication and the electoral process in recent years.

As Table 1–1 indicates, public officials have altered the legal environment in which campaigns are conducted by amending the Communications Act of 1934 in 1959 to permit more extensive coverage of political candidates, by transforming the delegate-selection process for presidential nominating conventions, by enacting campaign finance legislation that has altered the flow of campaign contributions and the expenditure of campaign funds, and by reinterpreting broadcast regulations to make the broadcasting of face-to-face candidate debates more attractive. Candidates and other campaigners have introduced new forms of

TABLE 1–1   Milestones in the Development of Modern Campaign Communication, 1952–1980

1952	Richard Nixon's "Checkers" speech; first use by presidential candidates of televised spot advertisements.
1956	Publication of *The American Voter,* ushering in the empirical study of citizen voting behavior.
1957	Supreme Court ruled that broadcasters would not be held liable for content of campaign commercials.
1959	Enactment of exemptions to equal-opportunities provision of the Communications Act of 1934.
1960	First televised presidential debate; publication of the first *The Making of the President* book, transforming press coverage of election campaigns; first use of election-night network news projections.
1961	First live televised presidential press conference.
1963	Expansion of network news to thirty minutes.
1964	Redefinition of libel in *New York Times* v. *Sullivan*; first televised presidential adversary commercial (Daisy Spot); formation of News Election Service, permitting news organizations to acquire timely vote returns.
1968	First year of extensive coverage of national nominating conventions by network news; first use of exit polling by CBS.
1969	Publication of *The Selling of the President, 1968,* describing candidate control of campaign communication; attack by Spiro Agnew on the liberalism of the "Northeastern establishment" press.
1972	Presidential primary process fundamentally changed by Democratic party reforms; national campaign finance legislation took effect.
1974	Publication of *The Boys on the Bus,* an influential critique of campaign news coverage.
1976	Federal Communications Commission reinterpretation of candidate debate regulation; spending limitations in effect during the presidential general election for the first time; network news regular primary-night news coverage; publication of *The Unseeing Eye,* a critique of network news campaign coverage.
1980	Exit polls used to project election results; extensive political advertising by political action committees.
1984(?)	Networks cease gavel-to-gavel coverage of nominating conventions.

campaign communication by using spot ads since 1952, participating in televised debates since 1960, devising controlled formats that have the appearance of spontaneity, and producing advertising by noncandidate organizations. Journalists, too, have contributed to the changing shape of campaign communication by extending and expanding their news coverage of campaigns, altering their coverage to meet the criticisms leveled by critics and analysts, encouraging and covering candidate debates, using public opinion polls to project and explain electoral outcomes, and developing procedures for projecting election returns.

These rapid changes in campaign communication have come from a variety of sources. Innovations in campaign communication over the past three decades have left the electoral process in a state of flux. Before accepting this observation as valid, however, it would be useful to consider why so much change has been taking place at this time.

Although it is difficult to say with certainty what the main factors have been in the development of modern campaign communications, there are a number of plausible explanations. First, *the rules by which the election game is played have recently changed.* As a result of a reform movement within the Democratic party, most state election laws have been changed in the last fifteen years. These changes have increased both parties' reliance on primaries for the selection of convention delegates to the national nominating conventions and have attempted to make these primaries a more meaningful expression of public sentiment by making uncommitted delegate slates more difficult to establish, setting the dates of primaries closer to the date of the nominating convention, and substituting the proportional allocation of delegates for winner-take-all rules. As a result, the nomination process has become more newsworthy to journalists by becoming more visible, less ambiguous, more conflictual, and more evenly spaced through time.

In addition, the reform activities of public interest groups and the need to relegitimize the electoral process after the Watergate scandal led to substantial changes in campaign finance legislation during the 1970s. This legislation has altered campaign contribution patterns and the level of campaign expenditures that can be made by candidates' campaign organizations. This in turn has changed the communication strategies of candidates by increasing the amount of paid advertising at the subpresidential level, where few spending limits exist, and increasing the need for free news coverage at the presidential level, where spending limits represent a stringent constraint.

Finally, there have also been significant changes in the federal government's regulation of the broadcast media's involvement in election campaigns. During the 1950s public officials made both the news coverage and paid advertising of election campaigns much more attractive to broadcasters. In 1957 the U.S. Supreme Court decided that broadcasters could not be held liable for the content of political spot ads, a decision necessitated by the fact that broadcasters were prevented from censoring the content of material that they themselves did not produce. In 1959 Congress enacted amendments to the equal-opportunities provision of the Communications Act of 1934 that allowed broadcasters to cover the activities of political candidates in news formats without having to worry about responding to equal-time requests for free time by all other candidates for that office. These two decisions made involvement in election campaigns much less risky for broadcasters.

More recently, two other public policy changes increased the attractiveness of campaign communication. In 1964 the U.S. Supreme Court changed the interpretation of libel, making it more difficult for a public official or public figure to pursue successfully a libel suit against a journalist, and creating the opportunity, at least, for election coverage to become more robust and critical. In 1976 decisions by both the Federal Communications Commission (FCC) and the U.S. Supreme Court created the opportunity to broadcast candidate debates without fear of an equal-time complaint, thus making candidate debates a more attractive format for broadcasters.

Although most of these legal changes have occurred as a result of broadcasters' desire to be less constrained by broadcast regulation, the effect of the changes has been to make spot ads, candidate debates, and regular coverage of campaign activities more attractive to journalists. These formats have, in turn, become more prevalent than ever, and have altered the flow of campaign communication available to the public.

A second major reason for the recent change in electoral communication is that *the public has also changed*. The U.S. electorate is less partisan now than it was a few decades ago—in some ways, less partisan than it has ever been in the twentieth century. Numerous public opinion surveys and analyses of voting returns have documented that the public currently has a less positive feeling about the two major parties, is less closely identified with either of the major parties, and displays less partisan voting behavior both over time and in any given election than used to be the case. Consequently, the electorate is more "up for grabs" in every election, and winning electoral coalitions have to be constructed more purposefully with election-specific communication. In the past, the electorate's voting behavior was more durable—one might even say habitual—and a candidate could count on stimulating a certain proportion of the vote through appeals to enduring cleavages and group identifications (such as party loyalty). Today, however, such appeals are insufficient. More citizens approach an electoral choice indifferent, undecided, and disconnected from an enduring pattern of voting behavior, hence increasing the importance of campaign communication in each election. It is unclear whether the decline in partisan attachments was originally the cause, or the result, of the new style in campaign communication. Nevertheless, it is a change that has current implications for the campaign messages and communication tactics of candidates.

Finally, campaign communication itself has also changed recently, in part because *the behavior of media organizations has changed*. Part of this change involves the economic health of major news organizations, patterns of media ownership, and the discovery that campaign news can make money. The media industry has experienced a recent period of ownership consolidation and merger, resulting in networks and newspaper chains with substantial resources at their disposal. These media conglomerates can afford to assign reporters to travel around the country with a candidate, can commission expensive public opinion polls, and can build computer models to project election results based on scattered returns. The media have also discovered recently that the coverage of presidential primary results and the televising of candidate debates (though not, apparently, the telecasting of the national nominating conventions) will not only satisfy the FCC's requirement for public affairs programming, but can also contribute to the network's profit-loss statement. In 1976, for example, the ratings for the Tuesday night primary returns coverage exceeded those for NBC's "The Tonight Show," CBS's movie offerings, and ABC's "Wide World of Entertainment." This undoubtedly justified the $5 million spent by the three networks on their primary night coverage.[1] Since most media organizations are primarily profit-oriented, it would be surprising if journalists covered campaigns in a way that significantly damaged the revenue position of their news organization. Recent experience with campaign coverage, however, suggests that it can make a positive contribution to revenues.

Another aspect of the change in the behavior of media organizations is that journalists themselves seem to have become both more cynical and more introspective. Watergate continues to have an effect on journalists, making them both more skeptical of public officials and political candidates, and more concerned with preventing manipulation by candidates. In addition, the publication dates of four books were included in the milestones listed in Table 1–1 because they have affected the way in which journalists approach campaign coverage. Theodore White's *Making of the President* books led to attempts by journalists to probe beneath the surface of a candidate's campaign organization; Joe McGinniss's *Selling of the President, 1968,* has led to continuing analyses of the advertising strategies of candidates; Timothy Crouse's *Boys on the Bus* has led to attempts to prevent "pack journalism"; and Patterson and McClure's *Unseeing Eye* led to an attempt by network news organizations to enrich the substance of their campaign coverage.[2] As a result, there is some evidence that news coverage of campaigns has become less positive and more analytical, and that journalists are themselves dissatisfied with the collective result.

All these changes—in statutes and regulations, citizen attitudes, and journalistic perspectives—have influenced current campaign communication and have transformed the electoral process. An understanding of their origins and implications is a major goal of this book, as we consider in turn the behavioral response of candidates, journalists, and the public.

Elections as Communication Processes

The second major theme of this book is that campaign communication results from the interaction among a number of important participants, with each participant contributing something to the overall communication pattern, and with no single participant dominating the process. The major participants are candidates and their campaign organizations, journalists, active citizens, and passive citizens. Since each of these participants has different goals and motives, each approaches the election campaign from a different perspective and makes a different contribution toward electoral communication.

The most obvious participant in electoral communication is the candidate and his or her campaign organization. Although the candidate's primary short-term goal is to communicate with voters in such a way that he or she wins election to a particular office, candidates (and others in their campaign organizations) have long-term goals as well. Some candidates, for example, want not only to win the present race, but also to do so by such a large margin that their reputations are enhanced. This allows them to become more influential officeholders, increases the possibility of a future bid for higher office, and discourages future challenges. For example, some observers have explained the various campaign-related illegalities of Richard Nixon's 1972 campaign as a desire for as large a victory margin as possible in order to strengthen the president's reputation and power. In a similar fashion, analysts of congressional elections maintain that incumbent members of Congress attempt to discourage qualified challengers by maintaining large victory margins.[3]

Candidates also use electoral communication to advance their policy preferences or ideological perspective. Although winning is the primary goal of most major-party candidates, in every election year some candidates with little chance of winning participate in the electoral process to persuade the citizenry of the correctness of their views. It is often argued that Barry Goldwater, Republican candidate for president in 1964, was more interested in articulating his conservative belief system than in winning the election. More recently, Ellen McCormack, a candidate for the Democratic presidential nomination in 1976, entered the campaign primarily to express her antiabortion attitudes; John Anderson persisted in his 1980 presidential bid in order to present his policy alternatives to the U.S. public.

Finally, professional campaigners not only want their client-candidate to win, but they also have the goals of future business and the enhancement of their professional reputation in mind. Their involvement and conduct in a campaign is also often motivated by such long-term considerations.

Candidates, as the focus of attention during election campaigns, make the primary active contribution to the flow of communication. They bring their own personal values, policy preferences, personality traits, and political experiences to the campaign, and are important decision makers regarding where to campaign, what to say and not to say, and how to attract attention. Candidates also choose their staff and, increasingly, their campaign consultants, who bring with them their own experiences and ideas about effective communication strategies and the allocation of scarce political resources. A tremendous amount of time, effort, and money goes into the development by the candidate and the campaign staff of an effective plan for the content, timing, and targeting of campaign messages.

Although candidates and their staffs are primarily responsible for the active stimulation of campaign communication, they are seldom unconstrained in what they say and do. Campaign strategy also involves anticipating the goals, motives, and interests of other participants in the electoral process and adjusting one's communication before delivering any messages. Journalists make an important contribution to the flow of electoral communication both by devising their own campaign-related messages and by influencing candidates' choice of campaign behavior.

Journalists do not share the candidate's primary goal of securing electoral victory. More often, they are motivated by their attempt to survive and prosper within their own media organization and career path, by a diffuse belief in their role of informing the public, and by their own personal candidate and policy preferences. Although most journalists are primarily concerned with pleasing their immediate superiors (editors, producers, and so on) and enhancing their own professional reputations through their coverage of election campaigns, others are influenced by more personal preferences. For example, Henry Luce, former publisher of *Time* magazine, is said to have personally favored Dwight Eisenhower's presidential candidacy in 1952, and to have influenced *Time*'s political coverage to advance this cause.[4] More recently, William Loeb, publisher of the New Hampshire *Manchester Union Leader*, made his political preferences known in both the editorial and the news columns of his newspaper. More than one journalist has also admitted the appeal and personal rewards of an assignment to cover the successful presidential campaign of a political underdog.[5]

The primary contribution that journalists make to electoral communication is their determination of what is newsworthy about a particular campaign. They decide which candidates are newsworthy, what campaign activities and statements to cover, and how campaign behavior ought to be interpreted.

The first decision that journalists and their superiors make about an election campaign is whether it is newsworthy at all. In general, presidential campaigns receive the most news attention in the daily media, with senatorial, gubernatorial, and mayoral races receiving much less attention and most other campaigns relegated to neighborhood weeklies and local-origination cable television stations. In recent years journalists have also had to decide *when* a campaign becomes newsworthy. Coverage of delegate-selection processes during presidential nomination campaigns has begun earlier and earlier with each successive election, causing candidates to adjust their strategies. As candidate campaigning in turn has begun earlier and earlier, media organizations have had a difficult time deciding when to start selling advertising space or time, when to start daily coverage of campaign activities, and when to restrain coverage of an incumbent officeholder who is using his or her position to stimulate free coverage and advance an impending reelection campaign.

Journalists also decide *which* candidates are newsworthy. Very few elections involve only two candidates. Many nomination campaigns attract a number of candidates, and many general election campaigns have several minor-party candidates. For example, recent presidential nomination campaigns have involved numerous announced candidates, and recent general election campaigns have included the third-party candidacies of George Wallace in 1968 and John Anderson in 1980, as well as a handful of other minor-party candidates who succeed in getting on the ballot in numerous states. Obviously, a candidate who is ignored will have a difficult time producing the voter awareness necessary for electoral success. Consequently, in a presidential campaign the period before the first convention delegate is selected has become a crucial stage in which candidates attempt to convince political columnists and journalists with national reputations that their candidacies are credible and interesting enough to be covered. The term *invisible primary* has been applied to this significant stage of the presidential selection process.[6]

Journalists also decide which campaign activities and statements are newsworthy enough to be covered. Candidates have become fairly proficient at staging so-called media events, such as walking across one's district, performing different jobs on different days, or donning scuba gear to dramatize a concern for water pollution. All campaigns, however, involve a struggle to define, on both the candidate's and journalist's part, those features that are newsworthy. For example, during the 1976 presidential campaign journalists thought that Jimmy Carter's statements concerning adultery and Gerald Ford's assertion regarding Eastern Europe were more newsworthy than either candidate did. Candidates often complain that their discussions of policy issues are ignored by journalists and that journalists are unduly interested in conflict, minute changes in a candidate's positions over time, and catching the candidates in embarrassing mistakes. Journalists, on the other hand, respond that candidate messages are deceptive, innocuous, repetitive, and boring, and that undue reliance on candidate messages forfeits journalistic responsibilities.

Finally, journalists also make decisions concerning the themes with which to treat a campaign. Accounts of campaigns do not start from scratch each day; they build on a limited number of themes that, once established, constrain coverage of a campaign. In 1976, for example, Democratic candidate Fred Harris was portrayed as a populist candidate who was "too radical to win"; Democratic candidate Henry Jackson was considered a "humorless, somber and dull" campaigner; and Republican candidate Gerald Ford was a "bumbler and fumbler."[7] In 1980 John Anderson was an eccentric if noble enigma; Ronald Reagan was foolish and guileless; and Jimmy Carter was a vindictive, manipulative, and petty incumbent.[8] Similarly, the 1982 congressional elections were commonly portrayed as a referendum on Reaganomics. Once themes such as these are established, it is difficult for a campaign or a journalist to alter them.

The discretion exercised by journalists is important, for journalists and candidates have different perspectives on what campaign coverage should include. As two political observers have concluded:

> That the media link candidates and public does not mean that they are neutral conduits. Far from it. Media-candidate relations are an ambiguous mixture of conflict and cooperation, support and destruction. The reason: the needs of the media and the objectives of candidates differ. The candidates strive to flood television and the press with selective information conducive to their election. Reporters and editors want news—defined as conflict, controversy, duplicity, scandal. They probe for candidates' weaknesses, deceptions, closeted skeletons. Candidates and their aides try to impose their definitions of what is important in an election on the media. They assert the primacy of the issues which favor them. . . . The media varyingly accept, ignore, or reject these attempts while seeking stories of their own devising.[9]

Candidates and journalists contribute to the flow of campaign communication by virtue of their roles and occupations. The public, however, also contributes to campaign communication. Since the involvement of the public varies, the contributions of *active* and *passive* publics will be discussed separately.

Only a small proportion of citizens are active in campaigns in any way other than voting. This group is disproportionately influential, however, since active citizens contribute money, volunteer to perform various tasks for candidates, publicly endorse candidates, and communicate with the passive citizenry. A candidate's inability to appeal to political activists severely limits the amount and type of campaign communication in which he or she can engage. In fact, some campaign strategists suggest that a campaign should proceed at two different levels, one directed toward the active citizenry and one toward the passive citizenry. Part of the success of the various New Right political action committees (PACs) in the 1980 senatorial elections lay in their ability to accumulate substantial resources from among the active citizenry. During presidential nomination campaigns, decisions by active citizens to stop contributing money to a particular candidate may be enough to doom the candidacy to failure.

The three groups discussed so far—candidates and their organizations, journalists, and active citizens—make a visible, active, explicit contribution to campaign communication. The fourth and most numerous group, consisting of passive citizens, contributes in a less active fashion.

Most citizens take only one action during an election campaign—casting a vote. These passive citizens, however, also contribute to campaign communication through their historical voting behavior, their media exposure habits, and their political preferences.

Campaigns with adequate financial resources spend considerable time and expense studying the behavior of the passive citizenry while developing the campaign's communication strategy. This analysis includes exploring the past voting behavior of the constituency to assist in the geographical targeting of campaign messages; determining the media exposure patterns of the constituency to inform the targeting of campaign messages through different media; and surveying the political interests, perceptions, and preferences of the constituency. In addition, media organizations are increasingly using polling information to enhance their coverage of election campaigns. As a result, passive citizens have substantial input, albeit of a passive nature, into the process by which campaign communication is formulated. In fact, cynics view election campaigns as processes in which candidates first find out from citizens what they want and then tell them that that is what their candidacy will deliver.

None of these four electoral participants can unilaterally alter the flow of campaign communication. Candidates behave the way they do in part because of the preferences of journalists and citizens. Journalists behave the way they do in part because of the presumed preferences of citizens and the behavior of candidates. Finally, citizens—both active and passive—behave the way they do in part because of the communication engaged in by candidates and journalists. One of the main goals of this book is to explore and analyze the interactions among these participants and the flow of communication that results.

The Effects of Campaign Communication

The third main theme of this book is that electoral communication influences the attitudes and behaviors of the U.S. populace. Although it is commonplace to presume that electoral communication exerts a direct and profound influence on the distribution of votes cast, this is by no means the only—or even necessarily the most important—consequence of electoral communication. Campaign communication may have other consequences at least as significant as influencing the distribution of votes cast and the determination of electoral winners. For example, the flow of electoral communication has implications for the political knowledge of the electorate, apart from how this awareness is used to guide a vote choice. Since a recurrent theme of democratic theory is the extent to which the political awareness of the citizenry qualifies it for a part in public decision making, inquiry into the level and ease of change in this awareness is important. Further, since election campaigns are thought to be one process by which political communication informs the citizenry, an exploration of the extent to which current electoral communication accomplishes this goal would be useful. Even though campaign communication is, in a complex way, the result of the preferences of campaigners, journalists, and the active and passive public, the end result of the communication process will not necessarily contribute to the ideal of an informed public. We will analyze, then, the extent to which electoral communication contributes to the pool of useful information available to the public.

Electoral communication might also affect the organization of citizen belief systems, again without necessarily affecting the distribution of the vote in a direct and straightforward way. A large body of research has found that the public's belief systems are unstable, complex, and nonideological. If so, then it is difficult to know what to infer from the outcome of election campaigns. That is why public officials and political observers are fond of discussing—and can seldom reach any agreement regarding—the "meaning of" or the "nature of the mandate conferred" by an electoral outcome.[10] An understanding of how the public responds to campaign communication will help us also understand what the populace is attempting to communicate with its ballots.

Electoral communication might also affect citizen perceptions regarding the legitimacy of the political regime and constitution, and thereby have a long-term, direct effect on the stability and form of the political system. Apart from the individual outcome of any given election campaign, campaigns might also reinforce or increase support for whomever the eventual winner is, the office being contested, the rules by which election campaigns are conducted in the United States, and identification with the nation-state itself.[11] These effects, which presumably persist long after a given officeholder has been replaced, and affect a wide range of citizen behaviors, could dwarf the importance of casting particular votes for particular candidates.

Finally, electoral communication could also affect the behavior of political elites and political activists, and thereby contribute to a transformation of political institutions. In the United States the functions and activities of political parties, interest groups, and social movements have been altered by the patterns of electoral communication. Since members of Congress and the president are important participants in the electoral process, those institutions might also be transformed by the flow of electoral communication. Scholars have already attributed the atrophy of political parties, the fluctuating fortunes of the U.S. presidency, and the "collectively irresponsible" behavior of the U.S. Congress to the changing shape of electoral communication.[12]

When campaign consultants claim that they can elect anyone to public office if their advice is followed to the letter, they make an extremely exaggerated and self-serving assessment of the impact of campaign communication on voting behavior. On the other hand, when scholars and pollsters limit their inquiry into the effects of electoral communication to the ability to alter the distribution of the vote cast, they run the risk of missing more enduring and significant phenomena. One of the goals of the following chapters is to redress this focus and entertain a number of possibilities regarding the effect of electoral communication.

In the pages that follow, we will discuss the contributions of a number of actors to campaign communication and the effects and meaning of this communication. We will begin by exploring the behavior of candidates, campaign consultants, and journalists; turn next to an investigation of the effects of electoral communication on the awareness, belief systems, and voting behavior of the electorate; and conclude with a look at the influence of campaign communication on the meaning of the electoral process more generally.

Notes

1. Edwin Diamond, *Good News, Bad News* (Cambridge, Mass.: MIT Press, 1978), Chap. 3.

2. Joe McGinniss, *The Selling of the President, 1968* (New York: Trident Press, 1969); Timothy Crouse, *The Boys on the Bus* (New York: Ballantine Books, 1974); Thomas E. Patterson and Robert D. McClure, *The Unseeing Eye* (New York: G. P. Putnam's Sons, 1976).

3. Gary Jacobson, *The Politics of Congressional Elections* (Boston: Little, Brown, 1983).

4. Doris Graber, *Mass Media and American Politics* (Washington, D.C.: Congressional Quarterly Press, 1980), p. 160.

5. Richard Reeves, "Score One No Vote for Brown," *Philadelphia Inquirer,* May 6, 1979, p. 9-M.

6. Arthur Hadley, *The Invisible Primary* (Englewood Cliffs, N.J.: Prentice-Hall, 1976).

7. Diamond, *Good News*, pp. 16–17.

8. Michael Jay Robinson, "A Statesman Is a Dead Politician: Candidate Im-

ages on Network News," in Elie Abel, ed., *What's News* (San Francisco: Institute for Contemporary Studies, 1981).

9. David L. Paletz and Robert M. Entman, *Media, Power, Politics* (New York: Free Press, 1981), pp. 32–33.

10. For a discussion of this issue, see Philip E. Converse, "Public Opinion and Voting Behavior," in Fred I. Greenstein and Nelson W. Polsby, eds., *Handbook of Political Science: Nongovernmental Politics*, Vol. 4 (Reading, Mass.: Addison-Wesley, 1975).

11. Benjamin Ginsberg, *The Consequences of Consent: Elections, Citizen Control and Popular Acquiesence* (Reading, Mass.: Addison-Wesley, 1982).

12. David Mayhew, *Congress: The Electoral Connection* (New Haven: Yale University Press, 1974); Jacobson, *Congressional Elections*.

2
Candidate Communication: The Development and Content of Candidate Appeals

The problem of the political communicator, the candidate and his staff, is to somehow communicate effectively. By effective communication I mean communication that influences the vote of that viewer. That's what a political campaign is about. It's not to amuse or enlighten the press as much as it is to communicate effectively to the voter.

> —John Deardourff, quoted in *Nominating a President*

The key decision-makers in most contemporary major-office campaigns are no longer party chieftains but political consultants.

> —Robert Agranoff, *The New Style in Election Campaigns*

. . . the most striking feature of candidates' rhetoric about policy is its extreme vagueness. . . . Presidential candidates are skilled at appearing to say much while actually saying little.

> —Benjamin Page, *Choices and Echoes in Presidential Elections**

What's wrong with the growth of political ads is . . . the way they encourage politicians to follow their constituencies rather than lead them. All political ads are based almost entirely on the results of polling, and they stress only those points that the pollsters tell the admen will evoke a response from the voters.

> —Nicholas Lemann, "Barney Frank's Mother and 500 Postmen," *Harper's*

---

*This and subsequent excerpts from *Choices and Echoes in Presidential Elections* (Chicago: University of Chicago Press, 1978), by Benjamin J. Page, are reprinted by permission of the University of Chicago Press.

The primary contributors to campaign communication are candidates and their campaign organizations. It is candidates and their staffs, after all, for whom the outcome of the campaign has the most immediate, direct, and material effect. In this chapter we will discuss the *process* by which candidate communication is developed and the *content* of the messages that candidates deliver to the public.

The Goals of Candidate Communication

In developing their campaign communication, campaigners are motivated by both short-term and long-term goals, and are constrained by a number of factors. The obvious short-term goal of most campaigners is to maximize the number of votes received by a candidate and to win election to public office. Although candidates usually need only a plurality of votes to win, thereby making it unnecessary to *maximize* one's vote totals, there are several good reasons that candidates desire larger victory margins. For one thing, the more convincing an electoral victory, the less likely it is that a serious challenge will appear in the next election. Second, a resounding victory may catch the attention of other political elites, increase the winner's prestige, and suggest the possibility of achieving higher elective office. Third, the more comfortable the margin of victory, the easier it is to raise campaign contributions the next time around. Although some contributors follow a marginal-effect strategy in which money is contributed to candidates in extremely tight races, most large contributions are funneled into safe races in which the payoff on the investment is more certain.[1] Finally, winning an election in a convincing fashion gives a public official more influence while in office. Impressive victory margins permit a winner to claim that he or she has a mandate for particular policy proposals and that other political actors would do well to defer to the victor's opinions. In the aftermath of the 1980 election, this claim was often made by the Reagan administration and the Republican party. In fact, part of the explanation for Reagan's policy successes in 1981 lies in the credibility of claims that Reagan's *margin* of victory over Carter, coupled with Republican gains in the U.S. Senate, meant that the populace had given its approval to the Reagan policy proposals. For all these reasons, then, candidates typically desire a victory margin greater than what is minimally necessary to win.

Campaigners also typically have long-term objectives beyond winning a particular campaign. Candidates may anticipate a future campaign for the same or some other office and consequently wish to attract the attention of journalists, activists, contributors, and the public in a way that will pay off in the future. Some candidates and campaigners—usually those with little chance of winning the immediate campaign—see an election as an opportunity to educate citizens concerning some matter of public policy. For example, in 1972 Congressman Paul McCloskey challenged Richard Nixon for the Republican presidential nomination in order to focus attention on the Vietnam War, which McCloskey opposed. In every presidential campaign there are candidates from parties such as the Socialist Labor party, Libertarian party, Communist party, and Prohibition party, who have little chance of winning the election but who use the campaign period to present their views to the public. Finally, other campaigners, particularly paid organizers and consultants, are concerned with developing contacts and reputations that will ensure continued business in future election years. At times these motivations will affect the nature of the communication used by campaigners in particular election campaigns.

Campaigners are seldom completely free to communicate with the public in any way they desire. They are constrained by the preferences, interests, and expectations of citizens; by their own previous behavior; and, it must be recognized, by their own values and ideology. In any particular election a candidate is also constrained by the preferences of the party and interest group members who actively support his or her candidacy, and by the communication of other campaigners.[2] Within these constraints, campaigners develop strategies of communicating with both active and passive segments of the public. Communication with the active citizenry—so-called opinion leaders, potential campaign contributors, volunteer workers, journalists—is designed to acquire political resources that may in turn be used to communicate effectively with voters. Communication with the passive citizenry involves attempting to encourage citizens to assume the costs necessary to cast a vote for the candidate.

The Development of Candidate Communication

In the U.S. electoral system candidates initiate most campaign communication. That is, candidates themselves must usually say or do something for any campaign communication to take place. Recent experience with incumbent presidents running for reelection (Nixon in 1972, Ford in 1976, Carter in 1980) has shown that when a candidate decides *not* to initiate this communication—by pursuing the so-called Rose Garden strategy of remaining in the White House and attending to presidential duties—a dearth of communication about that candidate is the typical result. As we will see in subsequent chapters, journalists are not apt to initiate campaign communication on their own in the absence of visible candidate activities. It is with good reason, then, that our discussion of campaign communication begins with the actions of candidates and their staffs.

THE ORIGINS OF CANDIDATE COMMUNICATION

The immediate goal of candidates and campaigners is to devise messages that will motivate voters to vote for that candidate. Toward this end, campaigns develop communication strategies, themes, and specific messages, and attempt to convey them to the citizenry.

Candidate messages have their origins in a number of different places. Candidates bring to a campaign their own experience and opinions concerning what messages have worked in the past; what messages other officeholders have used; what messages significant political actors (campaign contributors, party leaders, other opinion leaders) are expecting; and what messages they themselves would feel comfortable delivering. In addition, no campaign is a completely static enterprise, devised in July and carried out through November. Events occur and messages are devised by opposing candidates, creating a need to respond to messages, alter them, and devise new messages during a campaign.

Although candidates are clearly important contributors to the development of campaign messages, there is some evidence that they are not as important as they used to be. Recent U.S. (and foreign) election campaigns have seen the increased involvement of new types of decision makers in developing campaign communication.

PUBLIC OPINION AND CANDIDATE COMMUNICATION

One significant change in the conduct of contemporary U.S. campaigns is the increased reliance on public opinion polls for both the development and the evaluation of candidate messages. Although candidates have always been concerned about the interests, preferences, and desires of the electorate and the likely impact of campaign messages on them, the amount of systematic probing of these attitudes has undergone a quantum leap in the last two decades. More and more candidates are hiring paid pollsters to help them decide what to say to voters and to help inform them of whether the messages are working. Even by 1966, for example, almost all winning Senate contenders and gubernatorial candidates, and about half of the victorious U.S. representatives, had used commissioned polls.[3] In the typical contemporary million-dollar statewide campaign, anywhere from $50,000 to $80,000 is now allocated to polling.[4] In 1980 Carter spent $2 million and Reagen spent $1.3 million on polling of the $29.4 million available to each of them.[5]

Pollsters collect extensive information on citizens' concerns, their perceptions of the candidates, the extent of their political knowledge, and the attributes they think a public officeholder should possess. Such information is obviously helpful to candidates. In an election district primarily concerned about levels of property taxes and the availability of jobs, it would probably make little sense for a candidate to talk about legalizing marijuana or withdrawing troops from South Korea. Similarly, a candidate who is perceived to be honest will pursue a different campaign strategy than will one who is perceived to be crooked. In the former case the voluntary publication of one's income tax returns would probably have a marginal effect at best; in the latter case it could be a highly successful campaign tactic.

The information gleaned from polling operations influences the development of general campaign strategy and specific candidate messages. Recently, presidential campaigns have become the most reliant on measures of public opinion in the development of candidate communication. A few examples from recent presidential campaigns will illustrate the connections between public opinion, campaign strategy, and the content of candidate communication.

• Richard Nixon's 1968 presidential campaign was heavily dependent on the analysis of public opinion data and the advice of professional media consultants. Figure 2–1 presents excerpts from the campaign strategy devised for both the nomination and general election campaigns by advertising adviser Harry Treleaven. Notice that the first four paragraphs of the nomination campaign strategy discuss the broad parameters of public opinion and the public mood of the country. These observations were based on Treleaven's intuition, personal observations, and reading of public opinion polling data. The remainder of the nomination campaign statement goes on to develop the popular perceptions that it would be both *possible* and *useful* to create or modify, and the specific messages or themes that might be used to shape these perceptions.

The general election campaign statement is also filled with references to popular perceptions and the type of perceptual change that would be possible and useful to accomplish. Here, too, it is easy to see that observations of and assumptions about public opinion are important elements in the formation of the overall communication strategy.

• In 1976 Harry Treleaven had a new challenge: He became the mastermind behind Ronald Reagan's contest with incumbent President Gerald Ford for the Republican presidential nomination. Treleaven's reading of popular preferences indicated that the Reagan candidacy presented two problems for him to try to overcome with his advertising: the fact that Reagan was perceived as an actor, with all that profession's associations with artifice and insincerity, and the strong mood of political cynicism in the country at large. Treleaven's solution was to produce a series of ads, edited from press conferences, in which Reagan answered questions from the audience and delivered brief samples of his anti-big-government rhetoric. These ads showed Reagan's warmth and sense of humor in a format that had the looks—and credibility—of a news program.[6]

● Despite Treleaven's efforts, Reagan lost the 1976 Republican presidential nomination to incumbent President Gerald Ford. Prior to the general election campaign, Ford's advisors produced a 120 page strategy memo, analyzing the public's perceptions of the strengths and weaknesses of Ford and Carter, and suggesting possible communication messages and themes for the fall campaign.[7] The analysis included a list of the undecided public's positive and negative perceptions of both candidates. For example, Carter was perceived as a family man, with quiet strength and strong spiritual and moral values, but lacking humility and experience. Ford was perceived as hard-working, safe, and honest, but also as indecisive, inconsistent, and boring. The analysis continued with a listing of the "actual" (as opposed to perceived) strengths and weaknesses of both candidates, and concluded with the following summary of the perceptual situation. (This and subsequent excerpts from the 1976 Ford strategy memo appeared originally in *Running for President 1976: The Carter Campaign,* copyright © 1977 by Martin Schram. Reprinted with permission of Stein and Day Publishers, New York.)

Summary Chart

Ford/Carter Perception—National Survey

FORD

Positive: Honest and decent.	But primaries raise problem of political honesty.
Question: Intelligence.	Is he competent or intelligent enough to be president? Is he sensitive to how all this relates to average individual?
Negative: Leadership.	Weak, indecisive, lacks vision.

CARTER

Positive: Religious, ethical, conservative, regular Democrat.	He supports traditional American values—he has a conservative lifestyle. He's a Democrat, but not an extremist.
Question: Deceitful.	Is he some kind of fanatic who might be dangerous?
Negative: Inexperienced, lacks record of accomplishment, and is vague and not specific.	Is he up to the job? We don't know enough about him. Why is he avoiding clear expression of issues?

The campaign memo then shifted focus to a discussion of the implications of the public's perceptions and the actual strengths and weaknesses of the two candidates for campaign strategy and candidate communication. This is what the Ford strategists concluded needed to be accomplished with the candidate's campaign communication:

A. General Goals
  1. Cause the swing voter to reevaluate the President. This will take an "attention getter" (such as a good acceptance speech) so that people

The proposition for the Nixon for President primary advertising can be stated like this:

There's an uneasiness in the land. A feeling that things aren't right. That we're moving in the wrong direction. That none of the solutions to our problems are working. That we're not being told the truth about what's going on.

The trouble is in Washington. Fix that and we're on our way to fixing everything. Step one: move LBJ out, move a Republican president in.

And of all the Republicans, the most qualified for the job by far is Richard M. Nixon. *More than any other Republican candidate for the Presidency,* Richard Nixon will know what has to be done—and he'll know the best way to get it done. We'll all feel a whole lot better knowing he's there in Washington running things instead of somebody else.

A proposition has to be supported in the advertising by facts. What are our facts? What does Richard Nixon have that makes him "the most qualified by far?"

Experience. On the national scene. In foreign affairs. He knows how the Federal Government works, and how to make it work for the people. He's got it all over the other candidates in this respect.

Knowledgeability. Resulting from his experience. His travels. His conversations with the world's thinkers and achievers. His years of intensive study.

Intellectual ability. Formidable. A disciplined mind. Able to cope with the big problems, come up with new answers. Can more than hold his own in his dealings with other world leaders.

Acceptability. Where it counts. In the capitals of the world. In the top circles of business, politics, the professions. Not always loved, he is universally respected. Not glamorous, he does have a certain star quality going for him. Most doors are open to him.

Ability to form a top team. Running the country is not a one-man job. You have to have expert help—and Richard Nixon knows where the talent is. He can bring the best minds in the country into government, get them to working on our problems. He won't have to depend on home-town pals; he has ranged too far for too long to be thus hampered.

Toughness. A good man to have on your side. Won't be shoved around. Will stick to what he believes. Can he be brainwashed? Try.

Integrity. Although there were some doubts in the past, these

FIGURE 2–1 Communications Strategy for Nixon Presidential Campaign, 1968.

have been dispelled by the years. Richard Nixon is now generally regarded as honest, a man who levels with people. (The way he is handled from now on should strengthen that impression—particularly important in light of the credibility issue.)

Conscientiousness. He is serious. Hardworking. Selfless. Thorough. When you've got Nixon on a problem, you've got the best of Nixon.

Vigorous. He is young, healthy, energetic—not really a big advantage over the other Republican candidates, who are equally vigorous, but still a fact.

Party unifier. Self-explanatory. Probably not of much use in advertising. . . .

GENERAL ELECTION STAGE

Now to the heart of our problem; how do we convince people that Richard Nixon is the man who can effect the changes the country wants?

Two ways. First, we must overcome the negative anti-Nixon feeling that persists in so many minds. It is very difficult to get a man's opinions considered or even listened to if he is not liked. However, our experience in the primary campaigns showed us that we CAN change people's attitudes toward Nixon—that most people don't really know what Nixon today looks and sounds like, and when they do, when they're shown the new Nixon, they start coming around to our side. Therefore, during Phase One at least, exposure of the 1968 Nixon is a first priority of the advertising.

The second way we can convince people that Nixon's the One is to present his stand on the important issues. Most people have only a vague idea of Nixon's position—many people have a distorted impression—few people know exactly where he stands. In fact, one of the things many people don't like about Nixon is that they consider him too general in his views—not evasive but unspecific and inclined to be self-serving in his statements. The facts belie this, of course—and letting the public know precisely the Nixon position is a major objective of the advertising.

This means we should immediately list the issues we want to deal with and the Nixon stand on each, phrased as succinctly as possible and in terms that will have the most real meaning for the average voter.

(Incidentally, the above should be done state by state, as the issues and emphases will probably vary.)

FIGURE 2–1   Continued

Source: Joe McGinniss, *The Selling of the President 1968* (New York: Trident Press, 1969), pp. 172–174. Copyright © 1969 by Joemac, Inc. Reprinted by permission of Simon & Schuster, Inc.

will reevaluate their assumptions about the President's personal characteristics and once again begin to listen to what he has to say.

2. Develop a major and highly disciplined attack on the perception of Carter. We must close the gap between Carter's perception and his actual weaknesses. He must be seen as:

- An unknown. A man whose thirst for power dominates. Who doesn't know why he wants the Presidency or what he will do with it.
- Inexperienced.
- Arrogant—(deceitful).
- Devious and highly partisan (a function of uncontrolled ambition).
- As one who uses religion for political purposes; an evangelic.
- As liberal, well to the left of center and . . . the old-line Democratic majority.
- Carter's campaign must be linked (in the public's mind) to Nixon's '68 and '72 campaigns—very slick, media-oriented. A candidate that takes positions based on polls—not principles. . . .

Strategy Specifics (Actions Aimed at Specific Objectives)

A. Establish leadership qualities:

- Avoid self-deprecating remarks (Ford not a Lincoln) and acts (being photographed with a cowboy hat).
- Carefully plan, prepare and execute *all* on-camera appearances. The President should be seen on television as in control, decisive, open and candid. Prep time (15–30 minutes) should be built into the President's schedule (with Bill Carruthers) immediately preceding on-camera events. For example, the President should rehearse his Acceptance Speech (before departing for Kansas City), using a teleprompter and video tape.
- Use ads and advocates to compare the President's personal characteristics and experience with Carter's.
- The President must not go on the attack personally (not only because it results in a negative voter reaction) because the country does not want strident, divisive tactics. The country is coming together (as we saw over the 4th of July weekend) and part of this healing process is a rejection of politicians who are perceived to be aggressive attackers. . . .

Attack and Carter's Reaction

1. Background

Carter's popularity is based primarily on his perceived credibility, but it is very soft. The voter's perception of Carter can be substantially changed.

Our basic objective should be to change the perception of Carter:

— move him to the left on social issues and away from traditional American values;
— identify him as a partisan democrat; and
— show that he is devious and arrogant, driven by personal ambition in ruthless pursuit of power.

We cannot wait much longer before launching the Carter attack—he is building a very substantial lead and is beginning to look like FDR in the polls.

. . . But the attack in the South must be on issues. We should not attack him *personally* there since this would cause a backlash of regional pride. It must be a respectful disagreement on a high plane. (An example of how *not* to attack Carter is Senator Dole's line on *Face the Nation* (7/18): "He is Southern-fried McGovern.") . . .

Finally, we should try to characterize Carter's campaign as a mirror image of Nixon's '68 and '72 campaigns. The following similarities should be pointed out:

- A candidate who tries to be all things to all people.
- Avoids specifics on issues (RN—'68 campaign).
- Driven by personal ambition—harsh and manipulative.
- Secretive and surrounded by a protective and fiercely loyal staff. (One problem we face is the fact that in general the press likes the Carter staff. This may well change as he adds people and pressures increase.)

Clearly the Ford campaign's understanding of public opinion was instrumental in the development of campaign themes and appeals.

• On the Democratic side in 1976, the Carter campaign was also significantly shaped by a cadre of advisors and consultants attuned to public opinion, especially Gerald Rafshoon, Carter's media producer; Hamilton Jordan, Carter's chief aide; and Patrick Caddell, Carter's public opinion pollster. A remarkable feature of the Carter campaign is that his advisers actually began developing their 1976 campaign strategy in *1972*. The following excerpts from campaign strategy memos, written by Rafshoon and Jordan *three years* before the first delegate would be selected for the 1976 Democratic nominating convention, show the attention to and concern for popular perceptions of Carter. (These excerpts appeared originally in *Running for President 1976: The Carter Campaign*, copyright © 1977 by Martin Schram. Reprinted with permission of Stein and Day Publishers, New York.)

Rafshoon:

As for a national image . . . I believe that despite the accusations of backsliding by the liberal press, that Jimmy's image in national circles and in the media has not changed much since inauguration. He is still the man who said the time for racial discrimination is over. . . . He still has a Kennedy smile. . . . *What he does not have is much depth to his image. He is not as well known as many other big-name politicians in the U.S. and is not known for the heavyweight ideas and programs that he is capable of articulating.*

Getting this across should be the No. 1 priority now. The first phase of any Carter campaign should be to formulate a heavyweight program and project a heavyweight image, all at the same time, trying to infect other southern states and other regions with the Jimmy Carter "Good guy" brand of populism. It will take more than the hand-shaking and the projection of "I understand the problems" of the "average man" image to put Carter over. *This is still his greatest asset and it must be projected but he will also have to convince the press, public and politicians that he knows how to run a government (he has a record to prove this).* . . . He knows about the problems of the cities . . . the races . . . the economy . . . and the problems of the world, national defense, foreign affairs.

Timing

1973 will be a very quiet year on the political front but there are a lot of preparatory things that can be done. This is the phase when Jimmy's accomplishments in Georgia—such as reorganization, control, ecology, and the upgrading of positions for blacks—can be heralded nationally. I see 1973 as the year in which Carter is projected as the heaviest of the governors in accomplishments and the year in which the rest of the country gets a good look at him as a governor. It's really his last chance for this because in 1974 we will have mid-term elections and he needs to shift gears then for another phase of his publicity.

In general, I see the publicity phases as follows:

Phase I 1973: Projection of the Carter record and knowledge.

Phase II 1974: Carter as a leader in the Democratic Party and someone involved in bringing it back.

Phase III 1975: Carter as a heavyweight thinker, leader in the party (denote in Phases One and Two) who has some ideas for running the country and is going around the country talking about them and who may have presidential ambitions.

Phase IV 1976: Carter—a presidential candidate.

Each of these phases runs into the succeeding phase and is an integral part of the overall buildup. They all cannot be accomplished at the same time but they all must be accomplished at the time allotted in order to evolve into the next phase. Phase I must be accomplished early enough to make the others work.[8]

Jordan:

. . . I believe that Rafshoon's comments and overview are excellent. In keeping with his strategy and sense of timing, it is necessary that we begin immediately to generate favorable stories and comments in the national press. Stories in the *New York Times* and *Washington Post* do not just happen, but have to be carefully planned and planted.

I would hope that we could relate the accomplishments of your administration to the theme that revitalized state government is the key to solving many of the problems in this country today as has been demonstrated in Georgia by Gov. Jimmy Carter. The thrust of your national press effort should be that state government is working in Georgia and is solving the problems in meeting the needs of ordinary citizens. By emphasizing this theme and making your own political plans a secondary consideration, I believe you would have the forum and excuse you need to appear on television talk shows, write articles for national publications and serve as an obvious example that revitalized state government is where the action and the interests are. . . .

. . . I believe that you should attempt to develop the image of a highly successful and concerned former governor of Georgia and peanut farmer living in a small rural town, speaking out on the pertinent issues of the day. Once your name begins to be mentioned in the national press, you will not lack for invitations and opportunities to speak in major groups and conventions. . . .[9]

Rafshoon, Jordan, and increasingly Caddell continued to be influential as Carter's nomination campaign strengthened. In two appraisals of the campaign in March and April 1976, for example, Caddell opined, on the basis of his survey data, that the campaign had neglected to develop adequate campaign themes and had allowed Carter to be portrayed as "fuzzy on the issues." This was a problem that was to frustrate the Carter campaign throughout 1976:

Speeches, Issue Themes—This area of the campaign is the one in need of the most attention. We have passed the point when we can simply avoid at least the semblance of substance. This does not mean the need to outline minute, exact details. We all agree that such a course could be disastrous. However the appearance of substance does not require this. It requires a few broad, specific examples that support a point and it requires a better definition of these priorities and approach. . . . We need to have set formal addresses—no matter how distasteful—maybe every 10 days, for the purpose of articulating thematic program approaches and priorities, and to satisfy the press, elites, and eventually the public that we are presidential and competent. Also, we need to utilize this approach to send "signals" to interested groups and particularly to the suspicious but open liberals. . . .[10]

These examples clearly indicate that an understanding of popular attitudes and perceptions is central to the development of campaign strategy and candidate communication. Before the campaign begins, the analysis of public opinion typically focuses on current popular perceptions and attitudes and how these might reasonably and usefully be changed during the course of the campaign. Measurements of and guesses about public opinion *during* the campaign are also used to judge the effectiveness of the candidate's communication. Sometimes campaign advisers criticize a candidate's behavior based on a presumption about the public's response, as this memo from Jordan to Carter in 1976 demonstrates:

I thought that the tone of your remarks last week in New Hampshire [was] highly partisan and un-Presidential.

I feel that you should re-examine the manner in which you publicly discuss Ford's relationship with Richard Nixon.

The American people perceive Gerald Ford as being an honest, well-intentioned man who inherited a job bigger than he can handle. They see many of the same attractive personal qualities in you, but have made the tentative judgment that you are more capable of leading the country than Ford.

I do not worry in the weeks and months ahead that we can clearly demonstrate that you are a better qualified person to lead the country and manage the government. I do worry that our campaign rhetoric might undermine the favorable personal image you have with the American voters. Any statements which are perceived to be—directly or indirectly— by the American people as being personal attacks on Gerald Ford will hurt us and help him.

I feel strongly that you should discontinue using the phrase "Nixon-Ford Administration." I believe that the Republican Party generally and Gerald Ford specifically can be held responsible for many of the problems facing our country today. The American people are ready to hold them accountable at the polls in November for the past eight years, but the phrase "Nixon-Ford Administration" suggests a very conscious effort on your part to equate Ford, the man, with Nixon, the man. This does not and will not wash with the American people and I believe that it will be generally interpreted as a personal attack on the integrity of Gerald Ford.

When I watched you say that on the news recently it sounded harsh and out of character for you. It certainly did not sound like a man who wanted to put Watergate behind us and unite the country.[11]

Regardless of whether the advice being offered concerns the development of or the change in campaign strategy, knowledge of popular preferences and expectations are never far from the strategic considerations.

● In 1980 the presidential campaigns of both Ronald Reagan and Jimmy Carter again relied heavily on the judgment and advice of their chief pollsters. Patrick Caddell, again Carter's pollster and strategist, developed a campaign strategy based substantially on his reading of public opinion poll results. Caddell has described the message objectives of Carter's 1980 campaign in the following way:

… there was no way we could survive either a primary or general election contest on the first three years of the Carter administration. . . . We had to make the (nomination) choice *not* President Carter's record, but Senator Kennedy's issue stands and ideology. . . . (In the general election) we had to keep the focus on the candidates and we had to try to keep it on the future as opposed to the past. If the election were based on the past, we would lose flat out . . . there was a lot of doubt about what would happen with Reagan as president. We tried to put him on the defensive on exactly what his programs would mean. . . . Our job was to make people make a choice between two candidates—two personalities—and, to the extent that we could, between two parties.[12] [This and a subsequent excerpt from *Public Opinion* 3, no. 6 (December–January 1981) are reprinted by permission.]

Clearly Caddell had observed that perceptions of Carter's accomplishments in office were quite negative, but that there were also doubts about some of the personal characteristics of both Edward Kennedy and Ronald Reagan. These observations helped the Carter campaign decide what to talk about and what to ignore.

Richard Wirthlin, Ronald Reagan's chief pollster in 1980, also developed a campaign strategy consistent with his reading of popular perceptions. Wirthlin says the Reagan campaign attempted to

> focus the campaign on the issue of leadership. We knew that Reagan was viewed as decisive, as strong, and as someone who could get things done. We felt these qualities were good mirror images of some of the weaknesses perceived in the Carter administration. In addition to reinforcing our strengths, we also attempted to show the compassionate, human side of Ronald Reagan . . . [and] to highlight the perceived Carter weaknesses, primarily relating to his record.[13]

It is difficult to say exactly how much of candidate communication is the direct result of poll results and how much is uninfluenced by public opinion surveys. Candidates often ignore the advice of pollsters and advisers when it conflicts with their own intuition or judgment. In the 1976 Carter campaign, for example, Carter's aides had a difficult time convincing him that his use of the term "ethnic purity" in a news interview was causing problems and would have to be retracted, and that he would also have to clarify the comments made in his *Playboy* interview. Similarly, when Carter's campaign was slipping in October 1976, Pat Caddell failed to convince Carter that he should raise the issue of the Nixon pardon since it was their best issue among young and nonpartisan voters. Carter vetoed the idea because he did not want to produce a divided and bitter electorate.[14] Nonetheless, the ubiquity of polling information suggests that the public's expectations, preferences, and reactions are known and anticipated with much more precision (and expense) than has ever been the case before. Cynics would probably find ample evidence that campaigns learn through polls what the citizenry wants and then give it to them with their candidate's communication.[15]

THE ROLE OF PROFESSIONAL CAMPAIGN CONSULTANTS

The importance of the public opinion pollster is actually part of a broader phenomenon affecting modern campaigns. Increasingly, campaigns are being conducted by, or with the advice of, a new group of campaign decision maker: the professional campaign consultant. Candidates have always relied on the judgment and advice of other politicians, personal friends, and party workers. Now, however, candidates find that the expertise of the media producer, advertising executive, public opinion pollster, professional accountant, and computer programmer is increasingly necessary. A survey done in 1972–1973, for example, found that almost all senatorial, gubernatorial, and state attorney-general candidates, and half the secretary-of-state and state treasurer candidates, had hired at least one political professional. A 1970 survey of contested senatorial campaigns found that almost all had hired an advertising firm and a substantial minority had hired a pollster and a campaign management firm.[16]

There are two reasons for the emergence of political consultants. First, they possess the expertise necessary for using the complex tools of campaigning that now exist. The knowledge necessary to conduct a representative public opinion poll, to produce spot advertisements, to target campaign areas through computerized analysis of voting returns, to devise a campaign budget representing a rational allocation of resources, and to conduct a direct mail solicitation of funds is not generally possessed by the typical political candidate or party officeholder.

A second reason for the emergence of the campaign consultant is the weakening or disappearance of the party organizations that used to provide the information, advice, and resources necessary to the campaign. It is no coincidence that the first substantial participation of professional campaign consultants was by a firm called Whitaker and Baxter in California in the 1930s. California at that time lacked well-organized political parties as a consequence of Progressive party reforms that attacked partisan control over ballot access and patronage positions and of the population mobility in the area that made it difficult to establish party organizations based on personal contact. More recently, candidates often turn to professional campaign consultants in areas lacking an entrenched party organization (such as Republicans in the South and in Northeastern urban areas). Professional consultants fill the void left by the decline in party organizations, a decline that is then further accelerated by the delegation of political power and influence to nonparty campaigners.[17] As Theodore White, a close observer of the last six presidential campaigns, has discovered:

> New political advisers have developed whose professional cunning lies not, as it did in the Old Country, in cutting deals among the power brokers, but in manipulating television attention, baiting, diddling, and trying to befuddle those who allot time on television. The once-dominant finance chieftains of campaigning are now the paymasters of the television specialists at court; their chief obligation is to raise the money to buy television time.[18]

Professional consultants come in all shapes and sizes. Some perform political work exclusively, others only do it occasionally; some work only for candidates of particular parties or ideologies, others will work for anyone; some will take control over the entire campaign operation from the announcement of candidacy to the election-night celebration, others provide only one specialized service such as time-buying for media announcements or campaign finance accounting.

The range of services available is impressive. They include:

> advertising campaigns for radio, television and newspapers, including layout, timing and the actual placing of advertisements; public relations and press services, including the organization of public meetings, preparation and distribution of press releases and statements and detailed travel arrangements for the candidate; research and presentation of issues, including preparation of position papers, speech-writing and arranging for consultations between candidates and outside experts in appropriate areas of public policy; fund-raising solicitations, both by mail and through testimonial dinners and other public events; public opinion sampling to test voter awareness of the candidate, voter response to the campaign and voter attitudes on major issues; technical assistance on radio and television production, including the hiring of cameramen and recording studios for political films and broadcasts; campaign budgeting assistance designed to put campaign funds to the best possible use; use of data processing techniques to plan campaign strategy based on computer evaluations of thousands of bits of information; and mobilization of support through traditional precinct-level organization, door-to-door campaigns and telephone solicitation of votes.[19] [Reprinted with the permission of Congressional Quarterly Inc.]

Reliable information about the clients of professional consultants is hard to come by, but a rough indication of some of the involvement can be pieced together. It appears that the most active consultants work almost exclusively for candidates of one party and also for candidates of similar ideological leanings. Furthermore, statewide campaigns seem to rely more heavily than do local campaigns on consultants, and most consultants are confined to the region in which they are located.[20]

The reliance on campaign consultants has become so extensive that the political parties are trying to prevent consultants from preempting their participation in campaigns entirely. The National Republican Congressional Committee (NRCC) has been the most innovative in this regard, developing programs by which some of the expertise held by consultants is produced under the committee's auspices. In 1979 the NRCC devised a program in which six students would be selected for a six-month political advertising school and would be paid $150 per week to attend this school full time. They would be trained in the techniques of campaign advertising; examined and graded; asked to complete projects and take field trips (at the NRCC's expense); and, on successful completion of the program, would be placed on the NRCC staff at a salary of about $1,500/month. Their duties would then be to produce media advertising for 1980 Republican congressional candidates.

Candidates using professional consultants do not always win their elections. In 1970, for example, nine of the most active consultants won twenty and lost twenty-four of the races in which they were involved.[21] The importance of professional campaign consultants, however, should not be measured only by won-lost percentages; after all, consultants may be more often hired by candidates who face difficult campaigns. Rather, it is the prominence of the campaign consultant in contemporary campaigns that has attracted attention and raised some fears and doubts in the minds of political observers. Party officials and professional politicians tend to view professional consultants as a threat to their status, discretion, and expertise, and to claim that consultants' techniques are merely an expensive way of accumulating information that any worthy politician should already possess. Others worry that the electoral process itself is threatened by consultants since their intention is in some sense to manipulate the public. Our culture tolerates selling soap through carefully planned communication; selling political candidates in the same way is more suspect. Others point to escalating campaign costs and argue that the expense involved in using professional consultants is going to make the problem of financing election campaigns more serious. Still others worry that the main impact of the so-called new politics will be on the candidates themselves, who will increasingly be persons of wealth but not necessarily of political experience, vision, or intelligence. Whatever the relative merits of the various arguments, one thing is clear: The political campaign consultant is an increasingly important figure in the modern campaign. In fact, there is an organized association of political consultants, which holds an annual convention and plans to devise a code of ethics for the industry. A new profession has been born.

For our purpose, what is significant about the existence of professional campaign consultants is that they have an impact on the development of candidate communication. They have often had experience in dozens of previous campaigns and have formed their own beliefs about which messages will work and which will not. In addition, they hobnob with others in their profession, attempt to keep up with relevant social science research, and try to produce campaign results that will lead to more business in the future.

Not all consultants approach a campaign with the same view of the electorate and the same preference for different kinds of campaign messages. Some believe that voters are persuaded primarily by messages regarding the personal attributes of candidates:

> I think people have always voted for people. According to surveys, they have always voted on honesty, competence, and charisma, in that order. Many times issues are only used as a foil to express personal virtue. Our

candidates have been expressing personal qualities since we've been in business.[22]

Issues per se are not what move people to make their choice. The issue is the candidate's character, leadership and integrity.[23]

Voters are more influenced by perceptions of character and personality qualities than by whether they share their views on issues.[24]

Others, however, feel that voters are looking for information concerning the policy preferences of candidates:

I can't separate issue from personality. Candidates are in the business of issues. It's like trying to judge a lawyer who won't address himself to the law.[25]

Everyone is trying to put out the facade of honesty, purity and holiness. The public is not going to buy that any more than they buy the other crap they put out. What they're looking for is a candidate who's credible on any issue he talks about. They know the great white knight isn't going to ride down the trail.[26]

Regardless of which of these views is more accurate, both views carry implications for the development of campaign messages. If the first group of consultants had their way, we would expect candidate communication to focus on personality traits and other candidate characteristics. If the second group had their way, we would expect at least somewhat more discussion of the policy preferences or issue stands of prospective officeholders.

The Content of Candidate Communication

So far we have discussed the development of campaign communication strategies and candidate messages and the constraints on them. Now let us look more specifically at the types of messages relied on by political candidates. Although we do not have as much systematic evidence concerning the behavior of candidates as we would like to have, we can begin by analyzing the content of two increasingly prevalent forms of candidate communication: television spot advertisements and televised debates. (In Chapters 4 and 5 we will focus on the content of candidate messages as filtered through the journalists who produce campaign news coverage.)

To some extent each campaign is a unique communications event—a reflection of the history, experiences, and circumstances of those particular campaigners and that particular contest. Our goal here, however, is to discover the patterns in candidate communication that transcend the

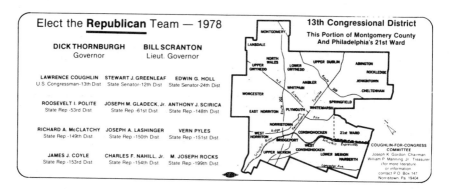

Partisan Ad

Narrator: A Wisconsin political quiz. You have sixty seconds to answer the following questions:

In the last six years, which party has twice raised taxes after promising no tax increases? The Republicans.

Which party was responsible for eliminating $322,000 in funds for campus security? The Republicans.

Which party refuses to enforce anti-pollution laws against Wisconsin's big industries? The Republicans.

Which party claimed a 3 million dollar surplus in 1968 and a 29 million dollar debt sixty days later? The Republicans.

Which candidate for Governor led the fight to raise the sales tax to 4%? Olsen.

Which candidate best promises a real change for Wisconsin? Lucey. November 3rd.

Partisan Debate Content

Carter: Mr. Ford takes the same attitude that the Republicans always take. In the last three months before an election, they are always for the programs that they fight the other three and a half years.

FIGURE 2–2   Partisan Campaign Appeals

circumstances of the particular campaign. We will do this by analyzing the *type of appeal* used by candidates to secure votes. The appeal reveals a candidate's assumptions concerning what a voter needs or wants to know as a guide in choosing candidates.

One type of appeal a candidate might use is a *partisan* appeal. This might involve identifying a candidate's partisan registration, mentioning other members of the same party, and describing the similarity between a candidate's characteristics and those of other party members. The use of such an appeal assumes that voters are motivated by partisan loyalties and that the voter would find it useful to know that a candidate is a "good Republican" or a "loyal Democrat." Figure 2–2 shows an example of a campaign flier and a television ad that are partisan in content, as well as an excerpt from the first presidential debate in 1976, in which Jimmy Carter links Gerald Ford with the Republican party.

A second type of appeal concerns the *personal characteristics of the candidate.* This type of appeal attempts to convince the voter that the candidate possesses qualities such as leadership, experience, honesty, and intelligence—or that the opponent does not. The use of this appeal assumes that the voter is motivated by perceptions of such qualities, and that particular qualities, characteristics, or traits are valued in the U.S. political context. Figure 2–3 contains an excerpt from a campaign brochure that focuses on the determination, integrity, and enthusiasm of a candidate; the text of a television spot ad that emphasizes the leadership, responsibility, and respect of a candidate; and excerpts from the 1976 presidential debates in which Gerald Ford claims to be experienced and Jimmy Carter questions Ford's leadership qualities.

A third type of appeal involves the transmission of information regarding the *demographic group identities* of the citizenry. The candidate is usually portrayed as understanding and sympathizing with the problems, goals, needs, or outlook of certain groups in U.S. society. Such an

Candidate Attribute Brochure Excerpt

. . . after 20 years of distinguished service in Austin, Bill Patman is ready to take the people's voice to Washington. And he'll take with him that same fighting spirit, that same dedication to principle, that same determination, that same integrity, and that same enthusiasm that have earned him a reputation as "the people's representative."

Candidate Attribute Ad

Narrator: There are times in our nation's history when leadership, responsibility and respect are measured not by age, but by ability. This is the time and this is the place. Kennedy, of Massachusetts.

Candidate Attribute Debate Content

Ford: For the last two years, I've been the President, and I have found from experience that it's much more difficult to make those decisions than it is to second-guess them. . . .

Carter: This kind of confusion and absence of leadership has let us drift now for two years with the constantly increasing threat of atomic weapons throughout the world.

FIGURE 2–3   Personal Attribute Campaign Appeals

Demographic Group Brochure Excerpts

With Jimmy Carter as President, Blacks are on the inside. Where it counts . . . Small Town America Can Depend On Jimmy Carter. A President From Rural America And For Rural America . . . Under President Carter's Leadership, Labor has a Partner in the White House . . .

Demographic Group Ad

Goldberg: So this fellow gets this letter: You have reached retirement age. We enclose a check for 20¢ and wish you well on your retirement.

Narrator: There is no man in or out of public life who has devoted more time or has been more successful in protecting the rights of the man who works. Goldberg, leadership for a change.

Demographic Group Debate Content

Carter: We could also help our youth with some of the proposals that would give to young people an opportunity to work and learn at the same time, just as we give money to young people who are going to college.

FIGURE 2–4   Demographic Group Campaign Appeals

appeal need not necessarily involve any oral communication; the visual presentation of a candidate with a member of a readily identifiable group may be sufficient to make the point. This type of appeal assumes that group identification is an important factor in voting behavior. Figure 2–4 contains excerpts from campaign brochures of Jimmy Carter that attempt to associate him with blacks, farmers, and workers; a television spot ad that contains some information pertaining to the candidate's concern for working people; and an excerpt from a 1976 presidential debate in which Jimmy Carter expresses his concern for the problems of the young.

The fourth type of appeal that candidates typically transmit concerns *issues* or matters of *public policy*. This type of appeal is more complex than the other three since there are a number of different ways in which candidates can discuss policy questions.

One type of issue-related appeal deals with the candidate's issue or policy concerns. This usually involves simply an expression by the candidate that he or she cares about some issue or, in the language of social scientists, that the issue is *salient* to the candidate. Such an appeal need not necessarily include any indication of what the candidate would propose doing about the issue or problem; it may focus primarily on who should be held responsible for a social problem.

The second type of issue-related appeal reveals a policy preference of the candidate, but only in the most *vague, ambiguous,* or *symbolic* way. A candidate, for example, may say that he or she opposes inflation or favors adequate medical care (who doesn't?). Appeals of this type are usually not particularly illuminating about the programs the candidate would actually propose or support.

The third type of issue-related appeal involves the articulation of more *specific policy proposals.* What separates this appeal from the previous one is that it is possible for the public to anticipate a fairly precise legislative or bureaucratic action consistent with the appeal.

Figure 2–5 displays some examples of issue-related campaign appeals. The first section of the figure contains an example of an advertisement in which a policy concern—medical care—is raised, but the candidate says nothing about what should be done about that issue; and an example of a statement during a presidential debate in which Jimmy Carter raises the issue of crime without saying anything further about it. Both examples attempt to increase the salience of, or attention to, an issue without revealing a policy *position.*

The second section of Figure 2–5 contains an excerpt from a campaign brochure, an advertisement, and an excerpt from a presidential debate in which candidates take a vague or ambiguous position on a public policy question. The brochure contains a whole series of proposals (an "end to special interest government," "tough new laws," "a change in our medical system," "sensible reductions," and "more aid to programs") that sound like policy positions but do not reveal very much about what policies the candidate would actually support. In fact, these proposals are so vague and general that it is difficult to imagine anyone disagreeing with any of them. The same is true of the advertisement, in which the candidate comes out in favor of "a decent retirement income and adequate medical care" but does not say how he would propose to accomplish these goals; and of the debate extracts in which both Carter and Ford make general, vague proposals (who could be in favor of government secrecy, opposed to personal privacy, or opposed to an educational system that allows children to improve themselves—at least in our culture?).

The third section of Figure 2–5 contains excerpts from a campaign brochure, an advertisement, and excerpts from presidential debates in which candidates do reveal fairly specific policy proposals. In each case it would be possible for a citizen to imagine a piece of legislation, executive order, or other governmental action that would represent the policies proposed by the candidates.

Candidates, of course, use more than one of these four types of appeals.[27] One or two types, however, may dominate a particular campaign or a campaign's use of a particular medium. Furthermore, patterns in the use of these different appeals reveal a good deal about what cam-

Issue Salience Ad

Hart: You don't have to be a young revolutionary to say something's wrong. We think that we're the healthiest people in the world—best medical system. Truth is, we're 18th among 23 of all the developed nations. We can do better than that.

Narrator: Phil Hart, the senior Senator from Michigan.

Issue Salience Debate Content

Carter: But I think that now is the time to heal our country after the Vietnam War, and I think that what the people are concerned about is not the pardon or the amnesty of those who evaded the draft, but whether or not our crime system is fair. . . . And the whole subject of crime is one that concerns our people very much. . . .

Vague Issue Position Brochure Excerpt

Here's Floyd Haskell's Program: Immediate reform of our tax laws to insure that no one is forced to pay more than his or her fair share . . . An end to special interest government that serves the well-heeled lobbyists better than the average working man . . . Tough new laws to clean up our air and water and protect what's still not polluted . . . A change in our medical system to see to it that costs are within reason and quality medical care is available to everyone— no matter who they are or where they live . . . Sensible reductions in our defense budget to cut out waste and streamline the military. More aid to programs that serve people.

Vague Issue Position and Demographic Group Ad

(Church shown with a group of old people)
Narrator: For them, his unequaled accomplishments on behalf of the elderly are more than statistics, for them they are life itself.

Church: They're proud people and they ought to be entitled as a matter of right to a decent retirement income and adequate medical care. That's a pretty modest program for a country as rich as ours.

Old Man: Boy, I guess that's correct.

Narrator: Frank Church, Idaho's man.

Vague Issue Position Debate Content

Carter: Our education system can be improved. Secrecy ought to be stripped away from government, and a maximum of personal privacy ought to be maintained.

FIGURE 2–5   Policy-Related Campaign Appeals

Ford: The member of a labor union must have his rights strengthened and broadened, and our children in their education should have an opportunity to improve themselves, based on their talents and their abilities.

Specific Issue Position Brochure Excerpt

There's only one sure way to create large numbers of new jobs for Americans, and that's through economic growth. A growing economy means increased investment, the expansion of industry, and the creation of new jobs—real, private sector jobs with a future.

That's how Ronald Reagan, himself a former union leader, sees the situation. And here is an outline of the program that he will, as President, formulate to get America's economy growing. It will include:

- A limit in the growth of government spending.
- Accelerated depreciation for industry, designed to spur job-creating expansion and investment in new plants.
- A balanced budget, to be achieved by controlling government spending coupled with economic growth spurred in part by tax rate reductions.
- Personal tax rate reductions aimed at increasing the incentive to work and produce, a vital component of any plan for economic growth.

Specific Issue Position Ad

(Mondale talking to workers. They tell him of their contributions to the pension fund of a local industry which is now moving out of town.)

Mondale: What's happening to you guys here is not just a scandal, it's a national scandal. No one, no employer should ever be able to get away with this. Here's what we want to do in our plan. First of all, we want the plan to vest—after you've been a certain number of years you got a legal right to that money.

Worker: That's correct.

Mondale: Secondly, it should be portable—that fifteen years oughta be added. . . .

Worker: You should be able to take it with you.

Mondale: Yes, it should be a right you carry with you. And then we need some rules to govern these pension funds because some of these funds are being raided: they're being used by the company to make money for themselves when the money's supposed to go back into that fund to make it secure for the people that are

FIGURE 2–5 Continued

Specific Issue Position Ad (Continued)

there. So we need control over these funds so they're run for the workers and not for somebody else.

Narrator: Mondale, of Minnesota.

Specific Issue Position Debate Content

Carter: Well, I think it is very difficult for President Ford to explain the difference between the pardon of President Nixon and his attitude toward those who violated the draft laws. As a matter of fact, now I don't advocate amnesty. I advocate pardon. There is a difference, in my opinion and in accordance with the ruling of the Supreme Court and, of course, the definition in the dictionary. Amnesty means that what you did was right. Pardon means that what you did—whether right or wrong—you are forgiven for it. And I do advocate a pardon for draft evaders.

Ford: In my tax reduction program for middle-income taxpayers, I recommended that the Congress increase personal exemptions from $750 per person to $1,000 per person. . . .

FIGURE 2–5   Continued

paigners assume motivates voters. Since candidates' selection of different appeals affects the kinds of information voters get, the pattern of candidate appeals will also have a profound influence on the beliefs and attitudes the public uses to make electoral choices.

We will now study some appeals presented by candidates in televised spot ads and televised debates. These sources are more readily available for systematic inquiry than are other forms of candidate communication, and they represent increasingly significant forms of candidate rhetoric.

CONTENT OF SPOT ADVERTISEMENTS

To see how candidates have used television spot advertising in a variety of campaigns, I have viewed and analyzed 156 different television spot ads. These ads represent a variety of electoral levels, competitive situations, and years. Although the sample analyzed unfortunately cannot be termed a representative sample of all ads ever shown (no such sample exists), the inclusion of a variety of campaign situations permits a more general view of campaign advertising than would be possible from studying a few campaigns in more detail.[28]

The four different types of candidate appeals described earlier—

TABLE 2–1   Content of Televised Political Spot Advertisements

Partisanship (%)	
Overt	9.6
Marginal	15.4
Nonpartisan	71.2
Bipartisan, cross-partisan	3.8
	100.0
Issue position (%)	
Specific	19.9
Vague	37.8
Salience only	19.2
None	42.3
	119.2[a]
Candidate qualities (%)	
Yes	47.4
No	52.6
	100.0
Groups (%)	
Yes	39.7
No	60.3
	100.0
$N = 156$	

Source: Adapted from Richard A. Joslyn, "The Content of Political Spot Ads," *Journalism Quarterly* 57, no. 1 (Spring 1980): 95. Reprinted by permission.

[a]This category sums to more than 100 percent since more than one type of policy appeal may appear in each ad.

partisan, candidate attribute, demographic group, and issue-related— were looked for in each of the 156 ads. Table 2–1 shows the distribution of the appeals that were found. Most of the ads contain some mention of issues, but usually only in order to show that a candidate is concerned about them. About half the ads focus on the personal attributes of the candidate, and fewer than half contain some demographic group information. About one-third of the ads contain vague or symbolic appeals concerning policy issues.

What the ads definitely do *not* contain are partisan and specific issue appeals. Only one ad in ten uses the partisan identification of the candidate; another 15 percent contain information from which the partisan identity of the candidate could be inferred if a viewer knew a little about politics. That leaves almost three-quarters of the ads with nothing to say about the candidate's political party. Similarly, only one ad in five contains information specific enough about the policy preferences of candidates that a viewer could use it to predict the candidate's future policy behavior. This conclusion has also been reached by a political analyst who claims to have viewed 1100 spot ads, both U.S. and foreign. Apparently, the policy content of British ads is far more programmatic than that of U.S. ads, and in the United States the policy content becomes even rarer and more ambiguous in campaigns for lower-level offices.[29]

The lack of specific issue position appeals in the ads suggests that public policy *positions* are less important to campaigners than are the impressions of candidates that policy discussions leave with the voters. The typical issue-related information mentioned in these ads would certainly tell a citizen little about what public policies to expect a candidate to support. Since politicians are supposed to be conversant on issues, however, and policy questions cannot be ignored completely, they are used to communicate something about the candidate as a person. As a member of one of the most active political consultant firms, commenting on a specific gubernatorial race, has put it:

> We are really stressing a personal quality of the governor and that was his leadership ability. And so, more often than not, the best approach is to stress a particular issue, but in so doing, highlight a personal quality of the candidate. And, that comes from first determining what issues are salient to voters and then determining what positive qualities your candidate has and see if there is an intercorrelation . . . what you're really saying to voters is this man, regardless of what the issue is, but certainly if it is this issue, he is thinking in a way that you can trust him . . . to make future decisions.[30]

Observing the general distribution of candidate appeals used in televised spot ads is an important first step in our attempt to understand candidate communication more generally. The next question that comes to mind is whether different types of candidates or candidates in different situations use different appeals.

We might initially ask whether the type of appeal used by Republican candidates differs from that used by Democrats. The answer is that it does not. The type of appeal used, however, does depend to some extent on the office being contested, the area of the country in which the campaign is taking place, and the year in which the ad was produced.

Gubernatorial ads contain more old-style—that is, partisan—appeals than the others do. This is probably a reflection of the fact that partisan organizations are more interested and active in gubernatorial campaigns than in many others. The gubernatorial constituency matches the important partisan geographical unit, and the patronage that comes with the statehouse is one of the few important partisan political resources that remains. Senatorial campaigns, on the other hand, are the least partisan of the three; most senatorial campaigns involve an incumbent who has reason to pursue a nonpartisan strategy, and most are only loosely tied to partisan organizations. There is little tangible reward for a partisan organization that is successful in electing a U.S. senator.

There is also a relationship between the geographic origin of television ads and the candidate appeals. Daniel Elazar has divided the United States into three different subcultures, each with a different view of politics, the political role of citizens, and the appropriate modes of conduct for public officials and governing bodies. The *moralistic* subculture, located in the New England and Northern-rim states, is characterized by ideological and policy-oriented politics with an expectation of active citizen participation. The *individualistic* subculture, located in the Middle Atlantic and Midwestern states, is characterized by partisan politics, with a partisan role preserved for citizens and partisan competition dominating the electoral arena. The *traditionalistic* subculture, located in the South, is characterized by elite-dominated politics with a very limited political role reserved for citizens and with factional conflict within a single dominant party the typical form of conflict resolution.[31] The television ads used by candidates in each of these subcultures reflect these subcultural tendencies: The ads from moralistic states contain more issue and demographic-group appeals, whereas those from states in the individualistic subculture are more apt to rely on partisan and candidate-oriented appeals.[32]

Perhaps the most interesting pattern in the content of ads is revealed when we look at ad content over time (see Table 2–2). Using 1969 as the dividing point, there seem to have been three recent changes in ad content. Ads have become less partisan, less filled with specific issue information, and considerably more group-oriented in recent years. This may reflect changes in candidate and consultant perceptions of the factors motivating voters. In the case of the transmission of partisan information, this shift in emphasis coincides with a decrease in voter reliance on partisan cues in voting at all levels.

Spot ads are a form of campaign communication that is completely controlled by the candidate and his or her organization. The appeals presented in ads are the ones candidates *want* to present, either because they are what candidates want to say or because they are what candidates think the citizens want to hear. As a result, the appeals used provide an excellent insight into the predispositions and assumptions of candidates and their staff.

The appeals made by candidates in televised spot advertisements also constrain the learning that the public is apt to experience during an election campaign. There are at least three notable ways in which the content of the spot ads described here delimits the public's political understandings.

First, the vast majority of spot ad appeals are candidate- rather than party-oriented. This means that the public is being asked to judge a candidate as a *person* rather than as the *nominee* or *representative of a political party* with a political history and enduring philosophical bent. Consequently, it is hardly surprising that public opinion researchers

TABLE 2–2   Relationship between Year and Content of Television
Spot Advertisements

	1960–1968	1970–1976
Partisanship		
Overt	15.1	7.2
Marginal	22.6	12.4
Nonpartisan	62.3	80.4
	100.0	100.0
Issue content		
Yes	79.6	75.5
No	20.4	24.5
	100.0	100.0
Issue position		
Specific	27.8	15.7
Vague	37.0	38.2
None	35.2	46.1
	100.0	100.0
Candidate qualities		
Yes	48.1	47.1
No	51.9	52.9
	100.0	100.0
Groups		
Yes	25.9	47.1
No	74.1	52.9
	100.0	100.0
	N = 54	N = 102

Source: Richard A. Joslyn, "The Content of Political Spot Ads," *Journalism Quarterly* 57,
no. 1 (Spring 1980): 97. Reprinted by permission.

have found that partisan cues and perceptions are decreasingly involved
in citizen evaluations of candidates for public office and choices between
them.

Second, most of the candidate-oriented appeals focus on the personal
characteristics, issue concerns, and group linkages of the candidate.
Such appeals are typically fundamentally noncontroversial and symbolic. In each case the appeal is to a norm or value that is part of a
cultural consensus. Candidate A is experienced, candidate B cares about
senior citizens, candidate C is concerned about high levels of crime.
Hardly anyone would disapprove of any of these appeals; they are all
attributes that the public considers good. What the citizen is typically left
to ponder, then, is not whether the appeal is good, or makes sense, or is
correct, but rather *whether or not it is believable.*

Third, the appeals used by candidates that relate to public policy
questions are not likely to assist the public in forming attitudes about

future policy alternatives or the policy preferences of candidates. Appeals that reveal the policy intentions of candidates are rare; most discussions of public policy issues focus instead on the issues candidates care about and the broad (hence vague and ambiguous) policy goals that the candidates approve of (prosperity, efficiency, economic growth, military strength, and the like). Such policy discussions may reassure the public that the policy viewpoints of candidates are acceptable, but they do little to allow voters (if they are so inclined) to choose a candidate on the basis of expected future policy actions and choices.

In short, some kinds of learning are encouraged by the appeals made in spot ads, and others are prevented.

CONTENT OF BROADCAST, FACE-TO-FACE DEBATES

As a form of candidate communication, debates differ from spot ads in that candidates are not in complete control of the messages that result. Although candidates rehearse answers to possible questions and replies to points likely to be emphasized by the opposing candidate, candidates never know for sure what they will be asked or what they will be accused of. Consequently, the content of candidate statements in debates is shaped less by advertising consultants and campaign advisers and more by the candidates' predispositions and the goals of the interviewers. What effect does this have on the type of candidate appeals presented in televised debates?

First of all, debates tend to be much more policy-related than spot ads are. Candidates are expected to be conversant on the "issues," and most interviewers participating in debates perceive their role as one of forcing candidates to reveal as specific and distinct policy preferences as possible. An analysis of the 1960 presidential debates between John Kennedy and Richard Nixon, for example, found that between 40 and 70 percent of the candidate statements (depending on how one type of statement is categorized) contained specific policy positions, the reasoning behind these policy positions, or the use of evidence to support the policy positions taken by candidates. Furthermore, this type of policy-related information was found to be much more prevalent during the 1960 debates than in either candidate's acceptance speech at his respective nominating convention. Policy-oriented appeals are also more prevalent in the opening statements of the candidate going first than in the closing statements of the candidate speaking last, since candidates may speak in a more general, vague, and ambiguous way when they know there will be no rebuttal.[33]

An analysis of the 1976 presidential debates found that they, too, tended to be issue-oriented. The interrogating reporters were found to have spent 92 percent of their time on issues, and the candidates responded with issue-related comments about 80 percent of the time.[34]

In order to demonstrate the contrast in the policy-related appeals made in debates and spot ads, the content of the nine presidential debates held during the general elections in 1960, 1976, and 1980 has been categorized using the same types of appeals used to analyze the spot ads (Table 2–3).[35] In general, all the televised, general election presidential debates have focused primarily on policy questions, though with varying degrees of specificity. Partisan, group, and personal attribute appeals have been a much less prominent feature of the debates than they have been of spot ads.

Although presidential debates have been concerned primarily with discussions of public policies, these discussions have sometimes been quite vague and general. Much of what passes for policy discussions includes the statement of consensually held goals such as full employment, economic growth, an equitable tax system, the elimination of governmental waste, and the development of a strong military capability. A significant portion of the policy-related discussion involves raising social, economic, or political problems without any subsequent discussion of what policies might be recommended to solve these problems.

Nonetheless, previous presidential debates have included the revelation of a number of fairly specific policy preferences by presidential candidates. Furthermore, debates contain more of this type of information than spot ads do. In 1960, for example, John Kennedy and Richard Nixon discussed fairly specific policy alternatives regarding the defense of Formosa, federal aid to education, medical care for the aged, presidential powers to deal with strikes, relations with Cuba, the oil depletion allowance, foreign aid, and nuclear testing. In 1976 Gerald Ford and Jimmy Carter debated policy concerning tax reductions, defense spending, gun control legislation, foreign relations with a number of countries, energy policy, revenue sharing, the Federal Reserve Board, arms reduction, and abortion. Finally, in 1980 Ronald Reagan and John Anderson debated tax policy, energy conservation and production, the reinstatement of the draft, military weaponry, and abortion; Ronald Reagan and Jimmy Carter debated tax policy, defense spending, minimum-wage legislation, nuclear arms reduction, energy production, Social Security, women's rights, and air pollution legislation.

In general, the types of appeals used in each of these three series of debates have been quite similar, but there is some intriguing variation. Partisan appeals have been much less frequent in the recent debates than they were in 1960, a pattern mirrored by the decline in the partisan content of spot ads. The discussion of specific policy positions, however, seems to have become slightly more prevalent in the recent elections than in 1960—a pattern exactly the opposite of what we found for spot ads. In the debates, unlike the ads, there has been no sign of an increased use of group-related appeals. These changes in the type of debate appeals may have contributed to the decline in party-related

TABLE 2–3 Content of 1960, 1976, and 1980 Presidential Debates

	Partisan	Group	Personal Attributes	Issues			Unclassified
				Salience	Vague	Specific	
1960							
First (domestic)	27.1	13.8	9.8	11.3	40.6	12.7	5.3
Second (open)	16.8	2.5	15.0	14.3	32.3	27.6	7.4
Third (open)	9.0	2.0	16.4	8.7	43.4	22.9	6.1
Fourth (foreign)	16.6	0.0	19.6	20.6	30.5	18.9	7.0
1976							
First (domestic)	7.4	7.3	10.9	8.0	31.5	30.8	4.0
Second (foreign)	3.2	6.1	17.1	8.4	42.6	24.9	2.5
Third (open)	1.7	7.6	22.8	10.1	23.1	21.1	11.5
1980							
First (Reagan-Anderson)	0.0	0.5	6.9	16.5	36.2	32.9	6.8
Second (Reagan-Carter)	4.8	6.1	12.9	12.7	33.8	28.3	6.4
Spot Ads							
1960–1968	37.7	25.9	48.1	14.8	37.0	27.8	—
1970–1976	19.6	47.1	47.1	21.6	38.2	15.7	—

TABLE 2–4 Candidate Appeals in Presidential Debates

	Kennedy	Nixon
Partisan		
First	23.9	30.4
Second	19.1	14.3
Third	6.1	11.5
Fourth	16.6	16.6
Group		
First	14.7	12.9
Second	1.6	3.5
Third	2.4	1.6
Fourth	0.0	0.0
Personal attributes		
First	5.6	14.1
Second	16.9	13.1
Third	17.2	15.8
Fourth	13.2	26.5
Policy salience		
First	14.3	8.3
Second	16.7	11.8
Third	16.1	1.9
Fourth	28.3	12.3
Policy vague		
First	41.1	40.0
Second	33.5	31.1
Third	36.8	49.4
Fourth	26.5	34.8
Policy specific		
First	11.6	13.8
Second	26.5	28.7
Third	30.9	15.6
Fourth	18.3	19.5
	Carter	**Ford**
Partisan		
First	7.5	7.3
Second	5.0	1.1
Third	2.5	0.7
Group		
First	8.6	5.7
Second	5.7	6.7
Third	9.4	5.6
Personal attributes		
First	13.6	7.7
Second	20.8	12.5
Third	25.6	19.4

TABLE 2–4   Candidate Appeals in Presidential Debates (*Cont.*)

	Carter	Ford
Policy salience		
First	10.6	4.8
Second	10.9	5.3
Third	15.5	3.9
Policy vague		
First	30.2	33.1
Second	42.4	43.0
Third	18.4	28.6
Policy specific		
First	25.9	36.9
Second	14.7	37.1
Third	14.2	29.1

	Anderson	Reagan
Partisan	0.0	0.0
Group	1.0	0.0
Personal attributes	6.0	7.8
Policy salience	24.6	8.5
Policy vague	21.1	51.2
Policy specific	37.5	28.3

	Carter	Reagan
Partisan	8.1	1.7
Group	8.1	4.2
Personal attributes	15.5	10.3
Policy salience	9.2	16.0
Policy vague	30.9	36.6
Policy specific	30.1	26.5

voting and the increase in policy-related voting that a number of observers have found in the U.S. electorate.

When we compare the debate appeals made by different candidates, the types of appeals used by each are usually quite similar (see Table 2–4). There are a couple of suggestive patterns, however. First, there is no particularly distinctive use of partisan appeals by any one candidate except for Jimmy Carter's greater reliance on them in both 1976 and 1980. This attempt to focus the campaign on partisan considerations was, of course, consistent with Carter's campaign strategy, as represented by his pollster, Pat Caddell, quoted earlier. Second, there is no candidate who relies on group appeals significantly more than any other, although Jimmy Carter also made somewhat more use of this kind of message in both 1976 and 1980. The most distinctive use of personal attribute appeals was also Jimmy Carter's reliance on them in 1976 (with leadership and Carter's "outsider" status the main topics), and in 1980 (with the attempt to portray Reagan as "dangerous").

There are two consistent patterns in policy-related appeals. Kennedy in 1960, Carter in 1976, and Reagan in 1980 all made greater use of policy *salience* appeals (messages simply defining something as an important *issue*) than did their opponents. All three were nonincumbents in each of these races. Challengers probably find it attractive to raise policy questions (usually policy *problems*) in an attempt to hold the incumbent responsible for them. Thus John Kennedy in 1960 held Richard Nixon responsible for an alleged drop in U.S. prestige abroad; Jimmy Carter in 1976 held Gerald Ford responsible for high rates of unemployment and a "disgraceful" tax system; and Ronald Reagan in 1980 held Jimmy Carter responsible for high rates of inflation. Although the incumbent may have had little to do with these issues and may in some cases be largely powerless to do anything about them, challengers hope to cast doubt on the incumbent's job performance by simply raising problems and attempting to assign blame to the incumbent. They usually refrain, however, from suggesting in any great detail what they would do about the problems they cite.

In contrast, incumbents are a little more likely to defend their previous performance with reference to specific policy proposals. This was particularly true of Gerald Ford's rhetoric in 1976, probably due in part to his attempt to pin a fuzzy-on-the-issues label on his opponent. John Anderson's rhetoric in 1980 was also somewhat more specific than that of either Reagan or Carter.

In thirteen of the eighteen candidate debate cases analyzed, the most prevalent type of appeal has been the *vague* policy preference one (and in four of the other five cases it is the second most prevalent type of communication). This category is a collection of vague policy goals; symbolic concepts (such as efficiency, fairness, and liberty); and diffuse criticisms. It is clearly a prominent type of appeal in both spot ads and debate utterances—one that is preferred by candidates in a variety of partisan, competitive, and institutional circumstances when they are in control of the campaign message.

A recent study of candidate communication has found that the vague policy appeal is by no means restricted to televised advertising and debate appearances. An analysis of *all* the campaign communication of John Kennedy and Richard Nixon in 1960 estimated that 23 percent of Kennedy's rhetoric and 16 percent of Nixon's focused on policy proposals, whereas almost half, on the other hand, focused on goals, problems, and past performances. A similar analysis of *all* the campaign speeches given by Hubert Humphrey and Richard Nixon in 1968 revealed that the typical issue was mentioned in only 5 percent of the speeches, and the issues most often discussed (Vietnam, inflation, law and courts) were mentioned in only 10 to 20 percent of the speeches. The author of this analysis, Benjamin Page, has concluded that

> the most striking feature of candidates' rhetoric about policy is its extreme vagueness. The typical campaign speech says virtually nothing specific about policy alternatives; discussions of the issues are hidden away in little-publicized statements and position papers. Even the most extended discussions leave many questions unanswered. In short, policy stands are infrequent, inconspicuous and unspecific. Presidential candidates are skilled at appearing to say much while actually saying little.[36]

This type of appeal is attractive to a candidate since it avoids controversy, avoids alienating those who disagree with him or her, and avoids establishing a public record with which subsequent performance can be compared. It may also be reassuring and comforting to the citizen to know that both candidates hold consensual values in the mainstream of U.S. political culture. It is hard to imagine, however, that such rhetoric allows members of the public, should they be so inclined, to learn anything new about policy alternatives or to base their electoral choice on those grounds. As Murray Edelman observed two decades ago, "most campaign speeches consist of the exchange of cliches among people who agree with each other. The talk, therefore, serves to dull the critical faculties rather than to arouse them."[37] There is little reason to believe that the situation has changed significantly in the past twenty years.

Conclusion

This chapter has focused on the communication strategies of candidates and other campaigners. Since candidates are the ones who typically initiate campaign communication and who need to develop the messages of a campaign, we concentrated on the origins and content of candidate appeals.

Campaign messages evolve from a complex and dynamic process involving candidate preferences, citizen predispositions, competitive challenges, and expert advice. The prevalence of public opinion polling and professional campaign consultants has meant that messages are now devised with greater information about the intended audience than ever before, and that the candidate's own intuition and predispositions may be less influential than in the past.

The candidate appeals used in two significant forms of campaign communication—televised spot advertisements and candidate debates—were analyzed for different candidates, and over time. These appeals most typically focus on personal attributes and the connections between candidates and demographic groups in spot ads, and on vague policy goals in debates. The policy discussion that takes place in these formats is occasionally specific but more often general, ambiguous, and vague, or used to convey an impression of the candidate's personal characteristics.[38] Furthermore, over time there apparently has been less use of partisan appeals in both spot ads and debates, less use of specific policy appeals in spot ads but more use of such appeals in debates, and more use of group-benefit appeals in spot ads.

The types of candidate appeals used are significant for many reasons. First, the type of appeal influences the nature of learning that is apt to take place among the citizenry during the election campaign. If most candidate appeals focus on personal attributes, for example, and other information is not forthcoming from other sources, this is probably what most citizens will learn about during the campaign. The inherent limits on the extent to which an election campaign can serve an educational function have often been detailed; the type of appeal used by candidates represents one important constraint on the educative effect of a campaign.

Second, candidate appeals undoubtedly affect the information that is salient to the voter and the relationships between different attitudes and the votes cast. Political scientists have argued for years over whether voters are more inclined to cast a vote based on party, policy, or personality grounds, and have gone to great pains to measure the contribution of each factor in different campaigns to the explanation of electoral choices. The simpler possibility—that the importance of these different attitudes to the voters is dependent on the selection of appeals used by campaigners—has seldom been seriously considered.

Finally, candidate appeals contribute to the meaning of election outcomes. Although we often speak of *mandates* for successful candidates, it is clear that if the salient candidate appeals and citizen beliefs have little prospective policy content, then the meaning of the mandate is unclear. In fact, if most candidate appeals emphasize vague but consensually held policy goals, or the personal characteristics of candidates, then it seems clear that the messages sent by voters could hardly represent a mandate for specific future policy choices.

Notes

1. For a general discussion of the motives behind campaign contributions in U.S. congressional races, see Gary C. Jacobson, *Money in Congressional Elections* (New Haven, Conn.: Yale University Press, 1980), ch. 4.

2. For an analysis of how the rhetoric of presidential candidates is shaped by partisan cleavages and candidate support groups, see Benjamin I. Page, *Choices*

and Echoes in Presidential Elections (Chicago: University of Chicago Press, 1978), pp. 152–153. For a discussion of the relationship between incumbent members of Congress and supportive members of the constituency, see Richard Fenno, *Home Style: House Members in Their Districts* (Boston: Little, Brown, 1978).

3. Larry J. Sabato, *The Rise of Political Consultants* (New York: Basic Books, 1981), p. 70.

4. Ibid., p. 80, and Robert Agranoff, *The New Style in Election Campaigns* (Boston: Holbrook Press, 1976), p. 36.

5. "Where the Polls Went Wrong," *Time*, December 1, 1980, pp. 21–22.

6. Edwin Diamond, *Good News, Bad News* (Cambridge, Mass.: MIT Press, 1978), pp. 32–34.

7. A larger portion of the memo is reproduced in Martin Schram, *Running for President 1976: The Carter Campaign* (New York: Stein and Day, 1977), pp. 253–268.

8. Ibid., pp. 52–53.

9. Ibid., pp. 55–56.

10. Ibid., pp. 101–102.

11. Ibid., pp. 222–223.

12. *Public Opinion* 3, no. 6 (December–January 1981): 2, 6, 10.

13. Ibid., p. 8.

14. These episodes are described in more detail in Schram, *Running for President*, pp. 121–124, 300–313, 332.

15. For a discussion of the use of polls by candidates, see Michael Wheeler, *Lies, Damn Lies, and Statistics* (New York: W. W. Norton, 1976), and Charles W. Roll and Albert H. Cantril, *Polls: Their Use and Misuse in Politics* (Cabin John, Md.: Seven Locks Press, 1980).

16. Sabato, *Political Consultants*, p. 12. See also Robert Agranoff, "The New Style of Campaigning: The Decline of Party and the Rise of Candidate-Centered Technology," in Agranoff, *New Style*, pp. 3–47.

17. Agranoff, *New Style*, pp. 3–4.

18. Theodore White, *America in Search of Itself* (New York: Harper and Row, 1982), p. 166.

19. Campaign Management Grows into National Industry," *Congressional Quarterly Weekly Report*, April 5, 1968, p. 708.

20. For a discussion of the relationship between political consultants and their candidate clients, see Sabato, *Political Consultants*, Chap. 1.

21. "Political Consultants: Mixed Results in 1970 Elections," *1970 Congressional Quarterly Almanac*, p. 1098.

22. Robert Goodman, quoted in "Campaign Consultants: Pushing Sincerity in 1974," *Congressional Quarterly Weekly Report*, May 4, 1974, p. 1105.

23. Gerald Rafshoon, quoted in Deirdre Carmody, "Ad Aides see Presidential Candidates as the Issues," *New York Times*, October 15, 1976, p. B5.

24. John Deardourff, quoted in James McCartney, "Ford's Campaign: It's a TV Show," *Philadelphia Inquirer*, October 11, 1976, p. A-8.

25. Charles Guggenheim, quoted in "Campaign Consultants," p. 1105.

26. Sanford Weiner, quoted in ibid., p. 1106.

27. Similar categories of advertising purpose are enumerated in Sabato, *Political Consultants*, p. 121.

28. Of the 156 ads, 49 are from presidential campaigns, 43 from gubernato-

rial campaigns, 62 from senatorial campaigns, and 2 from congressional campaigns. One hundred five are the ads of Democrats, 48 those of Republicans, and 3 those of minor-party candidates. Seventy-four are incumbent ads, 82 the ads of nonincumbents; 101 are ads of winners, 55 those of losers. For more information concerning this study, see Richard Joslyn, "The Content of Political Spot Ads," *Journalism Quarterly*, 57, no. 1 (Spring 1980): 92–98.

29. Sabato, *Political Consultants*, pp. 129–131, 148–151.

30. Interview with Paul Wilson from Bailey/Deardourff, Associates, Inc., by Michael Eng, a student of the author, December 1978.

31. Daniel J. Elazar, *American Federalism: A View from the States* (New York: Thomas Y. Crowell, 1966), and Daniel J. Elazar, "The American Cultural Matrix," in Daniel J. Elazar and Joseph Zikmund II, eds., *The Ecology of American Political Culture: Readings* (New York: Thomas Y. Crowell, 1975).

32. Richard A. Joslyn, "Manifestations of Elazar's Political Subcultures: State Public Opinion and the Content of Political Campaign Advertising," *Publius* 10, no. 2 (Spring 1980): 37–58.

33. John W. Ellsworth, "Rationality and Campaigning: A Content Analysis of the 1960 Presidential Campaign Debates," *Western Political Quarterly*, 18 (December 1965): 794–802.

34. David O. Sears and Steven H. Chaffee, "Uses and Effects of the 1976 Debates: An Overview of Empirical Studies," in Sidney Kraus, ed., *The Great Debates, 1976: Ford v. Carter* (Bloomington: Indiana University Press, 1979).

35. Debate transcripts may be found in Sidney Kraus, *The Great Debates* (Gloucester, Mass.: Peter Smith, 1968) for the 1960 debates; in George F. Bishop, Robert G. Meadow, and Marilyn Jackson-Beeck, eds., *The Presidential Debates* (New York: Praeger, 1980), for the 1976 debates; and in *1980 Congressional Quarterly Almanac*, pp. 127-B–137-B, and *Congressional Quarterly Weekly Report*, September 27, 1980, pp. 2863–2869, for the 1980 debates.

36. Page, *Choices and Echoes*, pp. 152–153.

37. Murray Edelman, *The Symbolic Uses of Politics* (Urbana: University of Illinois Press, 1964), pp. 17–18.

38. It may be, however, that candidate appeals during nomination campaigns contain more specific policy-related information, especially when candidates need to differentiate their campaigns from a host of others. Unfortunately, evidence regarding the nomination appeals used by candidates is fairly sparse. If the rhetoric of the Carter nomination campaign in 1976 is any indication, however, policy-related messages were *less*, not more, substantive early in the campaign.

3
Candidate Communication: Reaching the Desired Audience

*National political campaigns have become little more than a series of perfor-
mances calculated to attract the attention of television news cameras and their
audiences*
— Donald Matthews, "Winnowing," in *Race for the Presidency*

*The President's campaign must be television oriented. We must change the per-
ception of literally millions of voters, and this can only be done through the mass
media with the principal emphasis on television. This is true for coverage of the
President and media advertising.*
— Gerald Ford campaign memo, quoted in Martin Schram,
Running for President 1976

In Chapter 2 we discussed one aspect of candidate communication: the
development and content of the messages that candidates deliver to the
public in their quest for money, volunteers, and votes. In this chapter we
turn our attention to another aspect of candidate communication: delivering the messages to the intended audience.

Determining the Audience for Candidate Communication

Candidates seldom attempt to deliver their campaign appeals to the
entire populace, citizenry, or electorate. Rather, they usually think of the
audience in a more varied, differentiated way and develop, as part of
their campaign strategy, a plan for delivering messages to *portions* of the
public. There are two reasons for this. First, campaign resources are
typically scarce, creating the need to allocate resources in a manner that

will have the greatest payoff for the candidate's campaign. Second, campaigners presume that not all members of the electorate are equally susceptible to their candidate's appeals, and that concentrating one's communication efforts on the wrong portion of the public will result in minimal electoral gains. This second reason reflects the understanding that people come to a campaign with experiences, expectations, perceptions, and attitudes, and that they do not all respond to the same messages in the same way. Some are more attentive and receptive to some messages than to others, and some will perceive the same messages differently than will others.[1] Consequently, campaigners think of the most likely base of support as their target audience and attempt to deliver their campaign appeals to that audience.

There are a number of ways in which the match between campaign message and target audience can be conceptualized. One way of approaching communication with an audience is in terms of the public's *partisan predispositions*. Many voters have a psychological attachment or feeling of loyalty to a party label and are inclined to pay more attention to the campaign communication of their party's candidates than to that of the opponents.[2] For example, Republicans are more apt to attend the rallies and speeches of Republican candidates, read Republican direct-mail solicitations, and watch the Republican convention and half-hour shows of Republican candidates on television than are Democrats; and vice versa.[3] Furthermore, three decades of social science research about the voting behavior of the U.S. electorate has shown a strong relationship between these partisan predispositions and eventual candidate choices. Although there has been a considerable weakening in the public's loyalty to parties and reliance on party as a guide to candidate choices, partisan predispositions are still useful guides to the casting of many votes.[4]

In light of these communication-exposure and voting patterns, campaigners often prefer to concentrate their efforts on those who are predisposed in favor of their party label, and on nonpartisan or independent voters. The opposition's partisans are often left alone on the theory that they probably could not be convinced to defect from their partisan loyalties anyway, and that ignoring them might keep them uninterested in the campaign and hence less likely to vote. Target audiences, then, are often selected with an eye toward concentrating on those who have shown the most partisan support and/or the least partisan regularity in their voting over time. This is often done geographically, using voter registration figures and measures of ticket splitting or fluctuations in the partisan division of the vote over time as the indicators of partisan susceptibility to campaign messages.

Although the audiences of particular media outlets or programs are too diverse to lend themselves to this sort of partisan strategy, both statewide and nationwide campaigns concentrate on geographical areas where the partisan predispositions are thought to be the most promising. Presidential campaigns begin from the premise that some states are more winnable than others in terms of partisan loyalties and tendencies, and campaign appearances and advertising strategies are designed to win the largest and most competitive ones.[5] Similarly, in many statewide campaigns Democrats concentrate their efforts in Democratic (often urban) areas while Republicans concentrate on Republican (often suburban and rural) areas.

Since there are more Democratic than Republican partisans nationwide and in most states, Democrats are more likely to pursue vigorously a partisan-audience targeting strategy. Republicans, on the other hand, usually have to appeal to independents or nonpartisans *and* to some Democrats in order to achieve electoral success. In the 1972 presidential race, for example, Richard Nixon formed a Democrats for Nixon group within his campaign and produced a series of television advertisements blatantly appealing to Democrats for support. Similarly, the 1976 Gerald Ford campaign operated on the assumption that there was a 35 percent base Republican vote and a 40 percent base Democratic vote, and that the election would be "decided by the 25 percent 'swing vote' made up of Republican and Democratic defectors, the Independents and ticket-splitters."[6]

The decline in partisan loyalty among the electorate has created a growing independent/nonpartisan/ticket-splitting segment of the electorate, which has become the battleground of electoral politics and the target of campaign appeals. Many campaign consultants have developed complicated methods of defining the most fruitful constituencies with whom to communicate, based on indicators of independence, ticket splitting, and the like. Coincident with this focus on nonpartisans, of course, is the dearth of partisan candidate appeals discussed in Chapter 2.

A good example of (1) the importance of the independent vote, (2) the typical need of Republicans to capture some Democratic votes, and (3) the impact of this targeting approach on the content of candidate messages may be found in a 1980 campaign memo written by Ronald Reagan's campaign pollster, Richard Wirthlin, in early October. Wirthlin wrote that (This excerpt appeared originally in *Portrait of an Election,* copyright © 1981 by Elizabeth Drew, Inc. Reprinted by permission of Simon & Schuster, Inc, New York.)

> The strategy from the Convention until mid-September was to appeal to the Republican/Conservative political base. From mid-September until mid-October the principal political objective was to reach out to the undecideds and middle America. We broadened our appeal to the moderates, independents, and soft Anderson voters. Now during the last thirty-odd days of the campaign a serious effort must be made to secure the coalition, deal to strengths and avoid giving any voter a reason not to vote for Reagan. . . .

We Can Beat Jimmy Carter 21 Days from Now If We:

(1) Without alienating our base, expand it to include more:

- Independents
- Anderson voters, and
- disaffected Democrats
to offset Carter's larger Democratic base and the incumbency advantage.

We must shed every overt Republican symbol.[7]

Closely related to targeting the population in terms of partisan predispositions is the notion of dividing the population based on *predispositions toward a particular candidate*. Here again, the goal is to communicate with those who are supportive of or undecided about a candidate and to ignore, if possible, those who already have negative feelings. Since information of this type is not as readily available as the partisan indicators are, campaigns must rely on the distribution of votes for the candidate previously (if available), or on the distribution of votes in a previous race thought to be similar to the present one, or on information gleaned from a public opinion poll. This is one reason that so-called benchmark polls are so valuable to campaigns and that some campaign consultants refuse to work without one.[8]

In presidential elections since 1948, for example, between 54 percent and 78 percent of the electorate claim to have decided for whom to vote by the time the two major-party candidates were known, and prior to the beginning of the formal campaign period.[9] Consequently, presidential general election campaigns often concentrate on the minority of the electorate that is still undecided after Labor Day. Here again, the goal is to locate the target audience, either in a geographical or a media-exposure sense, and transmit the candidate's messages to them.

A third way of conceptualizing the audience for campaign communication is in terms of *political interest*. Some citizens are more interested in politics than others are, and political interest is related to a number of important campaign behaviors, including the willingness to read campaign literature and newspaper and magazine articles about the campaign; the likelihood of watching lengthy broadcast presentations; and the tendency actually to vote. In Table 3–1, for example, we can see that a majority of those who were very much interested in political campaigns in 1976 read campaign articles in magazines and regularly read about the election in the newspaper; almost all of the very much interested watched television news programs about the campaign. In contrast, only about 10 percent of those least interested in campaigns read campaign articles in magazines or regularly read about the election in the newspapers, and only about one-third of the least interested watched campaign programs on television. Table 3–2 shows that there is also a strong

TABLE 3–1   Selective Exposure to Modes of Communication, 1976

	Interest in Political Campaigns (%)		
Media Exposure	Very Much	Somewhat	Not Much
Watched several or a good many campaign programs on TV	89.4[a]	69.4	34.2[a]
Listened to several or a good many campaign programs on radio	41.3	30.5	14.3
Read several or a good many campaign articles in magazines	50.0	28.1	8.0
Regularly or often read about election in newspaper	64.6	31.0	10.8
Frequently or sometimes watch early evening national TV news	85.3	78.0	60.4
Frequently or sometimes watch late evening local TV news	77.8	70.9	55.2
Frequently or sometimes watch evening TV entertainment programs	61.1	66.0	60.5
Frequently or sometimes watch daytime entertainment TV	28.5	29.8	33.4

Source: Center for Political Studies, National Election Study, 1976.
[a]The table should be read this way: Of those who said that they were very interested in the campaign, 89.4 percent watched several or a good many campaign programs on television. Of those who said they were not much interested in the campaign, 34.2 percent watched several or a good many campaign programs on television.

TABLE 3–2   Relationship between 1976 Presidential Debate Exposure and Interest in Political Campaigns

Exposure to Presidential Debates	Interest in Political Campaigns (%)		
	Very Much	Somewhat	Not Much
None	6.6	16.0	39.4
One	6.0	13.5	16.2
Two	18.0	31.6	23.2
Three	24.0	16.5	10.1
Four	45.4	22.5	11.2
	100.0	100.1	100.1
	N = 722	N = 795	N = 358

Source: Center for Political Studies, National Election Study, 1976.

61

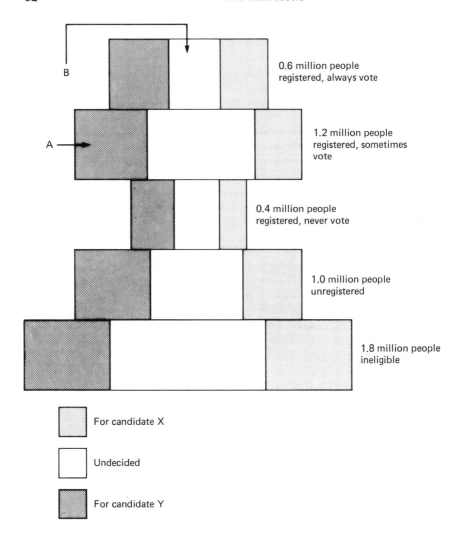

B

0.6 million people
registered, always vote

A —→

1.2 million people
registered, sometimes
vote

0.4 million people
registered, never vote

1.0 million people
unregistered

1.8 million people
ineligible

For candidate X

Undecided

For candidate Y

Source: Adapted from a lecture given by John Ashmore, of Matt Reese Associates, at Temple University, Philadelphia, Pa., fall 1981.

FIGURE 3–1   Example of Targeting Portion of Citizenry for Persuasive Campaign Communication, Missouri

relationship between political interest and watching televised presidential debates. Given that voter turnout rates are so low in U.S. presidential elections, and even lower in nonpresidential elections, it is understandable that campaigners would concentrate their efforts on reaching those citizens who are the most likely to vote. Persuading a citizen who is unlikely to vote to support a candidate has no payoff for the candidate on election day.

Sometimes both candidate predispositions *and* political interest are used to define a candidate's target audience. For example, a representative from Matt Reese and Associates, a prominent campaign consulting firm, once illustrated a way of targeting campaign messages to portions of the population of the state of Missouri (Figure 3–1).[10] First, the potential audience was broken down in terms of the likelihood of their voting (an indicator strongly related to political interest). Out of the 5 million residents of Missouri in 1980, 1.8 million were ineligible to vote and 1.0 million were eligible to vote but unregistered. Obviously, campaign communication with these groups could not possibly directly affect the distribution of the vote, although there is a possibility that these people could contribute to the campaign in other ways (new residents could contribute money, under-age residents could do volunteer work, and so forth). The remaining people were all registered to vote but could be further separated into categories according to the likelihood of their actually casting a vote. This left, in this case, only 0.6 million people who would almost certainly vote, and 1.2 million who might have voted, out of the 5 million with which Reese started.

The level of support for the candidate was then used to divide the population further into target groups. Some people in each of the previous categories were predisposed for the candidate, some were predisposed against, and some were undecided. (The exact proportion in each category can be acquired fairly easily from a public opinion poll. Here we will assume for illustrative purposes that the breakdown was approximately an equal three-way split.) Placing this division on top of the previous division resulted in fifteen categories to which the population was assigned.

Once the audience was thought of in this way, the strategy was then to communicate with those portions of the public thought to be important to the candidate. For Reese, two groups stood out: those supportive of the candidate who might vote (category A in Figure 3–1), and those who would probably vote but were undecided about whom to vote for (category B in Figure 3–1). In each case a candidate needs to be persuasive in only one way (*either* "vote" *or* "vote for my candidate") to achieve the desired goal; for all other groups either more change ("vote *and* vote for my candidate") or more difficult change ("change your mind about whom you support") must be accomplished. In the example used here, then, the goal became to find and communicate with the 0.6 million people (out of the 5 million residents Reese began with) targeted in this fashion.

A fourth way of selecting target audiences for campaign messages is in terms of the *demographic characteristics* of the population. Since considerable information is often readily available concerning the demographic makeup of a population, this information is sometimes used as indicative of a number of other traits. Some characteristics, such as education and income, are used as surrogate measures of political interest and the likelihood of campaign participation. Others, such as age, sex, race, occupation, place of residence, and religion are taken to be rough approximations of the interests, attitudes, and policy preferences of groups. Consequently, candidates often think of their constituencies or possible support groups in terms of their demographic characteristics, where those with certain traits are presumed to be interested in certain policies, to be supportive of a particular party, or to be responsive to certain messages.

There is considerable variation in the complexity and precision with which demographic targeting is done. For example, Richard Nixon's reelection campaign in 1972 used a complicated and empirically advanced strategy for selecting target audiences for mail and telephone appeals. A Nixon campaign aide, Jeb Magruder (who was later to become well known for his role in the Watergate scandal) described it this way:

> ... we took an area that according to the Census Bureau had income levels over $10,000, and then went back to the past voting behavior and found out where, say, the Reagan vote came in California. If the Reagan vote came in areas with incomes over $10,000, they were targeted as areas we were interested in. Or if our polls showed that we were going to do well with blue-collar, labor union workers, with certain demographic characteristics, we computerized the relevant information so we could pull it out by areas. Obviously, we got overlap, but we were able to target our mail and our telephone activities into those areas where we felt we had the highest potential opportunity. These included areas of the basic Republican constituency plus what we have called our emerging new majority, primarily the blue-collar, urban, ethnic-type people.[11]

Similarly, Gerald Ford's reelection campaign advisors in 1976 had a fairly clear and general sense of their target audience. In certain key states it was thought that (This excerpt appeared originally in *Running for President 1976: The Carter Campaign,* copyright © 1977 by Martin Schram. Reprinted with permission of Stein and Day Publishers, New York.)

> the target constituency in the suburbs for the President is the upper blue collar and white collar workers, often from a family which has risen in mobility in the last generation. These are independent minded voters, many of whom are Catholic. In addition, there is a weakness in Carter's support among Catholics and also among Jews. The upwardly mobile Catholics are a group becoming more independent and conservative, and they represent the key to victory in the northern industrial states where they are from 25–48% of the voters.[12]

In contrast, the demographic targeting of the George Wallace campaign during the 1972 Democratic presidential nomination campaign was a good deal simpler and more intuitive. As a Wallace media strategist put it, the Wallace campaign was directed at "the guy selling groceries or shoes or driving a truck."[13]

In 1980 both the Carter and the Reagan campaigns targeted demographic and geographic components of the electorate for special attention. The Reagan campaign thought that special gains in electoral support could be made among blue-collar/union voters, Catholics, and Southerners. The Carter campaign also recognized the importance of securing support from a number of demographic groups, as evidenced by this memo from pollster Patrick Caddell to Carter in June of 1980 (This excerpt appeared originally in *Portrait of an Election*, copyright © 1981 by Elizabeth Drew, Inc. Reprinted by permission of Simon & Schuster, Inc, New York.)

Looking at constituency groups one must be alarmed. Carter is having problems again with Catholics, Jews, liberals, the young, et al., particularly in the Northeast. . . .

In 1976 we were basically on our left in the general election. We were able to hold enough liberals, Jews, Catholics, etc. to win while Ford ate us up with Independents *and* Catholic suburbanites. We do not appear so fortunate in 1980.

First, although Reagan's blue collar strength has been much exaggerated in the primaries, he can hurt us with this group particularly in the blue collar metropolitan suburbs. In addition, the bad economic news has got to hurt and hurt badly. It could be seen not only in Reagan or Anderson defections but in lowered turnouts as well.

Second, Anderson cuts deeply at the moment into our liberal, young, upper class, suburban support. He cuts away people who would never vote for Reagan but *who may well stay* with Anderson because they perceive Carter to be a pale imitation of Reagan.

Third, I'm not sure the Jews will vote for Carter no matter what.

Fourth, one has to be concerned about the black vote—particularly the turnout.

Fifth, it is hard to imagine that Carter will surpass or even match his 1976 showing in the non-traditional Protestant, small town, rural communities of the North and Midwest, particularly farmers.

All of this raises some serious concerns. From this perspective, victory looks difficult. If Reagan cuts into blue collar conservative Catholic Democrats; Anderson pinches off liberals, Jews, and surburban independents; Carter does not surpass his 1976 showing among non-traditional groups—how does Carter win?

The answer is by no means hopeless. It requires a major strategic thrust with a conceptual plan as will be touched on in the next section. For this part (states and constituencies) a few points of targeting are important. First, Reagan is *not* going to take all the Ford 1976 vote. I suspect a lot of moderate upper income Independents and independent Republicans will have a difficult time with Reagan. This was evident in the primaries against Bush/Anderson. In fact the "equal" Anderson draw comes from many of those people. Unfortunately, the electoral break seems to be against us. Second, with the right strategy, signals and actions, many of the Democrats can be shored up.[14]

A fifth way of segmenting the audience for the purpose of communication is in terms of the *perceptions and attitudes of individuals*. For example, a campaign may wish to communicate with those who think crime is an important issue, or with those who think the opponent is indecisive. Such targeting can be achieved only with the aid of public opinion polls, and it is usually difficult to reach audiences targeted in these terms. No broadcast rating service collects information on the political perceptions or attitudes of the audiences of different programs, and no campaign poll can spend the time and money necessary to solicit the precise media-exposure habits of its sample. Consequently, campaigners often use demographic characteristics as surrogate measures of political attitudes, or rely on individual targeting and communication where resources permit and attitudinal information exists about individuals (such as magazine subscriptions, contributions to previous campaigns, or contact with an incumbent).

Ideology is sometimes used as a comprehensive conceptualization of the political values, interests, and attitudes of the electorate. In particular, candidates sometimes think of the public in terms of a unidimensional space with liberals and conservatives at opposite ends of a continuum. Such a conceptualization is used in conjunction with (1) a perception of the distribution of the constituency along this dimension, and (2) a decision regarding the optimum position along the continuum that the candidate should try to establish. Especially when a number of candidates are competing for the same office, campaign strategists conceptualize the situation in such ideological terms.

In the 1972 Democratic presidential nomination campaign, for example, there were many announced and possible candidates at the beginning of the nomination campaign. At one point or other, Edmund Muskie, Birch Bayh, Fred Harris, Harold Hughes, William Proxmire, Sam Yorty, Shirley Chisholm, Vance Hartke, Wilbur Mills, Henry Jackson, John Lindsay, Hubert Humphrey, Edward Kennedy, George Wallace, and George McGovern were all possible or actual contenders for the nomination. Although the field was rapidly winnowed to only a few of these candidates—in particular, Muskie, Jackson, Humphrey, Wallace, and McGovern—it was a situation ripe for ideological audience targeting. In fact, there is ample evidence that many of the candidates' strategists were thinking in these terms. One of Henry Jackson's advisers described their thinking prior to the Florida primary in this way:

> We looked ahead . . . to the Florida primary and which candidates were positioning themselves where. At that point, the line-up of Democrats in Florida looked something like: John Lindsay, George McGovern, Fred

Harris, Ed Muskie, Birch Bayh, and Harold Hughes, with very much of a question mark about whether Senator Humphrey was going to be in those early primaries or in any primaries at all. Given that line-up, exclusive of Senator Humphey's candidacy for a moment, there appeared to be a field well to the left of center; and a candidate who represented what we might call a centrist view might have a golden opportunity. He could pick up any votes to the right of center without actively campaigning for them, which would enable him to maintain all sorts of credibility with centrist, and even somewhat left of centrist, constituencies. Governor Wallace, of course, came into that race and markedly changed its whole complexion.[15]

Similarly, George Wallace's adviser recounted how Wallace "felt that there was probably a great void among Democratic prospects of centrist and right-of-center candidates and that there were a great number of Americans who did not love a candidate,"[16] and the philosophy of the McGovern campaign organization was that

> when you come to a nomination in the Democratic Party, there is, for all practical purposes, no center. Our strategy was always to co-opt the left, become the candidate of the liberal wing of the party, and then eventually get it down to a two-man race. It might be that Senator Muskie would opt for the right and successfully get it, and we would run against him in the later primaries. Or if Senator Humphrey beat Muskie, which is what happened in our judgment, we would run against Humphrey. We always knew it would be a two-man race between a liberal and a conservative. There was, in fact, no center, and it was just a question of whether or not we could win on our side and who would win on the other. We wanted Humphrey to emerge on the right.[17]

Although there is some disagreement in these examples concerning the ideological distribution of the pertinent electorate and the positioning of particular candidates, it is clear that all three candidates were thinking about their target audience in ideological terms.

Ideological views of the public also sometimes shape candidate communication during general election campaigns. In these two excerpts from the 1980 campaign memos of Ronald Reagan's and Jimmy Carter's pollsters, we can see the importance of viewing the potential target audience in ideological terms.

From the Reagan camp (Richard Wirthlin) (This excerpt appeared originally in *Portrait of an Election,* copyright © 1981 by Elizabeth Drew, Inc. Reprinted by permission of Simon & Schuster, Inc, New York.)

> While ideology does not cut strongly in the primary contests, it will be a major determinant in November. As the following table shows, the best predictor of vote between Reagan and Carter turned out to be a combination using ideology and party. Note that we have no opportunity to win the general election unless we pull substantial numbers of moderate ticket-splitters into our column.

Voter Types as Predictor of Reagan-Carter Vote (%)
(May 1979)

	%	Reagan	Carter	Undecided
Conservative Republicans	(22)	85	12	4
Moderate liberal Republicans	(7)	69	25	6
Conservative ticket-splitters	(13)	50	41	9
Moderate ticket-splitters	(17)	50	40	10
Conservative Democrats	(14)	37	58	5
Liberal Democrats	(22)	25	68	7
Non-Republican Blacks & Hispanics	(6)	17	78	5

Without question, the electorate must view Ronald Reagan in less extreme conservative terms in the fall if we are to win.[18]

From the Carter camp (Patrick Caddell) (This excerpt appeared originally in *Portrait of an Election,* copyright © 1981 by Elizabeth Drew, Inc. Reprinted by permission of Simon & Schuster, Inc, New York.)

President Carter faces an extremely difficult reelection. Struggling against a persistent defeated primary challenger, we face a united Republican party with a challenger posed to our right attempting to crowd our center. To our left, we face an Independent candidacy raiding our unhappy left leaning base and threatening the key electoral vote rich industrial belt. For a candidate who has often appeared a "remainderman"—taking the votes left over—a two front assault is of great concern. . . .

Given the nature of our opponents and our constituency problems, some attention needs to be given [ideological positioning]. Throughout his national political career Jimmy Carter has essentially dominated the center of American politics. So adroitly did he do so that liberals tended to view him as a liberal, conservatives as a conservative, etc. This positioning, while denying him hard core supporters, did permit maximum flexibility— Carter could slide left or right to meet any immediate challenge.

There are now two complications to this situation. First, Carter is in jeopardy of losing the center to Reagan. Surveys already indicate that Reagan is placed by the electorate as closer to them on general issues than Carter. Second, in a general election sense Anderson is assaulting much of Carter's natural liberal base whose normal certainty would allow Carter to move right toward Reagan. These factors are further complicated by the fact that Carter, to win, must hold the more conservative South *and* the more liberal blue collar Northeast. An all out move to secure one area could lead to an alienation of the other.[19]

Not all campaigns are equally explicit or systematic in targeting audiences for particular messages. Some candidates, particularly those who have been successful in the past, rely more on their own intuition and judgment than on public opinion polls and rating services to tell them with whom they should communicate. Others feel that they ought to communicate with a cross-section of the population and even make a special attempt to reach those who, by virtue of their low current levels of political interest, would be ignored otherwise. Still others develop atypical communication strategies in times of desperation or opportunity. Nonetheless, one of the primary thrusts of the new campaign technology and the use of the expertise of professional consultants lies in the latter's ability and inclination to help a campaign communicate with those segments of the audience most likely to be persuaded.

Methods of Communicating with the Citizenry

Once a campaign has chosen its target audience, decisions also have to be made concerning how the candidate will deliver his or her campaign messages to that portion of the public. A variety of communication modes are available to the political campaigner, including direct mail; phone banks; posters; bumper stickers; billboards; radio, newspaper, magazine, and television advertisements; the stimulation of news coverage; debates with the opposition; direct contact with voters; rallies and speeches; sound trucks; and personal canvassing. The selection of particular modes of communication is based on the cost and the cost-effectiveness of each method, the method's credibility and presumed effectiveness, the extent to which the campaign feels it is necessary to maintain control over the content of campaign messages, and the ability of a method of communication to reach the audiences targeted for the candidate's messages. Since few forms of communication are inherently superior to all others, the choice of communication forms involves intuition and past experience and usually results in a mix of various forms.

Methods of campaign communication may be divided into two categories: those that are *free* (such as an appearance on a news interview show or televised debate), and those that are *paid* for by the campaign (for example, all forms of advertising, direct mail, and personal contact). This distinction is not as clear-cut as it may seem, since candidates do spend money to conduct newsworthy campaign activities and to prepare for debate appearances. In the case of the so-called free forms of communication, however, the candidate is not in complete control of the message, and some other entity (such as a news organization or the League of Women Voters) is paying for a substantial portion of the complete cost of the communication.

PAID COMMUNICATION

All forms of paid communication involve delivering a message to an audience at a particular price. Consequently, the choice of particular methods of paid communication is often based on the cost, cost-effectiveness, availability, and presumed effects of the method, and on the ability of the method to reach a targeted audience.

Some forms of communication are more expensive than others. Printing a few thousand posters, hiring a sound truck for a few days, and delivering speeches at local shopping centers are relatively inexpensive endeavors. Placing advertisements in local newspapers, hiring campaign workers to contact large groups of people personally, and organizing an event of sufficient magnitude to achieve print or broadcast news coverage all require considerably greater monetary resources. Finally, purchasing large numbers of television spot ads and prime-time television slots requires still more money. The cost of methods of communication and the resources available to candidates are the first constraints on the choice of paid communication methods. Obviously, candidates are unable to use some methods of communication if their financial resources are insufficient. Hubert Humphrey had to cancel a series of television spot ads in the closing days of his extremely tight presidential campaign with Richard Nixon in 1968 because of a lack of money, and John Anderson continually scaled down his advertising plans and the size of his paid staff in 1980 when federal campaign subsidies and bank loans were not available before election day. Similarly, a number of announced presidential candidates in recent years have withdrawn from the nomination campaign because of a lack of money.[20]

Although the cost of different forms of campaign communication may be the most serious constraint on campaign plans, the cost-*effectiveness* of different forms is also an important consideration. Candidates are understandably interested in achieving the most effective communication for the least expense. For example, hiring a sound truck is cheap, but it also reaches few people. Purchasing a thirty-second spot on network television is extremely expensive (about $95,000 in 1983), but the number of citizens reached is much larger. Hiring enough sound trucks to reach an equivalent number of people would certainly be more expensive than purchasing the spot ad. Consequently, in terms of cost-effectiveness the spot ad is the better buy (provided, of course, the candidate has the necessary funds).

Campaign consultants help candidates select the methods of communication that are the most cost-effective. Borrowing from the concepts and experience of product advertising, political consultants evaluate the available paid forms in terms of their reach, frequency, cost per thousand, availability, and ability to reach specific audiences. *Reach* is the size of the audience touched by a particular form; *frequency* refers to the number of times a particular person will be communicated with throughout a campaign; *cost per thousand* is the amount of money that must be spent to reach 1,000 people; *availability* involves the lead time necessary to produce, reserve, and place a form of advertising; and the *ability to reach specific audiences* depends on the amount of available information concerning the composition of a medium's audience and the ability to use a method of communication to reach a particular targeted audience.

To illustrate the kinds of decisions that campaign consultants make for candidates, let us consider two examples.[21]

First, suppose you are the campaign manager for a congressional candidate in an urban/suburban district in 1984, and you are trying to decide how to spend your candidate's resources. You know that $2,000 will buy you 40,000 two-color brochures, 10,000 bumper stickers, 5,000 pieces of direct mail literature, and 10 strategically situated billboards. Assuming that you wanted to communicate with every registered voter (240,000 in the typical congressional district) in your district (the reach) once (the frequency), it would cost $12,000 for the brochures, $48,000 for the bumper stickers, $96,000 for direct mail, and $2,000 for the billboards. Clearly, the billboards and the brochures would be the best buy in terms of simply reaching the constituency.

Second, suppose you are the campaign manager for a presidential candidate in 1984, and you are intent on communicating with every Democratic voter in the Massachusetts primary (907,332 people voted in the 1980 Democratic primary, and I will use that number as the size of the target audience). At 20 cents apiece for bumper stickers, 5 cents apiece for a three-fold brochure, and 40 cents apiece for direct mail (including postage), it would cost $181,466 for a bumper sticker for everyone (excluding the cost of getting them *to* the voters), $45,367 for a campaign brochure for everyone (again excluding the cost of getting them to the voters), and $362,933 to send a piece of direct mail to everyone. In contrast, $100,000 would buy *fourteen* sixty-second commercials in top-rated, prime-time shows in the Boston metropolitan area. Thus the television advertising would seem to be the most cost-effective form of communication.

One important aspect of the cost-effectiveness of different forms of campaign communication is how well the market area of a medium corresponds to the election district under consideration. In a national campaign, of course, one can reach the potential electorate through network television with little wasted effort and few areas left out. In smaller election districts, however, it does not make sense to use the larger media outlets since much of the audience reached—and paid for—is outside the district and cannot vote for the candidate. In Philadelphia, for example, there are four U.S. congressional districts within the city limits and three VHF commercial television stations that cover the city and surrounding area. Congressional candidates who buy advertising on one of those stations communicate with many voters unconcerned with their race and unable to vote in it (although they could contribute money, volunteer to help with canvassing, and so on). Thus much of the money spent on such advertising would be wasted. Consequently, congressional candidates from urban districts usually spend

Copyright, American Map Corporation, New York, no. 18794

FIGURE 3–2   Media Markets across the State of Florida

more money on radio advertising than on television advertising, since the latter is considerably less expensive. Candidates for statewide office in New Jersey also repeatedly confront this problem: Since there are no commercial television stations in New Jersey that cover the state, buying television advertising means using Philadelphia and New York City television stations and paying to communicate with many Pennsylvania and New York State voters. The smaller the election district and the less congruent it is with a medium's markets, the less cost-effective that mode of communication is. The office walls of modern campaign consultants have maps showing the boundaries of the media markets across the country so that communication methods may be selected with the geographical correspondence in mind (see Figure 3–2).

The utility of different methods of paid communication also depends on the ability to reach the audiences that are targeted as being important to a campaign. Although it is difficult to draw general conclusions concerning the capability of different media in this regard, in general a medium is more attractive the more information there is about the makeup of its audience, and the more possible it is to segment the audience into those sharing similar traits.

One of the most attractive features of radio and television advertising is this ability to reach specific *targeted* audiences. We have seen that candidates often think of their target audience in demographic, geographic, partisan, and attitudinal terms; consequently, a method of communication that allows campaigners to reach such target audiences is a valuable campaign tool. Since there is a considerable amount of information on the demographic makeup of broadcast audiences, campaigners see in broadcast advertising a method of communication that allows them to communicate with otherwise difficult-to-reach or difficult-to-isolate audiences.

In demographic terms, broadcast advertising allows a candidate to select audiences with particular demographic makeups. If, for example, a candidate's campaign strategy indicates that women are an important portion of his or her constituency, ads can be placed during the afternoon on local television or adjacent to programs of interest primarily to women (such as "The Dinah Show"). If a candidate wants to communicate with men, ads can be placed during a World Series or NFL football game. If it is the politically interested a candidate wants to reach, ads may be purchased during "Face the Nation" or "CBS Reports." If a candidate wants to communicate with blacks, time may be purchased during black-oriented programming such as "Black Perspective on the News" or "What's Happening." Representatives of local media organizations and advertising time buyers have vast amounts of information at their disposal on the demographic makeup of their audiences and are quite willing—for a price—to advise a candidate on the appropriate placement of spot advertisements.

The radio audience is even more segmented than the local television audience. In many metropolitan areas the local radio situation is highly competitive and has led to a segmentation of the audience into several identifiable demographic categories. In such a situation political candidates can choose the audience with whom they wish to communicate based on their knowledge of the pivotal demographic groups in the metropolitan electorate, and their radio listening habits.

For presidential candidates, the ability to target advertising geographically is particularly important. Presidential elections are not won nationally; they are won within the boundaries of states, since that is where the popular votes are counted and the electoral votes assigned. Presidential campaigns often hinge on the result in a few competitive states with moderate to large numbers of electoral votes. Consequently, candidates usually reserve a large portion of their resources to use in the last weeks of the campaign in particular states that are thought to hold the key to electoral success. Picking up an additional 1,000 votes in Houston the day before the election does a presidential candidate absolutely no good if he or she was going to win Texas anyway—but picking up 1,000 votes in an undecided state like Ohio could mean a difference of 50 electoral votes (a transfer to 25 votes from one candidate to the other) out of a possible 538. Placing spot ads in Cleveland rather than Houston is a lot quicker and easier than flying one's volunteer workers from Texas to

TABLE 3–3   Nonselective Exposure to Television Ads

	Partisan Identification (%)		
	Democrats	Independents	Republicans
Nixon commercials			
Recalled seeing	45	45	34
Did not recall seeing	55	55	66
	100	100	100
McGovern commercials			
Recalled seeing	68	76	69
Did not recall seeing	32	24	31
	100	100	100

Source: Thomas Patterson and Robert McClure, "Political Advertising on Television: Spot Commercials in the 1972 Presidential Election," *Maxwell Review* 9, no. 2: 62. Reprinted by permission.

	Candidate Preference (%)		
	Favor Republican	Undecided, Won't Say	Favor Democrat
Relative exposure to broadcast advertising:			
Saw more Republican ads	31	27	32
Saw same number of each	48	53	37
Saw more Democratic ads	21	20	31
	100	100	100
	N = 177	N = 178	N = 157

Source: Charles K. Atkin, Lawrence Bowen, Oguz B. Nayman, and Kenneth G. Sheinkopf, "Quality versus Quantity in Televised Political Ads," *Public Opinion Quarterly* 37 (Summer 1973): 216. Reprinted by permission of *Public Opinion Quarterly*. Copyright 1973 by The Trustees of Columbia University.

Ohio to conduct door-to-door canvassing. In the closing days of the 1976 presidential election campaign, for example, Stuart Spencer, deputy director of the Ford campaign, estimated that there were thirty-one states in which the margin of support for the two candidates was within 3 percent.[22] This kind of information is used by campaign strategists to decide where to place their media "blitz" just before election day. In 1980 Reagan spent $6 million and Carter $4–5 million out of a total budget of about $16 million for media advertising in the last ten days of the election.[23]

    Another important aspect of this ability to use broadcast spot advertisements to communicate with certain portions of the citizenry is that candidates can communicate with undecided voters and independents. If exposure to campaign communication were completely voluntary, communication with nonsupporters and disinterested voters would be improbable.

    Table 3–3 shows this ability of spot advertisements. Ordinarily we would expect more Democrats to attend to the communication of Democratic candidates and more Republicans to attend to that of Republican candidates. During the 1972 presidential general election campaign, however, almost half of the Independents and Democrats recalled seeing some Nixon commercials, and over two-thirds of the Republicans and Independents recalled seeing some McGovern commercials. Similarly, in two 1970 gubernatorial races in Colorado and Wisconsin, candidates were also able to communicate through their broadcast advertising with undecided and opposition citizens. This capability is important for candidates and is an almost unique advantage of spot advertising. It also helps explain the dearth of partisan messages in political spots, which we noted in Chapter 2.

Broadcast spot advertising also lets candidates target their communication to categories of citizens who are presumed to have particular political interests or attitudes. A candidate running a statewide or nationwide campaign, for example, can place an advertisement expressing concern about crime in only those areas with high and/or rising crime rates. Time for an advertisement calling for increased Social Security benefits can be purchased only on those cities with a large proportion of elderly citizens, and time for an ad calling for increases in farm price supports may be purchased in those media markets covering rural areas. Thus a general capability is provided for communicating with targeted audiences in a way that is believed to be more meaningful to the audience and more advantageous to the candidate. The advertising times during and next to news and public affairs shows are particularly attractive to campaigners during a presidential nomination campaign, since they are thought to reach audiences that are the most likely to participate in the delegate-selection process. In fact, the ability to target messages is so attractive to campaign consultants that a number of them are currently developing expensive, computerized methods of matching audience information with public opinion results to enhance their ability to reach specific audiences.[24]

Of course, broadcast advertising is not the only method of communication that allows campaigners to target messages. Some campaigns have developed direct mail and phone bank operations that transmit a tailor-made message to each *individual* who meets some criterion of interest or predisposition (for example, a person who subscribes to a particular magazine, or is registered in a particular political party, or has contacted an incumbent previously on some issue).[25] Usually the number of people who can be reached with such techniques is quite small, however. Spot advertising combines the benefits of targeted communication with a reach (size of audience) that is significant. Lengthy paid broadcast programs typically attract fairly small portions of the prime-time television audience (usually around 15–20 percent) and about half the size of the audience of the preempted program. In other words, many citizens change the channel when their favorite show is preempted by a thirty-minute paid political broadcast. A spot ad during one of the more highly rated shows, however, would typically be seen by a larger proportion of the television audience (say, 35–40 percent), a difference that would amount to about 5 million viewers nationally.[26]

Although many candidates prefer personal contact with voters and numerous studies have shown that personal communication is more persuasive than mediated communication, constituencies have grown so large in this century that wide-scale personal contact is virtually impossible. Jim Wright, campaigning for the U.S. Senate in Texas in 1966, estimated that if he worked sixteen hours a day it would take him twenty-eight years to talk to every citizen in Texas for one minute.[27] It is no wonder, then, that candidates prefer to raise the money necessary to talk to the citizenry for a minute with a spot ad.

Paid broadcast communication, then, is attractive to campaigners in a number of ways. Its use can be allocated in a cost-effective manner, communication can be "narrow-casted" to segments of the citizenry, and experts are available who have had experience in its use and are willing to use their abilities to target this form of campaign communication. In addition, candidates (or their staffs) remain in complete control of the messages transmitted and need not be concerned with the distortion of the message by some other participant. As John Deardourf, one of the most prominent campaign consultants, has said, if a candidate has a message that he or she feels must absolutely get through to the citizenry, he or she would be well advised to pay the cost of transmitting it directly, without alteration by journalists or surrogate campaigners.[28]

FREE COMMUNICATION

Despite the attractiveness of paid communication, few candidates rely on it exclusively. Most candidates also devote substantial resources to designing messages or activities that will be considered newsworthy by journalists. Although this type of communication is riskier, since candidates relinquish control over the content to journalists, it has the advantage of being more credible (and hence, it is thought, more influential) and of transferring much of the cost of communication onto others (such as news organizations). Because of the spending limits now in force for presidential general election campaigns, presidential candidates are more desirous of achieving such free media coverage than they have ever been before.

Although we will discuss the way journalists cover election campaigns in detail in the next two chapters, a few remarks about *candidate* behavior are in order here. It is up to candidates to say or do something to attract free media coverage. On one level, this means timing campaign appearances to accommodate media production schedules; providing media representatives with typewriters, telephone lines, and press releases; and arranging the travel and accommodations of traveling journalists. One campaign consultant has summarized these considerations as the need to: "Be brief . . . be prompt . . . be early . . . and be visual."[29] On another level, however, it means providing stories that can be simplified and condensed, that contain conflict or drama, that present something novel or unexpected, and that lend themselves to stories about the likely outcome of the campaign. If a candidate wishes to deliver a message concerning offshore drilling, for example, donning a wetsuit and going for a dive will attract more media coverage than will holding a press conference or handing out a position paper.[30] A number of candidates have walked across their districts or performed different jobs for a day to symbolize their responsiveness and concern and to attract media attention, and candidates have gone so far as to hold a news conference in the nude (a female candidate for governor of California in 1974 for the Peace and Freedom Party); enter and exit from campaign appearances in a propane-powered balloon (an Oregon woman campaigning for governor in 1978); parachute into a campaign rally (a Montana candidate for the U.S. Senate); and campaign nonstop for thirty-seven hours (John Connally, a 1980 presidential hopeful) in order to attract news coverage.[31] In 1976 Jimmy Carter probably attracted more media attention by staying overnight in "regular citizens'" homes while campaigning than he did with all his position papers put together.

One arena in which the effort to stimulate media news coverage has taken on substantial significance is the earliest stages of presidential nomination campaigns. Months before the first votes are cast in an actual delegate-selection process, candidates are working behind the scenes to convince political reporters that their candidacy should be taken seriously. This period, called the "Invisible Primary" by one author, takes place beyond the view of the public and gives candidates varying amounts of preprimary publicity.[32] Since the "news-hole" for the presidential campaign is extremely small prior to the delegate-selection process and few media organizations assign reporters to the campaign that early in the process, receiving mention at this time is an important political resource.

Some presidential candidates are automatically considered newsworthy even before announcing their candidacies, by virtue of their standing in the polls, previous position, or present office. Incumbent presidents, U.S. senators, and politicians with large followings (Hubert Humphrey, Edward Kennedy, and Ronald Reagan, for example) fall into this category. Other politicians have to convince the media that they are viable, credible candidates who should receive media attention.

In the 1972 and 1976 campaigns for the Democratic presidential nominations, there were a number of announced and possible candidates for the nomination (for example, Edmund Muskie, Birch Bayh, Fred Harris, Harold Hughes, William Proxmire, Sam Yorty, Shirley Chisholm, Vance Hartke, Wilbur Mills, Henry Jackson, John Lindsay, Hubert Humphrey, Edward Kennedy, George Wallace, and George McGovern in 1972; Fred Harris, Birch Bayh, Morris Udall, Lloyd Bentsen, Terry Sanford, George Wallace, Edmund Muskie, Edward Kennedy, Hubert Humphrey, and Jimmy Carter in 1976). In the 1980 Republican presidential nomination campaign there were also a number of possible contenders (Philip Crane, Howard Baker, Robert Dole, John Anderson, Gerald Ford, and Ronald Reagan). At the time this book is being written there are already a number of announced candidates for the 1984 Democratic nomination (former Vice-President Walter Mondale, Ohio Senator John Glenn, California Senator Alan Cranston, Colorado Senator Gary Hart, former presidential candidate George McGovern, former Florida Governor Reubin Askew, and South Carolina Senator Ernest Hollings). In situations like these, journalists and news organizations have to decide who is credible, viable, and newsworthy, because they cannot afford to cover every candidate equally. (The fact that in each year it was the out-party that had the most candidates is not just a coincidence. Since the out-party lacks a recognized leader or incumbent, the nomination is more up for grabs.)

Jimmy Carter's strategy for receiving media coverage prior to the first 1976 delegate selection process is instructive. Reasoning that national media attention was unlikely unless some newsworthy theme could be established and until some level of support could be demonstrated, Carter attempted to achieve media mention through less visible means. In *1972*, Hamilton Jordan, Carter's campaign aide, wrote this memo suggesting how Carter could go about convincing important journalists that his was a credible and newsworthy campaign (appeared originally in *Running for President 1976: The Carter Campaign,* copyright © 1977 by Martin Schram. Reprinted with permission of Stein and Day Publishers, New York):

> . . . we should begin immediately to (1) generate favorable stories in the national press on the accomplishments of your administration, (2) develop and/or maintain a close personal relationship with the principal national columnists and reporters, and (3) take full advantage of every legitimate opportunity for national exposure as long as it is couched in terms of what you have accomplished in Georgia.
>
> We should compile a listing of regional and national political editors and columnists who you know or need to know. You can find ample excuse for contacting them—writing them a note, complimenting them on an article or column and asking that they come to see you when convenient. Some people like Tom Wicker or Mrs. Katherine Graham are significant enough to spend an evening or a leisurely weekend with. . . .
>
> Like it or not, there exists in fact an eastern liberal news establishment which has tremendous influence in this country all out of proportion to its actual audience. The views of this small group of opinion-makers in the papers they represent are noted and imitated by other columnists and newspapers throughout the country and the world. Their recognition and acceptance of your candidacy as a viable force with some chance of success could establish you as a serious contender worthy of financial support of

major party contributors. They could have an equally adverse effect, dismissing your effort as being regional or an attempt to secure the second spot on the ticket.

Fortunately, a disproportionate number of these opinion-makers are southerners by birth and tradition and . . . subconsciously desire to see the South move beyond the George Wallace era and assert itself as a region. . . . It is my contention that they would be fascinated by the prospect of your candidacy and would treat it seriously through the first several primaries.

In keeping with these recommendations, we should begin to:

(1) Foster relationships with political columnists that you know. Establish relationships with those you don't know.

(2) Utilize Don Carter's [a cousin, and publisher of the Lexington, Kentucky, *Herald*] contacts to create situations where you can get to know key people. For example, let Don Carter invite Tom Wicker and Max [Frankel] to spend a weekend visiting with both of you on Cumberland Island.

(3) Generate stories in national . . . trade magazines on particular accomplishments. . . .[33]

During Carter's campaigning in 1975 he met repeatedly with the editorial boards of local newspapers and broadcast stations in whatever states he visited. This laid the foundation for later media mention once voter support had been demonstrated.[34]

Often it is media mention, particularly in the *New York Times* or the *Washington Post,* or a media appearance that stimulates further news coverage. In the 1976 Carter campaign, for example, it was an article by R. W. Apple in the *New York Times* on October 27, *1975,* concerning the results of a straw poll in Iowa, that is credited with ending journalistic silence on Carter. In 1980 John Anderson's appearance in a candidate debate in Iowa in January was followed by a number of news stories that lifted him from obscurity. Such mention is not enough to secure a nomination, but it is a necessary condition for successful fund-raising and volunteer recruitment. Once news coverage begins, it tends to snowball unless a candidate withdraws or fails to demonstrate an enduring chance of winning the nomination.

During the general election campaign, the key to attracting news coverage lies in making a candidate's personal appearances newsworthy. In 1976 Hamilton Jordan devised a formula representing the value of each of Jimmy Carter's campaigners (Carter himself, his wife and children, Walter Mondale, and so on) and allocated those appearances in line with the strategic value of different states.[35] Carter's strategists eventually settled into a campaign travel schedule with a primary objective of having the candidate appear in three different media markets each day, a common practice nowadays.[36] At each stop a pseudoevent was conducted (sometimes consisting only of a brief speech at the airport), and then the campaigner was on to the next stop in the next media market.

One reporter covering the 1980 presidential election campaign observed that

> "All three campaigns herded the press around. When the plane landed, buses were waiting to take them to the 'event,' where they generally had to walk through a roped-off gauntlet of sign-waving, campaigning partisans. As soon as the candidate finished his speech, reporters then lunged back toward the buses to begin the whole process all over again."[37]

This frenzied travel allowed candidates to maintain "control over the all-important lead" and left "reporters engaged in a daily struggle to find a morsel, an unplanned quote, or a revealing statement."[38] This method of stimulating news coverage is typical for major-party candidates during a presidential general election, when journalists need candidates more than vice versa. During the nomination campaign and in nonpresidential races, however, news coverage is not so easily stimulated, and activities usually have to be considered exceptionally newsworthy to garner mention by the press.

Candidates will always be ambivalent about such free communication. It is definitely cost-effective and credible; yet it involves allowing others to exercise their discretion concerning the messages that are transmitted. Consequently, there is always a tension between the risk and the attractiveness of these forms of communication. Candidates attempt to control the content of debates, for example, by rehearsing, by attempting to anticipate the questions and the opponent's answers, and by answering questions that are never asked and ignoring those that are. They try to control the content of the news by staging pseudoevents and maintaining tight control over members of the campaign staff. These attempts are not always successful, however. In 1976 Gerald Ford's campaign advisers decided to decrease the amount of time spent striving for news coverage and increase the effort devoted to the production of broadcast advertising. The reason for the change was that the advertisements got them

> out of the almost impossible-to-control situation of the stump speech, which inevitably leads to the kind of strident anti-Carter stuff we don't want, and into a relaxed, informal, positive atmosphere that works well. The more stump speeches you book into a day, the greater the potential for trouble. He just gets wound tighter and tighter, and then he's not at his best.[39]

In 1980 part of Carter's reelection strategy was to place Reagan on the defensive by attacking him on certain issues, particularly on the possibility of war, through surrogate campaigners such as the vice-president. The networks, however, apparently ignored the statements of these surrogate campaigners, forcing the Carter campaign to change its strategy. As a result, Carter himself became more critical of Reagan, since he alone was able to stimulate news coverage.[40] The stridency of these attacks, many believe, had a damaging effect on perceptions of Carter, and caused an erosion in positive perceptions of him as compassionate and humane. Had the media not ignored the surrogate campaigners, the Carter campaign believes, their messages concerning their opponent would have been delivered more effectively to the citizenry.

Campaigners are always looking for ways to design communication that is both credible and able to be controlled by the candidate. One solution has been to produce television advertising that looks like news. For example, in 1968 the Nixon campaign orchestrated live broadcasts that looked like spontaneous question-and-answer sessions but were really carefully organized, rehearsed, and controlled productions.[41]

Although we have discussed the factors influencing the choice of both paid and free methods of communication in a very rational fashion, in an actual campaign there are usually healthy doses of intuition, repetition of past practices, and haphazard choice. Both candidates and professional consultants tend to repeat behaviors that they think have worked in the past, to copy the strategies of others in the profession and of opponents, and to include some of each type of communication because of uncertainty about the effectiveness of each. Nevertheless, there are some patterns in candidates' use of campaign communication methods that suggest the increased utility of particular forms in recent years. In general, campaigners have shown a strong preference in recent years for the broadcast media, for spot advertising, for face-to-face debates, and for communication that is independent of the candidate's organization itself.

Patterns of Recent Use in Methods of Communication

RELIANCE ON BROADCAST COMMUNICATION

One of the most dramatic changes in campaign communication in recent years has been the increase in candidates' reliance on the broadcast media. This reliance has two components: the increase in paid advertising time and the increase in time and energy devoted to stimulating broadcast media news coverage of candidate activities.

As constituencies have grown, political parties have atrophied, the number of people owning television sets has increased, and public policy decisions have made campaign advertising more attractive to broadcasters, candidates at all levels have increased their spending on paid advertising time. Figure 3–3 shows estimates of the amount of money spent on broadcast advertising in presidential general election campaigns since 1924 and in nonpresidential general election campaigns since 1956. Presidential broadcast advertising expenditures stayed fairly level from the 1920s through 1960. In 1964, however, spending was almost four times what it had been in 1960, and it almost doubled again in 1968.

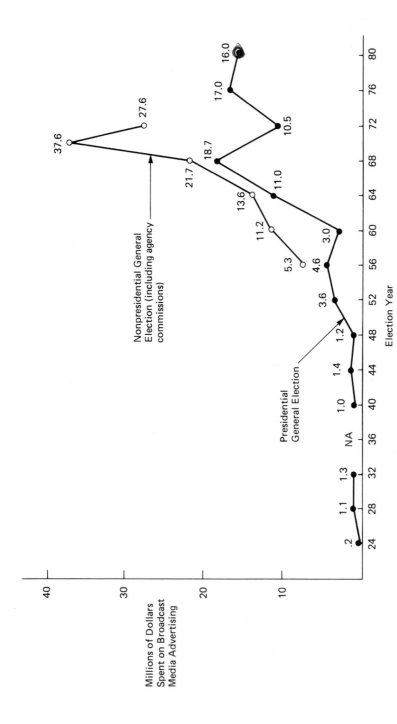

FIGURE 3-3   Trends in Campaign Spending on Broadcast Advertising

Source: Figures for 1924–1948 are from Herbert Alexander, *Financing Politics* (Washington: Congressional Quarterly Press, 1976), p. 27 reprinted with the permission of Congressional Quarterly, Inc.; figures for presidential funding for 1952–1976 are from Herbert Alexander, *Financing Politics* second edition (Washington: Congressional Quarterly Press, 1980). p. 10 reprinted with the permission of Congressional Quarterly Inc.; figures for nonpresidential spending for 1956–1972 are from Federal Communications Commission Annual Report, 1973, p. 207.

Nonpresidential spending (spending by all nonpresidential candidates) has also shown a substantial and continuous increase since 1964. (The temporary decline in broadcast advertising expeditures in 1972 was the result of federal legislation limiting broadcast advertising expenditures in that year.)

Inflation, population growth, and other societal changes can have an effect on broadcast expenditures that is independent of candidate behavior. Therefore, in Figure 3–4 the broadcast expenditures from Figure 3–3 have been standardized to their 1960 level and are compared with other indicators of related phenomena. This graph clearly shows that the post-1960 increase in broadcast advertising spending has been steeper than is accounted for by increases in the voting-age population, the number of television-owning households, an index of national advertising expenditures, and the consumer price index.[42]

Not only has total spending on the broadcast media increased recently, but the proportion of campaign resources committed to broadcast advertising by individual candidates has also increased. Reliable data on the proportion of a candidate's resources spent on various activities are hard to come by, but the available evidence demonstrates the extent to which the modern campaign relies on publicity in general and broadcast communication in particular.

The proportion of presidential campaign expenditures devoted to broadcast advertising has been increasing over the past two decades, from 34 percent of total expenditures in 1956 to 42 percent in 1964 and 1968.[43] In 1972, because of temporary spending limits on broadcast advertising and the huge sum of money raised by the Nixon campaign, broadcast advertising expenditures were a smaller proportion of total expenditures in that year (Table 3–4). In 1976, however, broadcast advertising expenditures came to almost half of both Carter's and Ford's campaign spending, and in 1980 both Carter and Reagan spent about $16 million on television advertising of the $29.4 million they had available to them.[44]

In general, the lower the level of political office contested, the smaller the proportion of campaign resources committed to broadcast advertising. The increased reliance on the broadcast media in nonpresidential campaigns is also evident, however. The proportion of campaign funds spent by all candidates for public office on broadcast advertising increased from less than 10 percent in 1956 and 1960 to 12 percent in 1964 and 15–20 percent in 1968 and 1972.[45] A typical $1 million statewide campaign now spends about 40 percent of its resources on broadcast advertising, and a typical $100,000 congressional campaign spends about 35 percent of its resources on broadcast advertising.[46]

Of course, the data on paid advertising actually underestimate the amount of resources committed by candidates to the use of the broadcast media because they completely ignore expenditures made to support the activities engaged in by candidates to stimulate so-called free news cover-

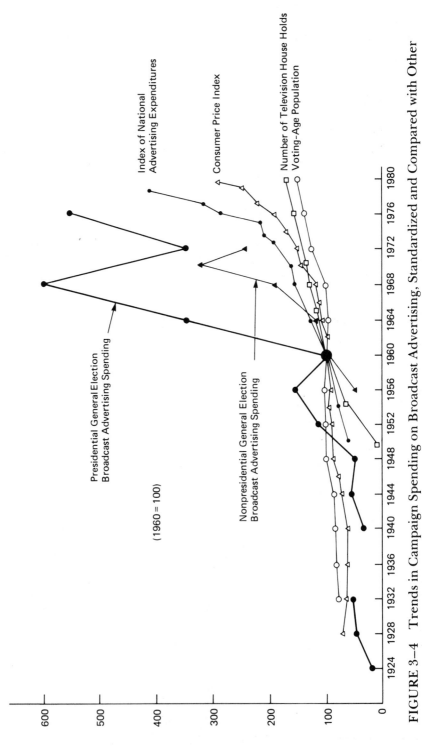

FIGURE 3–4 Trends in Campaign Spending on Broadcast Advertising, Standardized and Compared with Other Trends

TABLE 3–4   Money Spent by 1972 and 1976 Presidential General
Election Campaigns on Broadcast Advertising

1972	McGovern	Percentage of Total	Nixon	Percentage of Total
Total spending	$18,543,416	100	$61,400,000	100
Television time	4,071,088	22	4,277,000	7
Radio time	820,000	4	567,000	1
Television and radio production	792,596	4	1,000,000 (est.)	2
Total broadcast	$5,683,684	31	$5,844,000	10

1976	Carter	Percentage of Total	Ford	Percentage of Total
Total spending	21,800,000	100	21,786,641	100
Television time	7,819,091	36	6,385,000	29
Radio time	1,262,230	6	1,490,000	7
Television and radio production	483,822	2	1,200,000 (est.)	6
Total broadcast	9,565,143	44	9,075,000	42

Source: Herbert E. Alexander, *Financing Politics*, 1st ed. (Washington, D.C.: Congressional Quarterly Press, 1976), p. 31, and Herbert E. Alexander, *Financing Politics*, 2nd ed. (Washington, D.C.: Congressional Quarterly Press, 1980), p. 105. Reprinted with the permission of Congressional Quarterly Inc.

age. Political campaigns engage in a significant amount of travel and organize many scheduled events in order to produce broadcast news coverage. Personnel have to be paid, equipment rented, and airplanes chartered to campaign in this manner. If these expenses were included in the category of "broadcast media expenses," the proportions of such expenditures would increase further. In fact, most modern campaigns have become so oriented toward the broadcast media that it is difficult to separate out which expenses are for paid broadcast advertising and which are not. A substantial portion (typically about 25 percent) of newspaper ads, for example, are used to announce a political broadcast appearance.[47]

RELIANCE ON SPOT ADVERTISING

Not only have candidates become generally more attentive to the broadcast media for campaign communication, but broadcast *spot advertising* has also become a dominant type of broadcast communication. Whereas 85 percent of presidential campaign expenditures for paid television network time were for programs (thirty- and sixty-minute shows) in 1956, by 1968 only 52 percent went for programs and 48 percent for spots.[48] Similarly, nonnetwork advertising expenditures have gone in-

TABLE 3–5   Nonnetwork Expenditures for Types of Political
Advertisements

	Charges for Programs[a]	*Charges for Announcements*[b]	*Expenditure Ratio*[c]
	I. General Election		
1962	$2,498,296	$ 5,160,712	2.07:1
1966	2,280,393	9,670,915	4.24:1
1968	2,265,057	17,459,730	7.71:1
1970	1,271,019	23,292,981	18.33:1
1972	1,940,504	17,714,823	9.13:1
	II. Primary Election		
1962	$2,112,195	$ 2,762,941	1.31:1
1966	1,644,165	$ 5,325,632	3.24:1
1968	1,719,473	7,652,446	4.45:1
1970	1,070,650	10,715,404	10.01:1
1972	1,250,879	11,333,929	9.06:1
	III. Primary and General Election		
1962	$4,610,491	$ 7,923,653	1.72:1
1966	3,924,558	14,996,547	3.82:1
1968	3,984,530	25,112,176	6.30:1
1970	2,342,669	34,008,384	14.52:1
1972	3,191,383	29,048,752	9.10:1

Source: *Annual Reports,* Federal Communications Commission, various years.
[a]Broadcasts of ten minutes length or more.
[b]Broadcasts of five minutes length or less.
[c]Ratio of b to a.

creasingly for spot advertisements, with spot advertising representing 55
percent of general election expenditures in 1956, 67 percent in 1962, 80
percent in 1964, and 90 percent in 1972 (Table 3–5). In 1968 more than
half of the congressional campaigns used paid television or radio spots;
by 1972, 85 percent of U.S. Senate candidates and 53 percent of U.S.
House candidates had purchased at least some television spot time.[49]

We have already discussed why spot advertising is so attractive to
candidates and other campaigners. It allows candidates to communicate
directly with target audiences without the intrusion of journalists or
volunteer workers. Candidates can say or do what *they* want and, to a
certain extent, *to whom* they want.

VARIATIONS IN RELIANCE ON THE
BROADCAST MEDIA

Not all political candidates are equally apt to use broadcast advertising.
Some election districts are too small or poorly situated to permit a cost-

TABLE 3-6 Campaign Spending for Broadcast Advertising by
Level of Office, 1970 and 1972

	General Election (%)	Primary Election (%)	General and Primary Election (%)	Average General Election	N
1970					
Senate	28.3	24.9	27.1	$264,373	35
Governor	27.1	29.0	27.7	253,095	35
Lieutenant governor	3.0	5.5	3.9	32,205	31
House of Representatives	11.9	7.4	10.3	8,939	435
All other	29.8	33.1	30.9		
Total	100.1	99.9	99.9		
1972					
President and vice-president	28.4	16.3	24.0		
Senate	11.7	9.0	10.7	$131,390	34
Governor	11.8	15.2	13.0	236,973	19
Lieutenant governor	0.8	4.1	2.0	17,503	17
House of Representatives	12.5	12.6	12.5	10,936	435
All other	34.8	42.8	37.7		
Total	100.0	100.0	99.9		
1972 (excluding presidential spending)					
Senate	16.3	10.8	14.1		
Governor	16.5	18.2	17.1		
Lieutenant governor	1.1	4.9	2.6		
House of Representatives	17.5	15.1	16.4		
All other	48.6	51.1	49.6		
Total	100.0	100.1	99.8		

Source: U.S. Senate, Committee on Commerce, Hearings on Federal Election Campaign
Act of 1971 and 1973, Appendix A.

effective use of broadcast advertising, and some candidates lack the
resources necessary for a broadcast media strategy. In this section we will
investigate variations in the use of the broadcast media.

First, presidential candidates are not the only candidates to make extensive use of spot advertisements. In Table 3-6 we can see that broadcast advertising expenditures by presidential candidates only accounted

for about one-quarter of all such expenditures in 1972 and only about 28 percent of such expenditures in the 1972 general election. In fact, more spending was done on broadcast advertisements by the large number of lower state and local candidates in both 1970 and 1972 than by candidates for any other electoral office. Senatorial and gubernatorial candidates were substantial users of broadcast advertising in both 1970 and 1972, whereas candidates for lieutenant governor and the House of Representatives accounted for a smaller proportion of these expenditures.

Of course, one reason that lower-level state and local candidates account for so much broadcast advertising spending is that so many different candidacies are included in this category. If we calculate the average amount of money spent at the different electoral levels, we can see the level of spending that is typical for different offices. In 1970 the average senatorial candidate spent $264,373 in the general election; the average gubernatorial candidate spent nearly as much ($253,095). The typical candidate for the U.S. House of Representatives, on the other hand, spent only $9,000 on broadcast media advertising in the general election.

In 1972 average gubernatorial spending was very similar to that for 1970, but average senatorial spending was only half what it had been in 1970, reflecting the number of small states holding senatorial elections in 1972. Average media spending for the House of Representatives increased a little, to about $11,000. Unfortunately, there is no simple way to calculate an average expenditure for all the other state and local candidates. It is certain, however, that a very low average expenditure for many hundreds of candidates adds up to the substantial aggregate amount. Clearly, national and state candidacies have the most use for the broadcast media, but broadcast advertising expenditures are not restricted to those candidates.

Second, both Democratic and Republican candidates have been equally dependent on broadcast advertising. Although we often think of the Republican party both as the more affluent party and as the party with fewer strong party organizations across the country, Republicans have not made appreciably greater use of broadcast advertising than Democrats have. Table 3–7 shows broadcast advertising expenditures for Republican and Democratic candidates in selected campaigns since 1928. Of the nineteen comparisons possible, Republican candidates did spend more on the broadcast media in fifteen of them. In most of the cases, however, the differences are slight. The most serious imbalance occurred in the 1968 presidential campaign, when Richard Nixon outspent Hubert Humphrey 2 to 1.

We can also consider the partisan balance of broadcast advertising spending within each of the fifty states to see whether residents of particular states are exposed to the campaign communication of both parties.

TABLE 3–7   Partisan Balance of General Election Political
Broadcasting Expenditures
(in millions of dollars)

		Democratic Party Candidates	Republican Party Candidates	Other Party Candidates
1928	President	0.7	0.4	NA
1944	President	0.7	0.7	NA
1952	President	1.5	2.0	NA
	All offices	2.6	3.5	NA
1956	President	1.8	2.9	NA
	All offices	4.1	5.4	NA
1960	President	1.1	1.9	NA
	All offices	6.2	7.6	NA
1964	President	4.7	6.4	NA
	All offices	11.0	13.0	NA
1968	President	6.1	12.6	NA
	All offices	15.5	22.5	NA
1970	House	1.8	2.1	0.0
	Gubernatorial	4.1	5.7	0.1
	Senate	4.2	4.4	0.7
	All other state and local offices	4.3	4.4	1.1
	All offices	14.3	16.5	2.0
1972	House	2.3	2.4	0.1
	Gubernatorial	2.5	3.0	0.1
	Senate	1.8	2.5	0.1
	President	6.2	4.3	0.3
	All other state and local offices	4.7	5.3	2.5
	All offices	17.5	17.5	3.1
1976	President	11	12	NA

Source: Pre-1952 figures are from Herbert Alexander, *Financing Politics* (Washington, D.C.: Congressional Quarterly Press, 1976), p. 27; figures for 1952–1968 are from Herbert Asher, *Presidential Elections and American Politics* (Homewood, Ill.: Dorsey Press, 1976), p. 211; reprinted by permission of The Dorsey Press, copyright 1976; 1970 and 1972 figures are from U.S. Senate, Committee on Commerce, Hearings on Federal Election Campaign Act of 1971 and 1973, Appendix A. Reprinted by permission.

Of the 150 cases of state-level broadcast advertising spending available in 1966, 1968, and 1972 (50 states × 3 years), 76 show an imbalance in favor of the Republican party and 71 an imbalance in favor of the Democratic party (3 were perfectly balanced). Again, however, most of the cases were not extremely imbalanced. Only 28 (20 percent) of the imbalanced cases have imbalances of 2 to 1 or greater—20 of these involving a Republican advantage, 8 a Democratic one. Seven states show a Republican advantage in all three years (Arkansas, New York, Colorado, Oklahoma, Wyoming, Georgia, and Texas); seven states show a Democratic advantage in all three years (Kentucky, Mississippi, Maine, Nevada, Washington, Minnesota, and Utah). These are the exceptions, however: The overall pattern in most states in most years is one of fairly equally balanced expenditures.[50]

Of course, these aggregate statistics disguise individual campaigns characterized by gross inequality in broadcast advertising expenditures. For example, in the 1970 Senate race in Massachusetts, Edward Kennedy outspent his opponent on broadcast advertising $152,000 to $15,000; in the 1970 gubernatorial campaign in New York, Nelson Rockefeller outspent his opponent $1,182,000 to $365,000; and in the 1972 senatorial race in Tennessee, Howard Baker outspent his opponent on broadcast advertising by $163,000 to $51,000.[51]

Third, incumbents and open-seat candidates tend to spend more money on broadcast advertising than challengers do. In general, incumbents and open-seat candidates have more money to spend on campaigns than challengers do, and they spend more of it on broadcast advertising as well.[52] In 1970 gubernatorial campaigns, the average incumbent outspent the average major-party challenger $145,012 to $80,472; in 1970 senatorial campaigns the difference was $123,778 to $118,206; in 1972 gubernatorial campaigns the difference was $133,748 to $95,213; and in 1972 senatorial campaigns the difference was $74,268 to $50,969. Apparently, the ability to raise larger amounts of campaign contributions and the desire to maximize one's share of the vote leads to a greater use of broadcast advertising by incumbents.

Open-seat major-party candidates are also apt to spend considerable amounts of money on the broadcast media. The average expenditures for such candidates were: 1970 gubernatorial, $165,922; 1970 senatorial, $149,115; 1972 gubernatorial, $121,692; and 1972 senatorial, $68,874. These candidates also generally have more money to spend and apparently allocate a significant portion of it to broadcast advertising.

In general, then, candidates from large electorates, as well as open-seat and incumbent candidates, have been spending more money on broadcast advertising.

RELIANCE ON BROADCAST FACE-TO-FACE DEBATES

Another recent departure in campaign communication is an increase in candidates' participation in broadcast face-to-face debates. Although this use of the media does not afford the candidate as much control over the message as broadcast advertising does, candidates do have greater influence over the outcome of debates than they have in stimulating news coverage of the campaign. To the candidate, debates provide a relatively free means of communication and a sizable audience. To the broadcaster they provide a means of fulfilling responsibilities in the area of public affairs programming while preventing the sacrifice of audience ratings and advertising revenue.

One reason for the increased prevalence of candidate debates is that two recent policy changes have made face-to-face debates considerably more attractive to both broadcasters and candidates. One of these, a 1976 FCC decision sustained by the Supreme Court, holds that as long as broadcasters only *cover* face-to-face debates and do not *produce* them, their coverage will be considered "on-the-spot coverage of bona fide news events" and hence exempt from the equal opportunities provision of the Communications Act of 1934. Consequently, covering a debate between the major-party candidates for public office no longer creates a legal right for all other legally qualified candidates for that office to equivalent *free* use of that broadcast station. This has made the coverage of such debates considerably more appealing economically to broadcasters.

A second important policy change has made broadcast debates more attractive to candidates by limiting campaign spending. One of the features of the campaign finance legislation that survived Supreme Court review was the limitation on campaign spending during both the nomination and general election campaigns for presidential candidates accepting public subsidies. These limits have been set low enough to constitute a very real constraint on candidates and to force candidates to allocate their funds very carefully. Against this increasingly austere background of expenditure limits, at the presidential level at least, any form of campaign communication that is inexpensive or free or in which the costs are borne by others is highly valued by candidates. In 1976, for example, the League of Women Voters estimated that it cost them $322,000 to organize the series of debates between Jimmy Carter and Gerald Ford. Add to that the expense borne by journalists and media organizations for transmitting and covering the debates, and it is clear that candidates receive a substantial amount of exposure without much expense.

The inexpensive nature of debates makes them attractive to candidates, but the size of the audiences attracted by debates makes them almost irresistible. In 1960 it was estimated that the audience for each of the four broadcast presidential debates between John Kennedy and Richard Nixon was 70–80 million people and 55 percent of the adult population; that approximately 101 million people and 80 percent of the adult population viewed at least one of the debates; that 53 percent of television families watched three or four of the debates; and that 27 percent of television families watched all four debates.[53] The margin of victory in the popular vote between John Kennedy and Richard Nixon was 119,000 votes.

The 1976 presidential debates also attracted large audiences. Between 75 and 95 million people saw each of the presidential debates, and approximately 70 million people saw or heard the debate between vice-presidential candidates Robert Dole and Walter Mondale. This amounted to about two-thirds of all registered voters. According to one national survey of the voting-age population, 14 percent saw one of the four debates, 30 percent saw two, 22 percent saw three, and 34 percent saw all four.[54] In 1980 the Reagan-Carter debate attracted almost 59 percent of the television households, with very little tune out during the one and a half hours it was on.[55]

This audience is larger than would be achieved by any other form of communication. A half-hour, paid, prime-time television show in 1960 yielded an audience about one-third the size of the typical debate audience, and about 30 percent smaller than the usual audience of the programs preempted, whereas the debates attracted an audience about 20 percent *larger* than that of the entertainment programs preempted.[56] Compared with lengthy prime-time television programming, then, broadcast presidential debates clearly attract a much larger audience. Compared with a spot ad placed on a *typical* prime-time entertainment time slot, the debates also have reached slightly larger audiences. In fact, the debates reached a larger audience in 1960 than a spot ad placed during the World Series would have.

Recent elections have given ample indication that debates are being increasingly utilized by candidates. In 1978, for example, the two major-party candidates for governor of Pennsylvania engaged in a series of debates broadcast across the state; in New York the incumbent governor debated his major party challenger in sixteen televised debates, ten of which were seen almost statewide; in New Jersey the two major-party candidates for the Senate engaged in twenty-one debates across the state; and in Illinois the incumbent governor debated his major-party challenger. In both 1976 and 1980 there were debates between the presidential nominees, and in 1972 and 1980 there were debates among Democratic and Republican party candidates for the presidential nomination. In 1981 the two major-party candidates for governor of New Jersey also met in a series of televised debates.

Although many candidates, particularly those with little chance of losing and those with plenty of money, will still find debates too risky, it is clear that the legal and financial environment, especially at the presidential level, is much more conducive to debates than was true in the past. Since we saw in Chapter 2 that debates are at least somewhat more policy-oriented than other forms of campaign communication, the electorate is probably well served by the increased use of this mode of candidate communication.

INDEPENDENT CAMPAIGNING

Perhaps the most interesting recent innovation in campaign communication is the delivery of campaign messages by campaigners who are independent of candidates and their campaign organizations. Money spent for such communication is called an "independent expenditure" and has been defined by the Federal Election Commission as an expenditure "expressly advocating the election or defeat" of a candidate that is "not made with the cooperation, or with the prior consent of, or in consultation with, or at the request or suggestion of, a candidate or any agent or authorized committee" of the candidate.[57]

Although individuals have spent their own money to advocate the election or defeat of a candidate for some time now (then Governor William Shapp of Pennsylvania, for example, took out a full-page ad in the *New York Times* supporting the election of Jimmy Carter in 1976), the Supreme Court's decision to exempt such expenditures from a statutory limitation while keeping the limits on contributions to candidates has made a much more attractive form of campaign communication.

During the 1979–1980 election period, $16 million was spent "independently" by individuals, organizations, and political action committees, eight times more than was spent in 1975–1976. Of this amount, $13.7 million was spent to influence the presidential race, with most of it—$12.2 million—spent to promote the candidacy of Ronald Reagan. Considering that Reagan and Carter each had $29.4 million to spend during the general election, this represented a significant contribution to the flow of campaign communication.

At the senatorial level, most (78 percent) of the independent spending in 1979–1980 was intended to bring about the defeat of some candidate. The main targets of this spending were incumbents Frank Church ($339,018 spent against him), George McGovern ($222,044), Alan Cranston ($192,039), John Culver ($186,613), Birch Bayh ($180,723), and Thomas Eagleton ($101,794). Of these incumbents, only Cranston and Eagleton won reelection.[58]

For our purposes, the most notable consequence of independent campaigning is its notable contribution to the flow of campaign communication. Although data are unavailable regarding the proportion of independent expenditures that go to broadcast advertising, legally, all of this type of expenditure must go for campaign communication of one sort or another. In 1980 a number of independent spenders spent money on fairly extensive broadcast advertising campaigns. The most active independent broadcast campaigners were:

National Conservative Political Action Committee
(pro-Reagan, anti-Church, anti-Culver, anti-Cranston, anti-McGovern, anti-Bayh, anti-Eagleton, anti-Carter)

Fund for a Conservative Majority
(anti-Carter)
Americans for an Effective Presidency
(anti-Carter and pro-Reagan)

Although it is too soon to predict with certainty that such independent communication will increase in future campaigns, the regulatory environment in which campaign contributors and strategists operate is currently highly conducive to such activity. It is not yet clear whether the campaign messages of these independent campaigners will be significantly different from those devised by candidates and their advisers. In 1980 the spot ads of these groups tended to be less cautious, more policy-oriented, and more negative than we are used to seeing from candidates. In fact, many of the ads produced by these groups were denounced by their supposed beneficiaries.[59]

From the perspective of the citizenry, independent communication may prove beneficial if it turns out to be more specific, less cautious, and more comparative than the typical candidate message. If, however, it is also less accurate, more deceptive, and more symbolic, it will contribute little to the flow of useful campaign information. To candidates, independent campaigning is also a double-edged sword. It allows them to circumvent contribution and expenditure limits on campaign activity; but it also means the presence of highly visible messages that by definition cannot be controlled by the candidates. This permits a candidate's more zealous supporters inadvertently to devise campaign messages that antagonize a segment of the citizenry and actually work to his or her disadvantage.

Conclusion

In this chapter we have focused on the methods of campaign communication used by candidates and the ways in which campaigners think of the citizenry when they are attempting to direct their appeals where they will be the most effective. We have seen that candidates tailor their messages to specific audiences. This targeting may be done in a number of different ways, but typically it is done in terms of the partisan predispositions, political interest, political attitudes, and demographic characteristics of the electorate. Although targeting has been done geographically for years, it is increasingly being done in terms of media markets and station and program audiences. This is an area in which modern campaigns rely heavily on the advice of professional consultants.

We have also seen that candidates and their campaign staffs select communication forms on the basis of considerations of cost, cost-effectiveness, availability, and ability to reach certain audiences. Recent legal and political developments have led to an increased reliance on the broadcast media in general; on paid political advertising, stimulation of news coverage, and participation in debates in particular; and, most recently, on campaign communication whose origin is independent of a candidate's campaign.

One of the most important questions raised by the communications behavior of candidates is whether the U.S. polity is well served by the communication devised to reach, engage, and persuade them. On the one hand, modern-day campaign communication probably reaches more citizens more times with a greater sensitivity to the interests of the populace than ever before. Public opinion polling techniques give campaign strategists more systematic information about the citizenry than they have ever had before, and the reliance on the broadcast media probably means that more citizens are exposed now to a greater flow of campaign communication than ever before. One reason for this is that much campaign media exposure has become involuntary rather than voluntary through the use of spot ads. Another reason is that candidates have come to rely on methods of communication (news and debates) that are popular with the mass public. One suspects that advertisements in particular extend the acquaintance with some minimum amount of campaign information into portions of the citizenry that otherwise would have none.

On the other hand, some argue that the methods of communication used in contemporary campaigns are harmful to civic education and the electoral process. A number of arguments are often made: First, the increased reliance on brief campaign messages (spot advertisements) is thought by some to diminish the quality of candidate presentations and inhibit the discussion of substantive issues. Second, the increased reliance on broadcast (especially television) media rather than interpersonal or print communication is thought to accentuate visual symbolism and undercut cognitive thought and reason. Third, the increased reliance on paid advertising and stimulation of news coverage is thought to increase campaign costs (in the absence of expenditure limitations) to an exorbitant level. Although it is difficult to say whether the United States spends "too much" money on election campaigns (especially in a society that spends $7 billion a year on toys and $20 billion a year on weddings, and in which gamblers lose $1.5 billion each year in Atlantic City gambling casinos),[60] the upward spiraling of campaign costs is worrisome to many.

One implication of the new methods of campaign communication is that candidates probably have a greater capability now to communicate directly with citizens than ever before. This is both laudable, since it represents the free expression of political speech, and worrisome, since this communication may be misleading, deceptive, or untruthful. Hence, as candidates have increased their ability to control the flow of campaign communication, the availability of campaign communication that is *uncontrolled* by the candidate takes on added significance. Since for most U.S. citizens the primary competing source of campaign communication is provided by the mass media in various news formats, we turn to a consideration of that enterprise in the next two chapters.

Notes

1. For a concise discussion of these processes, see Jarol B. Mannheim, *The Politics Within*, 2nd ed. (New York: Longman, 1982), Chap. 6.
2. For a concise review of the literature on party identification, see Herbert Asher, *Presidential Elections and American Politics* (Homewood, Ill.: Dorsey, 1980), Chaps. 2, 3.
3. For example, see Wilbur Schramm and Richard F. Carter, "Effectiveness of a Political Telethon," *Public Opinion Quarterly* 23 (1959): 121–127, and Joseph T. Klapper, *The Effects of Mass Communication* (New York: Free Press, 1960), pp. 18–21. For a critical review of the selective-exposure thesis, see D. O. Sears and J. L. Freedman, "Selective Exposure to Information: A Critical Review," *Public Opinion Quarterly* 31 (1967): 194–213.
4. Asher, *Presidential Elections*, pp. 89–94. For an analysis of the recent decline in party as a voting cue, see William J. Crotty and Gary C. Jacobson, *American Parties in Decline* (Boston: Little, Brown, 1980), Chap. 2.
5. For four good examples of this sort of analysis, see the 1976 Ford and Carter campaign memos in Martin Schram, *Running for President 1976: The Carter Campaign* (New York: Stein and Day, 1977), pp. 239–250, 253–268, 386–391; and the 1980 Reagan and Carter memos in Elizabeth Drew, *Portrait of an Election* (New York: Simon and Schuster, 1981), pp. 351–362, 388–409.
6. Schram, *Running for President 1976*, p. 262.
7. Drew, *Portrait*, pp. 384–386.
8. For a discussion of this use of polls, see Charles W. Roll and Albert H. Cantril, *Polls: Their Use and Misuse in Politics* (Cabin John, Md.: Seven Locks Press, 1980), pp. 44–48.
9. Asher, *Presidential Elections*, p. 316.
10. This example was developed by John Ashmore, from Matt Reese Associates, in a lecture given at Temple University, Philadelphia, Pa., in the fall of 1981.
11. Quoted in Ernest R. May and Janet Fraser, eds., *Campaign '72: The Managers Speak* (Cambridge, Mass.: Harvard University Press, 1973), p. 194.
12. Schram, *Running for President 1976*, p. 263.
13. May and Fraser, *Campaign '72*, p. 10.
14. Drew, *Portrait*, p. 394.
15. May and Fraser, *Campaign '72*, pp. 38–39.
16. Ibid., p. 44.
17. Ibid., p. 73.
18. Drew, *Portrait*, p. 356.
19. Ibid., pp. 388, 402.

20. Both Republican Congressman Robert McCloskey and Democratic Senator Fred Harris, for example, dropped out of their respective parties' presidential nomination campaigns in 1972 because of a lack of money. See May and Fraser, *Campaign '72*, pp. 21, 286.

21. These examples were developed from information given in S. J. Guzzetta, *The Campaign Manual* (Alexandria, Va.: Campaign Publishing Company, 1981), and Adam Clymer, "Inflation and a Limit on Contributions Strain Presidential Hopefuls' Budgets," *New York Times*, February 4, 1980.

22. Lou Cannon, "As Nov. 2 Countdown Begins, Ford Camp Plans Media Blitz," *Washington Post*, October 22, 1976, p. A-2.

23. "Face Off," *Public Opinion* 3, no. 6 (December–January 1981): 63.

24. Conversation with a member of Campaign Group, Inc., a small consulting firm located in Philadelphia, Pa.

25. Larry J. Sabato, *The Rise of Political Consultants* (New York: Basic Books, 1981), pp. 200–204.

26. Delmer D. Dunn, Financing Presidential Campaigns (Washington, D.C.: Brookings Institution, 1972), pp. 35–40.

27. Ibid., p. 27.

28. As quoted in John Foley, Dennis A. Britton, and Eugene B. Everett, Jr., eds., *Nominating a President: The Process and the Press* (New York: Praeger, 1980), p. 75.

29. Robert W. Laird, "Running Under Wraps," *E.P.O.* 1, no. 1 (January–February 1979): 60.

30. F. Christopher Arterton, "The Media Politics of Presidential Campaigns," in James David Barber, ed., *Race for the Presidency* (Englewood Cliffs, N.J.: Prentice-Hall, 1978), pp. 28–29. See also the comments of Thomas Quinn, Jerry Brown's 1980 presidential campaign manager, in Foley, Britton, and Everett, *Nominating a President*, p. 59.

31. Sabato, *Political Consultants*, pp. 131–132, 154–155.

32. Arthur T. Hadley, *The Invisible Primary* (Englewood Cliffs, N.J.: Prentice-Hall, 1976).

33. Schram, *Running for President 1976*, pp. 56–57.

34. Arterton, "Media Politics," pp. 36–39.

35. Schram, *Running for President 1976*, pp. 248–250, 386–391.

36. Edwin Diamond, *Good News, Bad News* (Cambridge, Mass.: MIT Press, 1978), p. 79.

37. Joel Swerdlow, "The Decline of the Boys on the Bus," *Washington Journalism Review*, January–February 1981, p. 16.

38. Ibid., p. 17.

39. John Deardourff, Ford's television adviser, quoted in R. W. Apple, Jr., "Ford Tactic: TV Documentary Plus Chat with Sports Announcer," *New York Times*, October 25, 1976.

40. "Face Off," p. 10.

41. Joe McGinniss, *The Selling of the President, 1968* (New York: Trident Press, 1969).

42. The data for the consumer price index, voting-age population, number of television households, and index of national advertising expenditures were all taken from the 1980 *Statistical Abstract of the United States*, pp. 476, 515, 589, and 597, respectively. In each case the data were standardized to the 1960 figure.

43. Calculated from Dunn, *Financing*, p. 31.

44. Herbert E. Alexander, *Financing Politics*, 2nd ed. (Washington, D.C.: Congressional Quarterly Press, 1980), pp. 12, 104–108; and "Face Off."

45. Calculated from Dunn, *Financing*, p. 32; and Herbert E. Alexander, *Financing Politics*, 1st ed. (Washington, D.C.: Congressional Quarterly Press, 1976), p. 29.

46. Robert Agranoff, "The New Style of Campaigning: The Decline of Party and the Rise of Candidate-Centered Technology," in Robert Agranoff, ed., *The New Style in Election Campaigns* (Boston: Holbrook Press, 1976), pp. 3–47.

47. James J. Mullen, "Newspaper Advertising in the Kennedy-Nixon Campaign," *Journalism Quarterly* 40 (Winter 1963): 3–11; idem, "Newspaper Advertising in the Johnson-Goldwater Campaign," *Journalism Quarterly* 45 (Summer 1968): 219–225; idem, "How Candidates for the Senate Use Newspaper Advertising," *Journalism Quarterly* 40 (Autumn 1963): 532–538.

48. Dunn, *Financing*, p. 35.

49. Sabato, *Political Consultants*, p. 116.

50. For more details, see Richard A. Joslyn, "The Impact of Television on Partisan Politics," Ph.D. diss., Cornell University, 1977.

51. It would be worthwhile to update these expenditure data to more recent elections, but the FCC no longer collects information on the broadcast spending of individual candidates. Consequently, although the Federal Election Commission now releases detailed information on the overall campaign spending of political candidates, up-to-date data are unavailable on how much of the spending goes for broadcast advertising.

52. Gary C. Jacobson, *Money in Congressional Elections* (New Haven: Yale University Press, 1980), Chap. 5.

53. Frank Stanton, "A CBS View," in Sidney Kraus, *The Great Debates* (Gloucester, Mass.: Peter Smith, 1968), pp. 65–77; and Elihu Katz and Jacob J. Feldman, "The Debates in the Light of Research: A Survey of Surveys," in ibid., pp. 173–223.

54. 1976 Survey Research Center/Center for Political Studies election study.

55. "Opinion Roundup," *Public Opinion* 3, no. 6 (December–January 1981): 34.

56. Stanton, "A CBS View," p. 68.

57. Federal Election Commission, U.S., "Campaign Guide for Presidential Candidates and Their Committees" (Washington, D.C.: FEO, October 1979), pp. 9, 36–37. Also quoted in Sabato, *Political Consultants*, p. 281.

58. Mike Feinsilber, "They Spent for Their Candidates," *Philadelphia Inquirer*, November 29, 1981, p. 6-A.

59. *Dollar Politics* (Washington, D.C.: Congressional Quarterly, 1982), p. 86.

60. Al Haas, "Here Comes the Bride's Register Again," *Philadelphia Inquirer*, May 29, 1983, p. 6-G; Laurie Wegner, "How the Toy Industry Caters to Fantasies," *Philadelphia Inquirer*, May 29, 1983, p. 7-G; Fen Montaigne, "Making the Casino Work," *Philadelphia Inquirer*, May 29, 1983, p. 22-A.

4
Journalism, News, and the Coverage of Election Campaigns

A struggle over the content of political news has become the core of presidential nominating politics.
> —Donald R. Matthews, "Winnowing," in *Race for the Presidency*

The competitive nature of television makes us reach for the dramatic, for the conflict, for the confrontational, for the theater of politics. . . .
> —Bill Moyers, "ABC News Viewpoint"

. . . television news is not primarily information but narrative; . . . it is governed not by a political bias but by a melodramatic one.
> —Paul H. Weaver, "Captives of Melodrama"*

. . . I would question the use of the word objectivity. In my opinion there is no such thing . . . objectivity is not the ideal; fairness is.
> —David Brinkley, "ABC News Viewpoint"

In the preceding chapters we have seen that the ability of candidates to transmit their messages to the public has been enlarged recently in a number of important ways. The increased use of broadcast advertising (as well as direct mail and telephone canvassing) has permitted candidates to reach enormous audiences with messages that are completely controlled by the candidate. The use of broadcast debates and incumbent press conferences has also allowed candidates to communicate with the public in a substantially controlled format. Furthermore, the expertise and availability of paid political consultants has given candidates the ability to conceptualize and target audiences that are particularly important and to measure systematically the interests, preferences, and perceptions of those target audiences. Given this increased capability of

---

*This and subsequent excerpts from "Captives of Melodrama," are © 1976 by The New York Times Company. Reprinted by permission.

candidates to devise and deliver their own campaign messages, the contribution that journalists make to campaign communication is an important alternative source of information for the electorate. In this chapter we will discuss the importance of campaign coverage, how journalists decide what the news is, and how journalists go about covering an election campaign. In Chapter 5 we will take a closer look at the patterns in campaign coverage in recent years.

The Importance of Campaign Coverage

There are two reasons that the campaign communication provided by journalists is so important. First, unlike the communication explored in Chapters 2 and 3, the campaign communication of journalists is hardly ever designed to serve the interests of particular candidates.[1] The prevailing norm of U.S. journalism is that journalists should be detached, objective, and disinterested observers motivated primarily by a desire to inform the U.S. public accurately. Although this norm is violated, it is generally true that journalistic coverage of campaigns represents a perspective that differs from that of the candidates. Campaign coverage is far more apt to be critical of or unfavorable toward a candidate, to reveal a candidate's flaws and weaknesses, and to compare one candidate with another. Consequently, journalistic coverage of campaigns provides a needed corrective to the self-serving and strategically designed communication of candidates and their surrogate campaigners.

Second, journalistic coverage of election campaigns is important because for most citizens it is an influential way of experiencing a campaign. Many citizens are also exposed to the controlled communication of candidates, but few experience campaigns in any other way. At the presidential level, for example, only about 4 percent of the adult population regularly devotes time to party or interest group activities; only about 10 percent of the population does volunteer campaign work, donates money to campaigns, or attends rallies; and only 25 percent of the adult population regularly "talks politics" with others.[2] For the majority, awareness of an election campaign is entirely mediated, and campaign coverage is the only alternative for understanding electoral choices.

Journalists exercise political power through campaign coverage in a number of ways. The most obvious involves deciding how much coverage to give a campaign and the candidates involved in it. In general, candidates desire as much coverage as they can get (although coverage may be harmful if its content is unfavorable). A candidate who is ignored by the media has a difficult time becoming known to the public and acquiring important political resources such as money and volunteers. Such candidates have little chance of winning. In the beginning stages of presidential nomination campaigns, for example, a candidate's goal is typically to do something that will result in news coverage of the candidate and stimulate campaign contributions. These contributions can then be used for further campaigning, helping to convince the press and the public that the candidate is both credible and newsworthy. If "momentum" can be established in this way, a candidate can remain in the nomination process longer and will be able to sustain subsequent efforts to win convention delegates.

Journalists also decide which of many possible interpretations to give to campaign occurrences. Since an election campaign is a complex and ambiguous phenomenon, different people will draw different conclusions about its meaning. Some of these conclusions will be more advantageous for particular candidates than for others. Consequently, candidates strive to shape the interpretations and perspectives of journalists, and the extent to which they are successful is important both for their own campaigns and for our understanding. For example, presidential candidates are always concerned with how the results of presidential primaries are *interpreted*. Candidates want to be seen as winners who are gaining momentum. This results in a sort of game between candidates and the press in which presidential hopefuls attempt to keep press expectations about the likely success of their campaign in a particular primary understated so that the primary results will be interpreted as having shown the candidate doing "much better than expected." This interpretation was an important part of Lyndon Johnson's abortive campaign in 1968, when Johnson's defeat of Eugene McCarthy by "only" 50 to 42 percent in the New Hampshire primary was widely interpreted as a loss; of Edmund Muskie's collapse in 1972, when his 46 to 37 percent margin over George McGovern in the New Hampshire primary was also interpreted as a loss; and of the successful nomination campaigns of George McGovern in 1972 and Jimmy Carter in 1976, both of whom did much better than any journalist had expected prior to the nomination campaign.

Journalists also exercise discretion in how favorably candidates are presented in the news. Although norms of objectivity and balance prevent most campaign coverage from including bold, unchallenged assertions about and evaluations of candidates, a more subtle and pervasive "slant" or "theme" to campaign coverage is possible and is significant from so credible a source. During the 1980 presidential nomination campaign, for example, press coverage of Edward Kennedy changed from a theme of "Teddy the Klutz" to one of "Teddy the gallant loser," whereas coverage of John Anderson praised his personal qualities but focused on the futility of his presidential quest.[3] Such themes are clearly interpretive, transcend daily campaign activities, and can affect both popular understanding and candidate fortunes.

One campaign expert has asserted that "there isn't a newspaper today that doesn't pick targets and doesn't somehow give better coverage to some candidates whom they tend to support or tend not to support."[4] Such an assertion erroneously traces the tone of a candidate's coverage to the personal preferences of journalists. It is far more likely that the favorableness of a candidate's coverage results from candidate efforts to shape news coverage and the press's pursuit of their own objectives and themes. The favorableness of a candidate's coverage may well depend on how well a candidate fits the melodramatic needs of, especially, television news, or may reflect the cyclical tendency of the press to be the most critical of those candidates who are doing well.[5] George McGovern's campaign coverage was unfavorable in 1972, for example, in part because his original choice of a vice-presidential candidate, Thomas Eagleton, was ill advised; and Jimmy Carter's campaign coverage during the nomination process in 1980 was more favorable than it would have been otherwise because of his ability to manage the news regarding the Iranian hostage situation. This suggests that what is considered bias in news coverage is more often unintentional than deliberate on the part of journalists. Nevertheless, the favorableness of a candidate's coverage is just as significant whether it is intentional or not.

Finally, journalists (usually editors and publishers) contribute to campaign communication by endorsing candidates. Endorsements may in turn become important political resources beyond their direct effect on a medium's audience (as, for example, when Gerald Ford's 1976 presidential campaign produced a television spot ad listing a number of Georgia newspapers that had *not* endorsed Jimmy Carter). An endorsement is clearly a more direct statement of preference by a media organization than are the other areas of journalistic judgment discussed here. In recent years, most endorsements have appeared in the print media, since an endorsement by a broadcaster could trigger requests for free equal response time from each of the endorsed candidate's opponents.

What Is News?

In order to understand the way in which a journalist approaches an election campaign, we ought to consider how journalists generally decide what constitutes the news. To most journalists an election campaign is just one news assignment to be completed before going on to the next one. Therefore, the general approach to covering the news will influence a reporter's coverage of an election campaign.

News has been defined as a process by which journalists "concentrate on acquainting sizable audiences with timely information about events highly visible to newsmen."[6] This definition holds that journalists are essentially chroniclers of events. That is, some event has to occur or some activity take place before a phenomenon will be considered newsworthy. Journalists scan their environment in certain nonrandom ways in search of appropriate events to cover, and news coverage is a description of the unambiguous facts of the event and an interpretation of the meaning of those facts.[7]

Not all events are considered equally newsworthy by journalists. Nevertheless, the financial resources committed by the media to the coverage of presidential primary returns, presidential nominating conventions, general election campaign activity, public opinion polls, and election night returns indicate that election campaigns are generally considered to be newsworthy events.

Election campaigns fit the journalist's criteria for a newsworthy event in a number of different ways.[8]

1. Campaigns recur at specified times and involve a daily flow of discrete events. This means that cost-effective coverage may be planned in advance by news organizations. Generally, news organizations prefer to commit their resources in an orderly, predictable fashion to the coverage of events that have a high probability of resulting in an important or interesting, usable news story.[9]

2. Campaigns allow journalists to write stories filled with drama, whether real or contrived. Drama is considered an important aspect of the news, in part because it is thought to keep audiences interested in continuing news coverage.

3. Campaigns have measurable outcomes that represent a resolution or climax to the drama that has been unfolding. Presidential elections are now particularly useful in this respect because they involve a series of well-spaced delegate-selection processes over a span of several months. Consequently, the drama in a presidential campaign develops over a number of months, with periodic and discrete climaxes available as indicators of how the "actors" are doing.

4. Campaigns contain conflict. Conflict lends itself to dramatic portrayal, is fairly easy to cover, and is thought to be engaging to the news audience.

5. This conflict may often legitimately be presented as two-sided, thus making brief and recognizable summaries of the conflict possible and allowing news organizations to present campaign summaries and stories that are balanced.

6. There are many available and suitable sources of information about campaigns. This facilitates the journalist's task of putting together a news story based on the opinions of authoritative sources.

All these attributes make election campaigns a frequently covered portion of politics, eclipsing coverage of other political processes such as court decisions, bureaucratic rule-making, legislative bargaining, and social and economic change.[10]

The way in which journalists cover election campaigns is similar to the way they cover any ongoing newsworthy event. In the United States, journalistic accounts tend to be fact- and source-based, nonopinionated, interpretive, thematic, and dramatic. Let us discuss each of these characteristics in turn.

Perhaps the most important job of any journalist is to acquaint the audience with a body of unambiguous facts about a newsworthy event.[11] This is primarily due to the norm of "objectivity" in U.S. journalism, and the consequences of that norm for news coverage.

In the early days of the Republic, the press was much more partisan and ideological than it is today. There was no separation between news and opinion or commentary, and papers unabashedly expressed partisan and philosophical viewpoints. Over the years, however, newspapers have attempted to appeal to wider audiences; the policy of appearing dispassionate and balanced developed as a result of this economic need to avoid offending anyone. In the late nineteenth and early twentieth centuries this policy became embodied in journalism's adoption of a *norm of objectivity* to guide news-gathering activities. This norm, a reaction to perceived journalistic excesses at the time, rejected the notion of the opinionated or ideological reporter mixing news with commentary, and opted instead for a journalistic role that valued unbiased description, a fairly strict demarcation between news and opinion, and a concern for the transmission of as much factual information as possible. The adoption of this norm transformed the job of the reporter from that of commentator or advocate to one of interviewer, transcriber, or stenographer.[12]

One of the advantages of this normative change for journalism was that it produced a news product that was more credible and more acceptable to a mass audience of diverse viewpoints and attitudes. As a result, journalists became oriented toward an attempt to observe and transmit factual information about activities or events, and news became largely a chronicle of the activities of certain news-makers.

When the news that is being covered is an election campaign, the norm of objectivity translates into an attempt by journalists to transcribe, as completely and with as much detail as possible, what happens on the campaign trail. This means taking copious notes on every campaign appearance, press release, handout, and sentence uttered by the candidate and his or her staff; selecting a few of these that seem to be most notable; developing a theme around which to present these facts (which will become the news story's lead); and in this way summarizing the day's occurrences. A journalist files a story in this manner one day and then immediately devotes his or her attention to duplicating the process the following day.

For the journalist covering a newsworthy event, the facts presented are often the words spoken by so-called authoritative or informed sources. Although these utterances may well be personal opinions or preferences and may be factually inaccurate, once they are spoken to the journalist, they become facts capable of being transmitted to the news audience. Consequently, the availability of news sources and the willingness of news sources to speak with journalists are important aspects of news coverage, and news accounts may properly be described as fact- and source-based.

A second consequence of "objective" journalism is that most news coverage is nonideological or, perhaps more accurately, nonopinion- ated. Although it is impossible for a journalist to remain completely detached from his or her news coverage, or to submerge personal and cultural values entirely, it is still the case that *explicit* statements of *per- sonal* preference or opinion are seldom found in U.S. news accounts.[13]

From time to time the press is charged with violating its norm of objectivity and with implicitly and subtly presenting an ideological— usually "liberal," "liberal-intellectual," or "countercultural"—slant.[14] This slant is usually thought to result from the personal attitudes and values of the people attracted to a career in journalism, and from the socialization process and reward structure of the (particularly the Wash- ington) press corps. The ideological bias in turn is thought to influence the amount of coverage political actors receive, how positive this cover- age is, and what interpretations of events are presented. Empirical re- search on the content of news coverage, however, has cast doubt on this ideological interpretation. Although there *are* values, themes, and slants to the news, they do not appear to be primarily personal ones, or to be ones that may be understood simply as "liberal" or "conservative."

There are exceptions to this general rule, of course. Opinion maga- zines (*New Republic, National Review,* and *The Progressive,* for example) are ideological and opinionated, and syndicated columnists often assert their own personal world views. In the columns and news stories of most daily news journalism, however, personal statements of ideological pref- erence are difficult to find.

The norm of objective journalism has been a serviceable one for the U.S. press. It has allowed contemporary news to take on a detached, balanced flavor quite unlike the partisan press of the early 1800s or the sensationalism of the penny press of the mid-1800s. It has also trans- formed journalism into a respectable occupation with a professional status; it has often deflected controversy and criticism away from jour- nalism, and it has been partially responsible for the expansion of news to a wide segment of the U.S. population. Although the norm has been under attack in recent years, it is still a dominant one within journalism, is still taught as the goal in journalism schools, and is used as a defense against criticism of news coverage. Its significance in the coverage of election campaigns is that it leads to campaign coverage that is event-, fact-, and source-oriented and discourages the expression of explicit opinions and personal preferences by journalists.

Despite the fact that news accounts tend to be fact-based and usually do not contain the journalist's personal ideological preferences, journal- istic accounts are also not simply detached, impartial descriptions of the day's events. Rather, journalists also provide their audiences with interpretations, themes, and dramatic accounts of the newsworthy events they cover.

Interpretation involves organizing, selecting, and extrapolating from a body of facts to the underlying *meaning* of those facts. For example, when a journalist writes that the most notable thing about the day's events is that George Bush has gained momentum and become a frontrunner, or that Jimmy Carter continues to use his incumbency to further his own reelection bid, or that Ronald Reagan continues to utter factual inaccuracies, or that Edward Kennedy is showing class and character in defeat, an interpretive statement about the meaning of the day's "facts" has been clearly offered. In each of these cases the journalist does more than simply transmit a body of disorganized facts to the audience. He or she also offers a judgment concerning the meaning of those facts.

When the press persists in interpreting the meaning of newsworthy events in a particular way over an extended period of time, we may also refer to a *theme* in news coverage. "Fanatical Iran," "Reaganomics," "turmoil in the Middle East," and "the taxpayer revolt" are all news themes that persisted for some time in the early 1980s and were used by journalists to give meaning to a number of discrete and possibly unconnected events and phenomena.[15] In campaign coverage, themes also tend to emerge. The 1976 presidential campaign was often understood to be a contest between a "Washington outsider" and an "honest but bumbling incumbent," whereas the 1982 congressional elections were often interpreted as a "referendum on Reaganomics."

Not all journalists provide the same mixture of description and interpretation in their news accounts. Wire service reports are probably the most descriptive because of their need to provide as complete a factual account of the day's occurrences as possible for their geographically dispersed and philosophically diverse clients. Television news reporters and weekly news magazine correspondents, on the other hand, more typically mix interpretation with their factual descriptions. The news coverage of daily newspaper journalists varies widely, depending on the size and policies of their particular paper, but mainly falls on the descriptive side of these two more extreme types.[16] The contrast between the styles of presentation of television news and the daily newspaper may be summarized in this way:

> . . . daily newspaper reporting at its most responsible has traditionally confined itself, when covering politics, to reporting those things that can be known with reasonable certainty: the outcome of elections, what the candidates say and do and the few generalizations that knowledgeable observers believe can be made about motives, plans and other intangibles.
>
> In the world of television news, by contrast, the diversity, complexity and uncertainty of the real world become all but invisible. They are re-

placed by the false simplicity and clarity of what TV news, assuming a posture of omniscience, pretends to know in sharp detail, about the politician's every important action, secret hope, fear, plan and motive.[17]

The distinction between legitimate interpretation and unacceptable personal commentary is difficult to make. Journalists who stray too far from the fact-oriented news called for by objectivity may find that there is a price attached to being more outspoken. Timothy Crouse, in his book on press coverage of the 1972 presidential campaign, gives two examples of journalists attempting to present what they considered to be legitimate deductions from a body of evidence concerning the campaign of then President Richard Nixon. In one case, a story by Jules Witcover about Nixon's decision not to hit the campaign trail was refused by Witcover's editors at the *Los Angeles Times* because it was an "opinion" story, relying too much on his own analysis and not enough on the conclusions expressed by others (which constitute "facts" and hence meet the criteria for objective reporting). In another case, Cassie Mackin filed a story for NBC News accusing Nixon of misrepresenting Democratic nominee George McGovern's policy positions. Her story moved Herb Klein, presidential press secretary, to complain to NBC News, and led to NBC's ordering Mackin to spend the following day collecting evidence to support her story.[18] Clearly, the norm of objectivity, though permitting a certain amount of journalistic interpretation, prevents campaign coverage from becoming consistently bold, one-sided, opinionated, and personal.

Finally, news accounts, particularly television news stories, tend to be dramatic narratives rather than simple summaries of a disjointed set of facts and quotations. Drama is thought by the press to be engaging to news audiences, and it provides journalists with a familiar framework within which to portray an otherwise complicated and confusing phenomenon.[19]

As a literary form, drama has a number of familiar features. First, "intensified peril is a basic ingredient."[20] News-makers are portrayed as threatened by outside forces, or embarked on a journey or quest of uncertain and possibly dangerous outcome. Second, the story line involves rising action, climax, and falling action. Journalists create expectations concerning the importance of crucial events in resolving a situation, and then cover those crucial events in a climactic fashion. For example, a congressional vote or summit meeting is often presented as a crucial resolution to a public policy issue or international episode, and a particular presidential primary is portrayed as the crucial climax of a candidate's campaign.

Third, news-makers are given roles, characters are developed, and portrayals of important actors take shape over time. Hence a president may be thematically portrayed as "beleaguered," or as "a firm and resolute commander-in-chief," or as "making a political comeback." During election campaigns the roles of "front-runner," "also-ran," and "sure loser" are parceled out by journalists to candidates.[21] Fourth, to a journalist, observable conflict is one of the handiest ways of presenting either a real or a contrived drama. Using conflict may simply mean reporting the charges and countercharges/responses made by newsmakers and ensuring that the sides involved in the conflict are roughly evenly balanced.

Of course, the particular conflicts that are judged to be newsworthy at any point in time are subject to journalistic discretion. At times journalists have presented racial conflict as being the most important; at other times it has been age-based (young versus old), geographic (Frostbelt versus Sunbelt), partisan (Democrats versus Republicans), ideological (New Deal liberals versus neoconservatives), institutional (White House versus Congress), or personal (Ronald Reagan versus Tip O'Neill) conflict that has been judged to be newsworthy. During campaigns, of course, conflict between candidates—and between and within candidate organizations—is used to dramatize a campaign efficiently.

Finally, news drama also sometimes involves the creation or accompaniment of a hero who rises above the others in his or her quest for some goal. Although heroes are few and far between in the world of political journalism, some politicians have been given something like heroic portrayals (for example, Dwight Eisenhower, John Kennedy; and, more recently, Sam Ervin, William Simon, and William Ruckelshaus). During campaign coverage "heroes" are typically candidates who do unexpectedly well and embody a number of American virtues (such as humor, folksiness, or honesty). Although the hero may falter, may have weaknesses and vulnerabilities, and may become a tragic figure, the portrayal corresponds to a literary narrative.

This suggests that an analysis of news coverage that focuses only on the facts transmitted or on the balance of opposing viewpoints will miss much that is important. The themes, portrayals, and dramatic narratives that journalists use to give meaning to newsworthy events also contribute to popular understanding.

One consequence of journalists' reliance on interpretation and drama is that news-makers continually attempt to shape the narratives, themes, and portrayals used by journalists in their news coverage. Candidates emphasize certain themes and attempt to present themselves as possessing heroic attributes; other campaigners and news sources attempt to influence the interpretation that is given to newsworthy events. All candidates have become proficient at staging pseudoevents for the purpose of stimulating news coverage with advantageous themes and portrayals. For example, one campaign strategist tells a story about how U.S. Senate candidate John Tunney almost drowned when he dove into the Santa Barbara Channel to *dramatize* his opposition to offshore oil drilling.[22]

In summary, then, news coverage is typically fact-based and nonopinionated but also interpretive, thematic, and dramatic. Journalists select the facts and symbols to be transmitted to their audiences; organize and amplify them in a way that produces coherent, interesting, and dramatic stories; and present a simplified, engaging, and understandable account of complex and ambiguous phenomena. In the process they render political judgments that might not be shared by all and that delimit our understanding of newsworthy events. Despite the fact that journalists claim that they are being detached, fair, and objective, the themes, portrayals, and stories they choose to use have important consequences for the received images of a remote populace. Since election campaigns are just one type of newsworthy event covered by journalists, these general features of news accounts are important for an understanding of campaign coverage as well.

How Journalists Cover Election Campaigns

An election campaign could be covered in a number of different ways. It could be viewed as a choice between two sets of policy preferences represented by the candidates' political values and priorities; it could be viewed as another in a continuing series of choices between two political parties, each with a history of governmental action and interest representation; it could be viewed as a choice between different persons, each possessing a different combination of personality traits and personal qualities; it could be viewed as the expression of social conflict between citizens with different interests and motives; or it could be viewed as a political ritual, designed to legitimize the political system and reinforce the notion of authority based on popular consent.

Journalists typically do not view election campaigns in any of these ways. Instead, a campaign is usually viewed as a contest between two candidate organizations in which the primary motivation is securing votes and in which the candidates' daily campaign activities are judged within the context of this motivation. Hence the candidate travels around all day giving speeches, being interviewed by reporters, and staging pseudoevents, with the press following him or her every step of the way and spending most of their time pondering the likely effect of all this activity on the candidate's chances of winning. Policy pronouncements, by this logic, are treated not so much as insights into what might be expected from the candidate if elected, as for what they reveal about a candidate's tactical ploys for support. As political scientist Thomas Patterson has observed, "although journalists consider the campaign to have more than ritual significance, they tend not to view it primarily as a battle over the directions of national policy and leadership. It is seen mainly as a power struggle between the candidates."[23] (This and subsequent excerpts from *The Mass Media Election* (New York: Praeger, 1980), by Thomas Patterson, are reprinted by permission.)

The way in which resources are allocated by media organizations for the coverage of presidential election campaigns shows the importance of this approach to elections. The usual method of covering presidential campaigns is for a media organization to assign a reporter to travel with a particular candidate wherever the candidate goes. This means riding on the same plane with the candidate; staying in the same hotel as the candidate; attending all of the candidate's speeches, rallies, news conferences, and other appearances; following the candidate's motorcade on a press bus; and, in general, doing as much traveling as the candidate does. (Those media outlets that cannot afford to assign one of their reporters in this way use the wire service reports of United Press International and Associated Press reporters for their campaign accounts.) This one-on-one coverage has a number of implications for the type of campaign coverage that results.

One consequence of this way of covering election campaigns is so-called pack journalism—the tendency of most reporters traveling with a candidate to write about the campaign in very similar fashion. The notion of pack journalism suggests that the campaign coverage that appears in the daily press varies little regardless of the particular reporter or media outlet.

Pack journalism stems from many sources. One is that all the reporters traveling with the candidate have approximately the same material available from which to write their stories. Everyone has the same handouts, press releases, and texts of speeches; everyone observes the same campaign activities on a given day. When something happens on the campaign trail that all the reporters cannot attend or observe (such as a trip by helicopter somewhere) a few journalists are selected to attend and write a collective pool report that is distributed to the rest of the group. The norms of pool coverage dictate that reporters selected for the pool may not include anything in their stories that was not written up in the pool report. In addition, the reporters are continually interacting—discussing the events of the day, trying out new theories or explanations with each other, and comparing perceptions. Eventually they all start to believe the same rumors, subscribe to the same theories, and write the same stories.

A second reason for pack journalism is that most of the reporters have been trained to write news stories in a similar fashion. Most newspaper articles, for example, are written in an inverted pyramid style in which the main point or theme of the story (the *lead*) is placed in the first paragraph, and supporting details are filled in later on. Consequently, the reporter's main quest is for the lead—the most newsworthy theme or angle on which to write. Once the lead is found, filling in the supporting details is fairly routine.

On the campaign trail, some journalists are acknowledged to be the principal lead finders. The rest of the reporters check their leads against those of these authorities. In 1972 Timothy Crouse found that Walter Mears, the number-one Associated Press reporter on the campaign trail, was the acknowledged leader of the pack and helped other reporters decide what the most important meaning of a campaign activity was.[24]

Still another reason for pack journalism is that editors compare the stories written by their own reporters with those written by wire services. When there is a significant discrepancy, the editor may call the reporter and ask for a justification for the interpretation offered. How much discrepancy between the two sources will be tolerated by the editor depends on the faith the editor has in his or her own reporter's judgment. Some editors accord their reporters a large amount of leeway, but inexperienced reporters fear the editorial callback and may try to ensure that their accounts do not vary substantially from those of the wire services. As one journalist has observed: "The editors don't want scoops. Their abiding interest is making sure that nobody else has got anything that they don't have, not getting something that nobody else has."[25] (This, and subsequent excerpts from *The Boys on the Bus* [New York: Ballantine Books, 1974], by Timothy Crouse, are reprinted by permission of Random House.)

A second implication of the way in which the media cover election campaigns is that the traveling journalists sometimes infer the candidate's qualities and chances of electoral success from the quality of the candidate's press operation. Since all the journalists know is the isolation of travel on the campaign trail, and since they suspect that the way in which the press is handled indicates something about the organizational ability of the candidate and his or her staff, there is a tendency to conclude that a sloppy press operation means inefficiency and electoral defeat, and a smooth, efficient press operation means efficiency and electoral success. In 1972, when Humphrey and McGovern were contesting the California primary, Crouse found that the press operation of McGovern was far superior to Humphrey's and that reporters were impressed by the efficiency and organization of the McGovern campaign. During the general election campaign, however, McGovern's press operation did not compare favorably with then President Nixon's. The Nixon press operation was

> Manipulative, frustrating, and sometimes downright evil; but it was always professional. From Nixon on down, the people in the White House knew the art of feeding news to the press at a proper digestible rate, doling out just the right amount at the right time. The McGovern people never mastered this technique. McGovern's press secretary was never around. There never seemed to be enough filing time. Reporters who had to write in the afternoon kept getting assigned to afternoon pools.[26]

If nothing more were at stake here than the convenience of a group of reporters, this contrast would be unimportant. The skill of the press operation, however, can affect media perceptions of the candidate and influence the types of messages journalists can communicate about a campaign. In political campaigning, where the control of information is crucial to a candidate's strategy and most journalists' insight comes from the campaign trail, an inability to control the flow of information may be treated by journalists as a sign of candidate weakness or inefficiency.

A third consequence of one-on-one coverage of a candidate's campaign travel, particularly in the early stages of the presidential nomination campaign, is that after a while there is a tendency for reporters to hope that their candidate will be the winner and to perceive events in that light. For a reporter on the winner's bus (or plane), the travel and filing of copy will be more exciting and interesting; the accumulation of knowledge will be considered more worthwhile; there will be more of a "news-hole" reserved for that reporter's contribution; the reporter's name will become known and additional career opportunities will open up; and the reporter may possibly be assigned to cover the candidate as an incumbent officeholder, thus ensuring continued career advancement. In 1976, for example, a number of reporters, including James Wooten of the *New York Times*, Jack Nelson of the *Los Angeles Times*, Judy Woodruff of NBC, Sam Donaldson of ABC, Eleanor Clift of *Newsweek*, and columnist Richard Reeves were all advantaged by Carter's victory, either because of books they were writing or because their assignment to his campaign led to attractive assignments at the White House.[27]

It is difficult to tell how much this winner's phenomenon influences campaign coverage. At most, reporters may develop a tendency to ignore indications that the candidate they are covering is a likely loser. Outright promotion of a candidacy or substantial overestimation of a candidate's chances of victory are quite rare, although at least four reporters covering McGovern in 1972 (Mary McGrory of the *Washington Star*, Jim Naughton of the *New York Times*, Dick Cooper of the *Los Angeles Times*, and Adam Clymer of the Baltimore *Sun*) entertained the possibility of a McGovern victory in the final days of the campaign.[28] What seems more likely is that reporters have a vested interest in an interesting campaign and may cover a particular candidate's quest more gently because of its contribution to a good story. Crouse argues that such was the case during the final days of the 1972 Democratic presidential nomination campaign:

> In California, there was sometimes a feeling of general giddiness on the McGovern Bus. McGovern was so close to victory, and if he won the nomination it would be perhaps the most sensational political story since Lyndon Johnson took himself out of the running in 1968. No one wanted to spoil a story that good.[29]

Richard Reeves has claimed that a similar phenomenon was working to then California Governor Jerry Brown's advantage in 1980. Reeves argued that one reason journalists paid so much attention to Brown's bid for the 1980 Democratic presidential nomination was that his presence in the campaign made the nomination contest much more interesting.

A fourth consequence of the standard form of media coverage of election campaigns is that the reporters' existence is so confining, isolating, and exhausting that it is unclear whether they are capable of providing any fresh insights or useful information to the U.S. electorate. All these reporters know is the daily travel of the candidate—the continual movement from hotel to hotel, airport to airport, campaign stop to campaign stop—and the daily rhythm of stump speeches and press releases. They lose touch with their families and friends, they seldom have time to find out what the campaign means to the citizenry, and they know little about other events occurring elsewhere or even about the campaigns of other candidates. Timothy Crouse has claimed that during the 1972 presidential campaign

> the reporters attached to George McGovern had a very limited usefulness as political observers, by and large, for what they knew best was not the American electorate but the tiny community of the press plane, a totally abnormal world that combined the incestuousness of a New England hamlet with the giddiness of a mid-ocean gala and the physical rigors of the Long March.[30]

In addition to the isolation of the reporters traveling with the candidates, the physical deterioration that this travel causes makes it difficult for reporters to function. Travel itself can be exhausting; this kind of travel—hectic, frequent, and virtually meaningless—soon becomes boring, disorienting, and emotionally taxing. A typical day on the campaign trail involves little sleep, early rising, hastily gulped fast-food meals, plane and bus rides, the consumption of liquor, the continual processing of information and writing, and late hours. Candidate organizations keep their candidates moving continuously from one media market to another because the candidate's presence is thought to be so precious. This takes a serious physical toll on the capabilities of the journalists traveling with the candidate. By the last few weeks of the campaign, when the public may be the most interested in what reporters have to say, the media may be incapable of thinking coherently or imaginatively.

The discussion so far has implied that journalists have always covered election campaigns in exactly the same way, but this is not the case. Throughout the last two decades several changes have taken place in campaign coverage, often as a result of some unpleasant experience in the previous campaign or some criticism of press conduct. In a few cases the publication of a book has revealed some aspect of a campaign that had not received much attention previously and has caused an adjustment in news-gathering procedures.

Campaign coverage was altered after 1960 as a result of the first of Theodore White's *Making of the President* books. White wrote about the campaign as a novelist would, complete with good guys and bad guys, conflict and suspense, and rich detail concerning the political decisions and personalities of the candidates and their staffs. Readers found his books engaging and revealing, not only because much of his information had not appeared in daily press reports of the campaign, but also because the style of presentation was dramatic and entertaining.

The media response to White's series of books was chagrin at having been scooped and a commitment to prevent it from happening again. The Associated Press told its reporters that "When Teddy White's book comes out, there shouldn't be one single story in it that we haven't reported ourselves." Abe Rosenthal, the managing editor of the *New York Times*, told his reporters and editors: "We aren't going to wait until a year after the election to read in Teddy White's book what we should have reported ourselves."[31] This has produced a level of press scrutiny of candidates quite unlike any that had been observed in the past, with attention to the smallest detail, intrusions into the candidate's privacy, the probing of the inner workings of the campaign organization itself, and the extension of campaign coverage many months before election day.

Other books and events have altered media coverage of campaigns in like manner. The political conflict in the streets of Chicago during the 1968 Democratic convention indicated to the media that they should devote more attention to the preferences and attitudes of the electorate; as a result, reporters started doing door-to-door canvassing of voters and articles on the "mood of the country." More recently, many news organizations have extended this logic by conducting large-scale voter surveys during the nomination and general election campaigns.

Journalists have also become more attentive to the campaign strategies and communication techniques of candidates, and have begun depicting and analyzing them in their news stories. Joe McGinniss's *Selling of the President, 1968*, an account of the Nixon advertising effort in 1968, demonstrated to the media that they ought to pay more attention to the media strategies of the candidates. The Watergate episode in 1972–1973 contributed to a general movement toward "adversarial" or "investigative reporting."[32] For example, in 1980, while accompanying Jimmy Carter on a campaign swing through Philadelphia, Leslie Stahl of CBS News included in her story a comment on the motive behind Carter's activities.

> What did President Carter do today in Philadelphia? He posed, with as many different types of symbols as he could possibly find. There was a picture at the day-care center, and one during the game of boccie ball with the senior citizens. Click, another picture, with a group of teenagers. And then he performed the ultimate media event, a walk through the Italian market.[33]

Such a story would have been highly unusual twenty years ago.

In the aftermath of the 1972 presidential campaign, news coverage was sharply criticized by a number of analysts for being inaccurate and uninformative. This led to a determination by the press to avoid repeating the same mistakes in 1976. Consequently, journalists embarked on the 1976 campaign with a number of changes in mind: to avoid predicting the wrong winner (like Muskie in 1972) again; to avoid ignoring any of the important candidates (such as George McGovern) again; to prevent the candidates from manipulating them and controlling the news; to go beyond reporting who is ahead and who is behind to probing the personalities and policy preferences of the candidates; to escape the isolation of the campaign trail and experience the meaning of the campaign in other ways; and to cover the fund-raising strategies and media tactics of the candidates.[34] In 1980, as a result of the criticism that the press coverage of the early primaries in 1976 handed the Democratic nomination to Jimmy Carter, the media also attempted to revise previous practices by exhibiting a tentativeness in interpreting primary results, and a quicker tendency to scrutinize *critically* the behavior of front-runners.[35]

In some ways both candidate behavior and campaign coverage in 1980 differed from the process described earlier. Apparently the candidates did not follow the hectic, breakneck pace of public appearances in 1980 that had characterized previous campaigns, and several of the journalists with national reputations (including David Broder and Haynes Johnson of the *Washington Post*; Jules Witcover, then of the *Los Angeles Times*; and syndicated columnists Rowland Evans and Robert Novak) spent a fair amount of time away from the campaign trail to avoid the isolation of that method of covering a campaign. In addition, the campaign activities planned by candidates in 1980 were designed more to appeal to the needs of television journalists and less to those of print reporters:

> Campaigns are organized for pictures, not words or ideas. In fact, the Boys-on-the-Bus—the romantic truth-tellers licensed to lurch from coast-to-coast with presidents and would-be presidents—have become irrelevant. Reporters for newspapers and magazines have been nudged, literally and figuratively, to the back of the bus by the steady, inexorable encroachment of television. . . .[36]

In many important respects, however, press conduct during the 1980 campaign was a continuation of practices first revealed by Crouse in 1972. There were still a tendency toward pack journalism, the isolation of the campaign trail, the reduction of reporters to the role of stenographers of relatively meaningless tidbits of information, and the attempts by candidates to control the messages transmitted about their campaigns. In fact, a number of journalists have observed more continuity than change in recent campaign coverage.

Haynes Johnson of the *Washington Post* noted in 1983:

I'm afraid [pack journalism] still exists today and you're still hurtled on a cylinder tube throughout the night, never get off, you see only your colleagues and your candidates, and you live in an unreal world—you don't know where you are when you touch down. . . .[37]

Joel Swerdlow commented (on the 1980 campaign):

The dominance of television images, lack of access to the candidates, door-stopping, and isolation bred a peculiar form of pack journalist. No pack existed in the sense of everyone copying CBS or the *New York Times*. The process was more insidious. It grew from using the same rules of objectivity and newsworthiness to piece together a story from the day's meager morsels.[38]

Conclusion

In this chapter we have discussed how journalists go about determining what is newsworthy in their environment and how this perspective influences their approach to the coverage of election campaigns. We have seen that the prevailing conception of a campaign as a power struggle between candidate organizations directs the attention of journalists to certain features of a campaign and that covering presidential election campaigns by assigning reporters to travel the campaign trail with candidates further shapes campaign coverage. Furthermore, we have seen that the news coverage of election campaigns is apt to be fact-, source-, and event-oriented and nonopinionated—yet also interpretive, thematic, and dramatic. In the next chapter we will consider more carefully the patterns in the coverage of recent (mainly presidential) election campaigns.

Notes

1. There are exceptions, of course. *Time* and *Life* publisher Henry Luce, the Whitney family's *New York Herald Tribune*, and the Scripps-Howard newspapers have been credited with advancing the Republican presidential candidacies of Wendell Wilkie in 1940 and Dwight Eisenhower in 1952, and with resisting the presidential candidacy of Robert Taft from 1940 to 1952. More recently, the late William Loeb, publisher of the *Manchester* (N.H.) *Union-Leader*, was never bashful about revealing his political preferences. In 1976 Loeb called then President Gerald Ford "Jerry the Jerk," and in 1980 he wrote that Republican candidate George Bush was a "spoiled little rich kid who has been wetnursed to succeed and now . . . thinks he is entitled to the White House as his latest toy." See Jeff Greenfield, *The Real Campaign* (New York: Summit Books, 1982), pp. 44–45, 97.

2. William H. Flanigan and Nancy H. Zingale, *Political Behavior of the American Electorate* (Boston: Allyn and Bacon, 1979), pp. 161–164; and Robert S.

Erikson, Norman R. Luttbeg, and Kent L. Tedin, *American Public Opinion* (New York: Wiley, 1980), p. 5.

3. Greenfield, *The Real Campaign*, Chaps. 4, 6.

4. J. Joseph Grandmaison, quoted in John Foley, Dennis A. Britton, and Eugene B. Everett, Jr., eds., *Nominating a President: The Process and the Press* (New York: Praeger, 1980), p. 25.

5. Paul H. Weaver, "Captives of Melodrama," *New York Times Magazine*, August 29, 1976, p. 6; and Michael J. Robinson, "A Statesman Is a Dead Politician: Candidate Images on Network News," in Elie Abel, ed., *What's News* (San Francisco: Institute for Contemporary Studies, 1981).

6. Bernard Roshco, *Newsmaking* (Chicago: University of Chicago Press, 1975), p. 19.

7. Paul H. Weaver, "The Politics of a News Story," in Harry M. Clor, ed., *Mass Media and American Democracy* (Chicago: Rand McNally, 1974), pp. 85–112; and Weaver, "Captives of Melodrama."

8. David L. Paletz and Robert M. Entman, *Media, Power, Politics* (New York: Free Press, 1981), p. 29.

9. Edward J. Epstein, *News from Nowhere* (New York: Random House, 1973).

10. Herbert Gans, *Deciding What's News* (New York: Pantheon, 1979), Chap. 1.

11. Weaver, "Politics of a News Story."

12. For a historical account of this process, see Michael Schudson, *Discovering the News: A Social History of American Newspapers* (New York: Basic Books, 1978).

13. Robinson, "A Statesman."

14. Robert D. Novak, "The New Journalism," in Clor, *Mass Media*, pp. 1–14; Peter B. Clark, "The Opinion Machine: Intellectuals, the Mass Media, and American Government," in ibid., pp. 37–84; William E. Simon, "You Can't Trust the News," *Saturday Evening Post*, December 1980, pp. 20, 22, 26, 128; and Edith Efron, *The News Twisters* (New York: Manor Books, 1971).

15. Epstein, *News from Nowhere*, Chap. 8; see also Robert R. Smith, "Mythic Elements in Television News," *Journal of Communication* 29, no. 1 (Winter 1979): 75–82.

16. Thomas Patterson, *The Mass Media Election* (New York: Praeger Publishers, 1980), pp. 25–28.

17. Weaver, "Captives of Melodrama," p. 6.

18. Timothy Crouse, *The Boys on the Bus* (New York: Ballantine Books, 1974), pp. 115–116, 280–282.

19. For an interesting perspective on the dramatic imperative of television news, see Dan Nimmo and James E. Combs, *Mediated Political Realities* (New York: Longman, 1983), Chaps. 1, 2.

20. Weaver, "Captives of Melodrama," p. 6.

21. Ibid.

22. Thomas Quinn, quoted in Foley, Britton, and Everett, *Nominating a President*, p. 59.

23. Thomas E. Patterson, *The Mass Media Election* (New York: Praeger, 1980), p. 22.

24. Crouse, *Boys on the Bus*, pp. 21–22.

25. Ibid., p. 10.

26. Ibid., pp. 360–361.

27. Richard Reeves, "Score One No Vote for Brown," *Philadelphia Inquirer*, May 6, 1979, p. 9-M.

28. Crouse, *Boys on the Bus*, pp. 363–368.

29. Ibid., pp. 71–72.

30. Ibid., p. 369.

31. Crouse, *Boys on the Bus*, p. 36.

32. For a thorough and provocative analysis of the move toward adversarial journalism, see Paul H. Weaver, "The New Journalism and the Old: Thoughts after Watergate," *The Public Interest* 35 (Spring 1974): 67–88.

33. "ABC News Viewpoint," April 21, 1983, p. 6 of the transcript.

34. Donald Matthews, "Winnowing," in James David Barber, ed., *Race for the Presidency* (Englewood Cliffs, N.J.: Prentice-Hall, 1978), p. 55.

35. Robinson, "A Statesman."

36. Joel Swerdlow, "The Decline of the Boys on the Bus," *Washington Journalism Review*, January–February 1981, p. 15.

37. "ABC News Viewpoint," April 21, 1983, p. 9 of the transcript.

38. Swerdlow, "Decline," p. 18.

5
Patterns in Campaign Coverage

One of the consequences of the campaign finance laws that was overlooked at the time . . . was . . . to shift the power of carrying the message from the candidate himself to the news media.
— Richard Stearns, quoted in *Nominating a President*

. . . television hypes each primary election, attributing earthshaking significance to each outcome.
— Paul H. Weaver, "Captives of Melodrama"

The Nixon campaign was viewed more favorably and less unfavorably than the McGovern campaign on each of the major networks.
— Richard Hofstetter, *Bias in the News*

The (television network news) viewer tuning in for facts to guide his choice would . . . have to pick his political nuggets from a great gravel pile of political irrelevancy.
— James David Barber, "Characters in the Campaign," in *Race for the Presidency*

. . . we tend to concentrate not on those issues that are likely to affect the governing of the country for the next four years, but upon the men who are contending with each other for the nomination. There is a lot of short-term emphasis on personalities, who's ahead, who's behind, who wins this primary, who wins that primary; and I think a lot of that is insignificant for the big story.
— Bill Moyers, "ABC News Viewpoint"

In the previous chapter we discussed the general orientation of journalists toward news-gathering and the way in which the press approaches the coverage of election campaigns. In this chapter we will focus more specifically on the effects of this news-gathering approach on campaign coverage. We will limit our discussion primarily to the coverage of presidential election campaigns, since most of the studies of campaign coverage have been conducted at that level. By proceeding chronologically through the nomination campaign, nominating conventions, the general election campaign, and election night coverage, we will be able to see the many ways in which the press makes significant political judgments during its coverage of election campaigns.

The Nomination Campaign

Media coverage of presidential nomination campaigns may be more important than that of any other portion of the entire presidential selection process. It is at the nomination stage that most candidates are eliminated and the choices narrowed down to a very small number. Which choices are provided to the public out of all those who are legally qualified to be president may be far more important than which of the choices is eventually selected. In this context, then, the coverage of the presidential nomination campaign takes on added significance.

The presidential nomination process has become an extremely complex and lengthy one in recent years. It involves the selection of delegates from each of the fifty states and other territories to a national nominating convention in a process that now takes well over six months to complete. In recent years there have been two major changes in this nominating process. First, federal campaign finance legislation has made public money available, on a partial matching basis, to qualifying candidates for the two major-party nominations, and has forced fairly stringent expenditure limitations on those candidates who accept this public money. Second, the delegate-selection process in each of the states and territories has become subject to national party regulation. As a result, the delegate-selection process has become more visible, open, and up for grabs than ever before in U.S. history. One consequence of these two changes is that more candidates are initiating campaigns for their party's nomination. Another consequence is that news coverage of the delegate-selection process has become both more voluminous and more significant.

Although the first actual delegates to the national nominating conventions are not chosen until February of the presidential election year, campaigning by candidates and coverage by the media actually begin well before that. In the year preceding a presidential election year, candidates and their staffs are involved in a complex process of courting favor with those few national reporters and columnists who cover national politics continuously. Arthur Hadley has called this period the "invisible primary" and has described it as follows:

> To court Apple, Lydon, Broder, and others, the candidates and their staffs go through intricate mating dances. Lunches with the candidates in their offices, tidbits about the campaigns saved for each reporter exclusively; breakfast appearances with groups of reporters that either include the top correspondents of the *Times* and the *Post* or their friends; ap-

proaches to them through third parties to plant ideas in disguise. . . . Later in the campaign, if he gets that far, the candidate must be careful not to turn the majority of the press against him by playing favorites to the few. But in the opening days, when only the few cover him, he must save what little he has for the *Times*, the *Post* and the news magazines, again, not so much to get coverage for its own sake, but because mention leads to TV time.[1]

The invisible primary is a stage of the nomination process in which candidates are trying to establish their credibility as viable candidates with a chance of winning the nomination. Media attention at this stage can lead to the accumulation of other political resources, such as volunteers, money, endorsements, and further media coverage.

The name of the game in the preprimary campaign is to get free TV time on the nightly news and programs like "Meet the Press" and "Face the Nation." This can be done by receiving mention in the *New York Times*, the *Washington Post*, *Time*, or *Newsweek*; by participating in some newsworthy activity; or by improving one's standing in the Harris or Gallup poll. Between 1972 and 1976, for example, presidential candidates George Wallace and Jimmy Carter attempted to keep their names in the news—and hence in the public's mind—by appearing at dinners held throughout the country and by keeping the national press informed of accomplishments while in office (refer back to Hamilton Jordan's ideas for stimulating prenomination news coverage of Jimmy Carter in Chapter 3).[2] Of course, there is a certain amount of circularity to news coverage. Once a candidate has received some, he or she is likely to receive more; receiving the first significant amount of coverage is the most difficult.

One of the ways in which the press decides who should receive media coverage during the invisible primary is by relying on the support for a candidate in Gallup's or Harris's list of presidential contenders. Generally, the more support a candidate demonstrates in these initial polls, the more coverage that candidate's activities will receive. Of course, receiving significant support in the preprimary polls is not a necessary condition for a viable nomination campaign: Neither George McGovern, nor Jimmy Carter (in 1976), nor George Bush received much support in preprimary polls. Still, if a candidate desires media coverage during the invisible primary stage, one of the surest ways of achieving it is by being on the pollsters' list of presidential contenders and demonstrating significant and growing support.

Another way in which the press decides whose campaign should receive preprimary coverage is by attending preprimary political gatherings and measuring the support for candidates there. On October 29, 1979, for example, Florida's Democratic party held a series of county meetings at which an informal, nonbinding straw poll for presidential candidates was taken. Although no delegates were selected at this point, both Jimmy Carter and Edward Kennedy spent over $400,000 to try to influence the result, and the news media gave the event front-page coverage. Carter's ability to demonstrate substantial support in this straw poll helped alter the then prevalent perception that Kennedy would be the Democratic party's nominee.[3]

A few weeks later a similar event shaped news coverage of the 1980 preprimary Republican campaign. At a state convention of Maine Republicans on November 3, 1979, a nonbinding straw vote for presidential contenders led to a rush of press coverage of George Bush. Bush won the straw vote (barely), resulting in a front-page *New York Times* headline declaring, "Bush Gaining in Stature as '80 Contender."[4] Headlines like those affect the likelihood of other journalists giving candidates a share of the scarce presidential campaign news-hole.

At the time this book is being written, the press is already involved in the process of judging the preprimary viability of candidates for the 1984 Democratic presidential nomination. On April 9, 1983, Massachusetts Democrats conducted a nonbinding straw vote at their state convention. Walter Mondale's victory in that poll (with 29 percent of the vote) stimulated a lot of press coverage of his presidential campaign. As one major metropolitan newspaper put it, "Mondale wins Mass. Straw Poll, Leaving Party Rivals Far Behind." One measure of the importance of this preprimary coverage is that is was estimated that Mondale, Ohio Senator John Glenn, and California Senator Alan Cranston each spent over $100,000 to influence these straw poll results.[5]

Media appearances also shape preprimary presidential news coverage. On November 4, 1979, when Edward Kennedy seemed to be winning the invisible primary for the 1980 Democratic presidential nomination, he appeared on a CBS news interview with Roger Mudd. His inability to answer questions on the program concerning his marital status, presidential aspirations, and behavior in the Chappaquiddick episode is generally acknowledged to have given his campaign a setback from which he was never able to recover. The program not only implied that Kennedy's behavior at Chappaquiddick was suspect:

> . . . the show . . . contained a scene in which the camera looked out from the driver's seat of a car as it drove toward a bridge at night lit only by the automobile headlights. The image suggested something tawdry and furtive, impressions magnified by Kennedy's hesitant and clumsy responses to Mudd's questions.[6]

It also established a theme in the press that Kennedy was a stumblebum.[7]

The invisible primary stage is important to candidates because it means they will enter the delegate-selection process with different amounts of campaign resources and media attention. For *most* journalists, however, the presidential nomination campaign begins in earnest when the process of selecting actual convention delegates begins. This process now takes about six months to complete and involves the selection of thousands of delegates in each of the states and territories. The first delegate-selection process in which actual delegates to the national nominating convention are chosen takes place in New Hampshire in February, although Iowa begins its delegate-selection process with local caucuses in January. Between these two states' activities and the eventual selection of all the more than 3,000 Democratic delegates and over 2,000 Republican delegates, each state and territory selects its delegates in a different way under different rules.

One of the most important decisions the news media make during the delegate-selection stage of the nomination is how much coverage to give each state's delegate-selection process. Media coverage of the earliest delegate-selection processes has increased tremendously in recent years. Coverage of the Iowa caucuses, for example, *totaled* 4 lines in *Time* and 72 lines in *Newsweek* in 1972. In 1976 the caucuses received about 900 lines of coverage in *Time* and *Newsweek* combined, and in 1980 this coverage had increased to 800 lines in *Time* and 900 in *Newsweek*.[8] This increased attention by the media has made the Iowa caucuses important far beyond the number of delegates at stake (50 for the Democrats, 37 for the Republicans in 1980). As we saw in Chapter 1, the press's increased interest in Iowa in 1976 led Morris Udall to change his campaign strategy and commit more resources to Iowa than he had originally intended. A number of presidential campaigners have admitted that if the press were not present to cover the Iowa caucuses, they would have little reason to be there either.[9]

The New Hampshire primary, the first primary in which convention delegates are selected, has also received a huge amount of media coverage disproportionate to the number of delegates at stake. In fact, if one compares the amount of coverage given different state processes with the number of delegates at stake, it becomes clear that the media are using different criteria of newsworthiness other than simply the number of delegates to be selected.

In 1976, for example, eight primaries were held between February 24 and April 6. The number of Democratic delegates at stake ranged from 274 in New York to 12 in Vermont, the number of Republican delegates at stake ranged from 154 in New York to 18 in Vermont, and the number of votes cast ranged from millions in New York to a few thousand in Vermont. Media coverage of these primaries, however, was not proportional to either the number of votes cast or the number of delegates selected (Table 5–1). The New Hampshire primary received twice as much coverage as any of the other primaries, even though very

TABLE 5–1   Media Coverage of the First Eight Presidential
Primaries, 1976

	Network News Stories	Delegates at Stake		Vote Cast		Number of Stories per Delegate
		(D)	(R)	(D)	(R)	
New Hampshire February 24	100 (30%)	17	21	82,381	111,674	2.63
Massachusetts March 2	52 (15%)	104	43	735,821	188,449	0.35
Vermont March 2	6 (2%)	12	18	38,714	32,157	0.20
Florida March 9	50 (15%)	81	66	1,300,330	609,819	0.34
Illinois March 15	38 (11%)	169	101	1,311,914	775,893	0.15
North Carolina March 23	19 (6%)	61	54	604,832	193,727	0.17
New York April 6	30 (9%)	274	154	3,746,414	N.A.	0.07
Wisconsin April 6	42 (12%)	68	45	740,528	591,812	0.37
	337 (100%)					

Source: Adapted from Michael J. Robinson, "Television News and the Presidential Nominating Process: The Case of Spring," Unpublished manuscript, 1976; and Michael J. Robinson, "TV's Newest Program: The Presidential Nominations Game," *Public Opinion* 1, no. 2 (May–June 1978): 41–46. Reprinted by permission.

Note: All three networks' nightly news stories combined, weekdays only.

little was immediately at stake in terms of delegates. The New York primary, in contrast, received less coverage than did five of the eight primaries, even though the most votes were cast and the most delegates were at stake there. In general, there is very little correspondence between the number of delegates at stake or votes cast in primaries and the amount of media attention they receive.

The reason for this discrepancy is that the newsworthiness of the primaries is judged by factors other than delegates or votes. New Hampshire is considered newsworthy because it is the first concrete indication of voter sentiment and it is the only delegate-selection process occurring on that day—a situation New Hampshire politicians have insisted on and Democratic party officials have permitted. As one analyst has observed:

Being first, it opens the year's political melodrama, introducing the characters, sketching the basic conflicts, and establishing the central themes. Winning there naturally gets magnified, the more so because whoever wins in New Hampshire never has to displace an existing front-runner. . . .[10]

Some primaries are more newsworthy than others because of the ambiguity of the primary results. In New York, for example, primary voters used to vote for delegate slates without any indication on the ballot of the candidate for whom the delegates are committed. Consequently, the results of this type of balloting were difficult to present. In 1976 the Wisconsin and New York primaries were held on the same day, with far more delegates at stake in New York than in Wisconsin. Nevertheless, Wisconsin received more media coverage, in part because New York lacked a direct vote for the presidential candidates.

Another factor that affects the amount of coverage accorded a primary is how many candidates are considering it important. If many of the announced candidates are seriously campaigning in a primary state, or if a candidate is venturing into what is considered to be hostile territory to contest a primary, or if a candidate has announced that a particular primary is crucial to his or her nomination campaign, the media are likely to take the contest more seriously and to cover it more extensively. In 1976, for example, the Florida primary was considered newsworthy because Jimmy Carter had established it as the battleground for his attempt to eliminate George Wallace from the presidential campaign.

Finally, a primary is apt to be more heavily covered if it is the only one on a particular day than if it is one of many held at the same time. In 1980, for example, these factors combined to affect the relative attention given to two delegate-selection processes held on the same day: the New Hampshire primary and the precinct caucuses in Minnesota, both held on February 26. (No actual convention delegates were selected in Minnesota on that day. As in Iowa, this was only the first stage in a multistage selection process.) Since Minnesota had three times as many delegates as New Hampshire, one would have thought that Minnesota's selection process would have received at least as much attention as New Hampshire's. No so—the clarity of results in New Hampshire (primary versus caucus); the immediacy of the consequences (in Minnesota the actual delegates would not be selected until much later); the continuation of past practices (journalists were used to covering New Hampshire); and even the geographical proximity to major media cities (New Hampshire to New York) led to greater coverage of New Hampshire. This media focus in turn clearly influenced candidates and their staffs. Tom Tripp, George Bush's Minnesota campaign manager, observed that

A lot of people are going to stay home on caucus night to watch the New Hampshire returns on television. New Hampshire is getting the attention because you guys [the media] say that's where the action is. You guys are the ones who've made New Hampshire important. Look, Walter Cronkite isn't going to be here [in Minnesota]. He's going to be in New Hampshire.[11]

A second, related judgment that journalists make during coverage of the nomination campaign is the *interpretation* of the results of the delegate-selection process in each state. The results in each state are seldom simply reported without comment, but are interpreted for news audiences and compared with journalists' expectations concerning the outcome. Thus the press's expectations are important, and candidates are continuously attempting to shape them to their advantage. Generally the press's expectations come from a combination of sources, including a knowledge of previous voting behavior in the state; preprimary state polls, which are considered moderately valid indicators of candidate support in each state; geographical location, in which states that are closer together are presumed to vote in a similar fashion; cost/benefit calculations, in which it is assumed that the more time and money a candidate spends in a particular state, the better he or she should do; and the predictions of candidates themselves.[12]

Journalistic expectations and dramatic perspectives serve as a basis for the interpretation of actual primary or caucus results. A candidate who receives 40 percent of the vote in a primary may be declared a winner if this is better than expected or if this makes the campaign more interesting. In 1968, for example, Eugene McCarthy lost to Lyndon Johnson by 7.7 percent in New Hampshire and was generally considered to have been the "winner" (because the small margin was so "interesting" and unexpected); in 1972 George McGovern lost to Edmund Muskie by 9.3 percent in New Hampshire and was also generally declared the "winner"; and in 1980 John Anderson came in second in both the Vermont primary and the Massachusetts primary on the same day and was considered that day's winner. In other words, to be declared a winner by the news media, one need not necessarily win a majority or plurality of the votes; sometimes just doing better than expected is enough.[13]

Let us take a closer look at how the news coverage of presidential nomination campaigns interprets the meaning of the outcomes of the earliest delegate-selection processes. In 1976, after the Iowa caucuses on January 19, in which precinct delegates were selected in a process that would eventually lead to the selection of 47 (out of 3,008) delegates to the Democratic national nominating convention, CBS correspondent Roger Mudd had this to say about the caucus results:

With 88 percent of Iowa's 2,500 caucuses in, no amount of bad-mouthing by the others can lessen the importance of Jimmy Carter's finish. He was the clear winner in this psychologically crucial test. With 13 projected national convention delegates, almost 28 percent of the total, Carter had opened ground between himself and the rest of the so-called pack. Birch Bayh did not finish his promised strong second. He had a weak one, he picked up six delegates, 13 percent. Morris Udall hoped to finish in the pack and did, no more, no less. Udall—three delegates, six percent. Sargent Shriver fell badly off the pace with two delegates, 3.3 percent. Shriver did not even hold his own with Iowa's Catholic Democrats. Henry Jackson, whose strategy did not include Iowa, got no delegates. So the candidate with that highly prized political momentum tonight is Jimmy Carter covered now by Ed Rable in New Hampshire. . . .[14]

Similarly, after the New Hampshire primary, NBC's Tom Pettit commented that "Carter emerges from New Hampshire as the man to beat"; *Newsweek* reported that "On the Democratic side, former Georgia Governor Jimmy Carter was the unqualified winner, with 30 percent of the vote in a crowded field." After the New York and Wisconsin primaries on April 6, *Time* concluded that "To stay in the race as a serious contender, he [Morris Udall] needed to win in Wisconsin. The narrow loss was only partially offset by his unexpectedly strong showing in New York."[15]

These reports are clearly interpretive. We are told that Iowa was a "psychologically crucial contest" and that Wisconsin was crucial to the Udall candidacy. In the case of Iowa that seems to be a strange claim, since no actual delegates were selected on that day and the Gallup poll of Democrats taken about that time indicated that at least six Democrats had more support for the nomination than Carter did nationwide. The claim about Udall after Wisconsin also seems strange, given the fact that at that point in the campaign the candidates differed little in delegate strength: Carter had accumulated about 220 delegates, Jackson about 160, and Udall about 120. Nevertheless, when the media announce that a contest is psychologically crucial or that a particular primary is important for a candidate's chances, the chances are that it *will* be more important to the candidate than would otherwise have been the case.

Often it is difficult to see why primary results are interpreted the way they are. We have already seen that Jimmy Carter's New Hampshire primary victory in 1976 (with 30 percent of the vote—23,000 votes—for 17 delegates) was followed by the interpretation that Carter had become the front-runner. One week later in 1976, however, Henry Jackson "won" the Massachusetts primary with 23 percent of the vote—163,000 votes—for 104 delegates. Yet press interpretations of this outcome were a good deal less dramatic than were those of the New Hampshire outcome. Instead of displacing Carter as the front-runner, Jackson was put "alongside Jimmy Carter in front of the Democratic pack," and the Massachusetts outcome was seen to have "scrambled the race and upset some of the early predictions."[16]

During the 1980 delegate-selection process the press also interpreted primary and caucus outcomes. Much of this interpretation involved the Republican campaign, since there were more announced candidates and the situation was more unsettled. As in 1976, the winner of the Iowa caucuses—George Bush—received a tremendous amount of press coverage and was also labeled "the principle challenger to front-runner Ronald Reagan" (in the words of CBS's Walter Cronkite). Tom Brokaw, on the "Today" show, called Bush's victory "a major upset" and referred to Reagan as the *"former* front-runner"; the *Boston Globe* speculated about Bush winning four straight delegate-selection processes and knocking Reagan out of the race; *Newsweek* put Bush on the cover with the headline "Bush Breaks Out of the Pack"; and *Time* featured contrasting photographs of a grinning Bush and a distressed Reagan and the headline "Bush Soars." NBC's Tom Pettit even went so far as to declare that "Ronald Reagan is politically dead"—a view he was to alter one month later, after the New Hampshire primary.[17] All this was on the basis of the vote for 37 out of 1,994 Republican convention delegates!

Similarly, Illinois Congressman John Anderson's vote totals in the March 4 Massachusetts and Vermont primaries in 1980 were interpreted by the press as having created a three-man presidential race. Although Anderson did not win either primary (the only time in 1980 that someone who did not come in first was declared a "winner"), the results were interpreted as taking "a little-known candidate . . . out of nowhere" and turning him into "one of the front-runners, jolting both Ronald Reagan and George Bush." The *New York Times* opined that the March 4 results made Anderson "a major candidate," and CBS's Bruce Morton called the Anderson vote a "spectacular showing."[18] This interpretation clearly hurt George Bush's campaign, since it deflected attention away from him even though he had won the Massachusetts primary and almost defeated Reagan in the Vermont primary.

There is some evidence that the media have lately become more hesitant to play this "expectation game" and to declare as winners other than first-place finishers (as we just saw, for example, the only time this happened in 1980 was in March with John Anderson).[19] The outcomes of delegate-selection processes, however, are still interpreted by the press for news audiences by assigning the roles of "front-runners," "strong challenger," "also-ran," and "sure loser" to candidates. Furthermore, one tendency in the coverage of delegate-selection outcomes remains. Despite the change in nomination rules and procedures so that most delegates are now allotted proportionally to candidates, the press continues to treat each primary as a winner-take-all situation in which most subsequent coverage focuses on the one candidate who came in first. In 1976, for example, 60 percent of the coverage after each primary in the first thirteen weeks went to the first-place finisher, regardless of the medium (network television, daily metropolitan press, and news week-lies).[20]

One of the most important consequences of the media's coverage and interpretation of selected portions of the nomination process is that the candidates who do well in some states receive a disproportionate amount of coverage. Since this coverage may translate into voter perceptions that a candidate is viable, the press's decisions about what parts of the process to emphasize and what outcomes to concentrate on can have a major influence on the outcome of the nomination process.

In 1976, for example, the major beneficiary of this selective coverage by the media was clearly Jimmy Carter. After the Iowa caucuses on January 19, 1976, from which only 47 delegates to the Democratic convention would eventually be chosen, and in which fewer than 10 percent of the state's Democrats participated and Carter was projected to have garnered no more than 28 percent of the vote, the media focused almost exclusively on the Carter candidacy. In the next week's *Time* and *Newsweek*, for example, Carter received 726 lines of coverage, compared with an average of 30 lines for each of his rivals; he received five times as much exposure as any of his rivals on television network news, and four times as much as his average opponent in the daily newspapers.[21] All this coverage occurred as a result of a process that meant the winning of 13 delegates out of the 1,505 needed for the nomination.

After the Iowa caucuses, New Hampshire's primary was the next big media event in 1976. There, Carter barely eked out a plurality victory (30 percent) over four liberal opponents, putting him in line for another 17 convention delegates at the most. For the media, however, it was a Carter story again: 2,600 lines of coverage in *Time* and *Newsweek* to 96 for Udall and 300 for all Carter's other rivals combined, three times as much television news coverage, and three to four times as much newspaper coverage for Carter as for his typical opponent.[22]

The end result of this coverage was that from February 23, 1976, to April 27, 1976, Carter was the presidential candidate covered most (Table 5–2). In fact, he received almost half the total coverage accorded to Democratic contenders in the spring of 1976 on television and in the newspapers, and over half the coverage in *Time* and *Newsweek*. This was despite the fact that during the same time period Henry Jackson had actually outpolled Carter in the six primaries he contested (New Hampshire, Massachusetts, Florida, North Carolina, Wisconsin, and New York) by a 1,880,664 to 1,597,186 margin. Following Carter's "win" in New Hampshire (total Democratic votes cast: 82,381) the New Hampshire result received 2,100 seconds of total news time on the three networks. Following Jackson's win in New York (total Democratic votes cast: 3,746,414) the New York result received only 560 seconds of coverage on the three networks.[23]

TABLE 5–2   News Coverage Received by Each of the Democratic
Candidates during the 1976 Primaries
(Percent)

	Network Evening Newscasts	Erie Times/ News	L.A. Herald-Examiner	L.A. Times	Time/ Newsweek
Brown	10	9	20	22	10
Carter	48	44	41	46	54
Church	8	7	8	7	5
Jackson	12	13	14	11	11
Udall	13	11	12	10	13
Wallace	5	12	2	3	5
Bayh, Harris, and Shriver	4	4	3	1	2
Total	100	100	100	100	100

Source: Thomas E. Patterson, *The Mass Media Election* (New York: Praeger, 1980), p. 46.
Reprinted by permission of Praeger Publishers. Copyright © 1980 by Praeger Publishers.

The amount of coverage given different presidential contenders in 1980 also varied considerably. On the Democratic side, news coverage focused almost exclusively on Jimmy Carter and Edward Kennedy, with Carter receiving the majority of the coverage. Given that Carter was the incumbent president at the time, this is hardly surprising. What *is* somewhat surprising is that Kennedy's coverage approached Carter's throughout April 1980. Probably the lingering aura surrounding any member of the Kennedy family and the subconscious desire to keep the Democratic nomination a good story combined to produce more coverage for Kennedy than would otherwise have been the case. California governor Jerry Brown never made much of a dent in this two-person media coverage.

On the Republican side, coverage focused on Ronald Reagan, George Bush, and John Anderson; but no Republican received as much coverage as Carter and Kennedy did during the invisible primary. Between February and April, Bush had a brief flurry of coverage and then practically disappeared, whereas John Anderson went from no coverage to parity with the other two Republicans. Throughout this period, Reagan did maintain a general superiority in coverage over the other two, but nowhere near as dramatic as Carter's advantage had been in 1976.[24]

So far we have considered mainly the quantitative and interpretive aspects of nomination campaign coverage. There is also a more qualitative dimension to press coverage of a nomination campaign that involves the way in which candidates and the process are portrayed.

Candidates differ in the ways in which their candidacies are portrayed and in how favorable those portrayals are. Furthermore, over time these portrayals may develop into themes that are used to capture and refer to different candidates. During the 1972 primaries, for example, on television news Senator Hubert Humphrey was portrayed as "the politician of the past," Senator Edmund Muskie as the "front-runner," Senator George McGovern as the "antiestablishment populist," and Governor George Wallace as "the creator of division and discord."[25] During 1976, Fred Harris was portrayed as the populist candidate who was too radical to win, Henry Jackson as dull and humorless, and Gerald Ford as a "bumbler."[26] In 1980 Edward Kennedy was portrayed first as "a klutz" and a "stumblebum" and later as a "classy loser"; Jimmy Carter's portrayal went from "a well-meaning boob sure to be denied renomination, to stern-visaged leader of a nation in crisis, to a cynical manipulator of images, blatantly using the White House for his political advantage"; coverage of Reagan emphasized his age and his questionable intelligence and grasp of issues; and coverage of John Anderson focused on "praise of his personal qualities" and "the fruitlessness of his quest."[27] (Michael Robinson has noted a similar phenomenon during the *general* election campaign in 1980. We will consider this possibility later in this chapter.)

Two studies measuring the tone of candidate coverage during the 1980 presidential nomination period have both found that candidate coverage was in general quite negative, but that it was far more negative for some candidates than others. Jimmy Carter's coverage was the most negative in 1980, whereas Edward Kennedy's coverage was extremely negative at the beginning of the nomination campaign but more positive later on. Ronald Reagan's coverage was moderately negative throughout most of the year; George Bush's coverage was slightly positive to begin with but negative by March; and John Anderson's coverage, noticeable only after February, was modestly positive at that point.[28]

What accounts for the differing portrayals of different candidates? One explanation is that the tone of campaign coverage is directly related to how likely a candidate is to win the nomination, with increased scrutiny of front-runners used by the media to prevent a media-generated momentum from developing for any candidate.[29] Hence Kennedy's coverage was the most negative in 1980, when he was the most preferred candidate among Democrats during the invisible primary, and became positive only once it was clear he had lost the nomination. Anderson's coverage was the most positive in the beginning when support was nil, became more negative when his support rivaled that of Carter and Reagan, and improved again when it was clear that he too would lose. George Bush's coverage rode a similar roller coaster: positive while becoming a front-runner, negative once he had attained that status (briefly), positive again after it became clear he would lose the nomination, and negative again after he was given the vice-presidential nomination.

Another possibility is that the tone of a candidate's coverage depends on how well that candidate fits the dramatic needs of journalists. Paul Weaver has suggested, for example, that in 1976 Jimmy Carter received more favorable coverage than did Washington Senator Henry Jackson because Carter embodied the media's myth of the nonpolitical politician: unsullied by Washington service, unattached to any of the Democratic party's interest groups, and unexpectedly popular with the people.[30] In 1980 the press's fascination with John Anderson can be explained in a similar way—as a result of the drama inherent in the unlikely prospect of a liberal candidate catching on in a party that was becoming increasingly conservative. During the concluding months of a nomination campaign in which both nominations had been decided early and no liberal candidate had survived, John Anderson gave the press something interesting to write about.[31] Whatever the accurate explanation for the variation in the nomination campaign portrayals of presidential contenders, it is clear that the press makes political judgments about candidates that affect both the fortunes of candidates and the understanding of the public. Two days after the press declared George Bush a legitimate challenger as a result of his Iowa caucus victory, for example, the Bush campaign had received $150,000 in contributions and triple the previous number of requests for press seats on the campaign trail.[32]

Finally, we ought to consider another qualitative dimension of media coverage of the presidential nomination campaign: whether nomination campaign news coverage provides news audiences with useful information. Since most citizens are ill informed at this stage of the campaign and are heavily dependent on news coverage for their insight into the different candidacies, the quality of campaign coverage has an important effect on the judgments citizens make during the nomination campaign.

Media definitions of what is newsworthy lead the media to focus on identifiable events and campaign activities rather than on the candidates' policy preferences and personal qualities. This means that most media coverage of nomination campaigns focuses primarily on the campaign strategy of the candidates and interpretations of how well each candidate is doing. Much less information is provided on what the selection of a particular person to fill the office of president would mean in terms of the individual's personal qualities and policy preferences.

In 1976, for example, *Newsweek* magazine presented precampaign sketches of eleven candidates in the January 12 issue. Fifty-eight percent of this material discussed the campaign approaches of the candidates; only 13 percent focused on ideology or issue stands, 8 percent on the geographic origins of the candidates, and 6 percent on previous campaign experience and personality factors.[33] In other words, if a citizen were looking for policy- or personality-related information, the chances of finding it there were slim.

The type of coverage that focuses on the "game" and "event" elements of the campaign, including who is ahead, who is behind, who is gaining, who is losing, what campaign strategy is being followed, and what the impact of campaign activities is on the candidate's chances of winning has been called *horse-race* coverage. During the 1976 nomination campaign, this type of news coverage amounted to about 60 percent of the coverage in television network news, weekly news magazines, and daily newspapers. This left only about 25 percent of the coverage for more substantive material. In addition, the interpretations of the results of primaries also emphasized strategic considerations such as a candidate's organization, financing, strategy, momentum, style, and vigor far more often (60 percent) than interpretations based on more substantive or enduring factors, such as a state's ideological predispositions.[34]

In 1980 the horse race also dominated most media coverage of the nomination campaign. On television network newscasts the coverage of the "race" became more prevalent than that of any other major issue category (including Iran, the economy, and all other domestic issues) by January, and increased in prevalence through April. Among a national sample of daily newspapers, a fairly constant 50 percent of all public affairs coverage was devoted to the race from November 1979 through April 1980. Of the media surveyed, only the *New York Times* covered other major issue topics, such as the economy and Iran, in about equal proportions to the horse race.[35]

This focus on the gamelike elements of the nomination campaign is clearly the result of the journalistic perspective on the campaign. Since the campaign is viewed as a strategic contest between candidate organizations in which the explicit daily activities of the candidates are the important data, most coverage of these daily activities will be embedded in the context of what they reveal about the candidates' electoral prospects. These activities are the most visible aspects of the campaign and constitute its indisputable facts:

> . . . the news is what happens. The news is what somebody says or does. The news is not a reporter's perception or explanation of what happens; it's simply what happens. That's horserace, granted. And I think there is a real question as to whether the proper role of an evening news service . . . is to give people the kind of in-depth examination of political and policy issues that has been suggested at least by implication . . . it is safer, in all candor, to stick to the horserace elements of the election and not go wandering off into the thickets of substance.[36]

Of all the patterns in news coverage of the presidential nomination campaign, this focus on the horse race may well be the most consequential. The nomination stage is important because most alternatives are eliminated at this stage. In addition, the nomination process has recently been opened up to more public participation; yet citizen interest and knowledge are probably lowest during this stage. If the flow of information concerning the candidate choices available is largely nonsubstantive, the apparent democratization of the nomination campaign may be of little consequence. As one observer has concluded:

> The power of the press rests largely on its ability to select what will be covered and to decide the context in which these events will be placed. Through this influence and because the press is guided substantially by its values, conventions, and organizational imperatives certain aspects of an election are magnified and others muted in news of the campaign. The press's version of election politics elevates competition over substance, outcomes over process, and the immediate over the enduring. While these favored aspects are not an insignificant part of the election, focus on them represents an unquestionably limited perspective.[37]

In the absence of more substantive information about the candidates, voters are left to form impressions of and judgments about candidates almost exclusively on the basis of how well the latter are doing in the race. In the opinion of one analyst:

> The failure to cover consistently and conscientiously the struggle among competing views about the nature of government—which was at the heart of the real [1980] campaign—effectively helped disenfranchise the voter *by stripping him of a reason to care about the outcome.*[38] [This and subsequent excerpts from *The Real Campaign* (New York, Summit Books, 1982), by Jeff Greenfield, copyright © 1982 by Jeff Greenfield, are reprinted by permission of Summit Books, a division of Simon & Shuster, Inc.]

The National Nominating Conventions

Coverage of the nomination campaign concludes and coverage of the general election campaign begins with the national nominating convention. To the successful nominee, the convention may be the most important communication event of the entire campaign. This is because convention coverage dominates the political arena for a considerable period of time; focuses almost exclusively on one candidate and party; and is practically free to the candidate since the federal government, the national party, and the media pay for a considerable portion of the cost. In 1980, for example, convention coverage amounted to more than forty hours of prime-time exposure, more prime-time exposure for the presidential campaign than in the rest of the year put together.[39]

National nominating conventions used to be rambunctious, unpredictable, and decisive affairs. Recently, however, they have become much less spontaneous and consequential. Because of changes in the delegate-selection procedures in the last decade, most convention delegates are now committed in advance to a presidential candidate; the convention serves to ratify and legitimize electoral decisions already made elsewhere. Although the nomination has been uncertain in some recent conventions (John Kennedy's in 1960 and Richard Nixon's in 1968, for example) there is typically little suspense now regarding who the nominee will be. Since 1952 neither major-party convention has needed more than one ballot to determine the party's nominee.

Despite this decline in the substantive importance of conventions, they still have a contemporary significance for presidential campaigns. They represent an opportunity for a massive dose of persuasive communication designed to improve support for the party and the party's candidates. In fact, the nominating conventions have been called "the greatest media events on earth"—an understandable label given the fact that *Time* magazine alone brought 130 people to the Democratic convention in 1972 and the three networks had staffs of 1,400 and spent $8 million on convention coverage. In 1980, 15,000 members of the press attended the Republican convention; the three networks reported spending $40 million on convention coverage.[40] Hence conventions represent a major opportunity to improve public impressions of a party through the coverage of convention activities.

The program of the convention is now planned with television in mind. Important events are timed to coincide with the time the maximum audience will be tuned in; "spontaneous" demonstrations are carefully planned in advance, organized, and timed; news "sources" are made readily available to newsmen; and conflict is kept behind closed doors. The podium has taken on the look of a blockbuster talent show, complete with emcees and guest stars. The Republican National Committee had the nominating convention of 1972 so well scripted in advance that it "instructed the speakers when to pause, nod, and accept 'spontaneous' cheers" and "stipulated that at a certain point, a demonstration would interrupt the convention secretary in midsentence."[41]

Of course, despite candidates' attempts to stage a nominating convention that benefits the nominee, they cannot always control all the significant events, behavior, and images that convention coverage transmits. In fact, the failure to capitalize on this opportunity for political persuasion has crippled several presidential campaigns even before the general election. The Democratic party's 1968 convention was marred by disorder and violence and prevented Hubert Humphrey from receiving a substantial amount of positive coverage. The 1972 Democratic convention was a disappointment for George McGovern's campaign, partly because his most important address, his acceptance speech, could not take place until after midnight, when the audience was extremely small. Ronald Reagan's nomination by the 1980 Republican convention was somewhat undercut by the speculation regarding Gerald Ford as a potential vice-presidential candidate. Jimmy Carter's 1980 renomination was distinguished by the failure of Edward Kennedy to indicate enthusiastic support for Carter's candidacy.

Despite the attempts of candidates and the media alike, the citizenry is losing interest in televised coverage of the conventions. In each presidential election year since 1952, the share of the television audience watching the conventions has declined until in 1980 it reached 50 percent. As a result, CBS has announced its plans to shorten its convention coverage significantly in 1984.[42] If the other networks follow suit, the effect on the presidential campaign could be substantial.

The General Election Campaign

With the conclusion of the national nominating conventions and the naming of the two major-party candidates for president, the journalist's approach to the campaign undergoes a partial change. The norms of what is newsworthy remain the same, as does the overriding concern with the campaign activity and strategic decisions of each campaign organization. The news-hole expands, however; the number of actors to be covered shrinks; and norms concerning the balance of the amount of coverage for each candidate are fairly well established. In addition, once candidates are nominated, journalists need the candidates much more than they did previously, and the relationship shifts in favor of the candidates.

One of the perennial concerns with general election news coverage is whether the campaign is covered in an unbiased, balanced, and fair manner. Candidates frequently argue that their messages are misstated and that their opponent is being treated too gently, and losing candidates often blame their defeats on journalistic treatment. When Richard Nixon made his famous "you won't have Richard Nixon to kick around anymore" statement to the press at the conclusion of his unsuccessful California gubernatorial election campaign in 1962, he was only expressing explicitly what many other candidates have felt about their treatment by the press.

Despite the prevalence of claims that general election campaign coverage is biased, it is difficult to demonstrate systematic bias. If one considers bias to be some consistent deviation from reality, then demonstrating bias would require a comprehensive and accurate measure of that reality. Given the inherently ambiguous nature of an election campaign and the tendency of different people to perceive the same occurrence in different ways, such "unbiased" measures of reality are hard to come by.

Doris Graber and Richard Hofstetter have attempted to clarify the conceptual problem of news bias by distinguishing between "structural" bias and "political" bias. Structural bias involves portraying candidates in a different light as a result of "the circumstances of news production," whereas political bias involves "slanting the news for partisan reasons."[43] At present there are powerful constraints on the media that discourage *political* bias. In the case of the broadcast media, federal regulations and audience-maximization incentives discourage content that might be considered biased, controversial, and unfair. Although the print media are free from such government regulations, they too are primarily concerned with maximizing their audience and, consequently, their advertising revenues. Most publishers are interested in producing a newspaper that appeals to Republicans and Democrats, liberals and conservatives alike. Neutrality rather than bias, balance instead of imbalance, would seem to be the best means of achieving this maximum audience. As we saw in Chapter 4, balance is also more consistent with journalism's norm of objectivity.

Structural bias, however, is another matter. Since different candidates participate in different kinds of campaign activities, different journalists cultivate different sources, and journalists are subject to the policies and expectations of their superiors, it is hardly surprising that some candidates are dealt with more favorably than others, and that there is some variation in the treatment of candidates across media outlets. Structural bias is caused not by the intentional, personal preferences of the journalist, but rather by variations in candidate behavior and media organization policies. In fact, some structural bias is probably inevitable in news coverage because of "the need to select and report a small body of information from a much larger universe of newsworthy events."[44] Let us begin this section, then, by investigating how much bias has been found in general election news coverage. We will consider two related areas: the amount of coverage given candidates, and the favorableness of the portrayal of different candidates.

One fairly straightforward way to see whether different candidates are dealt with differently by the press is to measure the amount of coverage given each of the presidential candidates during the general election campaign. In the last three decades a number of studies have done this for both print and broadcast media.

In general, almost all the research focusing on the amount of coverage given presidential candidates agrees on one major point: The amount of coverage for both major-party candidates is usually extremely similar. In fact, it is usually so evenly balanced that this balance is probably not completely coincidental. Rather, the norm of objectivity, the need to appeal to a mass market, and—in the case of the broadcast media—federal regulations make evenly balanced coverage of major-party candidates an important goal for most news organizations. Anecdotes describing editors measuring column inches of coverage with rulers and producers measuring coverage with stopwatches indicate that this goal is often an explicit one.[45]

Table 5–3 shows the results of just one of the many studies reaching this conclusion. The table compares the amount of campaign coverage given the presidential candidates in 1960, 1964, and 1968 in fifteen of

TABLE 5–3   Percentage of Space for Each Party, 1960, 1964, and 1968 Presidential General Election Campaigns, Prestige Press

	1960		1964		1968		
	D	R	D	R	D	R	A
Atlanta Constitution	60.2	39.8	53.0	47.0	36.4	34.6	29.0
Baltimore Sun	52.8	47.2	52.2	47.8	41.5	39.5	19.0
Chicago Daily News	48.4	51.6	53.9	46.1	39.0	33.9	27.1
Chicago Tribune	40.8	59.2	34.4	65.6	37.0	45.9	17.0
Christian Science Monitor	41.5	58.5	48.9	51.1	37.2	32.9	29.9
Des Moines Register	45.8	54.2	50.5	49.5	36.9	42.1	20.9
Kansas City Star	52.2	47.8	54.4	45.6	36.0	37.1	26.8
Los Angeles Times	45.2	54.8	49.9	50.1	48.1	32.7	19.1
Louisville Courier-Journal	54.5	45.5	57.8	42.2	39.4	30.2	30.4
Miami Herald	51.3	48.7	59.4	40.6	39.3	35.0	25.7
Milwaukee Journal	54.4	45.6	51.0	49.0	42.7	37.5	19.8
New York Times	50.3	49.7	57.0	43.0	43.9	38.0	18.0
St. Louis Post-Dispatch	54.6	45.4	52.0	48.0	44.2	36.6	19.2
Wall Street Journal	47.2	52.8	45.2	54.8	41.1	37.6	21.4
Washington Post	51.9	48.1	53.5	46.5	44.3	35.9	19.9
Average	50.2	49.8	51.9	48.1	41.4	36.8	21.8

Source: Guido H. Stempel, III, "The Prestige Press Meets the Third-Party Challenge," *Journalism Quarterly* 46 (Winter 1969): 704. Reprinted by permission.

Note: D—Democratic; R—Republican; A—American Independent.

the most prestigious daily newspapers. Most of this coverage looks evenly balanced. In 1960 only three of the fifteen papers gave one of the candidates more than 55 percent of the coverage; in 1964 only four papers gave one candidate more than 55 percent of the total coverage; and in 1968 the difference between the proportion of coverage granted the two major-party candidates exceeded 10 percent in only one case. Furthermore, the average coverage summed across the fifteen papers was extremely well balanced; only one newspaper was imbalanced in two different years (the *Chicago Tribune*, with Republican tendencies). Furthermore, the overall balance does not disguise imbalance in any particular section of the newspapers.

Similar results have been found for television news coverage. In the 1968 presidential election 37.5 percent of CBS's coverage went to Hubert Humphrey, 28.6 percent to Richard Nixon, and 24.8 percent to George Wallace (9.1 percent was mixed or covered minor-party candidates). The coverage advantage to Humphrey represented an additional total of twenty to thirty minutes over the course of the campaign, an advantage that could be of some consequence; but since both candidates received an almost identical amount of favorable coverage, the imbalance was probably not noticeable.[46]

Network news coverage of the 1972 presidential campaign was also evenly balanced. Coverage of the two major parties during September and October was very evenly balanced (a finding that also applied to the *New York Times* over this same period); and network news coverage during August, September, and October was also evenly balanced across the three networks (although McGovern did receive three times as much coverage during July as a result of the Eagleton episode and other summertime activities).[47]

This general finding of balanced coverage of major-party candidates, though apparently true in recent years for most major news outlets, has not always been true in the past and is not always true of less prestigious and less well known news media. Newspapers and news magazines have in the past been much more blatant in expressing political preferences and permitting these preferences to influence the coverage of election campaigns. Henry Luce, for example, is often credited with using his publications, *Time* and *Life,* to advance Dwight Eisenhower's presidential campaign. The *Los Angeles Times* is similarly credited with promoting Richard Nixon for a seat in the House of Representatives in 1946 and a U.S. Senate seat in 1950, and William Loeb was noted for promoting conservative presidential candidates in his New Hampshire newspaper (the *Manchester Union-Leader*).[48] In the last few decades, however, powerful social, economic, and legal incentives have caused a decline in such blatant advocacy.

The typical picture of balance in the amount of campaign coverage may also be more prevalent among the prestige press and for coverage of national campaigns than it is for other papers and other campaigns. Where a less prestigious paper is covering a local or state campaign, imbalanced coverage may be the norm, particularly if the paper's market exists in an area that favors one party. A recent study of newspaper coverage of congressional campaigns discovered that incumbents receive more coverage than challengers do during general election campaigns, especially when a contest is close.[49] It has also recently been reported that some local weeklies in upstate New York have had a policy forbidding campaign coverage of any local candidate not opposed to abortions, and that some small local papers in Kentucky and West Virginia have had a policy of selling *news* space to candidates. Although these examples may not be typical of all nonprestige news, it does appear that the norm of partisan balance is less strongly held in some media outlets.

Determining the balance of campaign coverage is fairly easy when there are only two major-party candidates for a particular public office. The situation becomes cloudier, however, when one or more minor-party candidates are involved in a political campaign. In 1968, for example, there was an unusually viable third-party candidate for president, Alabama Governor George Wallace; in 1980 independent candidate John Anderson made a serious race for the presidency. Since the media do not have a well-established norm to guide them in what to do in such cases, decisions about the amount of coverage show much more variation across news outlets.

The daily prestige press resolved the dilemma regarding Wallace in 1968 by providing him with a substantial but minority proportion of the campaign coverage. On the average, Wallace received 22 percent of the coverage, compared with 37 percent for Nixon and 41 percent for Humphrey, with coverage varying from 17 percent to 31 percent in each of the newspapers. There was at least one paper (the *Louisville Courier-Journal*) that gave Wallace even more coverage than it gave Nixon (Table 5–3).

Receiving that much coverage demonstrates one aspect of the success of the Wallace campaign. More typically, however, minor-party candidates are virtually ignored by journalists despite having legally qualified to appear on the ballot. For example, Eugene McCarthy, Roger McBride, Lester Maddox, Thomas Anderson, Peter Camejo, Gus Hall, Margaret Wright, and Lyndon LaRouche all received more than 40,000 votes for president in 1976 running as minor-party candidates; yet none of them received much news coverage.

A second way in which news coverage of general election campaigns might exhibit either political or structural bias is in the portrayal of the campaigns of particular candidates. Candidates usually believe that they are receiving less favorable coverage than they deserve, but systematically evaluating the tone of coverage in a more disinterested and objective manner is quite difficult.

There is considerable evidence that the portrayals of different candidates in the news do exhibit significant variation. Some candidates are dealt with more favorably than others, and more complimentary themes develop in the coverage of some candidates than others. Most of this variation seems to be the result of structural bias, originating with differences in candidate behavior (including candidate mistakes), the intrusion of real-world events into a campaign, and the application of newsworthiness criteria to different campaign activities.

One study of press coverage of the 1966 California gubernatorial campaign between Edmund G. Brown (Jerry Brown's father) and Ronald Reagan, for example, compared the coverage given the two candidates in two California daily newspapers. It was found that both the *Sacramento Bee* and the *Oakland Tribune* violated the norms of partisan balance and overall neutrality. The *Bee*, which endorsed Brown, contained much more news coverage favorable to him than to Reagan (63 percent to 26 percent, with 11 percent neutral). The *Tribune*, which endorsed Reagan, contained more coverage favorable to him than to Brown (40 percent to 28 percent, with 32 percent neutral).[50] This seems to be a case of partisan bias, since the coverage corresponded to the stated editorial preferences of the two newspapers.

Despite the special legal and economic constraints under which television network news organizations operate, there is also considerable evidence of variation in how favorably some candidates are portrayed in that medium. During the 1972 presidential campaign, for example, Richard Nixon apparently received more favorable coverage than George McGovern did. (According to one study, ABC and NBC covered Richard Nixon more favorably, and CBS covered George McGovern more favorably.[51]) In general a viewer who in 1972 "tuned in on all of the network stories about the candidates would leave with a more positive impression of Nixon than of McGovern," and would probably also have received the distinct impression that "McGovern's campaign was disintegrating right up to the election."[52] In addition, different film techniques used in the 1972 television news coverage led to the projection of different candidate images. Film coverage of George McGovern portrayed him in a more intimate and warm way due to the use of "tightshots" (close-ups of only a portion, usually the face, of an individual's body); film of vice-presidential candidate Sargent Shriver showed him "mixing with the people" and hence portrayed him as a "man of the people, who is loved by, and loves the crowds"; and film of Vice-President Spiro Agnew portrayed him as "the man of authority, who takes a political stand, who speaks from the feeling of an internal conviction predicated upon his ability and experience in making political decisions."[53]

Finally, network news coverage of the 1972 campaign also portrayed candidates differently by depicting the associations between the candidates and various demographic groups in different ways. Richard Nixon was frequently shown with famous, common, and cultured persons, and with experts, foreign officials, the military, and the wealthy. As a result, he was "somewhat more favorably linked to many groups than McGovern," including "not only traditional, more pro-Republican groups but also . . . several traditional, more pro-Democratic groups." On the other hand, McGovern was shown more often receiving the support of unorganized crowds, rallies, testimonials, and campaign contributors than Nixon was. Unfortunately for McGovern, however, such portrayals were an infrequent part of network news coverage.[54]

In 1980 it was also evident that television network news coverage of the general election campaign portrayed some candidates more favorably than others. In general, the tone of coverage of Jimmy Carter was the most negative during the general election period, coverage of Ronald Reagan the next most negative, and coverage of John Anderson the least negative. In addition, one researcher noticed what he believes to have been dramatic, literary portrayals of each of the three major 1980 candidates. In his view John Anderson was portrayed as a modern-day Don Quixote, tilting at windmills and dreaming impossible dreams; Ronald Reagan was portrayed as foolish yet humane, similar to Chauncey Gardner in the movie *Being There*; and Jimmy Carter was portrayed as a mean, vindictive, petty, and manipulative person reminiscent of J. R. Ewing on the TV series "Dallas."[55]

These dramatic portrayals of the 1980 presidential candidates are certainly negative ones. In fact, there is some evidence that campaign coverage of presidential candidates in general has become more negative in recent years. Newspaper commentary concerning the personal qualities of candidates was negative 41 percent of the time in 1969, 51 percent of the time in 1972, and 57 percent of the time in 1976.[56] In addition, Paul Weaver has argued that television news coverage of the 1976 presidential candidates treated them with condescension, contempt, and at times "naked hatred." Furthermore, according to Weaver, presidential candidates are usually portrayed as consumed by ambition; "endlessly, obsessively, even fiendishly calculating"; "driven by deep passions and uncontrollable compulsion"; and "incurably fractious."[57] In 1980, according to one close observer of campaign coverage, this phenomenon was furthered as "the determination of the press not to be manipulated by candidates and campaign staffs led to a disparagement of the entire process of choosing the President" and to a portrayal of the presidential selection process as "an unseemly, tedious, almost disreputable enterprise."[58] This is hardly a positive view of presidential contenders or the presidential selection process.

The negative portrayal of presidential candidates and the presidential selection process is probably part of a broader trend in U.S. journalism. For a variety of reasons, including several recent instances of governmental lying and secrecy, criticism of the press for being too gentle with governmental sources and officials, determination to avoid campaign manipulation, and pursuit of the time-honored but somewhat romantic myth of investigative journalism, journalism in general has become more skeptical and cynical about politicians and more adversarial toward governmental officials and candidates for public office.[59] When this new style of journalism is applied to the coverage of presidential campaigns, a less-than-favorable depiction of candidates results. Clearly, such portrayals could have effects on the public that go far beyond merely altering the distribution of candidate support and votes cast.

In our discussion of campaign coverage during nomination campaigns, we saw that most of the coverage consisted of horse-race news focusing on what campaign activities indicate about a candidate's chances of electoral victory. This is due to the journalist's conceptualization of an election campaign as a strategic contest between two organizations, the daily search for a story, the campaign trail environment, and the effects of pack journalism.

During the general election campaign, some things change: The newshole expands while the number of candidates shrinks, and the near weekly rhythm of delegate-selection results is absent. Nevertheless, the journalistic perspective on the campaign remains, as does horse-race coverage.

If television network news coverage is divided into three categories—campaign activity (winning and losing, strategy, logistics, appearances and crowds); campaign substance (candidates' issue positions, candidates' characteristics and backgrounds, and other issue-related information such as party platforms); and other miscellaneous information (campaign events calendar, election procedures)—then the bulk of general election coverage focuses on campaign activity (the horse race). In 1968 CBS news coverage of all three candidates concentrated heavily on whether the candidate was winning or losing; crowd response; the securing of endorsements; and campaign staff, style, and organization. Coverage of policy issues, such as the Vietnam War, civil rights, public welfare, or economic policies, was virtually nonexistent.[60] In 1972 about nine times as much general election network television news coverage was devoted to campaign activity as to candidate qualifications and backgrounds, and about four times as much time to campaign activity as to candidate issue positions. CBS presented the most coverage of issue positions, and ABC spent the most time on candidate qualifications and the most total coverage time; but the distribution of time across the three networks was very similar.[61] In 1976 about 50 percent of network news general election coverage went to campaign activity, 35 percent to campaign substance, and 14 percent to miscellaneous information. The focus on campaign activity was a bit more prevalent on network news than in either the *Los Angeles Times* or *Time* and *Newsweek,* and was somewhat less frequent in all three media (television, newspapers, and news magazines) during the general election campaign than during the nomination campaign. The coverage of the horse race, however, also seems to be greater now than it was during pretelevision campaigns.[62]

Comparable data for the 1980 election are not available, but a number of observers have stated that the horse race was just as prevalent in 1980 as in previous years. CBS news coverage included four times as many explicit references to the success or failure of a candidate as to all other candidate characteristics combined.[63] Media critic Jeff Greenfield has observed that

> the press devoted the overwhelming preponderance of its money and manpower to an attempt to . . . tell the American people what was going to happen. In contrast, it spent a relatively minor effort in communicating the most accessible sort of information: the performance, proposals, intentions, and assumptions of the candidates.[64]

Journalism's concern for the horse race was evidenced in other ways in 1980: with the publicity by ABC of a phone-in poll regarding who "won" the Carter-Reagan debate; with the reporting of the results of public opinion polls performed several times throughout the campaign; and, on election night, by NBC's use of exit polls to project the winner before enough actual votes were in.

This emphasis by the networks on campaign activity means that citizens wanting to learn about the candidate's qualifications or issue positions during the campaign would have to be either extremely lucky or unusually perseverant to find any of this material. In 1972, for example, each network devoted about thirty minutes *total* during the general election campaign to a discussion of Richard Nixon's issue positions and a *total* of between five and thirteen minutes to George McGovern's issue positions, depending on the particular network.[65] Obviously, this is hardly enough time to investigate fully most candidates' positions on most issues—and with such coverage spread over two months it is extremely unlikely that the typical citizen would even be exposed to it or would remember the content of such coverage. This type of coverage represented only 3 percent of all available news during this period.

The situation has been even worse with respect to network television news coverage of candidate qualities and characteristics. In 1972 each network devoted between five and fifteen minutes of coverage *total* during the general election campaign to Nixon's qualifications and a total of three to seven minutes to McGovern's.[66] For the citizen, looking or waiting for such content would truly be like looking for a needle in a haystack. It constituted 1 percent of all available news time during the 1972 general election campaign.

It is unclear whether print coverage of general election campaigns is as dominated by the horserace as television is. Patterson and McClure claim that it is; Doris Graber, however, has found that in newspaper coverage of the 1968, 1972, and 1976 campaigns, the most prevalent type of information transmitted involved the personal qualifications of the candidates. These qualifications have been of two main types: (1) personal capacities, including personality traits (integrity, reliability, compassion, and the like); personal style (forthrightness, folksiness); and personal image (ability to appear productive and fiscally responsible); and (2) professional capacities, including the capacity to conduct foreign and domestic affairs, one's political philosophy, and one's approach to government reorganization. In these three elections, most of the focus has been on *personal* rather than *professional* capacities, with the lion's share of the emphasis on a candidate's trustworthiness, strength of character, and compassion.[67]

The discrepancy between Graber's finding and that of Patterson and McClure is probably the result of different ways of categorizing news stories. Yet the discrepancy is really not that great, since Graber also finds that coverage of campaign "hoopla" and "horse race" is the most prevalent type of issues and events coverage, that it is about equally prevalent for newspapers and television, and that it has been increasing since 1968. Consequently, the more significant finding is not whether horse-race or personal-attributes information is more prevalent, but that this represents the vast majority of the news coverage available to the citizenry. Social problems, economic and foreign policy, domestic politics, and the political philosophies of candidates are almost completely invisible when compared to the prominence of campaign hoopla and candidate personality traits.

Not only is there a dearth of general election campaign coverage of public policy alternatives, but political issues and policy preferences are also covered only in a particular way. Television news has a tendency to limit issue coverage to one or two issues. These become *the* issues of the campaign, and they dominate what little issue coverage is provided. In 1972 television network news presented the contest between Nixon and McGovern almost entirely in terms of two issues: political corruption and Vietnam troop withdrawals. During the general election campaign, the three networks mentioned Nixon's and McGovern's stands on the issue of the Vietnam War eighty-three times, on the issue of political corruption twenty-four times, and on military spending twenty-two times. Coverage of all other issues was much more sporadic, with most issue positions mentioned only a handful of times.[68]

In terms of the *amount of time* devoted to candidate issue positions by network news, the 1972 campaign was also a two-issue campaign. Nixon's position on handling the Vietnam War received thirty-nine minutes of coverage, and his position on political corruption received fourteen minutes of coverage during the campaign across three networks. Most of Nixon's other positions received only a minute or two of coverage. Coverage of McGovern's policy preferences was even less visible. Only one issue received more than six minutes total coverage during the entire two-month general election period: his position on military spending.[69] It would be surprising, then, if citizens acquired any awareness of either candidate's issue positions as a result of network news exposure.

The news media also show a preference for a certain kind of issue coverage. Issues that neatly divide candidates, produce disagreement and argument among the candidates, and can be summarized with simple slogans are more apt to be covered than are other issues since the former lend themselves to the kind of dramatic storytelling that journalists are good at. In 1976, for example, half of daily press and news magazine coverage of policy issues focused on such clear-cut issues, as did two-thirds of network news coverage.[70]

The issues covered by the press are usually not those emphasized by candidates. Candidates tend to talk about vague, general policy objectives in an attempt to construct broad coalitions and avoid offending large segments of the electorate. Such rhetoric is seldom considered newsworthy by the press and is usually ignored. In fact, the issues that often dominate general election coverage are what have been called *campaign issues*—issues that "develop from campaign incidents, usually errors in judgment by the candidates."[71] In 1976 these included Ford's comment that Eastern Europe was not dominated by the Soviet Union, Carter's comment that he saw nothing wrong with preserving the "ethnic purity" of neighborhoods, and Carter's admission in a *Playboy* interview that he had "looked on a lot of women with lust." In 1980 good examples would be the maneuvering concerning John Anderson's debate partici-pation and Reagan's remarks blaming trees for pollution, calling the Vietnam War a "noble cause," and implying that Carter was too cozy with the Klu Klux Klan.

Campaign issues appeal to journalists because they can be dramatized, they allow journalists to control the flow of campaign communication, and they lend themselves to the kind of "action-reaction" or "I said–he said–I said" stories that are journalism's stock in trade. Their attrac-tiveness, however, means that the issues considered important by candi-dates and those covered in news coverage are likely to be two substan-tially different entities.

Journalists claim that the reasons for the dearth of issue related cover-age are that candidates are too ambiguous, general, and repetitive to permit anything else, and that candidates use issues in a manipulative fashion to advantage their own candidacies. For example, when defend-ing his network's performance during the 1976 campaign, Robert Chandler of CBS News had this to say:

> In April of last year, Governor Carter kindly consented to have lunch with a number of our correspondents and executives in New York. One of us asked him why he had not put forth any position papers during the pri-mary campaign, why he had not taken definitive stands and put out white papers and made specific proposals. His response was that the only presi-dents he knew of who had done that during the primary campaign were Presidents Dewey, Humphrey, and McGovern. He had no intention of dealing with the issues.[72]

James Gannon, executive editor of the *Des Moines Register*, has also placed the responsibility for the paucity of substantive issue discussion squarely in the lap of candidates:

> The press can't generate issues and manufacture issues if the candidates won't talk about them. In large measure they don't want to because they don't want to take hard stands they are going to be held to later. . . . You can try to do things in staged debates and that helps, but the candidates have to be willing to come in where the contest is and talk about what the people want to hear.[73]

There is some truth, of course, to what journalists claim. Candidates do articulate specific policy proposals, but typically not in situations that are highly visible to reporters. It has been estimated, for example, that in 1960 between 16 percent (Nixon) and 23 percent (Kennedy) of all the sentences uttered by the two presidential candidates on the campaign trail were devoted to policy proposals, but that these policy stands were seldom expressed in the standard campaign speech delivered five to ten times a day, day in and day out. Rather, they appeared in speeches before specialized audiences; in "candidate forum" responses to written questions posed by limited circulation magazines (such as *Medical Economics, Business Week,* or *Education News*); and in media interviews and debates.[74]

Part of the explanation for the infrequency of specific issue coverage, then, appears to be that the campaign speech is the dominant form of campaign communication, both for candidates and for journalists:

> The typical campaign speech, delivered to a partisan crowd in a shopping center or meeting hall, has virtually nothing to say about the specifics of policy. For many candidates it is the same speech (with minor variations) five to ten times a day, day in and day out. "The speech" is a distillation of punch lines with proven audience appeal, which the candidate has sharpened and polished since his first primary campaign, and which he can deliver by heart, without the artificiality of reading or the strain of continually facing fresh texts.
>
> The speech sometimes includes a reference or two to problems of special local interest; its punch lines allude vaguely to policy matters; but . . . the bulk of it deals with exceedingly broad questions of goals and performance: "Peace, Progress, and Prosperity." Only rarely do ordinary campaign remarks describe specific policies which the candidate undertakes to pursue.[75]

It is not only candidate behavior that explains the paucity of issue coverage, however. As a result of the prevailing approach to election campaigns, reporters are less concerned with the merits or demerits of policy proposals than with the political consequences of these proposals. Statements on issues are usually considered newsworthy only if they represent a *change,* an *inconsistency* with other positions, or an *impracticality* that reflects unfavorably on the intelligence of the candidate. As one campaign consultant has argued:

> I have been associated with many candidates who made a serious effort to present substantive policy statements on a variety of issues, and I have seen 100-page research documents presented for solutions on the Middle East and energy crisis and so forth. And there was also a deliberate attempt not to hype it, to present it as a serious substantive statement. It got virtually no coverage.[76]

There is much evidence that belies the journalist's claim that candidates make it impossible (rather than merely difficult) to concentrate on political issues. When journalists *have* had an opportunity to interrogate candidates and prevent the latter from completely controlling the flow of information, they do not show much enthusiasm for focusing on questions of public policy. For example, in 1976 seven presidential candidates appeared on ABC's "Issues and Answers," CBS's "Face the Nation," and NBC's "Meet the Press" during February and March. Such shows represent an excellent opportunity for the press to solicit the type of policy-related information that may be otherwise difficult to gather and unavailable for transmission. Despite this opportunity, 45 percent of the journalists' questions (and 42 percent of the answers) focused on the type of campaign activity, horse-race themes (victory prospects, strategy, organization, polls, finances) that we have found to be a dominant feature of news coverage in general.[77] Similarly, face-to-face candidate debates are usually far more policy-oriented than any other form of campaign communication. Nonetheless, the news media accounts that follow these debates typically focus on such things as the candidates' debate performance and perceptions of the debate winner rather than on issue-related information. Newspaper coverage of the first presidential debate in 1976 devoted only 22 percent of the space to issues, and only 16 percent of television news time was devoted to issues. Across all the debates, issue and policy coverage was estimated at 31–36 percent for newspapers, television news, *Time,* and *Newsweek*—despite the fact that the interrogating reporters spent 92 percent of their time on issues and the candidates responded with issue-related comments about 80 percent of the time.[78]

The *New York Times,* by contrast, stands out as an exception to this general pattern: 78 percent of its coverage of the debates focused on issues.[79] Finally, most presidential candidates have records of actions taken in some public office over the years. These could be used by journalists to introduce a discussion of candidates' policy preferences. Unless a candidate's *opponent* raises an issue of a candidate's conduct in office, however, journalists seldom use previous behavior as a guide to understanding the values and political philosophy of candidates.

It seems, then, that both candidates and journalists must share responsibility for the paucity of campaign coverage that focuses on policy alternatives and programmatic substance. For candidates, the design of pseudoevents and the repetition of vague stump speeches has served the purposes of stimulating daily news coverage and avoiding offending large segments of the electorate. For journalists, the description of campaign activities and concentration on the horse race provide a straightforward way to meet daily deadlines, prevent controversies over biased coverage, and—it must be admitted—make a campaign minimally interesting to the citizenry. The qualitative content of campaign news coverage, however, raises the possibility that the citizenry probably learns little about the candidates from its exposure to most campaign accounts. Doris Graber, for example, has concluded that "information is ample on personal qualifications of the major mainstream candidates and on day-to-day campaign events" but that it is "sketchy and often confusing on most professional qualifications, on substantive issues, and on the policy options involved in these issues."[80] James David Barber's indictment of television news coverage, with which we began this chapter, is still more severe. Jeff Greenfield's indictment of 1980 press coverage is even more troubling:

> So prevalent was the "spectator sport" analysis of the campaign that when the "issues" were covered, through the device of excerpted interviews with the candidates in the last weeks of the campaign, they almost seemed an afterthought, something divorced from the real election, which was, of course, solely a question of who would win what votes.
>
> Implicit in this sort of coverage was the premise that issues, the past records of the candidates, their intentions about the economy or social issues or foreign affairs were pure tinsel, the necessary but irrelevant trappings of a struggle for great power. For the voter, this view of politics carried with it a clear corollary: that the fight for the Presidency was a struggle fought far beyond the boundaries of home, family, job, neighborhood, community; a struggle about which a citizen had almost nothing to say. Convince a citizen that politics is indeed a spectator sport, and that citizen is left with nothing to do save cast a vote and stand on the sideline cheering and booing. But even this becomes difficult when a campaign is covered only tactically and strategically. A Pittsburg resident knows which teams to root for: the Pirates, the Steelers, and the Penguins. It goes with the territory. But who does a citizen cheer for in a campaign if he has no idea which candidate is speaking to his interest? How does a citizen know what the stakes are in a contest of political power if the link between citizen and presumptive President are never spelled out?[81]

Clearly, the most significant political impact of campaign coverage may be the learning that the campaign permits or encourages. We will return to a careful consideration of the educative value of campaign coverage in the next chapter.

Editorial Endorsements

So far we have considered only the political judgments that journalists make in their daily news coverage of presidential campaigns. This is the primary avenue through which journalists exercise influence, but it is not the only one. Another political judgment is offered by editors and publishers in their decisions concerning the endorsement of candidates for public office. Endorsements themselves are important political resources, since they may have some effect on undecided voters; they may also be used by candidates in an indirect way, as when Gerald Ford used Georgia newspaper endorsements of his candidacy in 1976 as the basis for a television spot ad designed to show that Jimmy Carter was not supported in his home state.

Although all media organizations have the legal right to endorse political candidates, the broadcast media seldom do so, because federal regulations hold that a broadcaster that endorses a candidate must grant free time to reply to all other candidates for that office. Since this could amount to an unprofitable use of a significant amount of air time, few broadcasters exercise this right. Most candidate endorsements appear in the print media.

Over the years the vast majority of newspaper endorsements have favored the Republican party, because most newspaper publishers are Republican identifiers. At the presidential level about three-fifths of the nation's dailies usually endorse the Republican candidate, with about one-fifth endorsing the Democrat and one-fifth endorsing no one. In terms of circulation this Republican advantage is even greater, with about 70 percent of the national daily press audience exposed to newspapers endorsing the Republican candidate. Since 1940, 1964 has been the only year in which a plurality of newspapers endorsed the Democratic candidate for president.

Although evidence is fragmentary, this Republican advantage probably also pertains in state elections. In the 1966 Michigan gubernatorial campaign, for example, twenty of twenty-six Michigan newspapers (seventeen dailies and nine weeklies) endorsed Republican George Romney for governor; none of the papers endorsed the Democratic candidate, Zolton Ferency.[82] It is hardly surprising, then, that Democratic candidates have considered access to the citizenry through the broadcast media to be absolutely necessary as a balancing force.

Given the fact that most editorial endorsements of candidates come just before election day and that voters base their candidate choice on a number of different factors, it would be surprising if endorsements themselves were a particularly significant form of campaign communication. Nonetheless, for those who are undecided or who have little information about an electoral contest, a newspaper endorsement in a well-regarded daily might be influential. In Chapter 7 we will return to this question and look at some evidence that endorsements can have a small but noticeable effect on voting behavior, particularly in lower-level campaigns.

Election Returns

Media coverage of election campaigns concludes with the reporting and projection of vote returns on election night. Over the span of U.S. electoral history, the amount of time elapsing between the casting of votes and the reporting of the returns has decreased significantly. The penetration of the broadcast media and the development of news services for the rapid reporting of returns have now made same-day reporting of returns commonplace.

Since 1964, however, a qualitative change in returns coverage has occurred. The news organizations of the television networks are no longer content merely to report the vote returns as they are tabulated. They are now interested in projecting election results as quickly as possible—and before their competition does—and in explaining the outcome of the election. To do this, each network has developed a computer-based model that takes a sample of actual returns, compares them with past races, and projects an eventual result on that basis. Although the models used by the three networks vary, they all involve the selection of so-called sample precincts and the analysis of returns in those precincts. In 1980, for example, CBS news relied on 4,000 key precincts out of a nationwide total of 175,000 precincts.

Ever since the networks began doing this sort of analysis, tremendous pressures have built up to be the first to announce the projected result. In 1980 the three networks spent $7 million on this election-night programming. This sort of competition derives not only from professional rivalries but is also thought by the networks to be an important ingredient in the ongoing promotion of one's own news show. NBC News, which has been the network to project the result first in the last three presidential elections, has used this "accomplishment" in advertisements urging viewers to tune in to the "NBC Nightly News."

Throughout the history of network projections, most projections of state-level results in both presidential and nonpresidential races have been accurate. In 1976 there were only two incorrect calls all year, and during the 1980 primaries there were no mistakes at all. CBS has had only one incorrect call in the past thirteen years.[83]

The *accuracy* of the network projections has never been particularly controversial, however. Rather, it is the *timing* of the projections that has caused problems. Because of the three-hour time differential across the forty-eight continental states, it is possible for returns to be collected and projections made before the polls have closed on the West Coast. This raises the possibility of West Coast citizens knowing the estimated electoral outcomes before they actually vote.

In 1980 the network projections caused more controversy than ever before, for a number of reasons. First, NBC's projections came sooner (8:15 P.M. Eastern Standard Time, 5:15 P.M. on the West Coast) than most projections have in the past, and were broadcast almost three full hours before most West Coast polls closed. Second, numerous West Coast races for the U.S. House were decided by narrow margins (less than 10 percent) in 1980; since about 15 to 20 percent of West Coast voters typically vote between 6 P.M. and 8 P.M., if the projections affected the voting behavior of West Coast voters, the outcomes of some of these races could have been altered by the projections. Third, there were anecdotal reports of West Coast voters leaving the polls without voting when the projections became known, and a subsequent CBS News–*New York Times* public opinion poll found that 10 percent of West Coast citizens claimed that they had not voted because of the network projections. Finally, 1980 was the first year in which a network based its projection on *exit polls* rather than actual returns. Exit polls are personal interviews conducted outside the polling places throughout the day by survey organizations. NBC used them to project the results in some states and to enable them to announce their projection one and a half hours before ABC and two and a quarter hours before CBS.[84]

As a result of the controversy over NBC's early projection in 1980, a number of legal reforms have been proposed to prevent early projections from influencing subsequent voting behavior. One of these would involve legislating a national poll-closing time so that no returns could be reported until all polls are closed. Other proposals would shift election day to Sunday, spread voting over two days, or make election day a national holiday so that a uniform closing time would not represent a hardship for workers. Still other proposals would prevent election officials from releasing returns or forbid the networks from issuing projections until the polls close.

Only the last proposal would prevent networks from using exit polls to project results, but it raises constitutional questions about the abridgment of First Amendment rights of freedom of the press. Depending on the voluntary restraint of networks, however, does not seem promising given the competitive pressure felt by the networks and their position that the news ought to be reported as soon as it is acquired.

Much of the debate over network projections involves presumptions about the behavioral effect of the projections on West Coast voters. In Chapter 7 we will return to this issue and review the evidence collected so far on this matter.

Conclusion

In this chapter we have seen a number of ways in which journalists' news coverage of election campaigns is influenced by the behavior of candidates and journalists alike. In the selection and presentation of news stories, journalists exercise significant but constrained political judgment when deciding which candidates will receive news coverage, how to interpret campaign events, how to portray the campaigns of different candidates, and the meaning of the election campaign itself.

Although it is fairly common to conclude that news coverage of election campaigns (or of any newsworthy event, for that matter) is a considerable distance from the "reality" of the campaign, it is more difficult to understand why and to what degree that is the case. Most commentators on this subject assert that the reason is "bias," by which they mean the manifestation and expression of the political values and preferences of journalists. Here we concluded, however, that a more likely explanation is that a combination of economic and political constraints, the norms of journalism as a professional activity, and the objectives and goals of journalists and the news organizations within which they work influence the news coverage of election campaigns. This is a position with which journalists typically only partially agree. They often cite the objectivity norm as evidence that their news reports do not contain explicit opinions or commentaries. Less often do they acknowledge that their news stories are interpretive, patterned, and reflective of their own perspectives and approaches. Furthermore, this conclusion that the patterns in news coverage are more typically the result of structural than of political bias does not absolve journalists of all responsibility for their actions. Whether intentional or not, patterns in news coverage have important consequences for citizen responses and the electoral process.

It is possible now to speculate about some of the consequences of the campaign coverage we have just described, particularly as it relates to the prospects of civic education during election campaigns. A number of possibilities are plausible. First, given the pattern in news coverage of delegate-selection processes and candidates during the presidential nomination campaign, it is likely that citizens will learn more about some candidates than about others during that crucial stage. In fact, the dearth of coverage given to many candidates means that some candidates will remain largely invisible to citizens throughout the entire nomination process.

Second, given the tendency of journalists to interpret the significance of campaign events and to portray the campaigns of different candidates with some variation (albeit of an implicit, subtle nature), we might also expect citizens to form more favorable impressions of some candidates than others and to have these impressions shaped by news coverage. In fact, given the proclivity of journalists to introduce and emphasize thematic contexts for candidate coverage, we might expect citizens to learn and react to these same thematic choices.

Third, given journalism's perspective on campaigns as candidate contests and the preference for the kind of campaign-related information to which that perspective leads, we might expect the range of learning exhibited by the citizenry during election campaigns to be extremely limited. The focus on the horse race and on personal rather than political attributes of candidates would seem to make learning about the governing capabilities and policy preferences of candidates extremely unlikely. What learning does occur, then, might be limited to perceptions of who is likely to win and the personal styles of presidential candidates.

Finally, journalism's recent disdain for political candidates and the presidential selection process would seem to affect the public's interest in, support for, and involvement with the electoral process. A portrayal of candidates and process that is largely negative and not unlike the coverage of any spectator sport would be likely to engender cynicism on the part of the U.S. public.

In the next chapters we will take up these hypotheses as we explore the public's response to the campaign communication we have discussed. There we will consider, among other questions, what citizens learn during election campaigns and to what degree the communication of candidates and journalists contributes to this educative process.

Notes

1. Arthur T. Hadley, *The Invisible Primary* (Englewood Cliffs, N.J.: Prentice-Hall, 1976), pp. 187–188.

2. Ernest R. May and Janet Fraser, eds., *Campaign '72: The Managers Speak* (Cambridge, Mass.: Harvard University Press, 1973), p. 37; and Martin Schram, *Running for President 1976: The Carter Campaign* (New York: Stein and Day, 1977), pp. 52–61.

3. Jeff Greenfield, *The Real Campaign* (New York: Summit Books, 1982), pp. 115–116.

4. *New York Times*, November 4, 1979, p. A-1.

5. *The Philadelphia Inquirer*, April 10, 1983, p. 3-A.

6. David L. Paletz and Robert M. Entman, *Media, Power, Politics* (New York: Free Press, 1981), p. 40.

7. Greenfield, *The Real Campaign*, p. 66.

8. Paletz and Entman, *Media, Power, Politics*, pp. 35–36.

9. "ABC News Viewpoint," April 21, 1983, p. 14 of the transcript.

10. Paul H. Weaver, "Captives of Melodrama," *New York Times Magazine*, August 29, 1976, p. 54.

11. Bill Peterson, "It Is Easy to Overlook Minnesota," *Philadelphia Inquirer*, February 24, 1980.

12. Donald Matthews, "Winnowing," in James David Barber, ed., *Race for the Presidency: The Media and the Nominating Process* (Englewood Cliffs, N.J.: Prentice-Hall, 1978); and John Foley, Dennis A. Britton, and Eugene B. Everett, Jr., eds., *Nominating a President: The Process and the Press* (New York: Praeger, 1980), pp. 8–18.

13. Thomas Patterson, *The Mass Media Election* (New York: Praeger, 1980), pp. 45–46.

14. Thomas E. Patterson, "Press Coverage and Candidate Success in Presidential Primaries: The 1976 Democratic Race," Paper presented to the American Political Science Association, 1977, p. 4.

15. Ibid.

16. Weaver, "Captives of Melodrama," p. 52.

17. Greenfield, *The Real Campaign*, pp. 38–50.

18. Ibid., p. 50.

19. Patterson, *Mass Media Election*, pp. 45–46; and William E. Bichter, "Network Television News and the 1976 Presidential Primaries," in Barber, *Race for the Presidency*, p. 93, pp. 79–110. See also Greenfield, *The Real Campaign*, p. 103.

20. Patterson, *Mass Media Election*, pp. 43–48.

21. Patterson, "Press Coverage."

22. Patterson, *Mass Media Election*, p. 45; and Paletz and Entman, *Media, Power, Politics*, p. 36.

23. Patterson, "Press Coverage."

24. Lutz Erbring, "Media Monitoring and Public Opinion Change in 1980," Paper presented to the American Political Science Association, 1981.

25. Doris Graber, *Mass Media and American Politics* (Washington, D.C.: Congressional Quarterly Press, 1980), pp. 174–175.

26. Edwin Diamond, *Good News, Bad News* (Cambridge, Mass.: MIT Press, 1978), pp. 16–17.

27. Greenfield, *The Real Campaign*, pp. 66–79, 85–90, 98–103, 112–129.

28. Erbring, "Media Monitoring"; and Michael J. Robinson, "A Statesman is a Dead Politician: Candidate Images on Network News," in Elie Abel, ed., *What's News* (San Francisco: Institute for Contemporary Studies, 1981), pp. 159–186.

29. Robinson, "A Statesman."

30. Weaver, "Captives of Melodrama," p. 56.

31. Greenfield, *The Real Campaign*, pp. 107–108.

32. Ibid., p. 40.

33. Lee B. Becker and Maxwell E. McCombs, "The Role of the Press in Determining Voter Reactions to Presidential Primaries," *Human Communication Research* 4, no. 4 (Summer 1978): 301–307.

34. Patterson, *Mass Media Election*, pp. 51–53.

35. Erbring, "Media Monitoring."

36. Roan Conrad, political editor, NBC News, quoted in *The Wilson Quarterly*, Spring 1977, p. 84.

37. Patterson, *Mass Media Election*, p. 53.

38. Greenfield, *The Real Campaign*, p. 26.

39. Ibid., p. 154.

40. Timothy Crouse, *The Boys on the Bus* (New York: Ballantine, 1974), pp. 140, 164–165; Frank Greve, "As Show Biz, It Was a Bomb," *The Philadelphia Inquirer,* July 20, 1980, p. 1-C; Greenfield, *The Real Campaign*, pp. 154–155, 175.

41. Crouse, *Boys on the Bus*, pp. 176–177.

42. Greve, "As Show Biz."

43. Graber, *Mass Media*, p. 168; and Richard Hofstetter, *Bias in the News* (Columbus: Ohio State University Press, 1976), Chap. 1.

44. Robert Shelby Frank, *Message Dimensions of Television News* (Lexington, Mass.: Lexington Books, D.C. Heath, 1973), p. 7.

45. For example, see Crouse, *Boys on the Bus*, p. 159.

46. Robert L. Stevenson, Richard A. Eisinger, Barry M. Feinberg, and Alan B. Kotok, "Untwisting *The News Twisters*: A Replication of Efron's Study," in Susan Welch and John Comer, eds., *Public Opinion* (Palo Alto, Calif.: Mayfield, 1975).

47. Frank, *Message Dimensions*; and Hofstetter, *Bias in the News.*

48. Graber, *Mass Media*, p. 160.

49. Susan H. Evans and Peter Clarke, "Press Coverage and Competition for House Seats: Another Incumbent Edge," Paper presented to the American Political Science Association, 1981.

50. Jules Becker and Douglas A. Fuchs, "How Two Major California Dailies Covered Reagan vs. Brown," *Journalism Quarterly* 44 (Winter 1967): 645–653.

51. Frank, *Message Dimensions.*

52. Hofstetter, *Bias in the News*, pp. 55–56, 62.

53. Frank, *Message Dimensions*, pp. 45–47.

54. Hofstetter, *Bias in the News*, pp. 60–67.

55. Robinson, "A Statesman," pp. 178–182.

56. Graber, *Mass Media*, p. 174.

57. Weaver, "Captives of Melodrama."

58. Greenfield, *The Real Campaign*, pp. 269–270.

59. Paul H. Weaver, "The New Journalism and the Old—Thoughts after Watergate," *Public Interest* 35 (Spring 1974): 67–88.

60. Stevenson et al., "Untwisting *The News Twisters.*"

61. Thomas E. Patterson and Robert D. McClure, *The Unseeing Eye* (New York: G. P. Putnam, 1976), pp. 27–46.

62. Patterson, *Mass Media Election*, pp. 21–30.

63. Robinson, "A Statesman," p. 161.

64. Greenfield, *The Real Campaign*, p. 269.

65. Patterson and McClure, *The Unseeing Eye*, p. 39.

66. Ibid., p. 34.

67. Graber, *Mass Media*, pp. 169–183.

68. Patterson and McClure, *The Unseeing Eye*, pp. 186–187.

69. Ibid., pp. 186–187.

70. Patterson, *Mass Media Election*, pp. 34–37.

71. Ibid., p. 34.

72. *The Wilson Quarterly*, Spring 1977, pp. 85–86.

73. James Gannon, quoted in Foley, Britton, and Everett, *Nominating a President*, p. 49.

74. Benjamin I. Page, *Choices and Echoes in Presidential Elections* (Chicago: University of Chicago Press, 1978), pp. 153–162.

75. Ibid., p. 110.

76. John Martilla, as quoted in Foley, Britton, and Everett, *Nominating a President*, p. 76.

77. Thomas E. Patterson, "The Media Muffed the Message," *The Washington Post*, December 5, 1976, pp. B1/B4.

78. David O. Sears and Steven H. Chaffee, "Uses and Effects of the 1976 Debates: An Overview of Empirical Studies," in Sidney Kraus, ed., *The Great Debate, 1976: Carter v. Ford* (Bloomington: Indiana University Press, 1979).

79. Robert G. Meadow and Marilyn Jackson-Beeck, "A Comparative Perspective on Presidential Debates: Issue Evolution in 1960 and 1976," in George F. Bishop, Robert G. Meadow, and Marilyn Jackson-Beeck, eds., *The Presidential Debates* (New York: Praeger, 1978).

80. Graber, *Mass Media*, p. 180.

81. Greenfield, *The Real Campaign,* p. 272.

82. Robert L. Bishop and Robert L. Brown, "Michigan Newspaper Bias in the 1966 Campaign," *Journalism Quarterly* 45 (Summer 1968): 337–338, 375.

83. "Election Night Razzle-Dazzle," *Time,* November 3, 1980, p. 75.

84. Larry Light, "Early Returns Inconclusive," *Philadelphia Inquirer,* August 16, 1981, p. 3-M; "Peacock's Night to Crow," *Newsweek,* November 17, 1980, p. 82; "Like a Suburban Swimming Pool," *Time,* November 17, 1980, p. 97; and Elmer W. Lower, "Is Television Undermining our Elections?" *TV Guide,* January 17, 1981.

6

The Effects of Campaign
News Coverage
on Citizen Beliefs
and Attitudes

*[Campaign] learning levels do not generally come close to the democratic vision
of voters who fully understand the issues, know the positions of the candidates,
and are able to evaluate them and judge the capabilities of the candidates to perform as promised. . . . Despite large amounts of available information, most people learn very few dimensions of the candidates' images and even fewer aspects of
issues.*

—David H. Weaver et al., *Media Agenda-Setting in a
Presidential Election*

*Primarily because network campaign news contains so little meaningful informa-
tion, it fails to have any meaningful effect on the viewer's feelings about the candidates and knowledge of the issues.*

—Thomas E. Patterson and Robert D. McClure, *The Unseeing Eye**

Introduction

In previous chapters we have discussed how candidates and other campaigners devise and deliver their campaign appeals, and how journalists
acquaint the public with what they—the journalists—consider the newsworthy features of a campaign. In this and the following chapters we will
investigate the public's response to this campaign communication. In
this chapter we will focus on the impact that campaign news coverage
has on the beliefs and attitudes of the citizenry. In subsequent chapters
we will discuss the impact of spot ads and candidate debates, and the
effect of campaign communication on the choices made by voters.

*This and subsequent excerpts from *The Unseeing Eye* (New York: G. P. Putnam's, 1976)
are reprinted by permission.

Measuring the effects of campaign communication on public opinion is difficult and complex. One barrier to understanding the impact of campaign communication is that to date there has been little competent empirical research on this question. Most of the research that has been completed has focused on presidential election campaigns, for example, and has concentrated on the effect of campaign communication on *voting behavior* rather than on citizen beliefs or attitudes. Furthermore, much of our current understanding of opinion change during election campaigns has been shaped by studies conducted prior to the introduction of television and prior to the changes in candidate communication and campaign news coverage described in previous chapters. Consequently, there are large gaps in our knowledge about the effect of campaign communication during modern campaigns on citizen beliefs and attitudes.

A second barrier to understanding the impact of campaign communication is the more general problem of demonstrating such *effects*. Candidates and campaign consultants obviously believe that campaign communication has substantial effects on public opinion, or Richard Nixon presumably would not have spent $61 million to get reelected to the presidency in 1972, nor would Jesse Helms have spent $6 million to get reelected to the U.S. Senate from North Carolina in 1978. The fact that candidates and consultants *believe* in the effectiveness of their communication, however, does not tell us much about exactly what those effects are.

Empirical demonstration that campaign communication has a particular effect on public opinion would ideally include prior specification of the hypothesized effect, measurement of the relevant opinions both before and after the campaign communication has occurred, a comparison of the opinions of those exposed to the communication with those who were not exposed, and the elimination of all other possible reasons that those exposed to the communication might differ from those unexposed. Considering the variety of opinions that might be influenced by campaign communication; the multitude of communication stimuli that might be studied (each spot ad shown, each television newscast, each magazine article?); and the difficulty of measuring the exposure of individuals to each of these communication stimuli, this method of demonstrating effects is well beyond the reach of most researchers. Those who have the resources for such extensive probing of the opinions of the body politic during an election campaign are usually connected with the campaigns of a presidential candidate, and their data are seldom made available for the kind of inquiry that is necessary to study the effectiveness of campaign communication.

Despite this pessimistic introduction, our understanding of campaign communication and the response of the citizenry during a modern campaign has been substantially increased in recent years. For example, we now have excellent studies of the effects of candidate debates because the timing, advance warning, and limited number of debates lend themselves to affordable research designs. Competent studies of the effects of news coverage and advertising campaigns are fewer but are increasing in both number and quality. Moreover, a shift in the focus of attention from the campaign communication of the presidential general election campaign to nomination and nonpresidential campaigns is well underway and is beginning to yield fresh insights into the process of opinion change. Consequently, we know much more about how campaign communication shapes the public's response today than we did just ten years ago.

Before we begin our review of the evidence regarding the impact of campaign communication, we should consider what we would expect this review to demonstrate. One way to approach this subject is to specify more precisely what we mean by a campaign communication effect. We may do this by considering the *kind of effect* we are talking about, what *source of communication* is thought to have the effect, and what *portion of the citizenry* is apt to be affected.

The *sources of campaign communication* thought to affect the public are the easiest to specify. In previous chapters, we have discussed how candidates for public office have come to rely more heavily on spot advertising and debate appearances as methods of transmitting their messages to the citizenry, and how journalism has been devoting more extensive resources to the news coverage of campaigns. At the higher levels of elective office, then, the most pervasive and potent sources of impact on citizen opinions ought to be paid candidate advertising, broadcast candidate debates, and daily news coverage. These are the three main types of campaign communication dealt with in this and the following chapter.[1]

The *kinds of effects* that these sources of communication might have on the public are more extensive and less certain. When we think about the effects that exposure to campaign communication has on the citizenry, we usually think first of the possibility that exposure alters the distribution of the votes cast. This is obviously one of the more significant and more noticeable effects that campaign communication can have, but it is by no means the only, the most likely, or even the most important one. Exposure to campaign communication may also affect the salience of political issues to the citizenry; levels of recognition and awareness of various candidates for public office; expectations concerning the likely outcome of particular campaign events (such as face-to-face debates) and of the election itself; perceptions of the personal characteristics and policy preferences of candidates; attitudes toward policy alternatives; and evaluations of the worth of the electoral process itself. Although many of these effects are significant because of their impact on electoral choices, they also have a bearing on how well informed the public is generally and on the legitimacy of elections as a means of resolving political conflict. Candidates and journalists are understandably concerned primarily with the short-term impact of these opinion changes on the casting of votes; but scholars are also interested in the long-term impact of these opinions on our understanding of the message sent by voters in casting their votes, and in the contribution made by elections to the achievement of an informed populace capable of self-government. In this chapter we will consider a number of these possible effects of campaign communication, with a special focus on what the citizenry learns from its exposure to campaign news coverage.

Finally, we should also consider the *portion of the citizenry* most likely to be affected by campaign communication. In thinking about the likely effects of exposure to campaign communication, there is a tendency to assume that the messages are "injected" into a defenseless audience, whose members then all react to the messages in more or less the same way. This "hypodermic needle" model of media effects, as the view has come to be labeled, is far too simple a description of how individuals respond to political information. Rather, campaign communication is used by individuals who differ in their interests, their attitudes and perceptions, the social milieu in which they live, and their reasons for using the mass media. This suggests that not all individuals will respond to the same campaign messages in the same way.

One way in which citizens differ is in their approach to mass media exposure. Different people make different "uses" of the mass media and receive different "gratifications" from media exposure.[2] For example, some individuals may watch television primarily to be entertained, whereas others watch it mainly to be informed. Similarly, some types of programming may be expected to entertain, other types to inform. Therefore, different people may be looking for and may remember different messages from campaign communication, depending on their reasons for using a particular medium or program.

The social milieu within which the individual operates also affects citizen responses to campaign communication. The "two-step flow" model of communication perspective, for example, has asserted that some people are directly exposed to campaign communication but that others experience it only secondhand through the perspective of "opinion leaders."[3] Anyone who has traced the accuracy of information transmitted through many different people knows that the information can be significantly altered in the process.

The two-step-flow perspective is just one of many approaches to information processing that recognizes the importance of a person's social context. In general, the social interaction that occurs during or subsequent to exposure to campaign communication may have a significant effect on how that information is processed and stored. One's daily contacts with friends, co-workers, and family members can reinforce, highlight, or contradict the meaning given to any form of campaign communication.

Finally, citizens also vary in the interests, perceptions, and predispositions they possess prior to encountering new (that is, campaign) information. These existing attitudes and beliefs form a perceptual screen that influences the patterns of exposure and attention to, and the interpretation and storage of incoming information.[4] These processes allow individuals to protect themselves from unpleasant information and to process and store information in a personally relevant fashion. These processes also mean that campaign communication may never reach the intended audience, may be ignored or distorted by the audience, and may be forgotten or stored in such a way that recall of the information is unlikely. Although there are ways of circumventing this perceptual screen (such as overwhelming it by saturating the individual with massive amounts of information—the so-called media blitz—or by sneaking the information past the screen when the person's defenses are down) an awareness of these processes should serve to temper expectations that a persuasive message will be received and perceived in a straightforward way by the intended recipients.

For example, people are more apt to be exposed to some campaign communication than to others. Some of this *selective exposure* is purposeful, as when a Republican decides not to watch the Democratic nomination convention; some of it is accidental, as when the bus one takes to work contains a poster promoting a candidate's campaign. In general, the selective exposure that is purposeful is used by individuals to filter out information with which they are likely to disagree or in which they are likely to be uninterested. Thus conservatives seldom read liberal magazines, Democrats seldom watch Republican election-eve telethons, and a candidate's supporters seldom read the opposition's direct mail appeals.[5]

In a similar fashion, people often *selectively perceive* the communication to which they are exposed. This usually involves an individual evaluating a message in such a way that it reinforces existing attitudes or makes sense within an existing belief system. Republicans and Democrats may perceive quite different messages from a Republican presidential candidate's debate performance. Democrats may perceive that the candidate was tentative and inarticulate; Republicans may perceive that he was cautious and temperate. What one person perceives as a bold proposal another sees as foolhardy nonsense; what one sees as progressive another calls radical; what one sees as admirable honesty another sees as manipulative artifice; and so on. It is by no means certain, then, that what a campaign communicator intends to be the message will be perceived to be the message by the recipient.[6]

Given these barriers to the receipt and understanding of any communication, it is clear that the probability of all citizens responding to campaign messages in the same manner is fairly low. Consequently, it is reasonable to expect that the effects of campaign communication will be different for different portions of the public.

In the remainder of this chapter we will review what we currently know about the effects of campaign news coverage on public opinion. Our discussion will consider how news coverage influences the public's beliefs and attitudes and what kinds of learning take place during election campaigns, largely presidential campaigns.

The Effects of Campaign News Coverage

Given the resources that candidates expend to influence news coverage of their election campaigns, and the resources committed by news organizations to the coverage of campaigns, it hardly seems necessary to consider whether all this activity has any effect on the beliefs and attitudes of the U.S. public. After all, most citizens depend on the media for most of their information about election campaigns and most citizens consider this coverage to be credible, trustworthy, and unbiased.[7] Furthermore, there are enough anecdotes of campaign news coverage apparently affecting the voting behavior of the electorate that it seems evident that news coverage shapes citizen perceptions and attitudes. For example, it is widely believed that the news coverage by the New Hampshire *Manchester Union Leader* in 1972 led to Edmund Muskie's tearful breakdown during a speech in New Hampshire, his less-than-impressive victory in the New Hampshire primary, and his eventual withdrawal from the 1972 Democratic nomination campaign; that the press's lack of access to Richard Nixon during the 1972 general election campaign contributed to his landslide victory; that the *New York Daily News* headline of a 1976 story regarding Gerald Ford's veto of the U.S. Congress's attempt to provide financial assistance for New York City—"FORD TO NY: DROP DEAD"—cost him enough votes in New York City to provide Jimmy Carter with his margin of victory in New York State and the resulting margin of victory in the electoral college; and that Edward Kennedy's appearance on a 1979 news interview show on CBS with Roger Mudd damaged his campaign for the 1980 Democratic presidential nomination.

These intriguing examples of the presumed effect of news coverage do not really tell us much about the *systematic* effect of news coverage on public opinion. What kind of news coverage (say, print or broadcast) has more effect? Does coverage of some election campaigns, or of some stages of an election campaign, have more effect than coverage of others? Are some beliefs or attitudes more easily influenced than others are? Are some citizens more readily affected than others? Indeed, is there evidence that news coverage has much of a systematic effect at all on the public; and to what extent can news coverage be said to produce an informed electorate?

Most of us probably suspect that news coverage is effective for changing campaign-related beliefs and attitudes, but there are several good reasons that these effects might be minimal. We saw in Chapter 5 that the content of most election coverage by the U.S. press focuses on campaign hoopla rather than on the substance of the electoral contest. It would be difficult to imagine the U.S. public learning much about the issue positions or ideologies of the candidates from this election coverage. Also we have seen (Chapter 3), that exposure to news coverage is selective in terms of both interest and partisan predisposition. Most citizens are far more interested in how their favorite football team is doing or in Ann Landers's response to her mail than in the activities of political candidates. Most people, moreover, are far more interested in what the candidate for whom they intend to vote is doing than in what the opponent is doing. Given that the time we spend monitoring news coverage and the amount of information we can store in our memories are limited, it may be that news coverage of election campaigns has little measurable effect after all. Empirical research suggests that news coverage of election campaigns does affect public opinion but that the effects are neither as pervasive nor as substantial as we might have thought.

AGENDA SETTING

One effect of campaign news coverage that has been fairly well documented is called *agenda setting*. Agenda setting is the ability of news coverage to affect the composition of the political agenda—that is, to influence those issues, events, themes, or persons that the public considers important enough to think and talk about. The agenda-setting hypothesis asserts that "increased salience of a topic or issue in the mass media influences (causes) the salience of that topic or issue among the public."[8] This does not mean that the media necessarily affect whether we approve of, say, Iran's seizure of U.S. citizens or the price of gold or the approval for flight of DC-10s; but tells us, rather, that these are the issues and events that are important at this time. That is, the media may not influence whether we favor military action against Iran, or the imposition of import duties, or the grounding of DC-10s, but instead encourage us to think about these things rather than other political issues such as the nutritional value of our food supply, the effect of minimum-wage legislation on minority youth employment, the construction of nuclear power plants, or the utility of various income tax deductions. Political activists recognize that to get their cause or issue on the political agenda is half the battle; once it is there, it is far more likely that something will be done about it. Similarly, political candidates recognize that the content of the political agenda can influence their electoral fortunes, since candidates usually benefit from the discussion of some issues (say, Democrats from the issues of civil rights and unemployment and Republicans from the issues of inflation and foreign policy) and suffer from the discussion of others. To many candidates, control of the political agenda during an election campaign is a crucial part of campaign strategy. For example, George McGovern's failure to place Watergate on the political agenda during the 1972 presidential general election undoubtedly damaged his presidential campaign; Ronald Reagan's ability to focus the 1980 campaign on what his pollster called the "pocketbook issue cluster"—inflation, taxes, unemployment—probably worked to his advantage.[9]

AGENDA SETTING APPLIED TO POLITICAL ISSUES

The evidence for an agenda-setting effect of the media usually involves demonstrating that the topics covered in various media during election campaigns coincide closely with those considered important or worthy of discussion by the public. For example, one early study of the ability of the news media to shape the salience of political issues interviewed 100 undecided voters (thought to be the most susceptible to media effects) in a town in North Carolina during the 1968 presidential general election campaign, and asked them to indicate the political issues with which they thought the government should be dealing. At the same time the content of news coverage of the presidential campaign in the six newspapers, two weekly news magazines, and two network news broadcasts available in the community was divided into fifteen different issue categories (foreign policy, public welfare, civil rights, and so on). When the measures of the issues emphasized in the news coverage were compared with those of the issues considered important by the respondents, "a very strong relationship between the emphasis placed on different campaign issues by the media (reflecting to a considerable degree the emphasis by candidates) and the judgments of voters as to the salience and importance of various campaign topics" was found.[10]

Although a number of other studies have also found that the issues covered by the news media and those considered important by citizens are often in substantial agreement, such evidence is really only a weak test of the claim that media coverage itself *causes* the issues covered to become more salient to citizens. It could be, for example, that the media are responding to the concerns of their audience and focusing on those issues about which the public is concerned; or it could be that both news coverage and the citizen agenda are caused by some third factor, such as real world events or conditions. For example, newspapers might cover unemployment and people might care about unemployment because a lot of people are unemployed—not because the newspaper has arbitrarily decided that it should cover unemployment.

Considerable research attempting to verify this agenda-setting effect of campaign news coverage has been conducted in recent years. Researchers have attempted to determine if people exposed to different news media (because they read different newspapers, for example) have different political agendas that coincide with the campaign news contents of their respective news sources, whether media content or the political agenda come first in time, and what the impact of real-world events is on this relationship. Although different methods of conducting agenda-setting studies have led to a variety of results and conclusions, at this point the following summary of the agenda-setting effect on issue salience seems warranted.

First, at any given point there is usually a strong relationship between the issue content of election news coverage (at least for television and newspapers) and the issue concerns of citizens. The two agenda usually match.[11] It is seldom the case, however, that the audiences of different media (say, one newspaper versus another or one television station versus another) have substantially different issue agendas, or that they match up better with their favorite medium than with the news coverage of some other medium.[12] One reason for this is that the issues covered by different media outlets are usually very similar. Another reason might be that the shaping of the issue agenda among citizens is a more indirect, social phenomenon influenced by the sum total of news coverage rather than the direct result of exposure to one particular news source. During the 1976 presidential campaign, for example, there was some evidence that newspaper coverage was shaping television coverage, which in turn affected the voters' issue agenda.[13]

Second, the salience of some issues is more readily affected by media content than is that of other issues. The salience of unobtrusive issues—those that citizens experience primarily through the media (foreign troop movements, honesty in government, space exploration)—is more easily influenced by media presentations than is that of the obtrusive issues about which citizens have independent, personal sources of information (inflation, product shortages, mortgage rates, crime, mass transit dependability).[14] For some issues, such as the cost of living, there is probably a constant level of salience that exists independent of media content.

Third, it is uncertain whether newspapers or television have more effect on issue agendas. Generally newspapers have more effect, but this is hardly conclusive. It is probably more likely that television has more effect for some types of issues and newspapers have more effect for other types. Television's agenda-setting effect may be more short-term and that of newspapers more gradual; television may affect what people *talk* about whereas newspapers may affect what they *think* about; and television may affect the most important issues on the issue agenda and newspapers may fill in the rest.[15]

Fourth, there is some variation in which individuals are more suscepti-ble to the agenda-setting effect. Prior sensitization heightens the agenda-setting function of news coverage, as does lack of political interest, lack of political partisanship, and reliance on other news sources. For ex-ample, a citizen who initially is more concerned about unemployment (perhaps his or her father was just laid off) or crime (a friend was mugged) is more apt to be affected by news coverage dealing with these issues than are people who lack this prior concern. Also, agenda setting seems to occur more among people who have a high "need for orienta-tion" because of a large amount of political interest but uncertainty about some political issue or topic.[16]

Fifth, we are still uncertain whether changes in media content typically precede or follow changes in issue salience. Sometimes the concerns of citizens change while the media stay the same; other times the media move from issue to issue while the citizenry remains preoccupied with the same issue for years.[17] Part of the problem is that we do not have a very good idea how much time usually elapses between the media's first coverage of an issue and the time the issue appears on the voters' agenda. Does it take two days, two weeks, two months, or two years to alter the issue agenda substantially? Some issues, like hostile missiles in Cuba, get on a political agenda within hours; others, like Watergate, may take many months.

At this point there is enough evidence, both systematic and anecdotal, to support the validity of the general notion that news coverage during election campaigns does shape the kinds of issues discussed and talked about by citizens. The agenda-setting effect, however, is not an irresist-ible, omnipresent one that occurs consistently across all issues, times, media, and people. Instead, it occurs more regularly for some issues at some times in some media for some people. This does not diminish its importance as much as it challenges researchers to figure out the circum-stances under which agenda setting most typically operates. No one could tell George McGovern, who failed to force Watergate, poverty, and income tax policy onto the political agenda in 1972, that agenda setting is not an important phenomenon; nor could anyone tell Jimmy Carter and Ronald Reagan that in 1980 it really did not matter whether it was unemployment and inflation, or nuclear proliferation, that was on everybody's mind. Clearly, the issues that are covered by the media can affect both popular understanding and electoral outcomes:

> The discretion that newspeople enjoy in selecting issues to highlight or ignore gives them the potential to influence the outcome of presidential elections. . . . By making choices among issues, often quite independently from the stated issue priorities of the candidates and even from the flow of

real world events, the media may determine which candidate is shown in the best light and, hence, elected.[18]

AGENDA-SETTING APPLIED TO THE AWARENESS OF CANDIDATES

Just as we speak of the media affecting the agenda of issues considered worthy of discussion and consideration, it is also possible that the media affect the agenda of political *candidates* who become part of the public's awareness. A candidate who is ignored by the media is unlikely to be considered an appropriate subject of reflection or discussion and is unlikely to be considered a legitimate candidate for public office. A candidate's failure to get on the political agenda during an election campaign dooms that candidacy to failure.

The news media's effect on the candidate agenda has become increasingly important during presidential *nomination* campaigns. In recent years a large number of candidates for president have struggled to receive any amount of news coverage in the brief news-hole devoted to campaign politics in the early months of the presidential campaign. Many candidates find it necessary to drop out of the race even prior to the beginning of the delegate-selection process because their campaign activities fail to stimulate news coverage and campaign contributions.

For example, during the 1976 presidential nomination campaign there were numerous candidates for the Democratic nomination. Journalists had to decide which candidates to take seriously and how much coverage each would receive. The media had to make these decisions based on some criteria (such as having qualified for federal matching funds or having received votes in the early primary and caucus states); and these decisions resulted in unequal coverage for the candidates in the early stages of the nomination campaign (refer back to Table 5–2).

The effect of this unequal coverage of candidates was the reshaping of the list of candidates considered by the public to be serious, legitimate, possible nominees. Between February and April 1976, months before the Democratic nominee was actually selected, citizens were becoming aware of and informed about some candidates more than others and were forming perceptions about which candidates were likely to win and which were likely to lose (Table 6–1). In every case, Jimmy Carter was the main beneficiary of these changes. His name recognition changed the most, and by April 17 it equaled that of such prominent politicians as Hubert Humphrey and George Wallace. Possession of some additional information about Carter also increased the most, until people knew more about him than about any other candidate except Humphrey and Wallace; and, probably most important, perceptions that he was the leading candidate changed to an incredible degree.

TABLE 6–1   Recognition, Information, and Perception of
Democratic Contenders for the Presidential Nomination, 1976
(*Percent*)

	February	*April*	*Change*
Name Recognition			
Carter	57	99	+42
Jackson	56	89	+33
Udall	64	90	+26
Harris	44	61	+17
Bayh	58	73	+15
Shriver	89	94	+ 5
Humphrey	99	100	+ 1
Wallace	99	100	+ 1
Possession of Additional Information		*March*	
Carter	40.5	79.0	+38.5
Udall	35.1	57.2	+22.1
Jackson	52.3	72.8	+20.5
Shapp	18.9	35.5	+16.6
Shriver	62.5	76.9	+14.4
Bayh	34.2	45.7	+11.5
Church	22.0	33.2	+11.2
Humphrey	79.3	89.5	+10.2
Harris	25.8	35.0	+ 9.2
Wallace	81.4	89.5	+ 8.1
Bentsen	19.5	21.3	+ 1.8
Perception of Candidate in Lead		*March*	
Carter	2.7	62.5	+59.8
Udall	0.6	4.0	+ 3.4
Wallace	1.2	0.0	− 1.2
Other	2.3	0.0	− 2.3
Jackson	6.9	4.0	− 2.9
Humphrey	14.3	1.8	−12.5
Don't know	72.0	31.1	−40.9
	100.0	100.0	

Source: Thomas E. Patterson, "Press Coverage and Candidate Success in Presidential Primaries: The 1976 Democratic Race," Paper presented to annual meeting of the American Political Science Association, 1977; and Lee B. Becker and Maxwell E. McCombs, "The Role of the Press in Determining Voter Reactions to Presidential Primaries," *Human Communication Research* 4, no. 4 (Summer 1978): 301–307. Reprinted by permission of International Communication Association.

Three of the other Democratic candidates in 1976 (Shriver, Humphrey, and Wallace) were already on the voters' candidate agenda as a result of previous political activity. Two (Jackson and Udall) made it onto the political agenda at the same time Carter did; five more (Harris, Bayh, Shapp, Church, and Bentsen) failed to make it onto the candidate agenda at all.

This significant change in public awareness over such a short period of time can be traced to a combination of political events and news coverage. By early April 1976, six delegate-selection primaries had been conducted and covered by the media. Jimmy Carter received a plurality of the votes cast in New Hampshire (30 percent), Vermont (46 percent), Florida (34 percent), and Illinois (48 percent), and a majority in North Carolina (54 percent); Washington Senator Henry Jackson received a plurality in Massachusetts (22 percent of the vote; Carter received 14 percent—good enough for a fourth-place finish). To some extent, then, the placement of Carter and Jackson on the candidate agenda was a reflection of their successes in these contested primaries. Recall, however, the media blitz that accompanied Carter's "victory" in New Hampshire; recall that between February and April Carter received three to six times more coverage than any other candidate did, and that Udall, Jackson, and Wallace were the only other candidates to receive any appreciable amount of coverage during this period (Chapter 5). There is no doubt that Jimmy Carter ran an intelligent and effective nomination campaign in 1976 and that his efforts contributed substantially to his nomination. Media decisions concerning campaign coverage also benefited Carter (and hindered other candidates), however, and placed him on the candidate agenda with remarkable speed.

An indication of the importance of news coverage for the 1976 Carter nomination campaign is given in Figure 6–1. There we can see the trends over time of four important political resources: news coverage given Carter in the *New York Times*; support for Carter among Democrats, as measured by the Gallup poll; the Carter campaign's ability to raise campaign contributions; and a measure of the distance between Carter's delegate total and that of his closest competitor.

In Figure 6–1 it is clear that news coverage of Carter became prevalent *before* he accumulated nationwide support, money, and delegates. News coverage of Carter became noticeable early in the campaign, increased throughout March and April, and appears to have been greater than both his share of support among Democrats and his accumulation of money. In fact, news coverage increased significantly at least one month before Carter's delegate total indicated that he would secure the nomination. It appears in this case, then, that news coverage led rather than followed other indications of campaign success. Our best guess would probably be that news coverage was a valuable and important aspect of the successful Carter nomination campaign in 1976.[19]

The connection between news coverage and public awareness of candidates was not only a Carter phenomenon, however. The change in public recognition of each of the presidential candidates in 1976 was closely related to the amount of news coverage that each candidate received. Furthermore, in 1976 it was newspaper reading, not television viewing, that contributed more to the public's awareness of presidential candidates.[20] Apparently television coverage of all but the most promi-

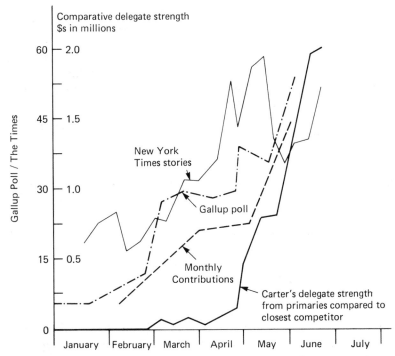

Source: John H. Aldrich, *Before the Convention* (Chicago: University of Chicago Press, 1980), p. 102. Reprinted by permission of the University of Chicago Press.
    Note: Financial data are from the Federal Election Commission's Form 3, line 15D (monthly matching funds subtracted). Gallup poll information is from the *Gallup Opinion Index* (Princeton, N.J.: The Gallup Poll), Report 127, February 1976, p. 21; and Report 133, August 1976, pp. 6–7, 12. Note that the Gallup poll curve shows the proportion of Democrats preferring Carter for the nomination at the time of each 1976 survey. The *New York Times* stories curve shows the proportion of *New York Times* stories about the active Democratic candidates each week that were about Carter. The contributions curve shows the contributions, in millions of dollars, that Carter received each month. The comparative delegate strength curve is a measure of the number of delegates committed to Carter relative to the number committed to the second-place contender and the number of delegates remaining to be selected. The number takes on a value of 1.0 when a candidate secures 50 percent of the delegates to the national nominating convention.

FIGURE 6–1   Jimmy Carter's Momentum

nent candidates was too fleeting, infrequent, and distracting to catch the attention of its audience, whereas the newspaper audience was more attentive and perhaps more interested.

The perceptual changes regarding who was the leading candidate also significantly benefited the Carter campaign in 1976. In an electoral situation in which voters have to choose one candidate from a group of many, and party loyalties are irrelevant, which candidates are known and which are perceived to be likely winners and losers become important influences on individual voter decisions (we will return to this point in Chapter 8). In 1976 most citizens had decided that Carter was the most likely winner by April, even though about 2,550 (85 percent) of the 3,008 delegates to the nominating convention remained to be chosen.

The ability of the news media to shape the candidate agenda also extends to general election campaigns. There the effect works a severe hardship on minor-party candidates and challengers to incumbents.

During each presidential election campaign there are often more than a dozen legally qualified candidates for the presidency for such so-called minor parties as the Socialist Labor party, the People's party, the Socialist Workers' party, the Libertarian party, the Prohibition party, and the National States Rights party.[21] Yet as far as the media are concerned, unless there is substantial evidence to the contrary, presidential campaigns are treated as contests between the two major-party candidates. Minor-party candidates are ignored. Publishers and editors argue that minor-party candidates are not serious and/or have no support and no chance of winning, so covering such candidacies is a waste of time or space that could be devoted to the coverage of major-party candidates. This claim, however, produces a self-fulfilling prophecy, since any candidate who is ignored by the news media because of a lack of support will surely have no support on election day.

We saw in Chapter 5 that news coverage of presidential general election campaigns provides a similar amount of coverage for the two major-party candidates but seldom covers any of the other candidates (Wallace's ability to receive media coverage in 1968 and Anderson's coverage in 1980 were notable exceptions). It is little wonder, then, that few Americans know anything about the minor-party candidates or consider casting a vote for one of them. This media control over the political agenda of candidates for public office, coupled with the U.S. electoral system of single-member districts and plurality decision rules, keeps electoral competition in the United States focused almost exclusively on candidates from the Republican and Democratic parties.

The 1980 presidential election contest provided an interesting example of the importance of being on the candidate agenda. Both major-party candidates, Ronald Reagan and Jimmy Carter, were quite well known at the beginning of the nomination campaign and had become recognized by over 90 percent of the voting-age population by the end of the campaign. Jimmy Carter, of course, was well known by virtue of having been the incumbent president for four years. Ronald Reagan, though slightly less well known, had become visible through previous nonpolitical activities and political campaigns.

In contrast, far fewer people were aware of John Anderson's independent campaign for president, and public recognition of his efforts never reached the levels for either Carter or Reagan. In New Jersey, for example, only about 30 percent of the population was aware of him in 1979, about half the population knew of him by the end of the nomination campaign, and 70 percent felt they were aware of him by the end of the campaign.[22] In short, about 20 percent of the voting-age population were well aware of Carter and Reagan but not of Anderson even by the end of his eleven-month campaign.

Increases in awareness of Anderson's campaign can be traced to three major events and, presumably, the news coverage associated with them. They were (1) the Iowa caucuses and Anderson's participation in the *Des Moines Register*'s January debate among Republican candidates, (2) Anderson's unexpectedly strong finishes in the Massachusetts and Vermont primaries in March, and (3) Anderson's televised debate with Reagan in September. Public awareness of the Anderson campaign increased shortly after each of these episodes, with the largest spurt of awareness following the Anderson-Reagan debate.[23] Nevertheless, Anderson was unable to orchestrate or participate in enough such events ever to overcome his initial disadvantageous position off the candidate agenda.

This phenomenon should not be taken as an intentional political bias of the media against John Anderson. In fact, as we saw earlier, in some ways the media's treatment of John Anderson in 1980 was quite gentle. Rather, this is probably nothing more than a reflection of the political realities of the U.S. political system. Most electoral competition, after all, does involve the two major parties. With the increase in the number of persons who eschew a partisan identification and who show an inclination to desert partisan loyalties when casting a ballot, however, there is an increased possibility of candidacies that do not come from either of the two major parties. How the media respond to this less partisan electoral environment and how tightly the two major parties are permitted to dominate the agenda of presidential candidates will profoundly affect the shape of future electoral competition in this country.

The importance of who is on the candidate agenda increases dramatically when one considers nonpresidential elections, where citizen interest and awareness are significantly lower than for presidential elections. In elections for U.S. congressional seats, for example, less than half of the voting-age population can recall the names of the congressional candidates in their district (although somewhat more claim to *recognize* the names when they are provided).[24]

One reason for this dearth of information about congressional candidates is the paucity of news coverage given congressional campaigns. In fact, a study of seventy-five selected congressional districts in 1978 found only about twelve articles and ads per race in the largest-circulation dailies in each area with any mention of either candidate or of the campaign more generally.[25] Since television markets typically do not match up well with congressional district boundaries, broadcast news coverage of congressional campaigns is also quite scarce. Furthermore, remember that what little coverage there is of congressional candidates is not given equally to both major-party candidates. Instead, congressional incumbents tend to receive almost twice as much campaign coverage as challengers do.[26] It is hardly surprising, then, that voters are much more aware of congressional candidates who are incumbents than they are of the challengers. In both 1978 and 1980, twice as many congressional voters recalled or recognized the name of the incumbent as recalled or recognized the name of the challenger, a considerable advantage in placement on the candidate agenda.[27] Although there are many reasons for this greater familiarity with incumbents (incumbent news coverage between campaigns, incumbent ability to spend more money and campaign more effectively, low quality of challenging candidates), there is strong evidence that the quantity of campaign news coverage given different congressional candidates is one factor. In fact, the ability to stimulate campaign news coverage seems to be particularly important for the campaigns of challengers, who typically begin a congressional campaign off the candidate agenda and often fail to make much headway in penetrating the awareness of the congressional electorate.[28]

As we shall see in Chapter 8, the dynamics of the vote choice are fundamentally different in the low-information context of a congressional election. Unlike presidential elections, in congressional campaigns one of the major-party candidates may not make it onto the agenda of candidates, leaving many citizens with a choice between a somewhat known and an almost completely unknown quantity. In such a case the identity of the known quantity is clearly important, and the contribution of news coverage to the visibility of candidates takes on added significance. Furthermore, if this is true in congressional elections, one can well imagine the importance of candidate agenda setting at lower electoral levels, where the information context is generally even poorer.

The ability of the media to affect the political agenda during election campaigns is a significant phenomenon. Influence over the candidate agenda is probably greater than the issue agenda, particularly in the early stages of a multicandidate nomination campaign and in nonpresidential elections, whereas influence over the issue agenda is greater for issues about which citizens have few independent sources of information than for those that citizens experience directly. This ability to affect what political issues we spend our time thinking about and discussing is an important one, as is the ability to stimulate greater levels of awareness of some candidates than of others.

AGENDA SETTING APPLIED TO PERCEPTIONS OF THE CAMPAIGN

Perhaps the most interesting and important variation on the agenda-setting thesis involves the relative salience of the ways in which the public thinks about an election campaign in general. As we discussed in Chapter 5, the news media emphasize the game elements of an election campaign (such as who is winning and what strategy is being pursued) over its substantive aspects (such as what policy positions the candidates are apt to prefer and propose). The media also emphasize *campaign* issues (such as Gerald Ford's 1976 Eastern European gaffe and Jimmy Carter's 1976 *Playboy* interview) over *policy* issues. This media agenda has also been found to be shared by the public. That is, most people talk and think about the *game* rather than the *substance* of the campaign, and about campaign issues rather than policy issues. Furthermore, the salience of these elements of the campaign parallels the treatment given by the news: heightened sensitivity for the game during the nomination campaign and increased concern for the substance (but still with a focus on campaign issues) during the general election.[29]

This is a worrisome finding. Although the *amount* of news coverage given presidential campaigns has increased in recent years, it may be that the qualitative nature of this coverage has deflected the attention of the public away from the substantive aspect of campaigns. In fact, there is some evidence that the substantive side of the campaign, as manifested both in the news and in the minds of the voters, is covered and thought about less now than it was thirty years ago.[30] If this is the case, then the ability of the news media to affect the salience of particular policy issues could well be less important than the ability of the news to remove policy issues from the voters' agenda entirely. Since an election campaign is an ambiguous and complex phenomenon, there is no certainty that it will be thought of by either journalists or citizens as an avenue for anticipating or influencing future policy decisions. In fact, we have seen that journalists seldom view a campaign as a policymaking exercise. This suggests that we should be particularly concerned, as we will be in subsequent sections, with what the public learns of a substantive nature from campaign news exposure.

PERCEPTIONS CONCERNING CANDIDATES

The ability of campaign news coverage to affect the agenda of issues and candidates is clearly an important one, but it does not exhaust the range of possible effects of news coverage. Another important way in which citizens might respond to news coverage is by altering their beliefs about the candidates. Of particular importance is whether news coverage contributes to more accurate perceptions of candidates or, put another way, whether citizens can be said to *learn* anything about candidates from campaign coverage.

Journalists are seldom bashful in claiming that their election coverage is complete, interesting, and valuable, and that the public achieves a deeper awareness of electoral contests through exposure to their news coverage. There are several reasons, however, that the citizenry might not learn much about candidates or the electoral process from the news coverage provided.

First, remember that exposure to news coverage is selective and that those who watch, listen to, or read a lot about ongoing campaigns tend to be the highly educated, the politically interested and active, and the politically partisan (refer back to Table 3–1). Consequently, it could be that those who watch and read a considerable amount of campaign coverage are those who already know a lot about the candidates and issues involved, whereas those who know the least at the beginning of a campaign are unlikely to learn very much from the news media during the campaign simply because they are not paying attention. In other words, given the voluntary nature of exposure to the news, and the types of people who are regular news users, campaign coverage may not *extend* awareness of the campaign beyond what already exists at the beginning of an election campaign. The already knowledge-rich may get richer while the knowledge-poor remain impoverished.[31]

Second, recall that our discussion of media coverage of election campaigns (Chapters 4 and 5) indicated that a large portion of news coverage focuses on the hoopla associated with campaigning—candidate travel, rallies, crowd reaction, polls, and speculation about who is winning—rather than on the candidates' personal attributes or policy preferences. Since this is true (at least at the presidential level) for both print and broadcast media, one wonders if citizens *could* learn very much from exposure to news coverage even if such exposure were frequent and attentive.

Third, there is some evidence that people simply do not remember very much of the news content they are exposed to. One study, for example, found that of the 437 news items available one day in the mass media to the residents of a particular city, the typical citizen could recall only 5 news items at the end of the day. Only 32 percent of the television news items, 19.2 percent of the radio news items, and 16.8 percent of the newspaper items were recalled by *somebody*.[32] Another study, which focused exclusively on television news presentations during an election campaign, found that, of the 20 news stories contained on the typical television network news show, viewers could recall only about 1 story themselves (more with some assistance from the interviewer). This was true even though respondents were interviewed less than three hours after seeing the network news show in question. Furthermore, recall was greater for weather and human interest stories than for any other type of news story.[33] Of the 297 times that issues were mentioned during the 1976 debates between Jimmy Carter and Gerald Ford, voters could recall barely 2 issue-related statements less than two weeks later.[34] It seems, then, that people have very selective memories, recalling only those news stories that are of the greatest relevance to their personal lives or of interest to them. For most people, unfortunately, news stories about election campaigns seldom meet these criteria.

Consequently, given patterns in exposure to news coverage, patterns in media coverage of election campaigns, and patterns in the recall of news presentations, it might be unreasonable to expect the public to learn very much at all from the news media during election campaigns. Many people, however, do claim to receive most of their information about current events from the news media, and we have just seen that the media are capable of affecting the political agenda of the citizenry. In fact, the public does learn certain things during the course of an election campaign from news coverage. What people learn, however, may not be what we would expect or hope for.

PERCEPTIONS CONCERNING THE HORSE RACE

One piece of information that the public clearly does learn about candidates from news coverage involves the horse-race aspect of the campaign. Citizens form impressions of the likelihood of a particular candidate doing well (securing the nomination or winning the general election) and of whether the candidate's prospects are improving or getting worse. These perceptions closely parallel the content of news coverage, they are most evident during presidential *nomination* campaigns, and television and newspaper coverage contribute about equally to them.[35] As we saw in the previous section (and in Table 6–1), in 1976 public perceptions regarding the strength of the Carter candidacy changed the most during the nomination campaign. Perceptions regarding the outcome of the Republican nomination in 1976 also followed news coverage, however, with Ford first thought likely to win, then Reagan (after his string of primary victories in April and May), and then Ford again.

In a similar way, public perceptions of which candidate has been helped by (or has "won") a campaign event such as a debate are also shaped by subsequent news coverage. In one of the most convincing demonstrations of the effect of campaign coverage, postdebate news coverage of the second Ford-Carter debate in 1976 significantly altered perceptions of who had won the debate, in Carter's favor.[36]

These perceptions of who the likely winner is would be inconsequential if they had no effect on other citizen attitudes or behavior. When the circumstances are right, however, these perceptions can alter levels of candidate support and the ability to attract votes. In 1976, for example, early perceptions of Carter's success made him a more attractive and acceptable candidate to Democrats and contributed to later primary victories. This does not always happen, however. When citizen preferences for candidates are more strongly held (as they were on the Republican side in 1976) and are based on a fuller awareness of what the candidates represent, perceptions of the likely outcome have little impact on support for a candidate. In fact, in that situation a candidate's (stronger) supporters show signs of overestimating (*mis*perceiving) their favorite's chances of success.[37]

Bandwagons *are* possible, then, and have occurred at the presidential level. Circumstances are not always ripe for their creation, however, or for them to alter the electoral outcome. In the absence of such conditions, learning about the horse race would seem to be interesting and entertaining to the public and perhaps even useful in conducting social discourse, but it is hard to see how it could help the electorate make informed choices between competing candidates or public policies.

Once we have dispensed with this horse-race learning, is there any evidence that the public forms any other perceptions of candidates based on campaign news coverage? The two most likely possibilities concern perceptions of the candidates' policy positions and perceptions of the candidates' personal attributes. Let us consider each of these in turn.

PERCEPTIONS CONCERNING CANDIDATE POLICY PREFERENCES

In Chapters 4 and 5 we saw that campaign news coverage contains a dearth of information about the policy positions of candidates. We also saw in Chapter 2 that candidates are wary of revealing definite and unambiguous policy positions in any but the most invisible of places. Given these conclusions, is it still possible that the public's perceptions of candidate policy positions are shaped by news coverage? Furthermore, are these perceptions accurate or are they confused and distorted?

In general, citizen perceptions of candidate policy positions correspond to how specific and distinct the candidates themselves are during an election campaign. In 1968 and 1976, for example, public awareness of the issue positions of the presidential candidates tended to be minimal. In 1968 citizen perceptions of both Richard Nixon's and Hubert Humphrey's positions on the Vietnam War were confused since neither candidate felt compelled (or able) to clarify the situation, and in 1976 voters were unaware of both Jimmy Carter's and Gerald Ford's issue positions.[38]

In 1972 and 1980, however, public awareness of candidate issue positions was much clearer and more extensive. In 1972 there was a fair amount of agreement on the policy preferences of George McGovern and, to a lesser degree, of Richard Nixon, particularly for those issues that they addressed frequently and clearly. In 1980 public perceptions of Carter's position concerning détente with the Soviet Union and both Carter's and Reagan's positions on defense spending became much clearer during the 1980 campaign, whereas perceptions of Reagan's positions on domestic services expenditures and détente became somewhat clearer. (Perceptions of both candidates' preference for reducing inflation or unemployment and Carter's position on domestic services expenditures, however, remained unchanged and muddied throughout the 1980 campaign.)[39]

The public, then, apparently responds to the clarity of the policy positions offered and, in some cases, increases the clarity and accuracy of its perceptions of candidate positions during the campaign. The role of the news media in shaping these perceptions is only now beginning to be understood, however. The evidence to date suggests that the print media, but not television, contribute to this type of learning.

In 1972 researchers· at Syracuse University interviewed a sample of respondents four times during the course of the presidential campaign (September, early October, late October, and November) and collected and analyzed the content of the news coverage and political advertising available to the respondents. They also determined the policy positions taken by Richard Nixon and George McGovern during the campaign on a variety of issues and were able to determine, on the basis of respondents' answers to their questions, the accuracy of citizen perceptions of the candidates' policy positions. The accuracy of these perceptions was determined at the beginning and the end of the campaign, and a comparison was made between the two measures to see if each individual's perception had become more accurate, become less accurate, or had remained unchanged. Then the respondents were divided into two groups, representing low and high exposure to television network news, so that the accuracy of their perceptions could be compared.[40]

Table 6–2 presents the results of this analysis. In general, across all the issues, those exposed to network news did not learn any more about the candidates' issue positions during the campaign than did those who were unexposed to television news. There are only three issues on which network television viewers formed appreciably more accurate perceptions than the nonviewers did (Nixon's position on foreign commitments and McGovern's positions on Vietnam withdrawal and taxes on upper incomes); on most of the issues there is little or no difference between viewers and nonviewers. Furthermore, there was no obvious subgroup of the population that increased the accuracy of their perceptions as a result of watching television network news. "Neither men nor women, the uneducated nor well educated, the poor nor the wealthy, the young, nor the old greatly improved their issue information by tuning in television news."[41]

The public did learn something from reading newspapers, however. When the same kind of analysis was done for nonregular and regular newspaper readers (Table 6–3), it was discovered that the perceptions of regular newspaper readers across all issues became more accurate than those of nonreaders on over half of the issues tested. Consequently, reading the newspaper, unlike watching television news, expands the breadth and depth of citizen awareness.

TABLE 6–2 The Impact of Network News Exposure on People's Issue Awareness during 1972 General Election

	Nonregular Viewers of Network News (%)	Regular Viewers of Network News (%)
Nixon policies:		
Vietnam War	4	11
Government spending	14	3
Military spending	27	36
Busing	35	35
China	38	32
Russia	25	28
Foreign commitments	37	50
Taxes on upper incomes	7	0
Law and order	2	−6
Jobs for the unemployed	15	16
Amnesty	41	49
Drugs	8	7
McGovern policies:		
Military spending	63	58
Vietnam withdrawal	38	67
Amnesty	38	31
Political corruption	−4	9
Taxes on upper incomes	14	40
Jobs for the unemployed	45	45
Average on all issues	25	28

Source: Thomas E. Patterson and Robert D. McClure, *The Unseeing Eye* (New York: G. P. Putnam's Sons, 1976), p. 50. Reprinted by permission.

Note: Figures represent percentage increase or percentage decrease (−) in people's issue information during the 1972 general election.

A similar study of the 1976 presidential campaign came to similar conclusions regarding the public's awareness of candidate issue positions. First, as Table 6–4 shows, hardly any learning of candidate policy positions occurred for those candidates who did not survive the nomination campaign. In contrast, many people did learn some of Jimmy Carter's and Gerald Ford's policy positions, although in general a majority of citizens failed to accurately identify even these candidates' policy positions after the year-long campaign. Furthermore, in 1976 as in 1972, exposure to television network news failed to increase the accuracy of citizen perceptions. Heavy viewers were no more apt than light viewers to improve the accuracy of their perceptions over the course of the campaign, regardless of initial levels of political interest. Regular use of the newspaper, however, did contribute to the accuracy of these perceptions.[42]

There are a number of reasons for television news's failure to influence the public's perceptions of candidate policy preferences. One is

TABLE 6–3   The Impact of Newspaper Reading on People's Issue
Awareness during 1972 General Election

	Nonregular Newspaper Readers (%)	Regular Newspaper Readers (%)
Nixon policies:		
Vietnam War	−5	22
Government spending	3	13
Military spending	21	34
Busing	31	43
China	19	51
Russia	12	41
Foreign commitments	22	62
Taxes on upper incomes	9	−1
Law and order	−12	10
Jobs for the unemployed	8	21
Amnesty	36	57
Drugs	2	12
McGovern policies:		
Military spending	50	67
Vietnam withdrawal	32	66
Amnesty	24	45
Political corruption	−1	11
Taxes on upper incomes	16	38
Jobs for the unemployed	48	43
Average on all issues	18	35

Source: Thomas E. Patterson and Robert D. McClure, *The Unseeing Eye* (New York: G. P. Putnam's Sons, 1976), p. 52. Reprinted by permission.

Note: Figures represent percentage increase or percentage decrease in people's issue information during the 1972 general election.

that candidate issue positions are seldom mentioned on network news. Most of the content of election coverage focuses on campaign hoopla, and it is the game aspect of the campaign that lingers in the minds of viewers. Second, what little mention there is of issues is brief and non-repetitive. The typical campaign news story is less than twenty seconds long—not exactly a format designed to encourage retention of content—and most network news stories about issue positions are buried in a news story about something else. As a result,

> television news provides an impossible learning situation. When the typical election issue is mentioned once a month, for less than twenty seconds in a mix of extraneous news material, the certain consequence is viewer ignorance. ABC, CBS, and NBC may have allowed Americans to "see" the campaign, but in so doing they have added nothing of substance to the voter's civic education.[43]

TABLE 6–4   Awareness of the Candidates' Issue Positions at
Different Times during the 1976 Presidential Campaign

| | Percentage Accurately Perceiving Candidate's Position on: | | | | | | | |
| | Public Works Jobs | | Defense Spending | | Welfare Spending | | Tax Burden | |
Candidate	Early	Late	Early	Late	Early	Late	Early	Late
Brown (Erie)	2	7	3	5	0	4	3	12
Brown (L.A.)	18	20	10	15	10	26	18	20
Carter	4	54	0	29	5	22	5	40
Ford	12	35	38	57	33	43	10	22
Harris	3	3	2	2	3	3	4	3
Jackson	6	12	5	9	0	1	5	10
Reagan (Erie)	11	11	10	30	19	21	10	11
Reagan (L.A.)	30	32	32	50	45	37	28	35
Udall	11	12	6	10	6	11	10	13

Source: Thomas E. Patterson, *The Mass Media Election* (New York: Praeger, 1980), p. 154. Reprinted by permission of Praeger Publishers. Copyright © 1980 by Praeger Publishers.

Note: *Early* denotes the first interview in which respondents were asked to identify the respective candidates' issue position. This was the February interview for all candidates except Brown and Udall, for whom the early interview was the one conducted in April. *Late* denotes the last interview in which respondents were asked about the respective candidate's positions. For Harris and Jackson, who dropped from the race halfway through the primaries, this was the April interview; for Udall, Reagan, and Brown, this was the June interview; and for Ford and Carter, this was the October interview. The respondents' perceptions of the candidates' position were measured on seven-point scales that had an alternative position on each end; for example, on defense spending, one alternative was "no increase in military spending is necessary," and the other was "spend much more on military defense." The position toward which a candidate leaned was determined from a content analysis of his campaign speeches; for example, Reagan stated that he supported increases in military spending. Respondents were considered to be accurate in their perceptions if they placed a candidate on any one of the three positions on the appropriate side of the scale; respondents also were considered to have an accurate perception if they placed a candidate at the scale's midpoint if his statements indicated qualified rather than full support for the position. The table proportions include a correction for guessing.

Finally, it must be acknowledged that most viewers watch television news passively and with less than full attention. "Busy lifestyles and the low priority people generally put on politics also contribute significantly to making political learning a small slice of the average individual's thoughts and concerns."[44]

This finding forces us to reflect on our long-standing beliefs about the news. Although print news does apparently contribute to the accuracy of citizen perceptions of candidate policy preferences, daily television news contributes little to the pool of useful information about candidates' issue positions. This does not mean that the public learns nothing from television news (we have just seen that candidate recognition and awareness of the horse-race aspects of election campaigns *are* shaped by television news shows). If the type of learning we want to occur during an election campaign involves policy-related perceptions, however, it seems unlikely that television news makes a significant contribution.

Actually, the effect of contemporary news coverage on the public's awareness of candidate issue positions is little different now than it was three decades ago. In a panel study of the *1948* presidential election, researchers also found that communication exposure can, in general, lead to more accurate citizen perceptions. Of course, in that election there was no network television news; the measure of communication exposure combined newspaper, magazine, and radio use.[45] Apparently the situation has changed little since then. The introduction of television news campaign coverage has added little to this type of citizen awareness, although the impact of television news on the public's agenda and on horse-race learning is sometimes powerful. In fact, it is possible that despite the increase in campaign expenditures, candidate travel, and journalistic attention, today's citizens are no more aware of the policy positions of candidates than were those of the 1940s.

There is one exception to this general indictment of television news. Coverage of live, extraordinary events, such as nominating conventions and candidate debates, does contribute to an increased awareness of candidate policy positions. We will discuss the impact of debates in the next chapter, but here we should acknowledge that in 1976 those who watched the nominating conventions on television did learn something about candidate policy preferences.[46] This suggests that the inability of regular television news to foster this type of learning is more a result of the way in which a news show is constructed and used by the audience than an inherent limitation of the medium itself.

PERCEPTIONS CONCERNING CANDIDATE ATTRIBUTES

The public might also use campaign news coverage to learn about the personal attributes of candidates. In fact, much of the concern about modern campaign practices has revolved around the so-called image-making practices of candidates and the effect that *television* news has on the public's perceptions of candidates. Because of the visual component of television news, the fact that film shots of campaigning candidates are a prevalent part of television news, the use of dramatic and thematic elements in television news stories, and the presumed ability of the television audience to use such fare to form judgments about the personal traits of candidates, television's image-making capability is often thought to be greater than that of the print media. If Michael Robinson's observations (Chapter 5) concerning the portrayals of candidates by television news organizations are even partially correct, we would expect the television news audience to sense these themes and integrate them into their belief systems.

Our approach to the evidence concerning the news's impact on perceptions of candidate attributes will be fundamentally different from that to the perception of policy preferences. In the case of policy preferences we were willing to identify actual candidate positions and were able to measure the accuracy of citizen perceptions. In the case of candidate attributes, however, we are much less certain of what a candidate's attributes really are, and we are less able to measure the *accuracy* of citizen perceptions. Instead, we will evaluate the effect of news exposure by its ability to *change* the distribution of public perceptions during a campaign. This is a fundamentally different approach to political learning.

There are any number of attributes or impressions of a candidate that citizens might use as a basis for evaluation. Candidates could be thought of in terms of their demographic characteristics (age, sex, race); group or social identity (religion, party identification); personal appeal (warmth, likability, honesty); and professional capabilities (experience, intelligence, administrative abilities). To date, most research on the formation and change of citizen impressions of candidates has distinguished between political/professional attributes and more personal or stylistic ones.

There are some continuities in the attributes emphasized in campaign communication and mentioned by the public (unfortunately, it is difficult to tell which causes which). Both candidates and citizens rely heavily on impressions involving political skills and abilities, such as knowledge, experience, and competence; and impressions concerning the more personal side of a candidate, such as honesty, integrity, decisiveness, warmth, and strength.[47] During the 1972 presidential campaign, for example, perceived competence (experience, ability); trust (honesty, integrity); and reliability (decisiveness) were the most prevalent standards used by voters to evaluate George McGovern and Richard Nixon.[48] During the 1980 presidential campaign, impressions of competence (knowledgeable, inspiring, strong leader) and integrity (moral, dishonest, power-hungry) described most perceptions of the personal attributes of Jimmy Carter and Ronald Reagan.[49]

There is also considerable variation over time in the impressions that the U.S. public has had of its presidential candidates. In 1956 and 1964, for example, incumbents Dwight Eisenhower and Lyndon Johnson were perceived to possess much more experience and ability than did Adlai Stevenson and Barry Goldwater. In 1972 George McGovern was perceived to be much weaker, more indecisive, and more inconsistent than Richard Nixon.[50] In fact, over the years there has been more variation in the evaluation of the personal attributes of the candidates than of any other attitude closely related to the presidential vote.[51]

Much of this variation in impressions of candidates occurs outside the campaign period. Politicians who become presidential candidates have usually been visible enough nationally prior to their nomination that the public already has some sense of their personal attributes. (George McGovern in 1972, Jimmy Carter in 1976, and John Anderson in 1980 were, however, notable exceptions to this rule.) Consequently, public impressions of most presidential candidates are not shaped anew by campaign communication. More typically, they are refined or filled in during the campaign.

Impressions of presidential candidates do not remain static during the campaign. One study of changes in citizen perceptions of presidential candidates during general election campaigns from 1952 to 1972 has found the following instances in which citizen evaluations changed by 10 pecent or more during the campaign: Hubert Humphrey became more positively perceived and George Wallace less positively perceived on experience/ability in 1968; Adlai Stevenson's (1956), Barry Goldwater's, and Humphrey's personal attraction became more positively perceived; Lyndon Johnson's and Richard Nixon's (1972) personal attraction became less positively perceived; John Kennedy's and Goldwater's background/character became more positively perceived; and Johnson's background/character became less positively perceived.[52] More recently, Gerald Ford's image became considerably more positive during the 1976 campaign, whereas Jimmy Carter's image became more positive during the nomination campaign but less positive during the general election campaign in 1976; Carter's image became less positive throughout the entire campaign period in 1980.[53]

The role of news coverage in the formation and change of these public perceptions is, unfortunately, unclear. Attempts to relate the amount and type of news exposure to positive or negative public impressions of candidates have generally failed to find consistent or robust relationships.[54] In fact, one study of the presumed image-making power of television news, conducted during the 1972 presidential election campaign, concluded:

> The long and short of images is that voters are not fools. Claims that the public's images can be manipulated by shallow television theatrics take the voters for dopes. The American voter judges presidential aspirants by politics, not entertainment. Voters arrive at their image of a candidate by judging where he stands politically and by assessing his significant accomplishments and failures. A smiling presidential candidate, engulfed by thousands of adoring admirers, may make for good television, but it is not the basis on which the electorate evaluates potential leaders. That evaluation is based on politics. Television's image-making power is a myth.[55]

It would be foolish on the basis of such little evidence to form such a certain judgment as that. The range of perceptual changes studied to date have been few, the research methods have been imprecise, and the electoral contests sampled have lacked variety. Although the evidence accumulated so far suggests that there is no simple, direct relationship between news exposure and citizen perceptions of candidates, a more subtle or complex pattern of influence may yet be found. Given that citizen impressions are varied and do show some tendency to change during a campaign period, there must be some explanation for the origins of these impressions. Isolating the influence of particular sources of communication, however, is very difficult.

Two careful attempts to measure the impact of news media on citizen images of candidates during the 1976 presidential campaign have reached some sensible conclusions about the impact of news exposure. In one, impressions of candidates were divided into "stylistic" (candidate mannerisms and performance) and "political" (leadership abilities, governing actions) types; the news media were found to be more important in shaping stylistic than political impressions. This was particularly true for Jimmy Carter (since few people had any prior basis for forming a *political* impression of him) and during the nomination campaign (since that is when the news media focused on stylistic portrayals). Impressions of Gerald Ford (and of other well-known candidates such as Ronald Reagan and George Wallace) were more political in nature and less susceptible to change consistent with news presentations.

If we also distinguish between the *structure* of citizen impressions (such as what attributes voters are using to evaluate candidates) and the *direction* of citizen impressions (that is, whether they are favorable or unfavorable), it is more difficult to discern an influence that can be attributed to news coverage. The ebb and flow of positive images of Carter in 1976 did coincide with news coverage during the campaign, but the change in impressions of Ford did not coincide with news presentations.[56]

In the other study, the impressions of Carter and Ford held by a group of Illinois voters throughout 1976 were compared with the coverage of the presidential candidates in the main locally available newspaper, the *Chicago Tribune*. Over the course of the entire 1976 campaign, Carter's coverage in the *Tribune* became more negative, whereas Ford's became more positive. Furthermore, these trends were closely paralleled by changes in the tone of the Illinois voters' impressions. The authors concluded that

> media agenda-setting (at least newspaper agenda-setting) extends to candidate image . . . and . . . media emphasis or de-emphasis of certain image attributes contributes to voter evaluations of candidates as well as to overall voter images of those candidates.[57]

One reason for the difficulty of measuring precisely the impact of news exposure on these perceptions is that the process of selective perception is involved in the formation of these impressions. That is, many, if not most, citizens following an election campaign have some predisposition in favor of one candidate or another and hence some interest in "learning" that their favored candidate possesses admirable qualities. In this area of perception, then, to perceive that a candidate lacks a valued attribute is to threaten the vote choice itself. As a result, different people use news reports in different ways to fill in, reinforce, and refine an existing belief system. The news provides citizens with ample messages with which to do this; only occasionally are these messages so consistent that the range of possible responses to the news is severely restricted. In fact, when one candidate's partisans become more favorable toward him or her and the opponent's partisans become more favorable toward the opponent (a familiar pattern), it could be argued that the news has had a significant effect despite the absence of any aggregate change.

An example from the 1980 presidential campaign nicely illustrates the importance of selective perception. In an elaborate tracking of citizen impressions during the year-long campaign, New Jersey citizens were asked about the candidates fourteen times between February and November.[58] When the percentage of respondents possessing favorable impressions of each candidate is presented separately for Republicans and Democrats, the pattern shown in Figure 6–2 emerges. A number of interesting things can be seen there.

First, at least among New Jersey citizens, Ronald Reagan was more positively perceived than was Jimmy Carter from March throughout the rest of the 1980 campaign. This was true among both the candidate's own partisans and the opponent's partisans.

Second, it is also clear that impressions of Carter became markedly less positive among both Democrats and Republicans between March and August, whereas impressions of Ronald Reagan remained more stable. Impressions of Carter then recovered somewhat during the fall campaign, but they never again reached the positive level of Reagan's.

Third, there is abundant evidence here of selective perception, particularly after the two candidates were nominated. Notice that in general a candidate is always more positively perceived by his or her own partisans than by the opposing partisans (this is as true for Carter as it is for Reagan). More important, however, notice how the perceptions of a candidate by the two partisan groupings diverge over the course of the campaign to create a picture similar to an open pair of scissors. In general, Republicans became more favorable toward Reagan while Democrats became less favorable, and Democrats became more favorable toward Carter while Republicans became less favorable, particularly once the general election campaign began. Clearly, not all citizens respond to campaign portrayals of the candidates in the same way.

Finally, although data such as these do not directly test the impact of campaign news coverage, the timing of changing impressions makes

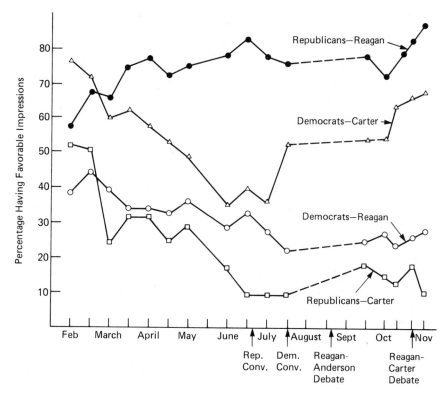

Source: Scott Keeter and Cliff Zukin, "The 1980 Presidential Election: Tracking Citizens' Opinions and Preference," Paper presented at the annual meeting of the Midwest Political Science Association, 1981. Reprinted by permission.

FIGURE 6–2   Change in Popular Impressions of Carter and Reagan during the 1980 Presidential Campaign among New Jersey Voters

sense when it is linked with visible campaign events. For example, favorable impressions of Carter plummeted after the unsuccessful Iranian hostage rescue attempt in April, and again—among Republicans—after the Reagan-Carter debate. What happened after each of the candidate's nominating conventions is even more instructive. In general, if selective perception is at work, we would expect a candidate to gain among his or her own partisans and lose among the other's partisans as a result of such an event. This is exactly what happened in 1980. Furthermore, the conventions had more effect on the partisans of the party holding the convention than on those of the other party. Democratic impressions during the Republican convention and Republican impressions during the Democratic convention remained quite stable (probably because they did not watch the opposing party's convention). Finally, it was the Democratic convention in 1980 that was associated with more opinion change.

Democratic impressions of Carter exhibited a 15–20 percent improvement (partly because Democratic impressions of Carter had eroded so seriously prior to the convention, whereas Republican impressions of Reagan had probably approached the maximum possible). It seems quite clear, then, that the nominating conventions in 1980 had a potent impact on the impressions citizens had of the candidates and that different citizens responded to the conventions in significantly different ways.

There have been very few studies of the effects of news coverage outside the presidential arena. This is because the campaign coverage of nonpresidential races is so sparse and because it requires substantial resources to study the news coverage and opinions of citizens across many states or election districts. Some preliminary evidence, however, suggests that news coverage during *congressional* campaigns also has a noticeable effect on the public's perceptions of candidate attributes.

As we discovered earlier, incumbents receive more campaign coverage than challengers do, and this contributes to greater public awareness of them. In addition, it has been found that the *tone* of campaign coverage is considerably more positive for incumbent candidates. In fact, incumbents are three times as likely as challengers to receive positive campaign coverage.[59] This is yet another asset for incumbents in congressional campaigns, and it translates into a more positive overall evaluation of incumbents than would be the case otherwise. Although a number of factors contribute to positive evaluations of congressional candidates (such as recognition of the candidate, personal contact with the candidate, constituent service, and party identification), the tone of campaign coverage is one of the more important ones.[60] Although the news media avow a norm of objectivity, congressional campaign coverage is not completely balanced and has important—though perhaps unintended—political effects.

It is still difficult to say exactly how much effect different news sources have on the public's images or impressions of candidates' personal attributes. It is plausible that citizens use news reports to form such impressions, but it is also likely that different citizens use the content of news coverage in significantly different ways. It is difficult to attribute the origins and change in citizen images to particular news stories or sources, although public perceptions of candidates often do coincide with news coverage of campaigns.

Despite the scarcity of empirical evidence regarding the impact of news coverage on public images of candidates, there is good reason to believe that such image making results from campaign coverage. Citizens show a tendency to evaluate candidates in personal rather than issue terms, news coverage contains far more information about candidate attributes than about policy positions, and the public may be better equipped to form impressions of persons rather than choose among policy alternatives. In short, *image* learning may be easier than *issue* learning.

> While personality assessments are made readily on the basis of past experiences, issue assessment is difficult because of the complexity of issues, the haziness of the candidates, conflicting appraisals, and a general feeling that promises of future performance are untrustworthy.[61]

Future research should provide a more reliable estimate than we have now of the impact of campaign news coverage on the public's impressions of candidates.

Conclusion

In this chapter we have discussed a number of possible effects of campaign news coverage on the opinions of the U.S. public. Although our inquiry was constrained by both the quantity and the quality of research conducted to date, a number of tentative conclusions are possible.

First, the evidence is strong that news coverage shapes both the candidate and the issue agenda. The shaping of the candidate agenda tends to benefit incumbent congressional candidates, major-party presidential nominees, and a presidential contender who becomes a "good story" during the nomination campaign. The shaping of the issue agenda limits the attention of the citizenry to a few newsworthy *campaign* issues, which may in turn influence electoral outcomes. The particular candidate advantaged by the shape of the issue agenda, however, is difficult to predict, since that depends on candidate messages and the thematic presentation of the issue by the news media. The shaping of the campaign agenda (that is, the perception of the campaign as a horse race) also constrains popular attention and discourse in a way that is likely to deflect attention away from the substantive aspects of an election campaign.

The evidence is also fairly clear that news coverage contributes only slightly to citizen understanding of candidate policy preferences. Although newspaper coverage and live coverage of nominating conventions do make some dent in citizen confusion and uncertainty, daily television news coverage apparently contributes little to this type of learning. Even the newspaper makes only a marginal contribution to policy learning, in part because such coverage is also dominated by hoopla, in part because of the vague and ambiguous language of candidates, and in part because of the citizenry's lack of interest in or familiarity with issue alternatives. Strange though it may seem, campaign news coverage may not generally extend public understanding of public policy questions.

The evidence is murkier regarding the contribution of news coverage to public impressions of candidates. Although it is reasonable to suspect that impressions are shaped by the news (where else could they come from?) and there is some evidence that news coverage shapes impressions of candidates, attempts to untangle the effect of particular news sources have generally failed. So far, it appears that the *stylistic* impressions of candidates are shaped by news coverage, particularly when little is known previously about the candidate, and that news coverage of peak events can shape citizen perceptions even of a relatively well known incumbent. Furthermore, there is evidence that citizens *use* (rather than *are affected by*) news reports to expand, refine, and fill in existing belief systems in a process that is complex and varied. The effect of the news on such global evaluations, then, is seldom direct, simple, or overwhelming; it is more often indirect, complex, marginal, and subtle.

The public's understanding of and response to an election campaign is shaped in important ways by how journalists view an election campaign. Journalists, however, are not the only contributors to campaign communication. In the following chapter we will consider the public's response to two sources of communication that are more within the control of the candidate. There we will discuss the effect of televised spot advertisements and broadcast debate appearances.

Notes

1. At lower levels of elective office, other sources of communication, such as personal canvassing, posters, brochures, telephone calls, and sound trucks might be more prevalent and potent. A consideration of the impact of these sources, however, would require a longer discussion than is possible here and would shift the focus away from the uses and effects of the *mass* media. Recent trends also indicate that independent campaigning may become an increasingly influential source of campaign communication. The phenomenon is so recent, however, that its potency is uncertain, and no research has been conducted into its effects.

2. For a review of this approach, see Jack M. McLeod and Lee B. Becker, "The Uses and Gratifications Approach," in Dan D. Nimmo and Keith R. Sanders, eds. *Handbook of Political Communication* (Beverly Hills, Calif.: Sage Publications, 1981).

3. Elihu Katz and Paul F. Lazarsfeld, *Personal Influence* (New York: Free Press, 1955).

4. For a more complete yet concise description of these processes, see Jarol B. Mannheim, *The Politics Within* (New York: Longman, 1982), Chap. 6.

5. For early statements of the selective-exposure phenomenon, see Paul Lazarsfeld, Bernard Berelson, and Hazel Gaudet, *The People's Choice* (New York: Columbia University Press, 1948), pp. 129–133; Bernard Berelson, Paul Lazarsfeld, and William McPhee, *Voting* (Chicago: University of Chicago Press, 1954), Chap. 11; Joseph T. Klapper, *The Effects of Mass Communication* (Glencoe, Ill.: Free Press, 1960), pp. 19–26; Herbert H. Hyman and Paul B. Sheatsley, "Some

Reasons Why Information Campaigns Fail," *Public Opinion Quarterly* 11 (1947): 413–423; and Wilbur Schramm and Richard F. Carter, "Effectiveness of a Political Telethon," *Public Opinion Quarterly* 23 (1959): 121–126. This literature is criticized in David Sears and Jonathan Freedman, "Selective Exposure to Information: A Critical Review," *Public Opinion Quarterly*, Summer 1967: 194–213, and is qualified in Thomas E. Patterson, *The Mass Media Election* (New York: Praeger, 1968), Chap. 8. A more recent statement on the applicability of selective exposure and attention in modern campaigns may be found in Garrett J. O'Keefe and L. Erwin Atwood, "Communication and Election Campaigns," in Nimmo and Sanders, *Handbook*, Chap. 12.

6. See Lazarsfeld, Berelson, and Gaudet, *People's Choice*, Chap. 9; Berelson, Lazarsfeld, and McPhee, *Voting*, Chap. 10; Hyman and Sheatsley, "Some Reasons"; Klapper, *Mass Communication*, Chaps. 2, 4; Thomas E. Patterson and Robert D. McClure, *The Unseeing Eye* (New York: G. P. Putnams, 1976), Chap. 3; Kurt Lang and Gladys Engel Lang, *Politics and Television* (Chicago: Quadrangle Books, 1968), Chap. 6; Patterson, *Mass Media Election*, Chap. 8; and Drury R. Sherrod, "Selective Perception of Political Candidates," *Public Opinion Quarterly* 35 (Winter 1971–1972): 554–562.

7. Roper Organization, *Changing Public Attitudes toward Television and Other Mass Media, 1959–1976* (New York: Television Information Office, 1977).

8. Donald L. Shaw and Maxwell E. McCombs, *The Emergence of American Political Issues: The Agenda-Setting Function of the Press* (St. Paul, Minn.: West Publishing Company, 1977).

9. Richard Wirthlin, quoted in Elizabeth Drew, *Portrait of an Election* (New York: Simon and Schuster, 1981), p. 380.

10. Maxwell E. McCombs and Donald L. Shaw, "The Agenda-Setting Function of Mass Media," *Public Opinion Quarterly* 36 (Summer 1972): 176–187.

11. See, however, David H. Weaver, Doris A. Graber, Maxwell E. McCombs, and Chaim H. Eyal, for a striking exception to this general pattern.

12. Jack M. McLeod, Lee B. Becker, and James E. Byrnes, "Another Look at the Agenda-Setting Function of the Press," *Communication Research* 1 (April 1974): 134–165; and Lutz Erbring, Edie N. Goldenberg, and Arthur H. Miller, "Front-Page News and Real-World Cues: A New Look at Agenda-Setting by the Media," *American Journal of Political Science* 24, no. 1 (February 1980): 16–49.

13. Weaver et al., *Media Agenda-Setting*, pp. 91–96, 106–107, 196.

14. Ibid., pp. 98–106, 129–133, 157–158, 197.

15. Shaw and McCombs, *Emergence*. See also Weaver et al., *Media Agenda-Setting*, pp. 50–54, 196.

16. Weaver et al., *Media Agenda-Setting*, pp. 96–98, 128, 153–154, 197.

17. Chaim H. Eyal, J. P. Winter, and W. F. DeGeorge, "The Concept of Time Frame in Agenda-Setting," in G. Cleveland Wilhoit and Maxwell McCombs, eds., *Mass Communication Review Yearbook*, Vol. II (Beverly Hills, Calif.: Sage Publications, 1981); James P. Winter, "Media-Public Agenda-Setting for Five Issues, 1948–1976," Paper presented to the Midwest Political Science Association Annual Conference, 1981; and Weaver et al., *Media Agenda-Setting*.

18. Weaver et al., *Media Agenda-Setting*, p. 206.

19. Apparently nothing of this sort occurred during the 1980 nomination campaign. Between February and June 1980 there was very little change in public awareness of Jimmy Carter, Edward Kennedy, Ronald Reagan, Walter

Mondale, John Connally, Jerry Brown, and Howard Baker. Only for George Bush and John Anderson was there some increase in public awareness during the nomination campaign, and in both cases one-quarter of the voting-age population was still uninformed about them in October. See Gregory B. Markus, "Political Attitudes During an Election Year: A Report on the 1980 NES Panel Study," Paper presented to the annual meeting of the Social Science History Association, 1981.

20. Patterson, *Mass Media Election*, pp. 110–114.

21. For the vote totals of minor-party candidates in presidential elections, see *Presidential Elections Since 1789* (Washington, D.C.: Congressional Quarterly, 1975).

22. Scott Keeter and Cliff Zukin, "The 1980 Presidential Election: Tracking Citizens' Opinions and Preference," Paper presented to the annual meeting of the Midwest Political Science Association, 1981.

23. Ibid.

24. Gary C. Jacobson, *The Politics of Congressional Elections* (Boston: Little, Brown, 1983), Chap. 5.

25. Edie N. Goldenberg and Michael W. Traugott, "Campaign Effects on Voting Behavior in the 1978 Congressional Elections," Paper presented to the annual meeting of the American Political Science Association, 1980.

26. Ibid.

27. Jacobson, *Congressional Elections*; Goldenberg and Traugott, "Campaign Effects"; and Gary C. Jacobson, "Candidates, Campaigns, and Contexts in Congressional Elections," Paper presented to the annual meeting of the American Political Science Association, Washington, D.C., 1980. See also Barbara Hinckley, *Congressional Elections* (Washington, D.C.: Congressional Quarterly Press, 1981), Chap. 2.

28. Goldenberg and Traugott, "Campaign Effects."

29. Patterson, *Mass Media Election*, pp. 98–100.

30. Ibid., p. 105.

31. See, for example, Weaver et al., *Media Agenda-Setting*, pp. 35–43, 202.

32. Alan Booth, "Recall of News Items," *Public Opinion Quarterly* 34 (Winter 1970–1971): 604–610.

33. W. Russell Neuman, "Patterns of Recall among Television News Viewers," *Public Opinion Quarterly* 40 (Spring 1976): 115–123.

34. Weaver et al., *Media Agenda-Setting*, pp. 21–24.

35. Patterson, *Mass Media Election*, pp. 119–122.

36. Ibid., pp. 123–125; and Frederick T. Steeper, "Public Response to Gerald Ford's Statements on Eastern Europe in the Second Debate," in George F. Bishop, Robert G. Meadow, and Marilyn Jackson-Beeck, eds., *The Presidential Debates* (New York: Praeger, 1980).

37. Patterson, *Mass Media Election*, pp. 125–132.

38. Benjamin Page, *Choices and Echoes in Presidential Elections* (Chicago: University of Chicago Press, 1978), pp. 179–184; and Weaver et al., *Media Agenda-Setting*, pp. 21–26.

39. Markus, "Political Attitudes"; and Page, *Choices and Echoes*.

40. Patterson and McClure, *The Unseeing Eye*.

41. Ibid., p. 54.

42. Patterson, *Mass Media Election*, pp. 153–165.

43. Patterson and McClure, *The Unseeing Eye*, p. 58.
44. Weaver et al., *Media Agenda-Setting*, p. 39.
45. Berelson, Lazarsfeld, and McPhee, *Voting*, p. 229.
46. Patterson, *Mass Media Election*, pp. 156–165.
47. Page, *Choices and Echoes*, Chap. 8.
48. Arthur H. Miller and Warren E. Miller, "Ideology in the 1972 Election: Myth or Reality," *American Political Science Review* 70 (September 1976): 832–849.
49. Markus, "Political Attitudes."
50. Page, *Choices and Echoes*.
51. Herbert Asher, *Presidential Elections and American Politics* (Homewood, Ill.: Dorsey, 1980), Chap. 5.
52. Dan Nimmo and Robert L. Savage, *Candidates and Their Images* (Pacific Palisades, Calif.: Goodyear, 1976).
53. Patterson, *Mass Media Election*, pp. 138–142; and Markus, "Political Attitudes."
54. Nimmo and Savage, *Candidates*.
55. Patterson and McClure, *The Unseeing Eye*, p. 73.
56. Patterson, *Mass Media Election*, Chap. 12.
57. Weaver et al., *Media Agenda-Setting*, pp. 185–192. The quotation is on p. 192.
58. Keeter and Zukin, "The 1980 Presidential Election."
59. Goldenberg and Traugott, "Campaign Effects."
60. Ibid.
61. Weaver et al., *Media Agenda-Setting*, p. 166.

7

The Effects of Spot Ads and Candidate Debates on Citizen Beliefs and Attitudes

Political ads are probably—message-for-message—more effective communicators than either product ads or televised news stories.
—Thomas E. Patterson and Robert D. McClure, "Television News and Televised Political Advertising"

The 1976 presidential debate produced a better informed electorate than would have been the case without them.
—Arthur H. Miller and Michael Mackuen, "Learning about the Candidates"

[The debates] offered the best opportunity in 1980 for the public to make a relatively informed judgment about who was worth voting for.
—Jeff Greenfield, *The Real Campaign*

In preceding chapters we have seen that the ability of candidates to present their campaign appeals directly to the voters has been increased in many ways. Policy decisions and changes in the public's media-exposure habits have made spot advertisements and candidate debates more prevalent in contemporary campaigns, and the expertise of the public opinion pollster and professional campaign consultant have permitted candidates to devise and deliver their campaign messages to the public more systematically. In this chapter we will discuss the impact of the two most visible forms of candidate-controlled presidential campaign communication—spot advertisements and candidate debates—on the perceptions and attitudes of the U.S. electorate.

The Effects of Political Broadcast Advertising

In many respects spot ads are an effective way to communicate political messages. Their appeals are typically brief, simple, and well illustrated; and they are presented in a context that is much less cluttered and distracting than the typical campaign news story. In addition, exposure to spot ads is involuntary; consequently, the audience exposed to spot ad messages is usually both larger and more representative of the entire electorate than is the audience for daily news coverage. Finally, since spot ads are shown many times, the chances are good that the message will be seen more than once by large portions of the audience. Since repetition is thought to be a key element of learning, frequent exposure to spot ads presumably increases the chances of the public becoming aware of their intended message. Consequently, although the public may also discount the content of spot advertisements because they are, after all, advertisements under the complete control of the candidate, it is at least plausible that the public learns something from advertising exposure.

Unfortunately, to date there are very few studies of what the public learns from the dozens of spot ads they are exposed to during each campaign period. The most extensive study completed so far was part of a study of the 1972 presidential general election campaign done at Syracuse University.[1] The Syracuse researchers investigated the impact of the advertising campaigns of Richard Nixon and George McGovern by measuring the public's beliefs, attitudes, and media-exposure patterns at different points during the campaign, and comparing these with the content of the presidential spot ads shown in the Syracuse area. The specific ads studied in most detail were Nixon's "Democrats for Nixon" ads. This was a series of ads designed to encourage traditional Democrats to defect from their partisan identification and vote instead for Richard Nixon. Let us consider in some detail what the public learned from this advertising campaign and supplement the results of this study with information from a handful of other pertinent studies of spot ads.

PERCEPTIONS CONCERNING CANDIDATE POLICY PREFERENCES

The 1972 Democrats for Nixon ads were unusual in their attempt to communicate the fairly specific policy positions of the presidential candidates. (As we saw in Chapter 2, most spot ads do not contain specific policy preference information.) In fact, this series of ads attempted to persuade the public that the presidential candidates preferred these policy alternatives:

1. George McGovern favors spending less money on the military.
2. Richard Nixon does not favor spending less money on the military.
3. George McGovern does not favor making people on welfare go to work.

In addition, the ads attempted to convince people that George McGovern "does not always make it clear where he stands."[2]

Since the researchers asked their respondents questions about each of these beliefs at both the beginning and the end of the 1972 campaign, the *change* in these beliefs could be measured and related to mass media exposure. Unfortunately, the researchers did not collect specific information about exposure to the presidential spot ads during the campaign. Consequently, they had to rely on a measure of exposure to prime-time television programming in general, assuming that the more prime-time television watched, the more spot ads were seen.

Table 7–1 shows the relationship between television exposure and the change in beliefs about the policy positions mentioned in these ads. There we can see whether most people changed their beliefs in the direction intended by the ads, and whether frequent television viewers changed their perceptions more than infrequent viewers did.

In general, frequent TV viewers were more apt to change their beliefs about the candidates in the direction of the ads than were infrequent viewers. Although the differences are not large, they are in the correct direction for three of the four ads. In particular, citizens were most apt to learn about the candidate's stands on military spending during the campaign, and those watching a lot of television learned more than did

TABLE 7–1   The Relationship between Voters' Belief Changes during the 1972 Presidential Campaign and Prime-Time Television Exposure

Exposure	Military Spending, McGovern	Military Spending, Nixon	Changing Stands, McGovern	Welfare, McGovern
High TV viewers	+29[a] (44–15)	+19 (43–24)	+3 (32–29)	−10 (28–38)
Low TV viewers	+11 (30–19)	+10 (34–24)	−8 (26–34)	−3 (30–33)

Source: Thomas E. Patterson and Robert D. McClure, "Political Advertising: Voter Reaction to Televised Political Commercials" (Princeton, N.J.: Citizens' Research Foundation, 1974), p. 20. Reprinted by permission.

[a]This is how the numbers in this table should be read. In the case of the ad about McGovern's position on military spending, 44 percent of the high TV viewers changed their perception in the direction of the ad, while 15 percent of the high TV viewers changed their perception in the opposite direction of the ad. The net "effect" of the ad among high TV viewers, then, was a 29 percent (44 percent–15 percent) increase in "learning."

those watching little television. The welfare ad seems to have been the least effective, apparently because it was contradicted by much of McGovern's own communication and because many voters did not find the ad believable. When both candidates' campaigns were transmitting similar information, however, as they were regarding military spending, the ads were apparently quite effective.

Not all people "learned" the same amount from the Democrats for Nixon ads. Those who had low levels of political interest were affected more by the ads than other voters were. This was because the level of awareness of candidate issue positions of low-interest voters was very low to begin with and also because a greater proportion of the campaign information of low-interest voters comes from advertising than is the case for more interested citizens. The more interested the citizen, the more likely he or she is to know the policy preferences of the candidates at the beginning of the election campaign, and the more likely he or she is to read newspaper accounts of the campaign during the campaign. For both reasons, the information contained in the spot ads is more apt to be redundant for the interested and informed than for the uninterested and uninformed citizen.

The Democrats for Nixon spots in 1972 were not the only ones that affected the public's perceptions of candidate issue positions. Similar effects were also found for voter perceptions on a number of other salient campaign issues in the 1972 campaign. Citizens exposed to many television spots increased the accuracy of their perceptions of candidate policy preferences in general more than those exposed to few television spots (Table 7–2). This was especially true for perceptions of both candi-

TABLE 7–2   The Impact of Political Advertising Exposure on People's Issue Awareness During 1972 General Election

	Exposed to Few Spots (%)	Exposed to Many Spots (%)
Nixon's China policy	20	41
Nixon's Russia policy	25	29
McGovern's military spending position	45	66
Nixon's military spending position	20	33
McGovern's tax policy	18	33
Nixon's stance toward political corruption	15	19
Nixon's Vietnam policy	4	11
McGovern's stand on Vietnam withdrawal	48	52
Nixon's policy on foreign commitments	34	44
Average on all issues	25	36

Source: Thomas E. Patterson and Robert D. McClure, *The Unseeing Eye* (New York: G. P. Putnam's Sons, 1976), p. 116. Reprinted by permission.

Note: Figures represent percentage increase in people's issue information during the 1972 general election.

dates' military spending position, Nixon's China policy, and McGovern's tax policy. Furthermore, this difference was more noticeable among those who did *not* also rely on the newspaper or television news for campaign information, suggesting that spot ads are most effective when they represent a significant, nonredundant source of campaign information.

It appears, then, that campaign spot ads contribute to learning about candidate issue positions *in certain circumstances.* That is, ads are most effective for those who know the least to begin with and for those who care so little about the campaign that they are exposed to hardly any other campaign communication. Also, ads are more effective when their content is credible (no one believed the Nixon ad claim about McGovern's position on welfare—"no presidential candidate, not even George McGovern would put half the country on welfare"[3]) and when they are consistent with other forms of communication. For those who are moderately informed or interested, and in those cases in which the advertising campaigns are making conflicting claims, the effect is minimal. *If* the perceptions gleaned from spot ads are accurate, and *if* the citizens affected by these portrayals would have remained uninformed otherwise, it could be said that these presentations actually contribute more to the ideal of an informed electorate than does either television news (as a result of its content) or newspaper coverage (as a result of the lack of exposure to it). Those, however, are two big ifs.

Unfortunately, there are no other comparable published studies of the effect of spot ad campaigns on citizen perceptions. Therefore, we are uncertain how general the type of effect documented in 1972 is. Most other studies of spot ads have corroborated the impact of ads on perceptions of candidate policy positions, but they have done so either by asking people if they *feel* more informed or by relating perceptions to exposure without considering the *change* in perceptions during the campaign period. For example, in a study of two gubernatorial contests in 1970, citizens *claimed* that ads were helpful in understanding candidate issue positions. This was particularly true if they also thought the ads were entertaining, if they paid close attention to the ads, and if they viewed the ads with the intent of receiving information from them.[4] A study of a 1974 congressional campaign between two nonincumbents also measured the accuracy of perceptions of the candidates' policy preferences directly and found more accurate perceptions among those exposed to a lot of radio and television advertising. Perceptions were also more accurate among those who reported an informational motivation for paying attention to advertisements.[5]

To date, however, we have very little evidence concerning the impact of spot ads on policy-related perceptions. Although the evidence so far indicates that the public does learn candidate issue positions from spot ads, there is good reason to be skeptical of such a conclusion. One reason for caution is that our review of the content of spot ads in Chapter 2 revealed that they seldom contain candidate policy positions. In this respect the ads produced by the presidential candidates in 1972 were atypical. It is difficult to imagine citizens generally learning candidate policy positions from the ads encountered in our previous analysis, few of which contain information about candidate policy positions.

Another reason for skepticism about the opportunities that ads provide for policy learning is that we must be careful what we consider a candidate policy position. There is a world of difference between citizens learning the message of an ad and citizens forming *more accurate* political perceptions. After all, some policy positions presented in ads are deceptive, distorted, or so general as to be meaningless.[6] For example, a study of the effectiveness of a television ad campaign during the 1975 Chicago mayoral election discovered that a series of ads were successful in communicating messages such as: "Which candidate would do the most to improve the public schools in Chicago?" "Which candidate would do the most to reduce corruption in city government?" and "Which candidate would do the most to stop wasting tax money on unneeded public employees?"[7] These perceptions could hardly be called *policy positions,* since they say nothing specific about the candidates' preferences for legislative or bureaucratic actions. They are, however, a prevalent type of spot ad message.

Until more research is done, then, we must reserve judgment about the effect of spot ads on the public's perceptions of policy positions. The Syracuse study of the 1972 presidential campaign suggests that if policy positions are presented in spot ads, the public is apt to learn them. Our earlier consideration of the content of a variety of spot ads, however, suggests that this type of content is the exception rather than the rule.

PERCEPTIONS CONCERNING CANDIDATE ATTRIBUTES

It is astounding that with all the concern about the use of political advertising to "merchandise" political candidates, social scientists have conducted little research on whether ads are effective in shaping the public's impressions of candidates. As we saw in Chapter 2, most ads do contain explicit messages about the personal characteristics of candidates. In addition, the *implicit* intention of almost all spot ads is to leave a favorable impression of the personality or character of a candidate for public office.

The most complete study of the effect of presidential spot ads on candidate images is again the Syracuse study of the 1972 campaign. The public's perceptions of a number of personal attributes of McGovern and Nixon were measured throughout the campaign. Then changes in

TABLE 7–3   The Impact of Political Advertising Exposure on
People's Images of Nixon and McGovern during the 1972 General
Election

	Pro-Nixon Voters		Pro-McGovern Voters	
	Exposed to Few Spots (%)	Exposed to Many Spots (%)	Exposed to Few Spots (%)	Exposed to Many Spots (%)
Nixon's image				
Experienced	40	77	30	44
Forward-looking	83	48	− 14	22
Confidence-inspiring	46	65	− 26	− 22
Trustworthy	26	33	− 50	− 30
Appealing	14	27	− 52	− 29
Compassionate	18	− 22	− 22	− 33
Not "political"	3	8	− 17	− 47
Average change	33	34	− 22	− 14
McGovern's image				
Experienced	− 11	− 38	− 4	40
Forward-looking	− 3	− 6	14	45
Confidence-inspiring	− 65	− 47	16	− 5
Trustworthy	− 33	− 45	15	14
Appealing	− 33	− 12	24	21
Compassionate	− 21	− 12	12	20
Not "political"	− 31	− 30	45	27
Average change	− 28	− 27	18	23

Source: Thomas E. Patterson and Robert D. McClure, *The Unseeing Eye* (New York: G. P. Putnam's Sons, 1976), p. 112. Reprinted by permission.

Note: Figures represent percentage improvement (+) or percentage decline (−) in people's images of the candidates during the 1972 general election.

these perceptions were related to television exposure as well as to other variables.

Table 7–3 shows the amount and direction of change in the public's perceptions of the personal attributes of both McGovern and Nixon during the 1972 campaign. Positive numbers indicate that the change was favorable for the candidate; negative numbers indicate that the change was disadvantageous to the candidate. The data are presented separately for frequent and infrequent television viewers, and for McGovern and Nixon voters.

In general, those exposed to many television spots were no more apt to change their image of either candidate in a consistent direction than were those exposed to few spots. On individual traits, there are some cases in which the heavy-exposure group changed considerably more than the light-exposure group did (McGovern on "experience" and "forward-looking" and Nixon on "experience" and "compassion"); but over the full range of attributes some changes are positive, some are negative, some pertain only for the candidate's supporters, and some only among the opposition. In fact, the most general finding is that the change in candidate images is related more to the candidate preference of the respondent than to anything else. The image of Nixon became consistently more positive among pro-Nixon citizens and more negative among pro-McGovern citizens, and the image of McGovern became consistently more positive among pro-McGovern citizens and more negative among pro-Nixon citizens during the campaign. This pattern led the authors to conclude that "by projecting their political biases, people see in candidate's commercials pretty much what they want to see."[8]

When one looks more closely at the data in Table 7–3, however, there is some circumstantial evidence that Nixon's advertising campaign was more effective than McGovern's in 1972. High television exposure was associated with positive change in the image of Nixon on "experienced," "confidence-inspiring," "trustworthy," and "appealing" among pro-Nixon citizens; and with a more positive or less negative change in the image of Nixon on "experienced," "forward-looking," "trustworthy," and "appealing" among pro-McGovern citizens. Exposure to the ads was not enough to create a positive image of Nixon in the minds of most McGovern supporters (except on "experienced" and "forward-looking"), but it did mute the more negative images of McGovern supporters who were unexposed to spot ads. The Nixon advertising campaign looks successful, then, if one credits it with this ability to cut into or deflect the process of selective perception so prevalent during election campaigns. The inability to make Nixon appear more compassionate is the only exception to this pattern. (There are some limits, after all, to what the public will believe.)

As for the McGovern advertising campaign, it too had some positive effects for the McGovern candidacy. It apparently produced a more positive image among supporters on "experienced" and "forward-looking" and a less negative image among the opposition on "confidence-inspiring," "appealing," and "compassionate." There is no case, however, in which nonsupporters had a positive image of McGovern. In summary, then, it appears that Nixon's ad campaign led to a more positive evaluation of him among his loyalists than McGovern's campaign did among his supporters, and to a less negative evaluation among his opposition than the McGovern campaign did.

There is some other fragmentary evidence concerning the impact of spot ad campaigns on public impressions of political candidates. The study of the 1974 congressional campaign mentioned earlier, for example, found that exposure to each candidate's ads was weakly related to general affect for that candidate, and that this relationship survived controls for campaign interest and other forms of communication exposure.[9] Similarly, a 1975 Chicago mayoral advertising campaign was effective in convincing voters that the candidate would be more effective in solving a number of urban policy problems, and that the candidate's opponent would do a poor job as mayor of Chicago.[10] In both these cases ad campaigns left some impression on the beliefs of the electorate.

To date it appears that spot ads have some modest ability to affect public perceptions of both candidates' policy positions and their personal attributes. Their effectiveness most likely stems from the fact that they reach an involuntary audience, their messages are repeated over and over again, and their content is artfully presented and well illustrated.

We will have to await further research on the impact of ad campaigns, however, before forming a more reliable and general assessment of their effect on candidate images. Just as it is hard to believe that ads leave absolutely no impression on the public, it is equally doubtful that the public's impressions can be systematically and significantly altered at will. As we discussed at the beginning of Chapter 6, campaign communication does not act on an unsuspecting, defenseless populace; rather, it interacts with a variety of social and psychological phenomena that protect individuals from facile manipulation. The fact that the public in general has fairly negative attitudes toward politicians indicates that candidate image making is far from completely successful.

Even if we were to conclude that spot ads are typically effective, it is doubtful that we should also conclude that they contribute very much to public understanding. The typical spot ad is too simple, too vague, and too misleading for us to equate perceptual change with *learning*. An occasional spot ad campaign, such as those of the 1972 presidential candidates, may help the public form more accurate perceptions of candidate policy positions; but the more typical effect seems to be to worry or reassure voters, to reinforce culturally held values, or to create and then debate nonissues. This is true not because spot ads inherently must have this effect, but rather because of the messages that are typically relayed in them by political campaigners. Regardless of how effective spot ads turn out to be, as long as their messages remain similar to those we looked at in Chapter 2, the opportunity for increasing popular awareness would seem to be slim indeed.

The Effects of Broadcast Candidate Debates

In the last few years, there have been nine telecast presidential debates during general election campaigns, one vice-presidential general election debate, a handful of debates among presidential contenders during the nomination campaign, and dozens of broadcast debates between nonpresidential candidates. The ten presidential general election debates took place as follows:

1960—Richard M. Nixon (vice-president) and John F. Kennedy (Massachusetts senator)

Date	Subject	Length (minutes)
1. September 26	Domestic issues	60
2. October 7	Open	60
3. October 13	Open	60
4. October 21	Foreign policy	60

1976—Jimmy Carter (former Georgia governor) and Gerald Ford (president)

Date	Subject	Length (minutes)
1. September 23	Domestic issues	90
2. October 6	Foreign policy	90
3. October 22	Open	90

Walter Mondale (Minnesota senator) and Robert Dole (Kansas senator)

1. October 15	Open	75

1980—John Anderson (Illinois congressman) and Ronald Reagan (former California governor)

Date	Subject	Length (minutes)
1. September 21	Open	60

Jimmy Carter (president) and Ronald Reagan

1. October 28	Open	90

Broadcast candidate debates are in many ways an unusual form of campaign communication. They are more policy-oriented than most other forms of campaign propaganda, they are voluntarily watched by many more citizens than voluntarily pay attention to any other form of campaign communication, they reach a representative cross-section of the U.S. electorate, and they provide an opportunity to compare candidates for public office. Some political observers have optimistically asserted that candidate debates contribute much to the wisdom of electoral choices. For example, Robert Sarnoff of NBC once wrote that presidential debates "will become a lasting political institution that will reinforce the vigor of our country's democratic heritage in the challenging years ahead,"[11] and Frank Stanton of CBS claimed in 1960 that the 1960 debates "not only brought an added voter participation . . . they brought a more thoughtful participation."[12] Such claims are reassuring but also self-serving. We need to evaluate the evidence regarding the effects of debate exposure to see if there is any reason for such optimism.

Do viewers or listeners learn anything from candidate debates that they did not already know? Do citizens' perceptions of the candidates change as a result of debate exposure? Do these perceptions become more accurate? Unfortunately, these questions are not easy to answer.

Measuring what the public learns from a debate involves solving at least three problems. First, some sort of baseline measure of awareness prior to the debate exposure is necessary; simply asking respondents after a debate if they have learned anything is not very precise or reliable. Measuring a citizen's level of awareness prior to a debate, however, may sensitize that person to certain types of information, may increase the attention paid to this information during the debate, and may result in more learning than would have been the case otherwise. This might lead us to overestimate the amount of learning that took place.

Second, there are a number of ways to measure "learning." Some researchers rely on answers to questions that have correct and incorrect answers and look for the accuracy of citizen responses. Some prefer to measure the ability of respondents to recall information spontaneously; others look for the recognition of information with some assistance from the interviewer. The amount of learning that is found depends very much on the way in which learning is measured.[13]

A third problem is to measure learning *from a debate* and to distinguish it from learning from other sources, from lucky guessing, or from educated guessing based on prior awareness. As we will see, even studies that attempt to measure learning within a few days of a debate have a difficult time distinguishing the learning that takes place as a result of the debate from that affected by media coverage subsequent to the debate. This problem becomes more serious the longer the time that elapses between a debate and the moment at which learning is measured.

Despite these problems with measuring learning, we know more about the impact of presidential debates than about that of many other forms of campaign communication. In both 1960 and 1976 dozens of presidential debate-related studies were conducted by academics, public opinion firms, and market research analysts. In 1960, thirty-one separate studies were reviewed in one volume, and in 1976 at least three dozen studies were conducted.[14] Also, the effects of broadcast debates are somewhat easier to study than are those of other forms of campaign communication because debates are relatively short; occur at the same time for all citizens; are usually known about in advance; and lend themselves to the sort of before/after, experimental/control group research design that is preferred by most social scientists.

PERCEPTIONS CONCERNING CANDIDATE ATTRIBUTES

In 1960 most of the debate research focused on the effect the debates had on citizen images of the candidates. Much of this research discovered that John Kennedy was the beneficiary of changes in citizen perceptions of his personal attributes. Before-and-after studies of the first debate, for example, revealed that the public came to view Kennedy as more industrious, tougher, more experienced, and more informed after the debate than before, whereas Richard Nixon was perceived to be more conservative, older, less experienced, and less active; but also tougher, wiser, and deeper after the first debate. Perceptions of both candidates on a number of attributes (honesty, sincerity, intelligence, imagination, and trustworthiness) were apparently unaffected by the debate.[15]

Before the first debate in 1960, public perceptions of the candidates were more positive among the candidate's own partisans than among those of the other party. In addition, perceptions of Nixon were more positive among Republicans than were perceptions of Kennedy among Democrats; and perceptions of Nixon among Democrats were more positive than those of Kennedy among Republicans. In short, impressions of Nixon were much more favorable than those of Kennedy before the first televised debate.

After the first debate in 1960, however, perceptions of Kennedy had improved on a number of attributes (industriousness, experience, toughness) among Democrats and had also improved markedly among Republicans. Nixon's image, on the other hand, remained fairly stable among Democrats and actually deteriorated slightly among Republicans. After the first debate, then, Kennedy had closed the gap on Nixon, although Nixon was still more positively perceived both by supporters and by opposing partisans. Kennedy's gain after the first debate was impressive but still left him with a less positive image than Nixon's.[16]

Overall, if one compares the perceptions of Kennedy and Nixon across a number of attributes with the public's perceptions of the ideal president, it is clear that perceptions of Kennedy moved closer to the ideal image after the first debate. Perceptions of Nixon, on the other hand, became more distant from the ideal image. Furthermore, this improved image of Kennedy is more striking when one realizes that it took place largely among undecided citizens and citizens preferring Richard Nixon for president.

After the first debate changes in the perceptions of the two candidates in 1960 were much smaller. In fact, profiles of personal attributes of both candidates look strikingly similar over time. There is some evidence that perceptions of Nixon's experience declined a bit after the second debate, that perceptions of Kennedy's experience increased a little after the fourth debate, and that perceptions of Kennedy's thrift and sincerity increased; but in general most attribute perceptions were quite stable in the aggregate over time after the first debate.[17]

In 1976 considerable research was also done on the effects of debate exposure on public perceptions of the personal attributes of Jimmy Carter and Gerald Ford. These perceptions were found to be even more stable in 1976 than they were in 1960.[18] In the context of this overall stability, Ford's image seems to have improved after the first debate, to have improved very slightly after the second debate (although there is some variation across different studies) and to have deteriorated a bit after the third debate. Carter's image, on the other hand, varied in different studies from much more positive to somewhat more negative after the first debate, and became substantially more positive after the third debate. In general, however, "these changes in candidate evaluation seem to have been either temporary, too slight to pick up retrospectively, or so multiply determined that they cannot be attributed solely to the debates."[19]

Looking at individual attributes, again the main finding is that changes in perceptions on most attributes were minimal and benefited neither candidate. What change there was suggests that Ford's image on certain "presidential" qualities (capability, decisiveness, strength) became more positive during the campaign, particularly after the first debate. Carter's image on more "personal" qualities (intelligence, empathy, honesty, trustworthiness), on the other hand, became more positive during the first and second debate period. These changes tend to be small, however, tend to vary across different studies, and cannot be attributed to debate exposure with any certainty.

In comparing the 1960 and 1976 debate studies, it is interesting to note that the respondents' images of the "ideal president" were quite similar in both years, and that there were marked similarities between the Kennedy-Carter and Nixon-Ford profiles. In both years "inexperience was the major liability for both Democrats; experience was the chief asset of both Republicans. Least liked in Nixon and Ford was their apparent conservatism; most liked in Kennedy and Carter was their appearance of being highly active.[20]

On the other hand, there were also two differences in public perceptions of the candidates in 1960 and 1976. Both candidates had more positive images in 1960 than did the two candidates in 1976. This is probably a reflection of the increase in political cynicism and distrust that occurred during that period. Also, the images of both candidates became less favorable throughout the campaign in 1960 (perhaps because initial impressions were unreasonably positive), whereas images of both candidates improved slightly in 1976 (perhaps because of initial levels of skepticism).

Although most studies of both the 1960 and the 1976 debates indicate that the impact of the debates on popular impressions of the candidates was minimal, there are some necessary caveats about this general conclusion. First, most of these results are based on aggregate perceptions for an entire sample. The fact that these aggregate perceptions stay the same over time does not mean all the individuals have remained unchanged. Some individuals may be concluding that a candidate is more experienced while others are concluding that he is less experienced than originally thought, as a result of debate exposure, with the changes canceling each other out. For example, when the perceptions of one group of citizens before the first debate in 1976 were compared with their perceptions at the end of the campaign, between 24 percent and 34 percent of the *individuals* changed their perceptions of Carter's and Ford's experience and trustworthiness during that time. Since many of these changes were in opposite directions, however, in the aggregate there was much less net change than there was individual change.[21] Consequently, individual changes in candidate images may be too inconsistent or idiosyncratic to show up in the aggregate in the typical sample survey.

Second, it is difficult to isolate the impact of debate exposure itself on perceptual changes (or lack thereof) because debate exposure is usually quickly followed by attention to news coverage of debates and to personal discussions about debates. Although it is plausible that changes occurring between two points in time are influenced by a major media event taking place within that time (particularly when the time span is short), perceptual changes could also be caused by coincident news coverage, personal discussions, or something else entirely.

For example, in 1976 there is evidence that voter perceptions of candidates were significantly altered by a *combination* of debate content and postdebate media coverage and interpretation. Voter reactions to the first and second debates of 1976 differed depending on whether the reaction was measured immediately after the debate or a few days later. Presumably, what caused the different reactions over time was exposure to secondary discussion and interpretation of the debates by both personal acquaintances and the media.

In 1976, those who were interviewed four to seven days after the first debate had different perceptions than did those interviewed immediately after the debate. Those interviewed later were less apt to perceive the debate as worthwhile, fair, and helpful; were more apt to perceive that Ford had done a better job and were more positive toward Ford; were more apt to perceive that Ford was the leader in the campaign; and were even slightly more apt to express a pro-Ford intention. After considering a number of possible explanations for differences in perceptions depending on when respondents were interviewed, it was concluded that the group interviewed later was responding to postdebate news coverage and personal discussion:

> The collective definition of the debate—the way it emerged in the public mind—did not depend solely on what each viewer had experienced by himself or herself in intimate communion with the tube. Rather, it developed over time by way of a process in which each person's impressions were constantly tested against those of others, including interpretative and analytic commentaries offered by authoritative mass media sources. Im-

pressions gained directly from the debate were accordingly modified and elaborated. Those that diverged too much from this consensus enjoyed little support and, consequently, were apt to lose out until they were no longer expressed. Persons within the controlled exposure conditions had given their evaluations without the benefit of any such give-and-take.[22]

Similarly, citizen perceptions after the second debate in 1976 were also found to vary with the amount of time that had elapsed between that debate and the measurement of perceptions. The most newsworthy portion of the second debate was Gerald Ford's comment about Soviet domination of Eastern Europe. A small group of debate viewers, whose reactions to the debate were being monitored as they watched, did not think the remark was extraordinary and did not respond strongly to it. Also, respondents who were interviewed immediately after the second debate did not volunteer much comment about the remark or give any other sign of being affected by the remark. Within a few hours after the debate, however, the responses of citizens began to change. The later citizens were interviewed after the second debate, the more apt they were to perceive that Carter had won the debate, to mention Ford's remark as something they remembered, to claim to have agreed more with Carter and to have disagreed with Ford, and to say they were going to vote for Carter. In this case, postdebate news coverage was clearly responsible for the alteration in public perception:

> the preponderance of viewers of the second debate most likely were not certain of the true status of Eastern Europe or, less likely, did not consider Ford's error important. Given the amount of publicity given to Ford's East European statements the next day by the news media and the concomitant change that took place, it is concluded that this publicity caused the change. The change probably was too rapid to be caused by interpersonal influence or by the classic two-step process. Rather, this is evidence of direct media influence. College-educated voters appeared to be a major group affected by the next-day publicity. . . . Women also seemed to be disproportionately affected by the next-day publicity.[23]

Just as Ford was advantaged by media commentary after the first debate, then, Carter was advantaged by commentary after the second debate. Since this effect could not have occurred without both the debate *and* the subsequent media coverage, we must attribute the result to the combined effect of both sources. The magnitude of these effects should remind us to consider carefully the way in which debates can *indirectly* as well as directly affect the perceptions of citizens, and should also warn us that the effect of debate exposure may be altered by other factors within brief time periods after a debate takes place.

Published research reports of the 1980 presidential debates are not yet available. There is some circumstantial evidence, however, that the

Reagan-Carter debate improved voters' impressions of *both* candidates. In interviews with Connecticut voters conducted one to three days before the debate and one to three days after the debate, it was found that after the debate respondents were more apt to consider Reagan forceful rather than rash and Carter careful rather than weak, and to perceive that Carter "understands the complex problems a president has to deal with" (there was no change on this for Reagan), and that both candidates had clear positions on the issues and spoke carefully. In addition, a nationwide poll conducted both before and after the Reagan-Carter debate found that after the debate the public thought that *both* candidates were *less* likely to "get us into a war." Unfortunately, since neither poll distinguished debate viewers from nonviewers, it is impossible to know how much of this change to attribute to the debate itself.[24]

In a more speculative vein, and in the absence of any empirical data on the public, a number of commentators have suggested that both the Reagan-Anderson and Reagan-Carter debates in 1980 worked to Ronald Reagan's advantage. Since so much of Jimmy Carter's reelection strategy in 1980 depended on portraying Reagan as incompetent, dangerous, and unacceptably conservative, Reagan's ability to deflect these suggestions and avoid the formation of these perceptions was probably crucial to his electoral success. Reagan's folksy tone, sense of humor, ease, and careful moderation of his issue positions in both the debates probably *prevented* the formation of the beliefs desired by and crucial to the Carter campaign.[25][6]

In general, then, presidential debates do not seem to *alter* public perceptions of the candidates drastically. With the exception of the first Kennedy-Nixon debate in 1960, and possibly the debates in 1980, there has been little evidence that the image of any candidate has been significantly changed by a debate performance. There are probably two main reasons for this. First, citizens are willing and able to interpret the meaning of a debate selectively to reinforce existing preferences. Consequently, Republican impressions of the Republican candidate may improve and Democratic impressions of the same candidate deteriorate. If the sizes of these two groups are similar, the net (aggregate) result will show no change.

Second, the presidential debates that have taken place so far have, in general, presented little new information to the citizen. The candidates have repeated campaign slogans and promises that have been made before, have carefully rehearsed and planned their debate peformance, and have generally looked and acted as we expected them to. Consequently, it is hardly surprising that the main response of the public has been to maintain rather than change their images of the candidates. If something entirely unexpected were to transpire during a candidate debate (for example, if a candidate told a sexist joke, used profane language, walked off the stage in a huff, admitted he was motivated by a desire for power, or broke into uncontrollable sobbing), we would hardly expect public perceptions to remain so stable. Ordinarily, however, candidate debate performances have been confined within much narrower and more conventional boundaries.

PERCEPTIONS CONCERNING CANDIDATE POLICY PREFERENCES

In contrast to the generally minimal impact candidate debates have had on the public's image of candidate attributes, presidential debates have allowed the public to clarify their perceptions of candidate policy positions. This is because debate discussions tend to be quite policy-oriented, and because debates attract into their audience people who are generally uninterested in and uninformed about campaign politics.

Very few of the 1960 debate studies investigated what the public learned about the candidates' policy preferences. Most of the research that did focus on policy questions simply asked citizens if they thought they had learned anything about candidate policy preferences without making an independent determination of the accuracy of these perceptions. Nevertheless, one review of the 1960 studies concluded that the 1960 debates made some issues more salient than others and caused some people to learn the policy preferences of the candidates.[26]

In 1976, however, there was much more interest in the perceptions of candidate policy preferences and in the debates' effect on these perceptions. Aggregate perceptions of the candidates' issue positions on the issues of unemployment, taxes, abortion, and defense spending were found to be highly stable during the 1976 campaign. At the individual level, however, there was a fair amount of change in the perceptions of candidate issue positions, and at least some of that change was related to debate exposure. The first debate, for example, clarified perceptions of candidate positions on employment policy, with between 20 and 30 percent of the respondents improving the accuracy of their perceptions on the issue after the first debate. Similarly, there were increases in the accuracy of voter perceptions of Carter's preference for government reorganization, and of both candidates' positions on tax reform and amnesty for Vietnam War draft evaders.

In contrast, citizens did not seem to learn anything after the first debate about issues that were *not* discussed in the first debate (a good indication that the learning was debate-related). On defense spending, the B-1 bomber, busing, gun control, national health insurance, and abortion, little learning took place around the time of the first debate, indicating that the amount of learning was related to whether the issue was discussed in that debate.[27]

Table 7–4 shows the effect of the first debate in 1976. Knowledge of the candidates' policy preferences was measured before the first debate

TABLE 7–4   Changes in Knowledge of Candidates' Stands on the Issues
(*Percent*)

		Postdebate 1		
	Predebate	*Total*	*Viewers*[a]	*Nonviewers*
Federal unemployment programs[b]				
Knowing Carter's stand	57.7	73.4[c]	76.3[c]	65.9
Knowing Ford's stand	28.8	43.6[c]	47.4[c]	33.3
Abortion amendment				
Knowing Carter's stand	30.8	34.7	38.1	25.6
Knowing Ford's stand	32.7	36.7	40.5	26.8
Tax reform[b]				
Knowing Carter's stand	59.6	75.4[c]	80.9[c]	61.0
Knowing Ford's stand	22.1	35.1[c]	35.5[c]	34.1
Controlling armed crime				
Knowing Carter's stand	21.2	25.9	26.5	24.4
Knowing Ford's stand	28.8	33.7	35.3	29.3
Federal reorganization[b]				
Knowing Carter's stand	50.0	75.4[c]	79.5[c]	64.6[c]
Knowing Ford's stand	23.1	41.1[c]	43.3[c]	35.4
Construction of B-1 bomber				
Knowing Carter's stand	43.3	36.0	37.7	31.7
Knowing Ford's stand	36.5	34.0	37.2	25.6
	N = 104	*N* = 297	*N* = 215	*N* = 82

Source: Lee B. Becker, Idowu A. Sobowale, Robin E. Cobbey, and Chaim H. Eyal, "Debates' Effects on Voters' Understanding of Candidates and Issues," in George F. Bishop, Robert G. Meadow, Marilyn Jackson-Beeck (eds.), *The Presidential Debates* (New York: Praeger, 1980), p. 135. Reprinted by permission.

[a]Viewers are persons either viewing or listening to at least fifteen minutes of the debate; nonviewers are all others.

[b]Issue was discussed in the first debate; the others were not.

[c]The probability of the difference between the predebate wave and postdebate 1 occurring by chance is less than .05.

and then compared for the same people with knowledge after the first debate. In addition, knowledge on issues covered in the first debate was compared with knowledge on issues that were ignored during the first debate, and gains in knowledge for debate viewers were compared with those for nonviewers. For the three issues discussed in the first debate (unemployment, tax reform, and government reorganization), awareness increased substantially, but for the other issues it changed very little. In addition, the knowledge gain was greater in every case for debate viewers than for nonviewers.

Neither the second nor the third debate had as much effect on citizen perceptions of candidate issue positions. The main issue-related information that was remembered after the second debate was Ford's Eastern European comment, in addition to a modest alteration in perceived military spending policies.

Another way of measuring the effect of debates is to compare the accuracy of perceptions at the beginning and end of the campaign and then see whether debate viewers' perceptions of candidate policy positions become more accurate than do those of nonviewers. When this was done in 1976, it was found that learning about the issues of employment, size of government, inflation, and military spending was related to debate exposure in 1976, even once the education, political interest, partisan strength, and other media exposure of the citizen were taken into consideration. Debate exposure was also related to the extent to which citizens perceived differences between the candidates on the question of unemployment and differences between the parties on inflation, unemployment, defense spending, and the size of the federal government: The more debates watched, the more difference perceived. This result also persisted after controlling for education and strength of partisanship; the relationship was stronger than with exposure to newspapers and television news; and the relationship was marginally stronger for those with low and medium political attention than for those with high political attention. This suggests that citizens do learn meaningful policy-related material from televised debates when the information transmitted is clear and is not entirely redundant to the individual.[28]

Finally, another 1976 study asked respondents to identify Ford's and Carter's positions regarding relatively obscure issues covered in only one of the presidential debates (registration of handguns, a constitutional amendment to allow voluntary prayer in public schools, the use of U.S. troops in Yugoslavia to counter a Soviet invasion, and a constitutional amendment giving states the right to set up their own standards for abortion). The accuracy of these responses was determined, and then the factors related to having accurate perceptions were explored. The more educated and more politically involved respondents had more accurate perceptions, but the one variable that best explained knowledge of the candidates' positions was a measure of debate exposure: The more debates watched, the more knowledgeable the respondent.[29]

It is particularly unfortunate that there are no published research reports yet available on the impact of the 1980 debates on the policy perceptions of the U.S. public. The policy positions taken in both the Reagan-Anderson and Reagan-Carter debates were unusually clear and distinct. As John Anderson said toward the end of the first debate, "Governor Reagan and I have agreed on exactly one thing; we are both against the imposition of a peacetime draft. We have disagreed, I believe, on virtually every other issue." The Reagan-Carter exchange involved an earnest attempt by Carter to defend his record as president and a fairly specific indication by Reagan of how his policies would differ. Given the programmatic nature of both debates and the large audiences attracted to both programs, it is quite plausible that the debates contributed to learning about the policy preferences of the presidential candidates.

In summary, then, it appears that televised presidential debates have helped citizens learn something about candidate policy preferences. Although this learning may not involve all issues mentioned in a debate; may involve a general rather than a precise perception of candidate issue positions (such as "he wants to provide government jobs," without knowing how many, to whom, for how long or at what cost); may not reach all citizens or even all viewers; and may not last much longer than election day, it does involve a fairly large minority of viewers' perceptions in those policy areas heavily concentrated on in the debates. In that respect, debates compare favorably with other modes of campaign communication in the extent to which they lead to the creation of an "informed" electorate:

> The 1976 presidential debates produced a better informed electorate than would have been the case without them. Watching the debates increased the level of manifest information that all citizens had about the candidates regardless of their education, political involvement, or general information-seeking habits . . . those individuals who watched the debators exhibited a heightened political awareness at exactly the time when political information is crucial—shortly before an election. In this respect democracy was well served, for without the debates a significant proportion of the electorate would have remained relatively uninformed about the candidates.[30]

Conclusion

In this and the preceding chapter we have considered the effect of three sources of campaign communication—campaign news coverage, broadcast spot advertisements, and televised candidate debates—on the beliefs and attitudes of the U.S. public. We have reviewed the existing evidence concerning the public's response to these sources of campaign communication and have considered the extent to which this communication contributes to public awareness.

Our first conclusion is that there is considerable stability to the public's beliefs and attitudes concerning political candidates, parties, and issues. Wild fluctuations in perceptions and preferences during the campaign period are rare; those politically significant changes in public opinion that do take place during a campaign generally occur within fairly narrow boundaries.

There are several reasons for this. One has to do with the way the public responds to campaign stimuli. We have seen that individuals maintain a significant degree of control over what they hear, see, and read, and the meaning they give to any messages encountered. We have existing values and attitudes, we have come to expect politicians to behave in a certain way, and we have our own history of previous political behavior. Campaign propaganda is responded to, or used, within the context of our own history and preferences and is personally attended, interpreted, and remembered. Consequently, many campaign messages are never received, are distorted, or are soon forgotten.

A second limit on the effect of campaign propaganda has to do with the flow of campaign communication. In the United States, campaign communication tends to be both *compartmentalized* and *balanced*. That is, most campaign communication is compartmentalized into regularly scheduled, predictable formats (such as news shows, newspaper columns, particular magazines, special television broadcasts, and so on), making it possible for citizens to maintain control over exposure to campaign communications and to ignore the campaign if they wish. Spot ads are the primary exception to this since they make exposure more involuntary, and the simultaneous broadcasting of debates or conventions by all three networks makes chance or casual encounters with campaign messages more likely. Nevertheless, the fairly strict separation of news from entertainment and the relegation of campaign coverage to particular locations and times makes it easy to restrict one's exposure to campaign communication. Further, the low priority that many U.S. citizens give to electoral politics means that many choose this intentional lack of exposure to campaign communication.

In addition, campaign communication also tends to be "balanced" or at least minimally diverse. News accounts, spot ad campaigns, and debate appearances are all generally balanced, at least across the two major parties during the general election. This means that the public is exposed to conflicting, contradictory viewpoints, within which one can find support for a variety of predispositions or prior belief systems. This makes unlikely a monopoly of campaign messages suitable for strongly affecting the populace in one direction. When campaign communication *is* unbalanced (as in the case, for example, of Jimmy Carter's 1980 failure to bring the Iranian hostage situation to a successful conclusion; of press commentary concerning Gerald Ford's Eastern Europe gaffe in 1976; or of George McGovern's controversial removal of Thomas Eagleton from the ballot in 1972), substantial changes in public opinion *are* more likely.

Our second major conclusion is that despite this general pattern of stability in citizen perceptions, there are a number of areas in which public opinion does change during an election campaign and where at least a portion of this change may be attributed to some form of campaign communication. News coverage is effective in (1) orienting the public's attention toward the game aspects of a campaign and in shaping horse-race perceptions of who is winning that game; (2) altering the makeup of both the candidate and the issue agendas; (3) developing popular, thematic impressions of political newcomers; and, (4) in the case of daily newspaper news, clarifying citizen perceptions of candidate policy preferences. The effects of spot ad campaigns are less certain, but at this point they seem to include modestly shaping popular impressions of candidates; reinforcing cultural values; reassuring voters that all candidates hold acceptable, consensually-held views; and, *when the content permits*, altering perceptions of candidate policy preferences. Presidential debates have in the past left popular images of candidates fairly untouched while showing a laudable capacity for clarifying candidate policy preferences.

Our third major conclusion involves the consequences of campaign communication for the notion of an informed electorate. To some degree campaign communication does contribute to public awareness. There are numerous limitations on the contribution that is made, however. Newspaper news is somewhat informative, but those who read it are already knowledge-rich. More people watch television news, but its content does not stimulate substantive learning. Spot ads can be effective, and they reach a large and diverse audience, but their messages are typically vague or symbolic and may be deceptive and misleading as well. Convention coverage helps people learn, but the party's supporters make up most of the audience. Only televised debates, then, combine the best features of each of these sources—large and diverse audiences, substantive and balanced content, an understandable and engaging format. Debates, however, are not part of every election campaign.

Campaign communication, then, at most makes the electorate only marginally more informed than it was at the beginning of an election campaign. Furthermore, this marginal gain in awareness is probably only true for presidential campaigns, since the flow of communication is so much less in nonpresidential campaigns. Even at the presidential level most citizens form very general evaluations of candidates ("I like him," "He is a good person," "I like his domestic policies") rather than specific ones. In 1976, "43% of the people in a nationwide poll could comment on only one of the candidate's strengths and weaknesses," and "less than 20% could state three or more likes or dislikes about either candidate. Such limited information prevented them from comparing candidates and choosing accordingly."[31]

This suggests that even a tiny morsel of meaningful information gleaned from campaign communication can be important because it may be all the voter has to work with, and that the ideal of an informed electorate making well-thought-out choices is seldom approached and gives us a misleading perspective on the meaning of elections more generally. Furthermore, it suggests that most campaign communication actually represents a constraint on the political awareness of the U.S. citizenry rather than a contributing agent for that awareness. If this is true, then a significantly different approach to elections, campaigns, and campaign communication may be necessary. Once we have considered the impact of campaign communication on voting behavior in Chapter 8, we will return to this possibility in the concluding chapter.

Notes

1. Thomas E. Patterson and Robert D. McClure, *The Unseeing Eye* (New York: G. P. Putnam's, 1976).
2. Thomas E. Patterson and Robert D. McClure, *Political Advertising: Voter Reaction to Televised Political Commercials* (Princeton, N.J.: Citizens' Research Foundation, 1973), pp. 14–17.
3. Ibid., p. 20.
4. Charles K. Atkin, Lawrence Bowen, Oguz B. Nayman, and Kenneth G. Sheinkopf, "Quality versus Quantity in Televised Political Ads," *Public Opinion Quarterly* 37 (Summer 1973): 209–224.
5. Charles Atkin and Garry Heald, "Effects of Political Advertising," *Public Opinion Quarterly* 40 (1976): 216–228.
6. See Robert Spero, *The Duping of the American Voter: Dishonesty and Deception in Presidential Television Advertising* (New York: Lippincott/Crowell, 1980) for a provocative and intemperate argument to this effect.
7. Ronald Mulder, "The Effects of Televised Political Ads in the 1975 Chicago Mayoral Election," *Journalism Quarterly* 56 (Summer 1979): 336–340.
8. Patterson and McClure, *The Unseeing Eye*, p. 113.
9. Atkin and Heald, "Effects of Political Advertising."
10. Mulder, "Effects of Televised Political Ads."
11. Robert W. Sarnoff, "An NBC View," in Sidney Kraus, ed., *The Great Debates* (Gloucester, Mass.: Peter Smith, 1968).
12. Frank Stanton, "A CBS View," in Kraus, *The Great Debates*.
13. Doris Graber, "Problems in Measuring Audience Effects of the 1976 Debates," in George F. Bishop, Robert G. Meadow, and Marilyn Jackson-Beeck, eds., *The Presidential Debates* (New York: Praeger, 1980).
14. For example, see the reviews and articles published in these three books: Kraus, *The Great Debates*; Sidney Kraus, ed., *The Great Debates, 1976: Ford vs. Carter* (Bloomington: Indiana University Press, 1980); Bishop, Meadow, and Jackson-Beeck, *The Presidential Debates*.
15. Richard F. Carter, "Some Effects of the Debates," in Kraus, *The Great Debates*.
16. Ibid.
17. Percy H. Tannenbaum, Bradley S. Greenberg, and Fred R. Silverman, "Candidate Images," in Kraus, *The Great Debates*, pp. 271–288.
18. Herbert W. Simons and K. Leibowitz, "Shifts in Candidate Images," in Kraus, *The Great Debates, 1976*.
19. David O. Sears and Steven H. Chaffee, "Uses and Effects of the 1976 Debates: An Overview of Empirical Studies," in Kraus, *The Great Debates, 1976*.
20. Herbert W. Simons and Kenneth Leibowitz, "Shifts in Candidate Images," in Kraus, *The Great Debates, 1976*.

21. Richard Joslyn, "Voter Belief and Attitude Change and the 1976 Debates," Unpublished manuscript.

22. Gladys Engel Lang and Kurt Lang, "The Formation of Public Opinion: Direct and Mediated Effects of the First Debate," in Bishop, Meadow, and Jackson-Beeck, *The Presidential Debates*, pp. 79–80.

23. Frederick T. Steeper, "Public Response to Gerald Ford's Statements on Eastern Europe in the Second Debate," in Bishop, Meadow, and Jackson-Beeck, *The Presidential Debates*, p. 101.

24. "Opinion Roundup," *Public Opinion* 3, no. 6 (December–January 1981): 28–35.

25. Jeff Greenfield, *The Real Campaign* (New York: Summit Books, 1982), Chap. 11, 12.

26. Elihu Katz and Jacob J. Feldman, "The Debates in the Light of Research: A Survey of Surveys," in Kraus, *The Great Debates*.

27. Arthur H. Miller and Michael Mackuen, "Learning about the Candidates: The 1976 Presidential Debates," *Public Opinion Quarterly* 43, no. 3 (Fall 1979): 326–346.

28. Ibid.

29. George F. Bishop, Robert W. Oldenick, and Alfred J. Tuchfarber, "The Presidential Debates as a Device for Increasing the 'Rationality' of Electoral Behavior," in Bishop, Meadow, and Jackson-Beeck, *The Presidential Debates*.

30. Miller and Mackuen, "Learning," p. 344.

31. Doris Graber, *Mass Media and American Politics* (Washington, D.C.: Congressional Quarterly Press, 1980), p. 185.

8
Campaign Communication and Voting Behavior

Newspapers' endorsements do influence presidential voting in their local communities.

—Robert S. Erikson, "The Influence of Newspaper Endorsements
in Presidential Elections"

. . . broadcast campaigning . . . is not the sole determinant of the outcome in any election . . . but in elections other than those for president . . . campaign broadcasting has the capacity to significantly affect the results.

—Gary C. Jacobson, "The Impact of Broadcast Campaigning on
Electoral Outcomes"

The first presidential debate of 1976 . . . did produce a better informed electorate. However, the debate had almost no impact on voting intentions.

—Alan I. Abramowitz, "The Impact of a Presidential Debate on
Voter Rationality"

In Chapters 6 and 7 we saw that campaign communication has a noticeable effect on many of the public's election-related beliefs and attitudes. Perceptions regarding the viability of different candidates, the policy preferences and personal attributes of candidates, and the salience of political issues are all significantly affected by campaign news coverage and candidate appeals. Since these opinions are related, in turn, to the public's decisions regarding electoral participation, campaign communication has an impact not only on the public's political beliefs and attitudes, but on the public's electoral *behavior* as well. Two types of electoral behavior will be discussed in this chapter: the decision whether or not to vote (turnout), and the decision to vote for a particular candidate (candidate choice).

219

Campaign Communication and Turnout

There is a great deal of contemporary concern about voter turnout in the United States. This concern is usually expressed in three ways. First, turnout levels in the United States are lower than most commentators find desirable. Second, it is often pointed out that voter turnout in the United States is lower than turnout in most Western European democracies.[1] Third, the recent downward-sloping *trend* in voter turnout in the United States is often pointed to with particular dismay.

HISTORICAL TRENDS IN VOTER TURNOUT

Figure 8–1 shows turnout levels in presidential and congressional elections since 1930. Although the historical trend in turnout levels is actually quite flat over this period of time, during the 1930s there was a general, gradual increase in turnout; during the 1940s there was a temporary dip in turnout; during the 1950s turnout was steady or slightly rising; and since the early 1960s turnout has declined. In addition, Figure 8–1 shows that presidential and on-year congressional (that is, congressional elections held in presidential election years) turnout levels are parallel, with on-year congressional turnout consistently slightly less than presidential turnout; and that off-year congressional (that is, congressional elections *not* held in presidential election years) turnout is typically 15–20 percent less than presidential turnout.[2]

INDIVIDUAL-LEVEL RELATIONSHIPS WITH TURNOUT

Since our goal here is to investigate the impact of campaign communication on voter turnout, we have to consider the reasons that individuals decide to vote. To date, researchers have discovered a number of individual characteristics and experiences that are related to turnout. These may conveniently be organized into three categories: relationships involving (1) the personal characteristics of citizens, (2) the political attitudes of individuals, and (3) the legal and political environment in which decisions to vote are made.

Of all of the *personal characteristics* related to turnout, an individual's amount of formal education has been found to be the most strongly and consistently related. The more education a person has, the more likely he or she is to vote. Once this relationship is taken into consideration, the effect of most other personal attributes is lessened considerably, but some interesting, though minor, relationships do remain between income, occupation, age, sex, marital status, race, and turnout.[3]

A number of *political attitudes* have also been found to be related to turnout. Among the most important are feelings of political efficacy, a

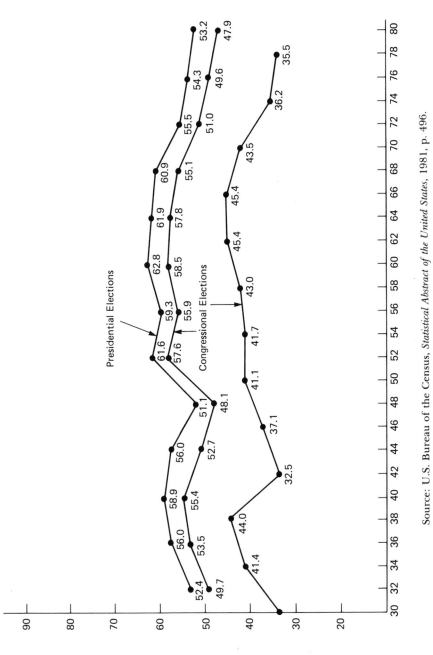

FIGURE 8–1 Voter Turnout, 1930–1980

Source: U.S. Bureau of the Census, *Statistical Abstract of the United States*, 1981, p. 496.

sense of civic duty, and the strength of party identification. In general, the stronger one's party identification, sense of civic duty, and political efficacy, the more likely one is to vote.[4]

Finally, the *political and legal environment* has been found to be related to turnout. The stringency of registration requirements, the political subculture of an area, and the level of partisan activity and competition in a locale are all related to turnout levels.[5]

Given the existence of these relationships, any direct effect of campaign communication on turnout is likely to be small. A number of analyses have concluded, however, that campaign media exposure does have a slight stimulating effect on voter turnout.

TELEVISION/NEWSPAPER AVAILABILITY AND TURNOUT

One way of estimating the impact of campaign communication on voter turnout is to compare the turnout rate of citizens who have certain media available to them during a campaign with the rate of citizens who do not. If the two groups of citizens are similar in all other important ways, then any difference in turnout could be attributed to the availability of the particular form of campaign communication.

At first, it might appear to be impossible to find or create a situation in which an entire medium or type of campaign communication is unavailable for a substantial segment of the public. Since the 1940s, however, there have been two types of situations in which events permitted just such a comparison.

One such circumstance arose in the early 1950s when half of the country was prevented from having television available for a period of four or five years. In 1952 the Federal Communications Commission ordered a freeze on applications for television broadcast licenses pending a review of frequency-allocation policy. This freeze was in effect during the presidential election campaign of 1952, the first presidential campaign in which television in general and paid spot advertisements in particular were used. In parts of the country this meant that some people had television signals available and some did not, as a result of their geographical location. Iowa was one state in which some of the counties were within range of a television signal while others were not.

This situation provided a natural exposed-to-television group and a natural unexposed-to-television group that depended on where a person lived. In addition, an approximation of a "before" and "after" measure of turnout could be obtained by comparing the turnout rates in 1952 (after exposure to television) with those of 1944 and 1948 (before exposure to television). This comparison showed that turnout in general increased in Iowa from 1944 and 1948 to 1952. It increased *more* (from 3 to 5 percent more), however, in those counties *with television* than in those without television.[6] Since we cannot be sure that the people living in the two sets of counties were identical in every way other than television availability, there may be another explanation for these differences (for example, the counties that had television might also have had more active party organizations in 1952). It is at least possible, however, that the availability of television in 1952 increased the turnout rate in parts of Iowa above the increase experienced in the rest of the state.

Another situation in which the effect of media availability can be studied occurs when a medium is on strike during an election campaign and hence is unavailable to the public in that locality. In Toledo, Ohio, in 1966, for example, the *Toledo Blade*, a monopoly newspaper, went on strike two weeks before an election for governor and state senator was to take place. This created a group of citizens (the 1966 electorate in Toledo) for whom exposure to newspaper coverage was impossible. When the turnout rates in 1966 for three statewide offices (governor, secretary of state, and treasurer) were compared with turnout for these three offices in two previous off-year elections, it was found that turnout usually ran about 3 percent higher in Lucas County (where Toledo is located) than it did statewide (55.44–52.42 percent). In 1966, however, turnout in Lucas County was slightly *lower* than turnout statewide even though one of the candidates for governor was from the local area.[7] This suggests that the absence of the daily newspaper depressed the Toledo-area turnout a few percentage points lower than normal.

In both these situations, then, the *presence* of a medium was associated with a slightly higher (3–5 percent) turnout rate. Given the impossibility of concluding for certain that it was media availability alone that caused the increased turnout rate, and given the fact that situations in which a medium is completely unavailable are rare, we must look at other evidence regarding the effect of campaign communication on turnout.

INDIVIDUAL MEDIA EXPOSURE AND TURNOUT

Another way to study the effect of campaign communication on voter turnout is to look for relationships between media exposure and turnout among individuals. In general, there is a persistent and significant relationship between media exposure in general, and newspaper exposure in particular, and turnout.

In the 1948 presidential election, for example, an "index of communication exposure"—consisting of exposure to radio, newspapers, and magazines (few people had television in 1948)—was found to be strongly related to turnout. Furthermore, this relationship remained after controlling for the respondent's political interest, and turnout rates were 15–30 percent higher for those with the most exposure to campaign communication.[8] One weakness of this study, however, was that it failed to control for many other attributes that we now know are related to turnout.

During the 1950s there were also modest relationships between campaign communication exposure and turnout. Both television viewing and reading a newspaper regularly were associated with voting, but radio exposure did not matter. Moreover, when the effects of watching television and reading the newspaper were combined, those watching television *and* reading a newspaper turned out at a rate of 83 percent, whereas those who just read a newspaper regularly turned out at a rate of 73 percent, those who only owned a television turned out at a rate of 61 percent, and those who *neither* owned a television *nor* read a newspaper regularly turned out at a rate of 41 percent. The main jump in turnout, then, occurred for those with some exposure to either television or newspapers. Newspaper exposure was the more potent force of the two, and exposure to both media was associated with higher rates of turnout than was exposure to either alone. These relationships also persisted after controls for the sex of the respondent, the rental value of the individual's home, and the individual's level of education were introduced.[9]

Finally, data from the presidential elections from 1960 to 1976 indicate that the frequency of reading about the campaign in the newspaper is strongly related to voter turnout. Furthermore, the fact that people have apparently been reading about the campaign in the newspaper less in recent years has been estimated to account for about 20 percent of the recent decline in turnout. Radio and television exposure, on the other hand, are apparently not important contributors to the recent decline in presidential turnout.[10]

The available evidence, then, supports the position that exposure to campaign communication stimulates voter turnout. Both the complete absence of a medium and low levels of exposure to the media in general are associated with a disinclination to vote. Newspaper exposure in particular seems to stimulate turnout, and a recent decline in newspaper reading is partly responsible for the post-1960 decline in presidential turnout.

So far we have considered only the possibility that campaign communication *stimulates* turnout. There is also some contemporary speculation that at least one form of campaign communication has a *depressing* effect on turnout.

ELECTION-NIGHT RETURNS AND TURNOUT

One of the post-1964 innovations in campaign news coverage (discussed in Chapter 5) has been the reporting of partial election returns as they are counted and the projecting of winners by the three television networks prior to the tabulation of the entire vote. In 1980 another innovation—the use of exit polls—further increased the networks' ability to make early projections.

The accuracy of these network projections has never been as much of an issue as the timing of the projections. Because of the time differential from the East Coast to the West Coast, many projections have been made over the years prior to the closing of the polls in the western United States. This has led a number of observers to express concern that people who have not yet voted in the Western states will perceive that their ballot is meaningless, resulting in a decline in turnout in those areas where voting has not been completed.

So far, however, the evidence suggests that there is little effect of election-night returns coverage on West Coast turnout. In 1964, for example, a survey of 1,704 California citizens who said the day before the election that they planned to vote found only 15 people who did not vote; none of those decisions could be traced to exposure to election-night vote returns coverage.[11] A similar survey of 364 California citizens found only 1 person who decided not to vote because of the early returns.[12]

In 1968 a comparison of the turnout rates of West Coast and East Coast citizens found that 4.3 percent of the Western respondents exposed to election-day returns decided not to vote, compared with 3 percent of the unexposed Western respondents. Of the Eastern voters, however, who could not possibly have been exposed to the returns before voting, 7 percent also decided not to vote at the last minute. Furthermore, since only 6 percent of the West Coast sample were exposed to the returns prior to voting, one would have to conclude that the evidence supporting an exposure-turnout relationship in 1968 was also negligible.[13]

Unfortunately, the evidence concerning the impact of returns coverage on West Coast turnout is not very good. Asking nonvoters to analyze the reasons for their own behavior is not a particularly valid strategy, and the number of respondents who can be interviewed in such cases is usually not large enough to provide an accurate estimate of the behavior of all eligible West Coast voters. There is a study of turnout in the 1972 election, however, that solves at least one of these problems by using interviews conducted with more than 90,000 people.

Nineteen seventy-two was a landslide presidential election in which both NBC and CBS were able to declare Richard Nixon the winner more than two hours before the polls closed on the West Coast. (NBC's call in 1972 was only fifteen minutes later than its call in 1980. In 1972, however, there was no concession speech soon thereafter by George McGovern, as there was in 1980 by President Carter.) By using the large sample of interviews conducted in 1972, and comparing the after-6-P.M. turnout rates of West Coast and non–West Coast voters with the after-6-P.M. turnout rates in 1974, it has been estimated that the after-6-P.M. West Coast turnout in 1972 was 2.7 percent lower than it should have been. This has been attributed to the election-night returns coverage.[14]

This estimate has been challenged in a study of turnout in the presidential elections from 1960 through 1980.[15] By comparing presidential and congressional turnout rates in Western states to those in non-Western, non-Southern states, and by analyzing the change in state-level presidential turnout rates over time, two researchers have shown that state-level turnout rates are not closely associated with returns reporting and early declarations of winners. This conclusion is based on the fact that (1) Western-state turnout has been lower than non-Western, non-Southern turnout in most of the presidential elections since 1960, *regardless* of whether early returns were involved; (2) the difference between Western and non-Western, non-Southern turnout is *less* in the years in which early projections were announced than in other years; and (3) the *change* in Western turnout from one presidential election to the next does not correspond to years in which early projections were made.

The evidence is mixed, then, regarding the impact of election-night returns on turnout. On balance, most of the evidence suggests that returns coverage does not depress West Coast turnout; at most, the measurable impact is small. Certainly, of all the explanations for individual turnout decisions and trends in aggregate turnout rates, exposure to election-night returns is probably among the least consequential.

In summary, then, campaign communication has a modest stimulating effect on turnout. Both the availability of media and the amount of exposure to television and newspapers are associated with higher turnout rates. Newspaper exposure has the greatest impact on turnout; radio and magazine exposure have no measurable effect. In addition, the recent decline in voter turnout may be attributed in part to declining levels of newspaper exposure.

There are a number of possible explanations for this stimulating effect on turnout. One is that exposure to campaign coverage itself activates the feelings of civic duty that are related to electoral participation. Another is that campaign communication stimulates campaign interest and strengthens party identification, both of which are related to turnout. A third is that the dramatic portrayal of election contests interests the electorate and indicates that a meaningful choice is involved. Whatever the accuracy of these explanations, voter turnout does seem to be partially responsive to the availability and awareness of campaign communication.

Campaign Communication and Candidate Choices in Presidential General Elections

The second major decision made in each election by the U.S. public involves selecting a candidate for whom to vote. Given the resources devoted to campaign communication by journalists, candidates, campaign consultants and other activists, it would seem to be hardly necessary to demonstrate that this flow of information has an impact on candidate choices. In the remainder of this chapter, however, we will see that the impact of campaign communication on the vote is often more indirect than direct, and that the effect varies with the electoral arena in which the vote is being cast.

A MODEL OF VOTING BEHAVIOR IN PRESIDENTIAL GENERAL ELECTIONS

Before turning to the role of campaign communication in the selection of presidential candidates, we first need to understand the bases for candidate choices more generally. Contemporary models of presidential voting are based on three main types of political attitudes. The public's attitudes toward political parties, toward political issues, and toward the candidates themselves are thought to exert the most *direct* impact on the vote, and to account for most of the variation in presidential voting.[16]

Party attitudes exert both a direct and an indirect impact on the vote. The indirect effect of party stems from the long-term identification with or loyalty to a political party that most voters have, and the fact that this identification is used by citizens to help understand and evaluate political personalities and issues. For example, if an incumbent president is not from the same party as some citizen, the citizen may selectively perceive that the incumbent is doing a poorer job than if he were from the same party. In this way, party preferences shape the other proximate attitudes (in this case, attitudes toward a candidate) that directly influence candidate choices.

Party identification can also have a *direct* effect on the vote. One way in which partisan attitudes can directly affect the vote is if a voter forms an evaluation of a candidate based simply on the candidate's party and his or her own party identification and bases his or her vote solely on partisan grounds. In addition, if the other attitudes toward the candidates and issues are balanced and the citizen is undecided about whom to vote for, party loyalties may be used by the voter to resolve the indecision. Presumably, voters break such ties by voting for the candidate of the voter's party.[17]

Attitudes toward candidates are the second proximate influence on the presidential vote. These attitudes involve evaluations of the professional capabilities, the personal character, and the political style of the candidates. They may be based on observation of a politician over a considerable period of time or derived from a more timely acquaintance with a candidate, and they may be shaped by partisan predispositions. The particular attributes that are used to judge candidates vary greatly across individuals and elections, although there are some enduring qualities that are sought in presidential candidates.[18]

Attitudes regarding issues are the third collection of attitudes thought to exert a direct effect on the vote. These attitudes may involve public policy questions, as well as less substantive campaign issues and more general social or political conditions. The attitudes may pertain to who should be held responsible for worrisome social conditions or who should be given the credit for improving some political problem, and they may concern both past policy performance or satisfaction and future policy proposals. The candidate or party given the most credit for solving social or political problems and the candidate or party proposing future policy actions that are most in agreement with the preferences of the electorate are thought to be aided by this category of attitudes.

If we were to diagram what we have described so far as a model of presidential voting, it would look like Figure 8–2. There we see that the

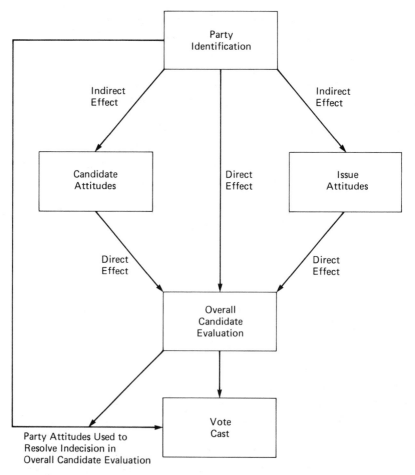

FIGURE 8–2   Preliminary Model of Proximate Attitudes Influencing Presidential General Election Vote

three categories of attitudes have a direct impact on the overall evaluation of the candidates, that party also has an indirect effect on the overall candidate evaluation via its effect on candidate and issue attitudes, that the overall evaluation of the candidates is related to the actual vote cast, and that party attitudes also affect the vote cast in cases where the overall evaluation of the candidates is balanced or indecisive.

Unfortunately, things are not quite as simple as Figure 8–2 implies. Voters do not form attitudes independently of each other or in quite the straightforward manner suggested so far. In fact, there are many interrelationships among the attitudes that have not yet been mentioned.

One complication not mentioned so far involves the tendency of voters to form a summary evaluation of the candidates *first* and then to adjust their other candidate, party, and issue-related attitudes to coincide with this initial evaluation.[19] For example, a voter may decide that he prefers candidate X, based on the candidates' personal traits, and then decide later that the candidate's policy positions are in agreement with his own. Similarly, a voter may decide that she prefers candidate Y (based on candidate X's inability to improve a social condition of interest to her) and then selectively perceive that candidate Y also possesses attractive personal attributes. Also, a positively evaluated candidate of the voter's party may strengthen the voter's party identification, and a negatively evaluated candidate may weaken the voter's party identification. In short, the process by which voters bring their attitudes into agreement is more dynamic and complex than the model in Figure 8–2 indicates.

There are two ways in particular in which voters bring their issue-related attitudes into agreement with their overall candidate evaluations. Essentially, a voter's evaluation of the issue attributes of opposing candidates consists of the voter's own policy stances, the voter's perceptions of the policy stances of the candidates, and the comparative distance between the two. Suppose that a voter decides whom to vote for before forming his or her attitudes regarding the issue positions of the candidates. This decision may be based on the voter's candidate- and party-related attitudes. The voter may then do two things. First, he or she may misperceive the candidate's issue positions as closer to his or her own than they really are. This is called *projection*. Second, he or she may decide that his or her own issue stances are really closer to the favorite candidate's issue stances than he or she originally thought. This is called *persuasion*. In these ways voters may form issue-related attitudes consistent with a candidate preference that are the *result* rather than the *cause* of candidate evaluations.[20]

Figure 8–3 displays a revised and more complex model of presidential voting behavior. It shows that comparative candidate evaluations may influence party, candidate, or issue-related attitudes, and that issue-related attitudes are made up of the voter's own issue stances and the

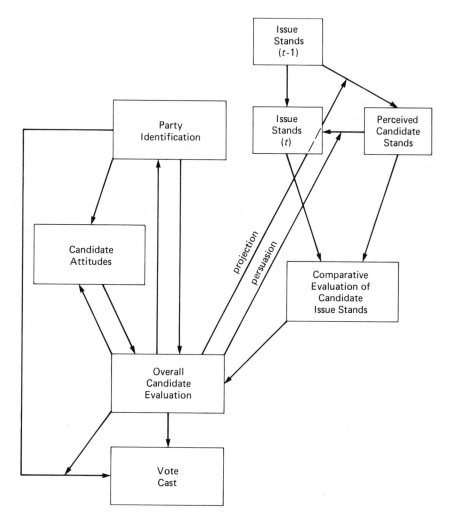

FIGURE 8–3   Revised Model of Presidential General Election Vote with Reciprocal Effects and Issue-Related Projection/Persuasion

voter's perceptions of the candidate's issue stances. It also shows that projection and persuasion may act to bring issue attitudes into agreement with candidate evaluations.

We now have a fairly complicated model of presidential voting that reflects a large body of empirical evidence regarding attitude change during campaigns and presidential voting. In fact, this model accounts very well for much of the variation in presidential candidate choices.

THE EFFECT OF PARTY, ISSUE, AND CANDIDATE ATTITUDES ON PRESIDENTIAL VOTING

There have been numerous attempts to measure the contribution that this trilogy of attitudes—toward parties, issues, and candidates—makes to the overall distribution of the presidential vote. Analyses of the public's votes for president since 1956 have led to a number of general conclusions.

First, the direct effects of the three types of attitudes account for most of the variation in presidential voting. In fact, when party identification is used to break any ties created by balanced evaluations of the two candidates, close to 90 percent of the presidential votes cast may be accounted for by the three proximate attitudes.[21]

Second, each of the three types of attitudes makes a significant contribution toward the explanation of overall candidate evaluations and electoral choices. Attempts to determine which of the three attitudes is most important, however, have produced contradictory results. Some analyses have found that the direct effect of candidate-related attitudes is the most important.[22] Others have argued that the effects of issue-related attitudes have been the most influential.[23] These differing estimates of the effect of each type of attitude reflect the different ways in which each of the attitudes has been measured and the differing relationships among the attitudes provided for in the models tested.[24] At this point the most sensible conclusion seems to be that each of the three attitudes makes a roughly comparable contribution to the votes cast, and that the importance of each varies with campaign developments.

Third, party attitudes do exert both a direct and an indirect effect on the presidential vote. The influence of partisan attitudes on attitudes toward issues and candidates means that the total effect of party attitudes is greater than the direct effect, and that partisan attitudes are roughly comparable to issue and candidate attitudes in explaining presidential votes.[25]

Fourth, there is evidence of significant reciprocal effects of candidate evaluations on the trilogy of attitudes. That is, not only do the three attitudes affect candidate evaluations, but candidate evaluations affect the three proximate attitudes as voters attempt to bring their belief systems into balance.[26] One implication of this is that models of voting behavior that assume that the attitudinal effect is in only one direction misspecify the dynamic nature of attitude formation and change.

Finally, there is also some evidence that both projection and persuasion are used by voters to bring their issue-related attitudes into line with their candidate evaluations. Of the two processes, projection seems to be the more prevalent.[27] In other words, voters change both their own policy preferences and their perceptions of the candidates' policy preferences to bring them into agreement with already existing candidate evaluations. Any models of voting behavior that fail to recognize that issue-related attitudes may be the result as well as the cause of candidate evaluations will tend to overestimate the impact of policy-related attitudes on candidate choices.

CAMPAIGN COMMUNICATION AND CANDIDATE CHOICES

Now that we have seen how contemporary approaches to voting behavior account for candidate choices in presidential general elections, we may consider the impact of campaign communication on voting behavior. In essence, the model of voting behavior we have been considering has no place for campaign communication as a *direct* effect on candidate choices, nor is campaign communication usually thought to exert a significant influence on party attitudes since party identification has usually been formed before any particular presidential election campaign. The main impact of campaign communication must be as an *indirect* effect on the vote via candidate and issue attitudes, and as a source of information used by voters to keep their attitude systems consistent and balanced.

We saw in Chapters 6 and 7 that campaign communication shapes citizen perceptions of the personal attributes and policy preferences of candidates. News coverage shapes at least the stylistic images of candidates and portrays candidates in thematic ways; broadcast debates alter the perceived issue positions of candidates. The impact of spot ads is less certain; the atypical issue-oriented spot ad campaign *can* alter citizen perceptions of issue positions, but it seems likely that such ads also transmit usable impressions of candidates. Furthermore, if we define *campaign* communication somewhat more broadly to include precampaign news coverage of incumbent administrations, it is clear that news coverage shapes voters' impressions of incumbents and satisfaction with current policy decisions and social conditions. Thus in many ways campaign communication can have an indirect impact on the vote by shaping candidate and issue-related attitudes.

It is also clear that campaign communication can be used by citizens to reinforce, form, or alter candidate evaluations. In fact, given the psychological tendencies of voters to rationalize their attitude systems into agreement, campaign communication may be generally used by most voters to reinforce rather than alter a candidate choice that has already been made.

There are three basic possibilities regarding the type of candidate choice a citizen may make *during* an election campaign. First, citizens may have a prior-to-campaign candidate choice predisposition (based, perhaps, on partisan loyalty or on a reaction to the performance of an incumbent seeking reelection) and may use the campaign to strengthen that predisposition. This may be done by projecting one's own preferences onto a candidate (this is most possible when information about the candidate is both meager and vague), by changing one's own attitudes to conform with those of the candidate, and by denying or ignoring information that might threaten the predisposition. If this is how a voter uses campaign communication, we would say that the vote has been *reinforced* by campaign communication.

Second, a citizen may enter the campaign with a well-defined set of attitudes—for example, strongly held policy preferences and/or a well-defined image of the traits appropriate for the office being contested—and use the campaign to form a candidate choice consistent with those attitudes. If the citizen is truly undecided before the campaign but has a set of enduring political attitudes that are used to make a candidate choice, we may conclude that campaign communication has *activated* the candidate choice of the voter.

Finally, a voter may enter the campaign with a candidate predisposition, discover that the preferred candidate is inconsistent with some attitude or attitudes, and change his or her mind about his preferred candidate. In this case we could say that the campaign has *converted* the voter.

Although precise estimates of how many citizens are affected by campaign communication in each of these ways are hard to come by, reinforcement and activation are apparently the most prevalent outcomes of campaign communication. (Whether a voter is characterized as having been reinforced or activated depends largely on when the campaign is thought to begin and when the first reading of candidate choice is taken. The further away from election day the first measure is made, the more likely a voter will be classified as *activated*.) For one thing, most voters claim to make their candidate choices very early in the campaign, long before much campaign communication has taken place (Table 8–1). Second, when the candidate choices of voters at the beginning of presidential campaigns are compared with their choices after the campaign, most voters stick with their precampaign choices or make candidate choices that are predictable from their predispositions.[28] Third, the aggregate distribution of candidate preferences tends to be most volatile early in the campaign, suggesting that candidate choices become firmer as the campaign progresses (Figure 8–4). Fourth, we now know that a fair amount of projection and persuasion does take place during a presidential campaign, and that candidate choices not only result from but also cause candidate-, issue-, and party-related attitudes.[29] In sum, activation and reinforcement seem to be more prevalent outcomes of campaign communication than conversion is.

This does not mean that campaign communication has no conversion potential. Although the aggregate distribution of the vote in Figure 8–4 is fairly similar throughout the presidential election campaigns of 1972,

TABLE 8–1 Time of Presidential Vote Choice, 1948 to 1980
(Percent)

Time of Decision	1948	1952	1956	1960	1964	1968	1972	1976	1980
Before conventions	37	34	57	30	40	33	43	33	42
During conventions	28	31	18	30	25	22	17	20	17
During campaign	25	31	21	36	33	38	35	45	40
Don't remember, not ascertained	10	4	4	4	3	7	4	2	1
Total	100	100	100	100	100	100	99	100	100
N	424	1,251	1,285	1,445	1,126	1,039	1,119	1,667	958

Source: Survey Research Center/Center for Political Studies election studies; reported in William H. Flanigan and Nancy H. Zingale, Political Behavior of the American Electorate, 5th ed. (Boston: Allyn and Bacon, 1983), p. 159. Copyright © 1983 by Allyn and Bacon, Inc. Reprinted with permission.

1968 (except for Humphrey), 1964, and 1960, in the other elections more significant changes in the vote intentions of the public are evidenced. Since one possible cause of these changes is campaign communication, we must acknowledge the conversion potential of the modern campaign. Furthermore, conversions are more important than either reinforcement or activation since they both subtract a vote from one candidate and add a vote to another candidate. When margins of victory are narrow, the conversion of even a small proportion of the electorate may determine the electoral outcome. Consequently, we should investigate the possibility that campaign communication alters the distribution of the presidential vote.

MEDIA EXPOSURE AND CANDIDATE CHOICES

Because of the *indirect* effect of campaign communication on candidate choices, and the tendency of voters to use campaign communication to reinforce candidate preferences and activate partisan and ideological predispositions, there are seldom strong relationships between campaign media exposure and candidate choices. Attempts to relate exposure to a *particular medium* or a *particular news source* with presidential voting have, for the most part, failed to find any significant relationships.[30] Nonetheless, there have been a few circumstances in the presidential elections of the last three decades in which exposure to a particular form of campaign communication was modestly related to the distribution of the presidential vote.

In 1952, for example, when part of the state of Iowa had television available and part did not, the low-television-density counties voted more Republican than the high-television-density counties did, compared with their voting behavior in the 1944 and 1948 elections. The difference between the two groups of counties was 2.4 percent, suggesting that having television available gave the Democrats a small advantage.[31]

We cannot be certain that the difference in candidate choices in these two groups of counties was due exclusively to the difference in television density. There may have been ways other than the availability of television in which the two sets of counties differed in 1952. Although long-standing differences may have been taken into consideration by using the 1944 and 1948 votes as baselines, other differences between the two groups of counties *in the 1952 campaign* may still account for at least a portion of the differences in candidate choices (candidate appearances, unemployment rates, local events, party organization activity, and so on). Nonetheless, this is one of the few cases in which the candidate choices of citizens with no television available have been investigated (finding such groups is virtually impossible now), and in which the re-

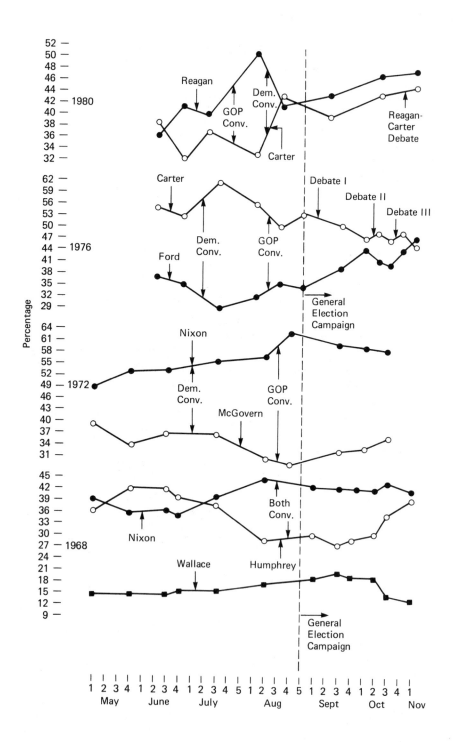

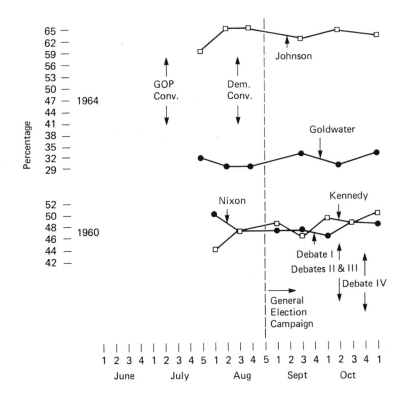

Source: Gallup Opinion Index, no. 183, December 1980. Reprinted by permission of the Gallup Poll.

FIGURE 8–4   Change in Support for Presidential Candidates During Campaigns, 1960–1980

sults suggest that a particular presidential candidate was aided by the availability of television.

In 1968 there was also some evidence that exposure to television was related to preferences for a presidential candidate. In that case the beneficiary was George Wallace. Among white Democrats, 18 percent of those relying exclusively on television for campaign information voted for Wallace, compared with 10 percent of those who watched hardly any television at all. Among white Independents, 27 percent of those relying exclusively on television voted for Wallace; only 12 percent of those who watched hardly any television did so. Furthermore, the relationship between television news exposure and voting for Wallace persisted after controlling for education and age. The explanation for this relationship was thought to be that network news coverage during this time had an anti-institutional bias, was focusing attention on social protest and the civil rights movement, and was fostering political cynicism. All of these were prominent elements of the Wallace campaign.[32]

Although there has generally been little or no relationship between exposure to a particular medium and presidential voting, there is some evidence that exposure to different newspapers has some impact on candidate choices. In fact, in many recent presidential elections there has been a relationship between the *editorial endorsement* policies of individual newspapers and the presidential votes of those who read them.

In each of the presidential elections from 1952 to 1972, there has been a relationship between the candidate endorsements of the papers read by voters and their presidential choices (Table 8–2).[33] In general, voters exposed to newspapers that endorsed the Democratic presidential candidate have been more apt to vote Democratic than those exposed to newspapers that either endorsed no one or endorsed the Republican candidate, regardless of the partisan identification of the respondents. This relationship has been strongest among Independents, suggesting that partisans resist the effect of newspaper endorsements but that undecided voters find a newspaper endorsement to be a credible voting cue.

Of course, since we cannot be absolutely certain that the *only* systematic difference between these groups of voters is the difference in newspaper endorsements, it is possible that these differences in voting behavior are not the *result* of the newspaper endorsements themselves. The endorsements may be partially due to the candidate preferences of the newspaper's readership, and the patterns in voting behavior may be due to aspects of the newspapers' content (news coverage, selection of columnists, distribution of political advertising) other than the endorsement itself. The fairest conclusion seems to be that the voting behavior of a *small* percentage of presidential voters may depend on the endorsement policies of the newspapers they read.

One reason that the effect of media exposure on candidate choice is so difficult to pin down is that this exposure takes place over a long period of time and is difficult to measure precisely. Measuring the effect of *broadcast debates* is easier since there have been few of them in past presidential campaigns. Also, the timing of presidential debates has generally been known well enough in advance that researchers could measure candidate choices both before and after debate exposure.

PRESIDENTIAL DEBATES AND CANDIDATE CHOICES

In 1960 four presidential debates were held between Richard Nixon and John Kennedy. Of the four, only the first one was associated with a noticeable change in support for the two presidential candidates.

The Gallup polls of vote intentions during the 1960 campaign (refer

TABLE 8–2 Voting for the Democratic Presidential Candidate by Newspaper Endorsements and by Party Identification, 1956–1972

	Party ID											
	Democrats				Independents				Republicans			
	Newspaper Endorsement				Newspaper Endorsement				Newspaper Endorsement			
Year	Dem.	Neither	Rep.	Diff. D-R	Dem.	Neither	Rep.	Diff. D-R	Dem.	Neither	Rep.	Diff. D-R
1956 (N = 969)	84	74	73	11	27	22	28	−1	0	4	5	−5
1960 (N = 451)	79	79	80	−1	61	—a	48	13	8	0	8	0
1964 (N = 972)	91	89	87	4	70	71	35	35	28	32	13	15
1968 (N = 939b)	62	65	69	−7	40	35	12	28	12	4	8	4
1972 (N = 778)	71	61	46	25	50	34	26	24	0	6	5	−5

Source: John P. Robinson, "The Press as King Maker: What Surveys from Last Five Campaigns Show," *Journalism Quarterly* 51 (Winter 1974): 593. Reprinted by permission.

a—Less than 10 respondents.

bPerceived newspaper endorsement, White voters only.

back to Figure 8–4) show that Kennedy picked up the support of 3 percent of the citizenry and Nixon lost 1 percent of his support during the first debate period. Given the margin of error of Gallup polls, however, and the fact that there had been a slight trend toward Kennedy *prior* to the first debate anyway, we cannot necessarily attribute all of the 4 percent net shift for Kennedy exclusively to the first debate. Furthermore, since many of those voters who shifted their vote intention after the first debate were Democrats, these voters might have eventually found their way into the Democratic camp anyway.

Nonetheless, studies of the vote intentions of citizens both before and after the first debate confirm that the debate helped Kennedy a bit. Although a majority of citizens maintained the same candidate choice both before and after the first debate, more people changed to Kennedy than to Nixon after the first debate. One study found that of the 24.5 percent of the respondents who changed their vote intentions, 15.1 percent of the changes favored Kennedy and 9.4 percent of the changes favored Nixon, for a net benefit to Kennedy of 5.7 percent. Furthermore, when we compare the changes in vote intentions before and after the first debate for debate viewers and nonviewers, viewers changed their vote intentions considerably more in Kennedy's direction than nonviewers did (Table 8–3). None of the other three debates had the noticeable effect on vote intentions that the first debate did. In each case changes in vote intentions benefited both Kennedy and Nixon equally, and the behavior of viewers and nonviewers alike was identical.

In 1976 there were three presidential debates and one vice-presidential debate. Gallup polls during the 1976 general election campaign (Figure 8–4) indicate that once both nominees were known, there was very little change in vote intentions from one Gallup poll to the next. In fact, the changes were so small that we cannot be sure they are accurate reflections of changes taking place in the larger population. If we take these changes literally, however, Carter lost 3 percent and Ford gained 4 percent after the first debate (but notice that the predebate survey was conducted almost one *month* before the debate); Carter picked up 1 percent and Ford lost 3 percent after the second debate; and Carter picked up 2 percent and Ford picked up 3 percent after the third debate. Since each of these changes correspond to the perceived winner of each, it may be that the change was real and was the result of the debates. In general, however, the changes are so small that such a conclusion is unwarranted.

If we look at the vote intentions of Democrats, Republicans, and Independents separately during the 1976 campaign, the first debate is the only one for which changes in vote intentions are noticeable (Table 8–4). During the first debate period (and the three-week period prior to it) Ford's support among all partisan groupings increased. Not only did he gain 7 percent of the vote among Republicans and 5 percent among

TABLE 8–3   Change in 1960 Presidential Vote Intentions, by Exposure to Presidential Debates

	First Debate		Second Debate		Third Debate		Fourth Debate	
	Viewers (%)	Nonviewers (%)	Viewers (%)	Nonviewers (%)	Viewers (%)	Nonviewers (%)	Viewers (%)	Nonviewers (%)
Unchanged	58	52	65	66	73	69	70	67
Change to Kennedy	25	25	17	17	14	15	16	16
Change to Nixon	17	23	18	17	13	16	14	17
Net gain for Kennedy	+8	+2	−1	0	+1	−1	+2	−1

Source: Elihu Katz and Jacob J. Feldman, "The Debates in the Light of Research: A Survey of Surveys," in Sidney Kraus, ed., *The Great Debates* (Gloucester, Mass.: Peter Smith, 1968), p. 210. Reprinted by permission of Indiana University Press.

Note: Based on special tabulations by Opinion Research of before-and-after interviews with the *same* individuals. Before and after the first debate, for example, 58 percent of the viewers indicated precisely the same commitment (on a nine-point scale); 25 percent made a change in Kennedy's favor (for example, from "leaning" to "strongly committed") and 17 percent changed in favor of Nixon.

TABLE 8–4 Distribution of 1976 Presidential Vote Intentions during the Campaign, by Party Identification

	Republicans			Democrats			Independents		
	Carter	Ford	McCarthy	Carter	Ford	McCarthy	Carter	Ford	McCarthy
Oct. 28–30	7%	90%	1%	80%	15%	1%	38%	49%	5%
Oct. 22–25	10	87	1	78	17	1	43	46	3
(Debate III)									
Oct. 15–18	7	85	a	73	16	1	33	53	3
(Mondale-Dole debate)									
Oct. 8–11	8	86	2	76	17	2	40	46	3
(Debate II)									
Sept. 27–Oct. 4	8	87	1	79	16	1	38	50	2
Sept. 24–27	9	87	a	76	17	1	36	45	5
(Debate I)									
Aug. 27–30	12	80	—	84	11	—	43	40	—
Aug. 20–23	11	77	—	78	14	—	40	37	—

					(GOP convention)					
Aug. 6–9	17	73	—	—	82	12	—	52	30	—
July 16–19, 23–26	21	68	—	—	84	10	—	60	30	—
			(Democratic convention)							
June 25–28	22	70	—	—	73	16	—	50	39	—
June 11–14	24	71	—	—	72	21	—	53	36	—
May 21–24	19	71	—	—	69	19	—	45	42	—
April 30–May 3	23	73	—	—	72	22	—	44	49	—
April 9–12	14	82	—	—	69	24	—	46	41	—
March 26–29	20	76	—	—	65	28	—	37	54	—
March 19–22	13	83	—	—	71	24	—	37	53	—

Source: Gallup Opinion Index, no. 137, December 1976. Reprinted by permission of the Gallup Poll.

Note: McCarthy was not included in trial heats until September. For each trial heat the percentage not shown was the vote for other candidates and those who were undecided.

[a]Less than 1 percent.

Independents, but he also picked up 6 percent among Democrats. Meanwhile, Carter was losing support among Independents (7 percent), Republicans (3 percent), and Democrats (8 percent). The first debate period in 1976 seems to have been an advantageous one for Gerald Ford, just as it was for John Kennedy in 1960. Unfortunately, we cannot tell from these data how much of this change to attribute to the debate itself.

The second and third debate periods showed much less change in aggregate vote intentions in 1976. There was virtually no change around the second and third debate periods as each candidate benefited from an increase in support among his own partisans (although Carter did pick up quite a bit of support among Independents). The vice-presidential debate had a minimal effect on the distribution of the vote intentions of partisans, although Ford did pick up quite a few votes among Independents during this period.

Aggregate poll results such as these show the overall change in vote intentions during the campaign period, but they do not tell us how many *individuals* have changed their intentions or whether debate exposure had anything to do with it. To investigate that question, vote intentions of the same citizens must be measured both before and after each debate.

In 1976 most respondents maintained their predebate vote intention after each of the Ford-Carter debates: Approximately 81 percent of the citizenry did so after the first debate, 78 percent after the second debate, and 87 percent after the third debate.[35] Furthermore, the strongest predictor of final vote intentions in 1976 was the *pre*debate vote intentions, and knowing whether a voter watched a particular debate or not did not help predict at all whether—or in what direction—a change in vote intention would take place. In fact, a comprehensive review of 1976 debate studies has concluded that "the debates seem to have played only a minor role in voter's vote choices."[36]

In 1980 there were two presidential debates: one between John Anderson and Ronald Reagan, and the other, just four days before the election, between Ronald Reagan and Jimmy Carter. Scholarly analyses of the effects of these two debates are not yet available, but there is some evidence that both debates benefited Reagan. The Reagan-Anderson debate was followed by a surge for Reagan in the Gallup poll (Figure 8–4), although we do not know whether debate viewers changed their vote intentions more than nonviewers did. The Reagan-Carter debate was also followed by a postdebate surge for Reagan that led to his unexpected margin of victory on election day. The role of the debate in this surge is unclear, however. Richard Wirthlin, Ronald Reagan's pollster, thinks the debate was primarily responsible for much of this last-minute surge. Patrick Caddell, Jimmy Carter's pollster, however, believes that the public realization that the hostages in Iran would not be home before election day had more of an impact on last-minute vote decisions.[37] Unfortunately, at this point no evidence capable of evaluating this debate is available.

Of the ten presidential general election debates held in 1960, 1976, and 1980, then, only a couple have clearly contributed to the significant alteration of voting intentions. This does not mean, however, that debates are inconsequential forms of communication. We saw in Chapter 7 that they contribute quite a bit to the education of the U.S. voter. Debates serve primarily to give voters more reasons to vote for candidates they were already predisposed to vote for anyway, rather than to convert voters from one candidate to another.

SPOT ADS AND CANDIDATE CHOICES

Given the resources committed by candidates to paid political spot advertising, there is surprisingly little research on the impact of advertising on candidate choices. We know that spot ads focus on the candidate-, issue-, and party-related attitudes that directly affect candidate choices; we also know that a substantial portion of the electorate *claim* that advertising helps them decide for whom to vote (in the 1972 presidential election, about 23 percent of those who changed their vote choice during the general election campaign gave some indication that their vote choice was influenced by advertising);[38] but we know much less about the contribution that advertising campaigns make to the distribution of the vote.

The Syracuse study of the 1972 presidential election campaign is almost the only one dealing with the effects of broadcast advertising on presidential vote intentions. In that election individual voter changes along a seven-point vote intention scale were found to be closely associated with changes in the beliefs and attitudes of the electorate. Since these beliefs and attitudes were in turn affected by spot advertising content, Patterson and McClure concluded that broadcast advertising does indirectly affect changes in the direction and strength of vote intentions.

Unfortunately, we cannot be certain in this case that the observed opinion change preceded the changes in vote intention, since the measures of these variables were taken one month apart. If a person changed both his or her opinions and his or her vote intention during this one-month period, it is impossible to tell which change occurred first or if both occurred simultaneously. More frequent monitoring of those attitudes and beliefs would be necessary (though extremely difficult) if such determinations are to be made. Although the possibility that spot advertising causes changes in vote intentions by altering beliefs and attitudes is plausible, we must reserve judgment for now about the strength and consistency of the effect.

Patterson and McClure themselves found some evidence that vote intention changes *preceded* belief-attitude changes in 1972. At the beginning of the general election campaign an abnormally high proportion of Democrats (34 percent in the Syracuse survey) had already formed an inclination to vote for Nixon; on election day almost all (91 percent) of those Democrats carried out their earlier decision and voted for Richard Nixon. Patterson and McClure think that one reason for such a high defection rate among Democrats was that the Democrats for Nixon advertising campaign provided justifications, rationales, and information to support the decisions of these Democrats. Defecting Democrats were unusually attentive to these ads and exhibited much higher rates of belief change in the direction of these ads than did any other group of voters: "Undoubtedly, many defecting Democrats found reinforcement for their voting decisions in the Nixon commercials. Most of these voters were voting against George McGovern as much as for Richard Nixon and the direct attack on George McGovern of many Democrats for Nixon commercials provided reasons for their decisions—and the comfort of knowing there were many other Democrats like them."[39]

In this case the change in vote intention (from a historical pro-Democratic tendency to a pro–Richard Nixon intention in 1972) *preceded* the advertising exposure. Consequently, we cannot say that exposure to Nixon's advertising campaign *caused* the change in vote intention; rather, it reinforced a change already made and, perhaps, prevented another change in vote intentions more in line with previous predispositions.

Unfortunately, the 1972 Syracuse study is about the only published attempt to determine the impact of advertising on presidential voting. Given the increased use of this form of campaign communication by voters, and the fact that this is a major way in which voters experience a campaign, we need to do much more research in this area.

ELECTION-NIGHT RETURNS COVERAGE AND CANDIDATE CHOICES

Finally, we should consider the impact of electon-night voting returns coverage on presidential voting. We have seen previously that the three television networks spend millions of dollars on their election-night telecasts of the vote returns so that they can project the eventual winner and analyze the reasons for the outcome. These broadcasts have involved the projection of presidential winners before the polls have closed on the West Coast. If those voters voting late on the West Coast hear these projections before voting, their candidate choices might be influenced. Both a bandwagon effect, whereby those hearing the vote returns will be more apt to vote for the winning candidate than they would have otherwise, and an underdog effect, whereby those hearing the vote returns will be more apt to vote for the losing candidate than they would have otherwise, have been suggested.

As was the case with election-night returns coverage and voter turnout, there is little evidence that this coverage alters the distribution of the vote cast. A 1964 survey of California citizens, for example, found that out of 1,212 respondents who expressed a vote intention in California the day before election day, a total of 3 votes were apparently changed because of the election-night broadcasts. In addition to these switchers, there were 161 respondents who were undecided about their candidate choice the day before election day but then cast a vote a day later. Of these 161 voters, 50 voted late enough in the day to have been exposed to East Coast vote returns. Of these 50, however, only 18 actually heard or saw any election returns coverage. Of these 18, 9 voted for Johnson, 5 voted for Goldwater, and 4 refused to disclose their votes. Since this proportion of Johnson voters (9/14) almost exactly matched the proportion of Johnson voters in the entire sample, there was little evidence for a returns-coverage effect.[40] Furthermore, in 1964 the margin of victory for the Democratic presidential candidate was so large in the West Coast states (18 percent in California, 27 percent in Oregon, and 24 percent in Washington) that election-night results could not possibly have affected the allocation of electoral votes.

The 1964 election was a landslide victory for Lyndon Johnson, and the presidential outcome was hardly surprising to those who had been following the campaign. What about a close election such as that of 1968, in which the outcome was in doubt up to the last minute? Research done in 1968 found that 6 percent of Western citizens were exposed to the election-night returns before voting and that, at the most, 0.7 percent of Western citizens were both exposed to election-day returns coverage and exhibited some change in voting behavior.[41] Since the margin of victory in 1968 was 3 percent in California, 6 percent in Oregon, and 29 percent in Washington, it does not seem that these telecasts could have affected the electoral vote in that year either.

Why do election-night broadcasts have such little effect? First, the proportion of the electorate that could be affected is quite small. When those voting early in the day and those who vote late but have not been exposed to returns coverage at the time the vote is cast are subtracted from the total West Coast electorate, only about 5–6 percent of that electorate is left. Second, even among those who could possibly have been affected by returns coverage, for many the information transmitted in the election night coverage is nothing new. In 1964 the early returns confirmed the Johnson landslide that had been expected prior to election day, and in 1968 the early returns confirmed the projected closeness of the race. Consequently, any candidate choices that were based on the likely outcome could have been made just as easily before election day. Those who might have thought in 1964 that voting would be a waste of time could already have decided that by the time the election-night broadcasts began. In 1968 those motivated to vote by the closeness of the contest did not need election returns to form this perception.

This suggests that early returns might have more effect when their reporting contradicts prior expectations. One wonders, for example, about the effect of the early returns in 1976, when everyone again expected a tight race. Because Carter's strength was primarily in the East, the initial returns gave the impression that he was on his way to an unexpected victory. Although network commentators were usually careful to point out this geographical factor, a California voter watching the East Coast returns might well have been surprised by what appeared to be an imminent Democratic victory. Since that piece of information was something new, one wonders what its effect might have been. This possibility is even more intriguing when one realizes that 7 percent of the 1976 presidential electorate claimed to have decided for whom to vote on election day, and that the margin separating the two candidates was 0.2 percent in Oregon, 1.7 percent in California, and 3.9 percent in Washington. Similarly, the 1980 returns quickly indicated that Ronald Reagan was winning by an unexpectedly large margin. Here, too, the returns coverage provided some "new" information. Furthermore, the 1980 projections were followed by a very early concession speech by Jimmy Carter, perhaps increasing the effect of the early network declarations.

A third reason for the failure of returns coverage to alter candidate choices generally is that voters decide for whom to vote for a myriad of reasons other than expectations about who is going to win. As we have seen, the presidential vote decision is based on a number of political beliefs and attitudes and is usually supported by enough reasons that the projected outcome is not enough to upset this decision. Furthermore, voters apparently use a number of attitude-formation and attitude-change processes to bring their attitudes into agreement. Consequently, for most voters, who is ahead and who is behind in a two-candidate presidential campaign is largely irrelevant to election-day behavior. There may be a few voters who exhibit underdog or bandwagon effects as a result of exposure to early returns, but in most circumstances they are too few to be important and they tend to cancel each other out anyway.

STRATEGIC VOTING

This does not mean that information about likely electoral winners and losers is always irrelevant in presidential general elections, however. In a multicandidate campaign there is good reason to suppose that this information has an important impact on the vote choice. Suppose, for example, that there is a three-person race between candidates A, B, and C, and that there is a citizen who prefers A to B and B to C. How will this citizen vote if he or she perceives that candidate A will be a likely loser? He or she might decide to desert candidate A and vote instead for candidate B in an attempt to prevent the election of C. To do otherwise would mean "wasting" his or her vote and helping C get elected. Such calculations are unnecessary in a two-candidate race, but in a three-candidate race they make sense.

An analysis of candidate choices in the 1968 presidential election between Richard Nixon, Hubert Humphrey, and George Wallace discovered that such "strategic voting" does in fact occur.[42] Fourteen percent of those voters who perceived that their first choice was behind in 1968 ended up voting for their second choice (compared with 5 percent of those who did not perceive their first choice to be behind). The proportion of voters who defected to their second choice in 1968 increased to 27 percent when the first choice was perceived to be behind both nationally and in the voter's state, and it increased still further to 36 percent when the first choice was perceived to be *far* behind and was only *slightly* preferred to the second choice.

A similar phenomenon was undoubtedly operating in 1980 among preferences for Jimmy Carter, Ronald Reagan, and John Anderson. Although Anderson was the first preference of many voters, as the campaign proceeded and evidence accumulated that he would not win, many of his supporters began considering voting for their second choice. Once these perceptions of electoral failure begin, they tend to snowball until the sure loser is left with only the firmest supporters. In 1980 this meant that John Anderson's first-choice support plummeted from over 20 percent in June to just above 5 percent in November.

Of course, in both 1968 and 1980 it was not the reporting of actual partial election returns that shaped these perceptions and caused the strategic voting behavior, but rather news coverage and the reporting of public opinion poll results. Unlike election-night returns broadcasts, the reporting of predictions, polls, and projections of how each candidate is doing does have important effects on the distribution of votes in multicandidate campaigns. In the next section we will see how important this effect can be in presidential *nomination* campaigns.

In summary, the evidence for a *direct*, straightforward effect of different types of campaign communication on presidential vote intentions in the general election is not particularly strong. We found some evidence for an impact of (1) television availability in 1952; (2) television news exposure in 1968; (3) the first televised debate in 1960 and the 1980 debates; and (4) exposure to different newspapers with different endorsement patterns. In general, however, it has been difficult to find a relationship between the type of news exposure, the amount of news exposure, debate exposure, election-night returns exposure, and presidential voting. We know little about the direct impact of spot ad exposure since we have very little evidence with which to even address the question.

Thus the real impact of campaign communication on presidential voting is an indirect one. Voters are not simply *exposed* to campaign communication, they *use* it. They are attentive to different portions of it; they perceive different meanings in it; and they categorize, internalize, and remember it in different ways. Some may discard a piece of information without further thought, whereas others use the same piece of information to reinforce or fill in an existing attitude system.[43] We ought not to conclude that just because there are few simple, direct relationships between campaign communication and presidential votes, therefore campaign communication has no impact. Rather, we should recognize the indirect, subtle, and complex ways in which the citizenry uses campaign information to guide, shape, and support voting decisions. If a citizen did not have campaign communication available at all, on what would an electoral choice be based?

Campaign Communication and Candidate Choices in Presidential Nomination Campaigns

The context in which voting for presidential candidates takes place during the nomination campaign is in many ways similar to that of general election campaign voting, and therefore we might reasonably expect the voters' decision-making process to be similar in both situations. There are, however, a number of significant differences in the nomination campaign that lead to a slightly different model of voter choice and a significantly different role for campaign communication.

First, nomination campaigns are more typically multicandidate campaigns that confront voters with a fundamentally different type of choice. Multicandidate campaigns encourage voters to decide not only whom they prefer, but also what the chances are that each candidate will win. In our electoral system the possibility of wasting one's vote on a loser is a real constraint on the behavior of voters.

Second, nomination campaigns are dynamic affairs in which the resources of candidates and the candidates appealing for votes are continually changing.[44] Consequently, not all nomination voters face the same choice situation.

Third, voting for presidential nominees typically takes place in a context in which one of the three main attitudes related to general election votes—party attitudes—is deemphasized. Since nomination voting takes place among partisans for members of one's own party, the electorate's voting behavior cannot be accounted for by party identification. This does not mean that all party-related attitudes are completely irrelevant for nomination choices, since some candidates may campaign more on their partisan service and identity than others do and voters may perceive some candidates as more representative of their party than others are. It does mean, however, that party-related attitudes will be much less important than they are later in the campaign.

Finally, nomination voting takes place in arenas characterized by even lower turnout rates than are typical of presidential general elections. Consequently, the ability of campaign communication to affect variations in turnout during the nomination campaign may also be more significant.

Given these differences between nomination and general election voting, what is the role of campaign communication during the nomination campaign?

First, the level of voter awareness of presidential candidates is an important factor in nomination campaign selections. Unlike presidential general election campaigns, where at least both major-party candidates are familiar to most voters, many candidates for presidential nominations fail to achieve even a minimum level of name recognition and awareness among the electorate. Not being recognized by the electorate is a liability to presidential candidates and limits the number of votes that a candidate can receive. Since we saw in Chapter 6 that the amount of news coverage given different candidates affects the level of voter familiarity with and recognition of candidates, this is one place in which news coverage has a fairly straightforward and direct effect on the vote intentions of (in this case, primary) voters.

This phenomenon was clearly at work during the multicandidate Democratic nomination campaign in 1976, and worked to the advantage of Jimmy Carter. Recall that (Table 5–2) press coverage of the early months of the 1976 nomination campaign focused heavily on Jimmy Carter and that, as a result, name recognition of Carter increased from February to June much more than it did for any other candidate. In fact, early campaign news coverage advantaged Carter so much that at the time of the Pennsylvania primary (April), 77 percent of a sample of respondents claimed they "knew something" about Carter, compared with 42 percent who knew something about Henry Jackson, 37 percent who knew something about Morris Udall, 21 percent who knew something about Frank Church, and 12 percent who knew something about Fred Harris. Similarly, in June (at the time of the California primary) 81 percent knew something about Carter, 34 percent knew something about Jackson, 37 percent knew something about Udall, 29 percent knew something about Church, and 16 percent knew something about Harris. Since as a rule primary voters do not vote for candidates they know nothing about, this edge in awareness was a definite advantage for Jimmy Carter. In the 1976 Pennsylvania primary, Carter apparently received 12 percent more votes "than he would have received if each candidate had been equally familiar to the voters."[45]

Name recognition or voter familiarity is not enough in itself to produce most primary votes. Nevertheless, the lack of such familiarity can be a serious handicap for any presidential candidate. Since familiarity is conferred largely by the news media, "the way in which the press distributes its coverage among the candidates can make a difference: its reporting helps to define voters' alternatives. . . . Under the appropriate conditions, such voters have a high probability of choosing the candidate emphasized by the press."[46]

Another way in which campaign communication during the nomination campaign shapes the votes of nomination campaign participants is by influencing the perceptions of which candidate is likely to be successful in the end. Since voters may have a preference ordering that involves many candidates but are only allowed to reveal one preference in the voting booth, voting for likely losers is discouraged. Voters recognize this, exhibit a willingness to consider the likely outcome when reaching their nomination vote decisions, and have shown a tendency to vote for non-first-choice alternatives. In a nomination campaign two types of likely-outcome attitudes are relevant: (1) perceptions regarding the likely chances of a candidate securing the nomination, and (2) perceptions of the likely chances that that nominee will win the general election.

Evidence for the importance of such strategic considerations was found during the 1980 nomination campaign.[47] During the early months of 1980, four different attitudes shaped voters' overall vote intentions among the candidates for the presidential nominations. One of these attitudes—overall *affect*—corresponds to the concept of candidate evaluation used in our model of general election voting behavior. Presumably it results from the same bundle of issue-, party-, and candidate-oriented attitudes discussed earlier. The other three attitudes, however, reflect the different context within which nomination behavior takes place, and suggest a different role for campaign communication during nomination campaigns. One of these attitudes is *candidate visibility*, which involves the proportion of citizens who are aware of a candidate. The second is *candidate viability*, a measure of the perceived chance a candidate has to secure a nomination. The third attitude is *electoral potency*, a measure of how successful the public thinks a candidate would be in the general election. Although the relationships between each of these attitudes and voter preferences for presidential candidates varied considerably for different candidates in 1980, both candidate viability and electoral potency were found to be related to citizen preferences.

This suggests that strategic considerations do make an important contribution to citizen preferences during the nomination campaign. Given what we have learned earlier about the impact of campaign news coverage on these horse-race perceptions, it is clear that campaign communication has an effect on preferences that is quite unlike its typical role in the general election campaign. Although it is impossible to tell how much of this effect may be attributed to print or broadcast news, daily campaign coverage or the reporting of poll reports, and news or candidate advertising, the effect of campaign communication in this stage is clearly significant.

This suggests that a model of citizen preferences during the nomination campaign must include elements of both candidate visibility and viability and must provide a more prominent role for campaign communication. A simplified diagram of such a model is provided in Figure 8–5, which shows how the viability and visibility of candidates affect candidate preferences.

Another way in which campaign communication during a nomination campaign shapes nomination vote intentions is by affecting the behavior of political activists. Campaign communication—particularly news coverage—may lead in turn to candidates' acquisition of other important political resources. News coverage, particularly if it is positive, can lead to the perception that a candidate is viable and to visibility for that candidacy. Political activists will be more likely to volunteer their time and effort for, donate their money to, and publicize their endorsement of a candidate who is perceived to have some chance of electoral success. In addition, a candidate's name will be more likely to appear on the Gallup poll's list of prospective nominees, and prominent politicians are more apt to agree to run as delegates for a candidate who is thought to be a likely nominee. Furthermore, each of these resources makes it possible for a candidate to achieve future electoral success and news coverage. In fact, the dynamics of a presidential nomination campaign are extremely important, and it is largely journalists and political activists who contribute *initially* to this process.

This suggests that news coverage during the nomination campaign is important not only for its direct impact on voter awareness of candidates and voter perceptions regarding who is likely to win or lose, but also for its indirect effect on the candidate resources acquired and available for future campaign efforts. Many candidates never receive the news coverage necessary to stimulate much resource acquisition and are winnowed out of the campaign before their candidacy has had much of an *electoral* test. In this way the behavior of voters in early delegate-selection processes affects (and usually delimits) the alternatives available later in the campaign. In 1976 the increase in news coverage of Jimmy Carter *preceded* increases in campaign contributions, Gallup poll ratings, and accumulated delegates.[48]

A final way in which the campaign communication of a nomination campaign can shape subsequent vote intentions involves the media event that marks the conclusion of the nomination campaign: the nominating convention itself. The trends in vote intention displayed in Figure 8–4

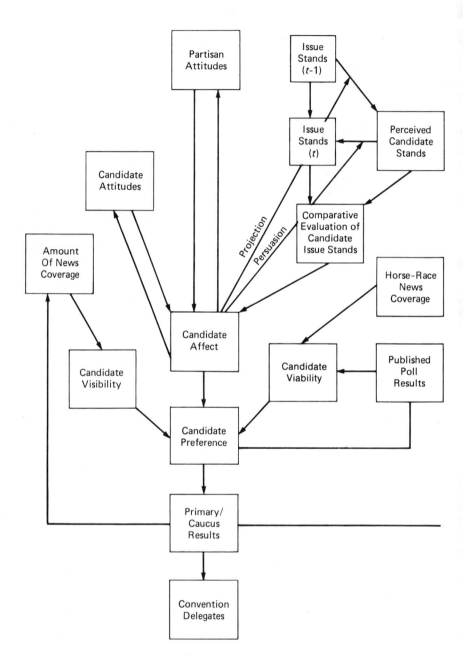

FIGURE 8–5   Model of Presidential Nomination Preferences

show that the convention period is a time during which vote intentions are unusually changeable. This is hardly surprising, since it is a time during which nominees become known (and other alternatives effectively eliminated) and one party dominates the flow of campaign communication for an extensive period of time. Furthermore, as we discussed in Chapter 5, parties and prospective candidates take elaborate steps to ensure that the nominating convention transmits a favorable image of both the party and the nominee, and journalists seem to suspend their more typically critical and skeptical approach toward candidates during this time.

Table 8–5 shows one rough indication of the importance of nominating conventions for presidential nominees. In 1972, 1976, and 1980—the only years for which satisfactory data are available—we can compare the preconvention and postconvention levels of support for presidential nominees. In all six cases analyzed there, the candidate nominated at a convention picked up support among the electorate (an average increase of 7 percent), and in five of the six cases the nominee's opponent also lost support (an average decrease of 4 percent). When these changes are combined, the net gain that the convention period has meant for recent nominees becomes substantial (an average of 11 percent).

The only exception to this pattern is the 1972 Democratic convention.

TABLE 8–5 Impact of Conventions on Presidential Vote Intentions

	Pre-convention Support	Post-convention Support	Change	Net Gain for Candidate of Convention	Net Gain Overall
1980 Republican					
Reagan	40	51	+11	+15	
Carter	37	33	−4		
1980 Democratic					4-Dem
Reagan	51	42	−9	+19	
Carter	33	43	+10		
1976 Republican					
Ford	32	37	+5	+12	
Carter	57	50	−7		
1976 Democratic					4-Dem
Ford	36	29	−7	+16	
Carter	53	62	+9		
1972 Republican					
Nixon	57	64	+7	+8	
McGovern	31	30	−1		
1972 Democratic					11-Rep
Nixon	53	56	+3	−3	
McGovern	37	37	+0		

That convention included fairly intense intraparty conflict and the inability of McGovern to use the convention to his advantage (his acceptance speech, for example, was given in the wee hours of the morning to a minuscule television audience). Therefore, it is hardly surprising that he failed to achieve the advantage usually experienced by successful nominees.

It is impossible at this point to estimate precisely how much of this change in vote intentions may be attributed to convention coverage. The data suggest, however, that the convention may be the most significant *single* communication event of the entire campaign. Convention coverage probably affects the voting intentions of wavering, undecided, or disgruntled partisans the most; but, after all, the votes of these groups are important to any presidential campaign. If a presidential nominee is unable to use the convention period to solidify the party, reassure the supporters of those candidates who lost the nomination, effectively criticize the opponent, and establish advantageous themes for the general election, then a significant opportunity will have been squandered.

Campaign communication seems to have a more direct and observable impact on candidate choice during the nomination campaign than during the general election campaign. The amount of news coverage is related to voter awareness of candidates and, particularly in multicandidate nomination campaigns, to voter willingness to consider a primary vote for a particular candidate. Both the amount and the favorableness of campaign communication also send messages to campaign activists (money contributors, volunteers, endorsers, journalists, pollsters, professional politicians, potential delegates) and influence a candidate's ability to accumulate political resources and to continue or expand campaign efforts. The nominating convention itself can be a time to reassure disgruntled partisans, persuade Independents and undecideds, and establish themes for the general election campaign. Considering the number of alternative candidates who are eliminated during the nomination campaign, a case could reasonably be made that the campaign communication of the nomination campaign has more of an overall effect on presidential selection than does the communication of the general election campaign.

Campaign Communication and Candidate Choices in Congressional Elections

Most of the research done on elections in the United States has focused on the presidential selection process. Most studies of voting behavior, candidate communication, and campaign news coverage have been confined to that electoral arena. In recent years, however, the availability of rich new sources of data have permitted the development of a small but informative literature on congressional elections. This research has suggested a number of ways in which campaign communication affects voting for congressional candidates.

To appreciate fully the role of campaign communication in congressional elections, one needs to understand the congressional election process as a dynamic one (see Figure 8–6). Central to current models of congressional elections is the observation that the types of candidates attracted to congressional campaigns greatly influence the flow of subsequent campaign information and the nature of the voters' choice.[49] Consequently, decisions made prior to the formal campaign period affect campaign communication in important ways.

Let us begin with two precampaign phenomena: the type of seat being contested, and the perceived vulnerability of the incumbent, if there is one. The *type of seat* involves whether the campaign is for the U.S. Senate or the U.S. House of Representatives, and with whether an incumbent is seeking reelection or not. The *perceived vulnerability of the incumbent* involves perceptions of whether the incumbent stands a chance of being defeated for reelection. This perception depends on a number of factors, such as the incumbent's involvement in controversial or scandalous behavior, redistricting of a congressional seat, events or conditions that disadvantage incumbents in general (such as economic depression) or incumbents of a particular party (such as Watergate's impact on Republicans), and the relationship between the incumbent and his or her constituency.

These two phenomena exert a strong influence on the types of candidates who are attracted to a particular congressional campaign. High-quality candidates—that is, candidates capable of accumulating substantial political resources and conducting a vigorous election campaign—are more apt to run for office when the office at stake is prestigious and the chances of winning are decent. For instance, such high-quality candidates are more apt to be attracted to a campaign for Congress when the seat is open (rather than held by an incumbent seeking reelection); when the seat is a Senate (rather than a House) seat; and when the incumbent, if there is one, is perceived to be vulnerable. In the absence of these conditions, the candidates attracted to congressional campaigns are more apt to be inexperienced and unknown, and are less able to conduct serious, visible, newsworthy campaigns. Politicians who might wage such a credible challenge, when faced with the wrong set of conditions, are apt to seek some other elective office or bide their time until conditions are more favorable.

The presence or absence of attractive candidates shapes the decisions of another set of political activists—potential campaign contributors—and the flow of money to congressional candidates' campaigns. Although some campaign contributions are not dependent on the perceived likelihood of a candidate winning and are used to reward and

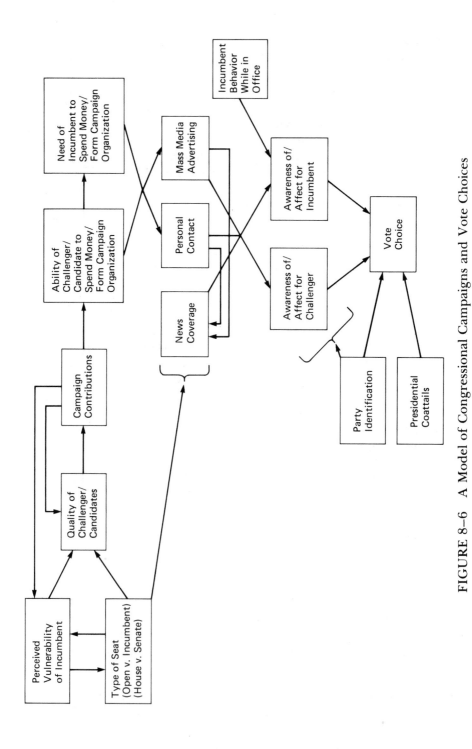

FIGURE 8-6   A Model of Congressional Campaigns and Vote Choices

purchase access to probable winners, many campaign contributors donate money where it will have the greatest chance of influencing the outcome. Disgruntled activists, in particular, often pursue the strategy of removing disliked incumbents from office; to do this in the most efficient way, they need to judge who among those they dislike is facing the most potentially successful challenge. Similarly, candidates for open seats attract a lot of campaign contributions since those races are perceived to be up for grabs and unusually sensitive to the competitive balance of political resources.

The ability to attract campaign contributions in turn affects the ability of congressional candidates to wage an effective campaign. The more money a candidate has to spend, the more visible a campaign will be. Money permits a candidate to purchase media advertising, to develop a personal contact organization, to hire the best campaign consultants, and thereby indirectly to attract news coverage. Those lacking such resources simply may never be able to achieve the level of awareness and recognition necessary for a viable, credible, vigorous campaign.

In the case of Senate seats and open U.S. House seats, usually both major-party candidates are able to solicit enough campaign contributions to run a visible campaign (both because these situations tend to attract experienced, capable, known candidates, and because such seats are thought by contributors to be more important and more winnable). In the case of U.S. House seats with incumbents seeking reelection, however, challengers' ability to raise and spend money varies tremendously. Experienced challengers facing vulnerable incumbents will be able to raise large amounts of money; inexperienced challengers facing secure incumbents will find fund-raising a difficult chore. In these incumbent-versus-challenger situations, incumbents raise and spend money in reaction to what their challengers are doing. That is, incumbents can almost always outspend challengers, but fund-raising is a grueling, distasteful task, and incumbents would just as soon do as little of it as possible. Therefore, incumbents will raise and spend money more only if they perceive that their challengers are doing the same. Large campaign expenditures by incumbents thus are not a sign of electoral strength, but of the existence of a vigorous and worrisome challenge. The main consequence of having an experienced challenger in a congressional race is not that he or she might outspend the incumbent but rather that both candidates will spend money at a significantly higher level.

The higher the level of campaign spending by congressional candidates, the greater the amount of advertising, personal contact, and news coverage for that congressional campaign. The flow of information that the electorate has available to it depends on a sequence of events, perceptions, and decisions by others (primarily potential candidates and campaign contributors) prior to the beginning of the formal campaign period. The attention given a campaign by journalists is also heavily dependent on the same set of prior decisions and actions. The amount of communication a candidate is able to purchase or stimulate (through paid advertising, personal contact, and news coverage) affects, in turn, the electorate's recognition of and affect for that candidate. It appears, however, that it is mainly the communication of *non*incumbents that alters the beliefs and attitudes of the electorate during the campaign.[50] Since incumbents have ample opportunities between elections to communicate with their constituencies, *campaign* communication has less of an effect on attitudes toward them. A challenger's communication, on the other hand, can have a marked effect on recognition of the challenger, affect for the challenger, and affect for the incumbent.

Finally, the strength of the candidate's campaign communication defines the nature of the choice situation for the congressional electorate. In the absence of visible communication from one of the candidates—usually a challenger—the voter's decision is basically a referendum on the incumbent. In the presence of balanced and visible communication from two candidates, however—which is usually the case in Senate races, races for open seats, and races with experienced challengers—the choice is more of a comparative one between balanced alternatives. This latter case is more similar to voting for presidential candidates, implying that a voting-behavior model similar to the one discussed earlier for presidential campaigns would be appropriate.

Given this view of congressional campaigns and elections, it is possible to see a number of ways in which mass media messages shape congressional voting. First, during the precampaign period, news coverage shapes perceptions regarding an incumbent's vulnerability. Coverage of an incumbent's role in a scandal, speculation on the impact of a redistricting scheme, and commentary on the incumbent's Washington activity and relationship with the district can clearly shape these perceptions. So can news reports of the intentions of interest groups to target an incumbent for defeat, as well as news coverage of social conditions and events for which a particular party might be held responsible. Given the importance of the type of candidate attracted to challenge an incumbent, and the importance of the incumbent's perceived vulnerability in affecting candidate recruitment, such precampaign news coverage can alter the entire nature of the subsequent campaign and election.

A second way in which precampaign communication can influence congressional voting involves news coverage, analyses, and commentaries on the initial campaign steps taken by congressional candidates (again, especially when that candidate is a House challenger). Reports on the visibility, vigor, and promise of a challenger's campaign will in turn shape the tendency of contributors to funnel money to or to make independent expenditures on behalf of a candidate. Volunteers and further news coverage might also be attracted by a candidate who seems to be mounting a credible campaign. In this way early efforts can feed back into later resource accumulation, thus improving (or dampening) the ability to expand a candidate's campaign.

A third way in which the mass media can affect congressional voting is through the campaign communication purchased and stimulated by candidates. Challengers' ability to buy campaign advertising and attract news coverage varies considerably. This in turn affects the electorate's recognition of and beliefs about candidates. In the absence of plentiful challenger resources, campaign communication is sparse and imbalanced in favor of the incumbent. In this situation the typically favorable attitudes toward an incumbent established during his or her tenure will remain unchallenged and unaltered, and the challenger's campaign will be seriously hampered. Although the content of campaign communication is clearly important, for the challenger of a House incumbent the *amount* of campaign communication is the initial barrier.

For Senate seats and open House seats, abundant and more evenly balanced campaign resources are more the norm and lead to a larger flow of campaign communication. In such situations the direction or qualitative nature of campaign messages is more important than simply the quantitative flow of information. In all cases, however, both the amount and the content of campaign communication influence the attitudes proximate to candidate preferences and votes.

Much of the preceding discussion is plausible but speculative. Empirical research on this whole process has been slow in coming, although it promises to be more plentiful in the near future now that data on the spending practices of candidates and the attitudes of congressional voters have become available. To date, what research has been done is consistent with the view of congressional campaigns just presented.

Little empirical research has been done so far on the impact of pre-campaign communication on the recruitment of candidates, public perceptions of the incumbents, or the distribution of campaign contributions. Some work has been done, however, on the impact of *campaign* communication on voter perceptions and preferences.

Levels of campaign spending are strongly related to voter awareness and attitudes toward candidates, and to candidate preferences. The amount of money spent by challengers is much more important than the amount spent by incumbents. In fact, there is some evidence that it is not who spends more or how much more is spent by one candidate that matters nearly as much as the *amount* of money spent by both candidates. Senatorial and open-seat candidates are usually able to spend large amounts of money and attract free news coverage; hence voter recognition and awareness are high. In incumbent-present House seats, however, awareness and recognition of the candidates depend on the amount of spending done by the challenger.[51]

Not only is total spending important for understanding congressional campaigns, but spending done specifically to purchase advertising has a noticeable impact on the distribution of the vote. In 1970 and 1972, the only years for which comprehensive media spending data are available, the *share* of broadcast spending by senatorial candidates was more closely related to the share of the vote received by the candidates than was either incumbency or party strength. In House races, incumbency was a far more important correlate of the vote, but the impact of media spending was still consistently positive and noticeable. Furthermore, the same general pattern was found for both primary and general election campaigns.[52]

There is also some evidence that news coverage of congressional campaigns is instrumental in shaping voter awareness, voter attitudes, and candidate choice. A study of contested 1978 incumbent-present campaigns discovered that the *amount* of news coverage given congressional candidates was related to the recognition of those candidates' names. This effect was stronger for challenger than incumbent recognition and was more noticeable than the effect of prior public service (the effect of controlled personal contact—say, through the mail or personal canvassing—was greater than for news coverage, however). Similarly, the *tone* of news coverage—that is, about whom the news coverage was more favorable—was found to have an effect on the favorableness of attitudes toward congressional candidates. In short, both the amount and the content of news coverage have been found to shape those perceptions and attitudes that affect candidate choices.[53]

The role of the mass media in congressional campaigns tends to be more similar to that in presidential primary than in presidential general election campaigns. News coverage in both settings has an important impact on the ability of candidates to acquire the political resources necessary for an energetic, visible, and enduring campaign, and on the electorate's awareness of different candidates. Perceptions of who is a likely winner and who is likely to conduct a viable campaign are central to the dynamics of both types of campaign and can affect the electorate's voting decisions both indirectly and directly. Varying amounts of pre-campaign awareness and attitudes combine with varying amounts and kinds of campaign communication to produce a variety of voter information bases and choice situations. Majority-party candidacies vary in viability and momentum in presidential primary and congressional campaigns in a way that is quite different from the situation in presidential general elections.

Conclusion

In this chapter we have summarized an enormous amount of material pertaining to the effect of mass communications exposure on the voting behavior of the U.S. electorate. In the process we have found a number of ways in which campaign and precampaign communication shape the choices made by the U.S. voter.[54]

First, mass media coverage of election campaigns leads to slightly increased rates of voter turnout. This effect is clearest when media coverage of election campaigns is unavailable, but it is also suggested by longitudinal studies of voting turnout and by individual-level relationships between media exposure and turnout. This effect is, however, modest, and tends to be smaller than the effects on turnout of education, political interest, political efficacy, strength of partisanship, the competitive environment, and registration requirements.

Second, we have seen that campaign communication during the presidential nomination process can have a significant effect on candidate preferences. News coverage, especially, can affect the public's awareness of candidates in a multicandidate race and their perceptions regarding the likely outcome of nomination campaigns. These perceptions can influence voter preferences and the behavior of campaign contributors and professional politicians. As a result, the process by which candidates for nomination are able to accumulate political resources and persist throughout a long nomination campaign is shaped in significant ways by campaign coverage. At the end of the nomination campaign, the nominating conventions represent an unparalleled opportunity for candidates to solidify partisan support and initiate general election campaign themes; changes in aggregate voter preferences indicate that the nominating conventions may be the most important communication events in the presidential selection process.

Third, we saw that campaign communication during the presidential general election campaign has more of an indirect than a direct effect on voter preferences. We have seen in previous chapters that campaign communication can influence candidate- and issue-related attitudes, and thereby affect candidate choices. Direct effects of campaign communication, however, are more difficult to document. With the exception of a couple of presidential debates and the tone of newspaper coverage, the messages delivered through the mass media are more typically used by voters to reinforce vote decisions already made and activate preferences already formed than to change candidate choices. This does not mean that presidential general election campaign communication is inconsequential; rather, it is a sign of the fact that presidential general elections are usually characterized by substantial and balanced information flows that encounter a *relatively* information-rich and predisposed electorate. Consequently, the effect of this campaign communication is more subtle, complex, varied, and indirect than it is in other arenas.

Fourth, we have suggested that campaign *and* precampaign communication is influential in congressional elections. Precampaign communication shapes the perceptions of potential candidates and campaign activists, which in turn affect voter awareness and evaluations of candidates.

Variation in the amount and tone of campaign communication across different competitive situations is extensive, and the campaign communication stimulated by challengers is a particularly important clue to understanding congressional election outcomes.

In this and preceding chapters we have discussed the nature of the campaign communication of journalists and candidates, and the effect this communication has on the perceptions, attitudes, and behavior of the U.S. electorate. In the final chapter we will return one last time to each of these topics and reflect on how campaign communication shapes the meaning of elections more generally.

Notes

1. For a graph presenting U.S. turnout rates from 1860 to 1964 and turnout rates in three Western European nations from 1948 to 1961, see William J. Keefe, *Parties, Politics, and Public Policy in America* (Hinsdale, Ill.: Dryden, 1976), p. 96. See also Ivor Crewe, "As the World Turns Out," *Public Opinion*, February–March 1981, pp. 52–53, for data on turnout rates in twenty-eight countries since 1945.

2. In the late 1800s, however, turnout rates were consistently above 70 percent (see Keefe, *Parties, Politics*). For what happened between 1900 and 1932, see Walter Dean Burnham, "The Changing Shape of the American Political Universe," *American Political Science Review* 59 (March 1965): 7–28.

3. Raymond E. Wolfinger and Steven J. Rosenstone, *Who Votes* (New Haven: Yale University Press, 1980), Chaps. 1–3.

4. Angus Campbell, Philip E. Converse, Warren E. Miller, and Donald E. Stokes, *The American Voter* (New York: Wiley, 1960), pp. 89–115. For an argument that most of the recent decline in turnout may be accounted for by declines in the strength of party identification and political efficacy, see Paul R. Abramson and John H. Aldrich, "The Decline of Electoral Participation in America," *American Political Science Review* 76, no. 3 (September 1982): 502–521.

5. Wolfinger and Rosenstone, *Who Votes*, Chap. 4; Ira Sharkansky, "The Utility of Elazar's Political Culture: A Research Note," *Polity*, Fall 1969, pp. 247–262; and Jae-on Kim, John R. Petrocik, and Stephen N. Enokson, "Voter Turnout among the American States: Systemic and Individual Components," *American Political Science Review* 69 (March 1975): 107–123.

6. Herbert A. Simon and Frederick Stern, "The Effect of Television upon Voting Behavior in the 1952 Presidential Election," *American Political Science Review* 40 (1955): 470–477.

7. Norman Blume and Schley Lyons, "The Monopoly Newspaper in a Local Election: The Toledo *Blade*," *Journalism Quarterly*, 45 (Summer 1968): 286–292.

8. Bernard Berelson, Paul Lazarsfeld, and William McPhee, *Voting* (Chicago: University of Chicago Press, 1954), p. 249.

9. William A. Glaser, "Television and Voting Turnout," *Public Opinion Quarterly* 29 (Spring 1965): 71–86.

10. Stephen D. Shaffer, "A Multivariate Explanation of Decreasing Turnout in Presidential Elections, 1960–1976," *American Journal of Political Science* 25, no. 1 (February 1981): 68–95.

11. Harold Mendelsohn, "Election-Day Broadcasts and Terminal Voting Decisions," *Public Opinion Quarterly* 30 (Summer 1966): 212–225. See also Douglas A. Fuchs, "Election-Day Radio-TV and Western Voting," *Public Opinion Quarterly* 30 (Summer 1966): 226–236.

12. Kurt Lang and Gladys Engel Lang, *Politics and Television* (Chicago: Quadrangle Books, 1968), Chap. 7.

13. Sam Tuchman and Thomas E. Coffin, "The Influence of Election Night Television Broadcasts in a Close Election," *Public Opinion Quarterly* 35 (Fall 1971): 305–326.

14. Raymond Wolfinger and Peter Linguiti, "Tuning In and Tuning Out," *Public Opinion* 4, no. 1 (February–March 1981): 56–60.

15. Laurily K. Epstein and Gerald Strom, "Election Night Projections and West Coast Turnout," *American Politics Quarterly* 9, no. 4 (October 1981): 479–491.

16. This approach may be found in any number of analyses of presidential voting behavior. Representative works include Herbert Asher, *Presidential Elections and American Politics* (Homewood, Ill.: Dorsey, 1980); Gregory B. Markus and Philip E. Converse, "A Dynamic Simultaneous Equation Model of Electoral Choice," *American Political Science Review* 73, no. 4 (December 1979): 1055–1070; Gregory B. Markus, "Political Attitudes During an Election Year: A Report on the 1980 NES Panel Study," *American Political Science Review* 76, no. 3 (September 1982): 538–560; Mark A. Schulman and Gerald M. Pomper, "Variability in Electoral Behavior: Longitudinal Perspectives from Causal Modeling," *American Journal of Political Science* 19 (February 1975): 1–18; Arthur H. Miller and Martin P. Wattenberg, "Policy and Performance Voting in the 1980 Election," Paper presented to the American Political Science Association, 1981; Arthur H. Miller, Warren E. Miller, Alden S. Raine, and Thad A. Brown, "A Majority Party in Disarray: Policy Polarization in the 1972 Election," *American Political Science Review* 70, no. 3 (September 1976): 753–778; Benjamin I. Page and Calvin C. Jones, "Reciprocal Effects of Policy Preferences, Party Loyalties and the Vote," *American Political Science Review* 73, no. 4 (December 1979): 1071–1089; and David E. Repass, "Comment: Political Methodologies in Disarray; Some Alternative Interpretations of the 1972 Election," *American Political Science Review* 70, no. 3 (September 1976): 814–831.

17. Markus and Converse, "Dynamic Model"; and Markus, "Political Attitudes."

18. Dan Nimmo and Robert L. Savage, *Candidates and Their Images* (Pacific Palisades, Calif.: Goodyear, 1976).

19. Markus, "Political Attitudes"; and Page and Jones, "Reciprocal Effects."

20. Markus and Converse, "Dynamic Model"; Page and Jones, "Reciprocal Effects"; Markus, "Political Attitudes"; Miller et al., "Majority Party"; and Repass, "Comment."

21. Markus and Converse, "Dynamic Model"; and Markus, "Political Attitudes."

22. Schulman and Pomper, "Variability"; Markus and Converse, "Dynamic Model"; Markus, "Political Attitudes"; Miller and Wattenberg, "Policy and Performance"; Samuel Popkin, John W. Gorman, Charles Phillips, and Jeffrey A. Smith, "Comment: What Have You Done for Me Lately? Toward an Investment Theory of Voting," *American Political Science Review* 70, no. 3 (September 1976): 779–805; and Repass, "Comment."

23. Miller et al., "Majority Party"; Page and Jones, "Reciprocal Effects"; Warren E. Miller and J. Merrill Shanks, "Policy Directions and Presidential Leadership: Alternative Interpretations of the 1980 Presidential Election," Unpublished paper.

24. Page and Jones, "Reciprocal Effects."

25. Markus and Converse, "Dynamic Model"; Markus, "Political Attitudes"; Miller et al., "Majority Party"; Miller and Wattenberg, "Policy and Performance"; and Miller and Shanks, "Policy Directions."

26. Page and Jones, "Reciprocal Effects."

27. Markus and Converse, "Dynamic Model"; Page and Jones, "Reciprocal Effects"; Markus, "Political Attitudes"; and Miller and Wattenberg, "Policy and Performance."

28. Berelson, Lazarsfeld, and McPhee, *Voting*; and Paul Lazarsfeld, Bernard Berelson, and Hazel Gaudet, *The People's Choice* (New York: Columbia University Press, 1948).

29. See the sources cited in notes 26 and 27.

30. Nimmo and Savage, *Candidates and Their Images*, Chap. 6.

31. Simon and Stern, "Effect of Television."

32. Michael J. Robinson and Clifford Zukin, "Television and the Wallace Vote," *Journal of Communication* 26 (Spring 1976): 79–83.

33. John P. Robinson, "Perceived Media Bias and the 1968 Vote: Can the Media Affect Behavior After All?" *Journalism Quarterly* 49 (Summer 1972): 239–246; and John P. Robinson, "The Press as King Maker: What Surveys from Last Five Campaigns Show," *Journalism Quarterly* 51 (Winter 1974): 587–594.

34. Paul J. Deutschmann, "Viewing, Conversation, and Voting Intentions," in Sidney Kraus, ed., *The Great Debates* (Gloucester, Mass.: Peter Smith, 1968).

35. Herbert W. Simons and Kenneth Leibowitz, "Shifts in Candidate Images," in Sidney Kraus, ed., *The Great Debates, 1976: Ford v. Carter* (Bloomington: Indiana University Press, 1979).

36. David O. Sears and Steven H. Chaffee, "Uses and Effects of the 1976 Debates: An Overview of Empirical Studies," in Kraus, *The Great Debates, 1976.*

37. "Face Off: A Conversation with the President's Pollsters: Patrick Caddell and Richard Wirthlin," *Public Opinion* 3, no. 6 (December–January 1981): 2–12, 63–64.

38. Thomas E. Patterson and Robert D. McClure, *The Unseeing Eye* (New York: G. P. Putnam's, 1976), p. 134.

39. Thomas E. Patterson and Robert D. McClure, "Political Advertising: Voter Reaction," Paper presented at the annual meeting of the American Association for Public Opinion Research, Asheville, N.C., 1973.

40. Harold Mendelsohn, "Election-Day Broadcasts."

41. Tuchman and Coffin, "Election Night Television Broadcasts."

42. Richard A. Joslyn, "Strategic Voting," Unpublished manuscript. See also Bruce E. Cain, "Strategic Voting in Britain," *American Journal of Political Science* 22 (August 1978): 639–655; Jerome H. Black, "The Multicandidate Calculus of Voting: Application to Canadian Federal Elections" *American Journal of Political Science* 22 (August 1978): 609–638; and Richard G. Niemi and William H. Riker, "The Choice of Voting Systems," *Scientific American* 234 (June 1976): 21–27.

43. For a concise but informative discussion of these processes, see Jarol Manheim, *The Politics Within* (New York: Longman, 1982), Chap. 6.

44. For a formal model of the process by which a candidate's resources change during the nomination campaign, see John H. Aldrich, "A Dynamic Model of Presidential Nomination Campaigns," *American Political Science Review* 74, no. 3 (September 1980): 651–669.

45. Thomas E. Patterson, *The Mass Media Election* (New York: Praeger, 1980), Chap. 10.

46. Ibid.

47. J. Merrill Shanks and Bradley Palmquist, "Changing Determinants of Candidate Preferences: Design Issues in Studying Electoral Behavior before and after the Major Party Conventions," Paper presented to the annual meeting of the American Political Science Association, 1982.

48. Aldrich, "A Dynamic Model."

49. This view of congressional elections is taken from the work of Gary Jacobson: "The Effects of Campaign Spending in Congressional Election," *American Political Science Review* 72 (June 1978): 469–491; *The Politics of Congressional Elections* (Boston: Little, Brown, 1983); and *Money in Congressional Elections* (New Haven: Yale University Press, 1980). It is also consistent, however, with Thomas E. Mann and Raymond E. Wolfinger, "Candidates and Parties in Congressional Election"; Alan I. Abramowitz, "A Comparison of Voting for U.S. Senator and Representative in 1978"; and Barbara Hinckley, "The American Voter in Congressional Elections"; all in *American Political Science Review* 74, no. 3 (September 1980).

50. Jacobson, "The Effects"; Jacobson, *Money*; Jacobson, *The Politics*; and Abramowitz, "Comparison of Voting"; Hinckley, "American Voter."

51. Jacobson, "The Effects"; Jacobson, *The Politics*; and Hinckley, "American Voter." See also John R. Johannes and John C. McAdams, "The Congressional Incumbency Effect: Is It Casework, Policy Compatibility, or Something Else? An Examination of the 1978 Election," *American Journal of Political Science* 25, no. 3 (August 1981): 512–542.

52. Gary Jacobson, "The Impact of Broadcast Campaigning on Electoral Outcomes," Paper presented at the annual meeting of the American Political Science Association, 1974.

53. Edie N. Goldenberg and Michael W. Traugott, "Campaign Effects on Voting Behavior in the 1978 Congressional Election," Paper presented at the annual meeting of the American Political Science Association, 1980. See also Johannes and McAdams, "Congressional Incumbency."

54. Although I have stopped short of discussing the impact of the mass media on voting behavior in nonfederal campaigns, there is some evidence that newspaper endorsements, telephone canvassing, and brochure drops have an impact on voter turnout and candidate choices in state and local elections. See, for example, William C. Adams and Dennis J. Smith, "Effects of Telephone Canvassing on Turnout and Preferences: A Field Experiment," *Public Opinion Quarterly* (1980): 389–395; Roy E. Miller and William M. Richey, "The Effects of a Campaign Brochure 'Drop' in a County-Level Race for State's Attorney," Paper presented at the annual meeting of the International Communication Association, 1980; Michael Hooper, "Party and Newspaper Endorsement as Predictors of Voter Choice," *Journalism Quarterly* 46 (Summer 1969): 302–305; and John E. Mueller, "Choosing Among 103 Candidates," *Public Opinion Quarterly* 34 (Fall 1970): 395–402.

9
Campaign Communication and the Meaning of Elections

Normatively speaking, consent from ignorance can never be genuine, no more so than conversion by the sword. Pragmatically speaking, an ignorant citizenry is dangerously unready when the time comes for choice, the key citizen choice being election.

—James David Barber, "Characters in the Campaign," in *Race for the Presidency*

In the preceding pages we have explored the origins, content, and effects of campaign communication. In the process we have focused on the news coverage of campaigns provided by journalists, the political rhetoric devised by candidates and their staffs and delivered directly to the public, and the attitudinal and behavioral responses of the citizenry to this flow of information. In this chapter we undertake our final and most difficult task: analyzing the implications of campaign communication for the meaning of elections more generally.

Historical Development in Campaign Communication

There have been a number of recent changes in the nature of campaign communication. Although comparisons with historical times for which memories are blurred and data are sparse are always risky, it appears that the U.S. electoral process has been significantly altered by modern campaign communication.

The recent change in electoral communication has both a quantitative and a qualitative dimension. In *quantitative* terms, the number of campaign messages devised and delivered by candidates has never been greater. Certainly more money is being spent by candidates on campaign communication than ever before, and the use of spot advertising, broadcast debates, and pseudoevents to stimulate news coverage means that the electorate is probably exposed to candidate messages more frequently than ever before. It is possible that in the late nineteenth and early twentieth centuries, when party organizations were at their strongest, candidate messages were delivered to as large a proportion of the eligible electorate as they are today. It is also likely, however, that those party organizations were not uniformly strong in all areas of the country or across time. Consequently, although the prominence of candidate (actually *party* at that time) communication may have occasionally reached the levels of contemporary campaigns, it is unlikely that the total amount of candidate-devised messages was generally as great as it is now.

In addition, the amount of campaign coverage provided by news organizations is probably greater now than ever before. Daily television news shows; press coverage of special events such as conventions and primaries; broadcast transmission of major speeches, news interviews, debates, and press conferences; and print coverage of the campaign in the daily press, weekly news magazines, and specialized opinion magazines have all combined to acquaint ever increasing audiences with at least a minimum of information about election campaigns. Again, it is possible that daily *newspaper* coverage of campaigns was more prevalent years ago when there were more daily papers in operation, but the contributions of other media to campaign coverage today more than make up for this loss.

There is also a *qualitative* aspect to contemporary changes in campaign communication. Not only is there simply more campaign-related information available to the public, but this information is qualitatively different. Generalizations here are particularly hazardous since there is little systematic data available on electoral communication prior to the television age. If thirty years is a long enough period to indicate trends in campaigning, however, then a number of qualitative changes are notable.

It may well be that today's candidate appeals are pretty much the same as they were in previous eras. Politicians have always promised peace, prosperity, and justice to the electorate; challengers have always attempted to blame incumbents for social problems and policy failures; campaigns have utilized nonsensical jingles, slogans, and image making throughout U.S. history; and, with a few notable exceptions, the natural tendency of candidates has typically been to avoid revealing specific, detailed policy preferences.

There are at least two ways in which contemporary candidate appeals are different, however. First, candidate communication is definitely much less party-oriented now than it was in the first half of the twentieth century. Party appeals are seldom visibly made by presidential candidates and are hardly ever the cornerstone of a presidential campaign.

Instead, candidate appeals usually focus attention on the *candidate* rather than on the party that nominated him or her, and attempt to create favorable *candidate* rather than party impressions. A number of researchers have argued that this leads to less party-based voting, more drastic fluctuations in the partisan division of the vote, more ticket splitting across electoral levels, and more cases of divided partisan control of governing institutions.[1] It may also leave incumbent officeholders more vulnerable to public dissatisfaction as the impressions that resulted in one's election typically turn sour and the public becomes uninterested in, skeptical of, or hostile toward officeholders.

Second, candidate messages are devised with much more awareness of and concern for public perceptions and preferences now than ever before. Candidate appeals are increasingly based on public opinion polls and delivered to targeted portions of a constituency. This may mean that the messages are more interesting, familiar, or persuasive to the public; and it may also prevent campaign rhetoric from being bold, provocative, or challenging. In the extreme case, if political leaders tell the public *only* what the public is comfortable with, political change becomes a less likely consequence of electoral politics.

Most of the qualitative change in campaign communication, however, is a result of the changing behavior of journalists. Here a number of observations seem warranted. First, I have commented many times in previous chapters about the tendency of the press to focus on "horse-race" aspects of campaigns. This focus leads to an emphasis on candidate prospects and strategy, indications of electoral strength and success, and a competitive struggle among journalists to be first to predict the electoral outcome. Furthermore, there is some evidence that the current presidential delegate-selection process and products of the public opinion-polling industry have allowed journalists to become even more obsessed with the horse race than ever before. This focus clearly delimits the understanding that the public is able to acquire during an election campaign and trivializes the significance of an election into little more than a spectator sport.

Second, journalists have shown a notable tendency recently to portray candidates and dramatize the electoral contest thematically. This tendency results from audience presumptions, economic incentives, and professional training; it yields campaign accounts that are candidate-, event-, and theme-oriented; exaggerates the significance of particular campaign episodes; constrains public awareness to impressions of a few "viable" candidates; and submerges programmatic and philosophical matters in a sea of metaphors and dramatizations. Although it is unclear whether this campaign coverage differs from the coverage provided in previous years, the presence of television news has probably made a major contribution to this development.

Third, there is some evidence that contemporary journalism approaches election campaigns with a much more skeptical, cynical, and derisive orientation than was true just twenty years ago. Portrayals of candidates have become increasingly negative, and the electoral process itself has been treated as a meaningless or unseemly exercise. This tendency may be the result of an emerging adversarial relationship between journalists and politicians, and it may have contributed to the decline in political efficacy and political trust of the U.S. public.[2] Although evidence for this effect is sketchy and adversarial journalism might also have beneficial consequences, the change in the *tone* of campaign coverage in recent years is surely a significant phenomenon.

Since we have only had about ten or fifteen years experience with the campaign communication of our new electoral process, it is unclear what the long-term consequences of these changes—both quantitative and qualitative—might be. The content of contemporary campaign communication, however, suggests a number of possibilities, mostly worrisome. Specifically, if current trends in electoral communication continue, we might reasonably expect the U.S. electorate of the future to be more cynical, less partisan, less frequently confronted with challenging political discourse, and more narrowly informed about the electoral choices available than was the case in the not-too-distant past. Any one of these consequences would have profound implications for the U.S. political process.

Elections as Communications Processes

We have also seen in the preceding chapters that the flow of campaign communication is the result of the contributions of a number of actors and that no one actor dominates this process. Even passive citizens affect campaign communication indirectly through public opinion poll results, historical voting returns, and media-exposure patterns. Furthermore, campaign communication can be seen as a process by which the main electoral participants come to a mutually satisfactory accommodation concerning the messages that will be delivered to the public. Candidates anticipate the behavior of journalists, campaign contributors, and voters when they engage in campaign activities; journalists have developed an informal set of norms that attempt to accommodate their need for daily newsworthy stories and access to news-makers with the candidates' desire for factually accurate and favorable coverage; and the public remains the final arbiter of which messages are attended to, ignored, distorted, remembered, and persuasive.

The end result of this interaction among campaign participants is that campaign communication is unlike what any one participant would unilaterally prefer. Candidates and journalists provide more campaign discourse than the public would probably independently desire or demand, the inquiries and commentary of journalists (in debate settings, for example) force candidates to reveal more specific policy-related preferences than candidates themselves would voluntarily reveal, and audience predispositions and economic considerations force journalists to be more circumspect and nonideological in their campaign coverage than they might be otherwise. In this way the net flow of campaign messages is shaped by a number of campaign participants with differing motives, goals, and roles.

The Effects of Campaign Communication

Of course, there is no guarantee that the communication that is acceptable to campaign participants will be optimal in any other sense. For example, it is not at all clear that contemporary election campaigns have the educative effect that is often ascribed to them. Candidates have devised forms of campaign communication that provide them with a satisfactory way to deliver their messages without having to reveal much in the way of policy specifics or without having to be too careful about the accuracy of the claims they make. Journalists have developed methods of campaign coverage that allow them to cultivate sources, compete for a portion of their organization's news-hole, avoid attacks on the legitimacy of their coverage, and interest a sufficiently large segment of the public in their campaign accounts without informing the public about the policy preferences and philosophical positions of the candidates. The public is probably fairly well satisfied with campaign communication that can be easily ignored, may be selectively perceived, and is generally reassuring. The collective outcome of all this mutually reinforcing activity, however, may be to constrain severely the educative value of the electoral process.

We have seen, after all, that although the direct impact of campaign communication on the voting intentions of the U.S. electorate is modest, the campaign does influence other popular perceptions and preferences. In particular, the public tends to learn horse-race information, to alter the salience of political issues and candidates for public office, to form stylistic impressions of political unknowns, and to increase slightly the accuracy of perceptions of candidate policy positions. The fact that most of this learning is shallow and superficial, or pertains mainly for the knowledge-rich, suggests that the educative effect of election campaigns is quite modest.

This raises the question of what U.S. elections actually accomplish and how the nature of campaign communication delimits the meaning of elections and the significance of electoral outcomes. Elections have always had a central position within the U.S. political system. From the early days of the Republic to the present, we have expected the electoral process to check the tyrannical designs of public officials, resolve divisive political conflict, ensure the representation of constituent interests, educate the public, and provide the public with an avenue for constraining the policy choices of public decision makers. It is quite possible, however, that what we hope elections do and what they actually do are two entirely different things.

In the remainder of this chapter we will analyze the meaning of U.S. elections by considering four different perspectives on campaign communication and the electoral process. This exercise will permit us to review what we have found to be the nature of campaign communication and to determine the impact of current campaign communication on the electoral process. At the conclusion of this analysis we should have a clearer understanding of the implications of contemporary campaign communication techniques for what we may reasonably expect elections to do in a political system such as our own.

Four Perspectives on Modern Election Campaigns

A perspective on elections is a general statement about the functions elections serve, the kinds of behaviors that are prevalent during election campaigns, and the significance of electoral outcomes. Such perspectives may contain both empirical generalizations about the frequency of certain behaviors and the consequences of electoral outcomes, and normative expressions of how elections ought to be conducted and might be improved. The fact that there are a number of different perspectives on U.S. elections suggests that the evidence for any one of them is not altogether convincing.

In the pages that follow we will discuss four perspectives on elections, which I will refer to as the *prospective policy choice* approach, the *retrospective policy satisfaction* approach, the *selection of a benevolent leader* approach, and the *election-as-ritual* approach. We will analyze the connections between the campaign communication we have been discussing and each of these perspectives, and we will discover that contemporary campaign communication is more consistent with some of these approaches than with others.

THE PROSPECTIVE-POLICY-CHOICE APPROACH

Americans are particularly fond of the notion that elections provide a mechanism by which the public can express policy preferences and constrain the future policy choices of public officials. We are often told that we can "send a message" with our vote, that this message can help shape future policy enactments by public officials, and that the aggregate message embodied in an election outcome confers a *mandate* on victorious candidates to pursue their policy preferences aggressively.

There are few political scientists who believe that elections are exclusively policymaking mechanisms. Many more political scientists, however, believe that this is a reachable goal with which the behavior of the U.S. electorate is more consistent than is often appreciated and toward which reform of the electoral process should be directed. Although numerous empirical shortcomings of this approach have been acknowledged, the normative hold of this approach on most Americans often leads to optimistic appraisals of the progress made toward the realization of this goal in the last twenty years, and to suggestions for reforming the electoral process so as to accelerate the pace of this presumed progress.

We will begin our consideration of the prospective policy choice approach by enumerating the empirical assertions and normative values expressed by those who believe that elections are mechanisms by which the citizenry can constrain the policy choices made by public officials.[3]

First, this approach claims that candidates ought to develop future-oriented policy proposals, present these proposals in an understandable way to the public during the course of the election campaign, and contrast their proposals with those of the opposition. That is, candidate policy proposals should be specific, visible, clear, and differentiated from those of the opposition. Nonprogrammatic appeals, or policy-oriented appeals that are vague, ambiguous, deceptive, or distorted, are inconsistent with this approach.

Second, this approach claims that the public will be attentive to the future-oriented policy proposals presented by competing candidates, and will accurately perceive the policy alternatives that each candidacy represents. This implies that the policy positions of the candidates will be readily accessible—via both candidate rhetoric communicated directly to the public and journalistic coverage of the campaign—and that citizens will perceive these policy choices accurately. The campaign will cause the public to learn something about what policy initiatives can be expected from the victorious candidate.

Third, this approach claims that voters base their candidate choice on their (accurate) perceptions of candidate policy preferences and will select the candidate who is closest to the policy preferences of the voter. This involves judging the distance between the voter's and candidates' policy positions and aggregating these proximities across a number of issues. In this way candidate choices become an individual-level referendum on policy proposals for the future.

Fourth, this approach concludes that if each individual vote is a choice between the "bundles" of policy preferences offered by candidates, then the summation of all votes cast represents a collective judgment concerning the policy preferences of the electorate. In this way the victorious candidate embodies the policy preferences of the public and has been granted the expressed seal of approval (mandate) for his or her policy preferences.

Fifth, this approach asserts that the victorious candidate should be emboldened by the policy mandate conferred on him or her, and ought vigorously to pursue his policy proposals. The expectation is that if he is successful, the public will have been represented and, presumably, satisfied. Although no one expects this postelection pursuit of policy initiatives to be easy, given the fragmentation of power in our system of government, the elected official is supposed to have the force of public approval behind his or her efforts.

In summary, this approach holds that elections may be viewed as a process by which citizens become informed about *future* public policy alternatives, by which citizens have the opportunity to choose a like-minded public official, and through which electoral outcomes shape future policy outcomes.

Although political scientists acknowledge that the evidence supporting each of the assertions enumerated here is far from compelling, those who study U.S. elections have also tended to use this set of claims as a basis for understanding and evaluating the electoral process. Since 1960, in particular, the question most frequently asked about elections is: "To what extent do elections allow the public to shape future policy choices?" The answer given tends to be that this approach is becoming a more accurate appraisal of contemporary U.S. elections.

Much of the post-1960 optimism concerning the validity of the prospective-policy-choice approach has come from unsystematic descriptions of the behavior of candidates. A number of recent electoral studies have made sweeping and unsupported assertions that candidate rhetoric has increasingly taken on the characteristics expected with this approach. These assertions have typically held that candidate rhetoric has become increasingly policy-oriented, that candidates are more willing to reveal specific policy proposals, and that the policy preferences of at least the major-party presidential candidates have become sufficiently distinct. Reviews of the 1964 election, for example, found that the candidates provided "sharply contrasting philosophies of government" with Goldwater in particular providing "an ideological stimulus" and a "meaningful test of liberal-conservative sentiment."[4] A review of the 1968 election argued that the candidacy of George Wallace "was reacted to by the public as an *issue* candidacy;"[5] and reviews of the 1972 election claimed that candidate "issue positions were unusually sharply defined,"[6] and that the election marked the end point of a twelve-year process during which there was an "upgrading in the quality of political rhetoric and debate" and an "increased articulation of the ideological differences between the parties."[7] This position was summarized nicely in a major study of U.S. public opinion that argued that candidates have shown an increased willingness to present voters with "meaningful bundles of issues," with positions "on the liberal-conservative continuum that [are] both unambiguous and fairly far from the center," with "issue choices," and with a "coherent set of issue positions."[8] The net result of these studies has been to raise the possibility that candidates are increasingly offering meaningful, clear, and distinct policy proposals to the electorate.

Complementing these assertions about candidate rhetoric is research claiming that the beliefs and behavior of the U.S. public have also changed significantly in the past two decades. This research has attempted to demonstrate that the ideological consistency of mass belief systems has undergone a quantum jump since 1964, that the public learns more about the policy preferences of candidates during a campaign than we originally thought, and that "issue positions" have been an increasingly important correlate of electoral choices. These changes in political behavior have been attributed both to the presumed change in candidate rhetoric discussed earlier, and to more general societal phenomena such as the emergence of new and less easily resolved policy issues and the increased education of the U.S. public.

The combination of altered candidate and citizen behavior has led a number of scholars to argue forcefully that the electoral process is showing a renewed ability to permit the public to make prospective policy choices. Some have argued that elections are now an arena in which political parties "stand as 'groups of like-minded men' offering particular stances toward public issues,"[9] and that candidate contests are now "fought along lines of deepening policy cleavages" with issues "expected to play an increasingly significant role in future elections."[10] In addition, some have argued that party victories "can now reasonably be interpreted as related to the mass choice of one set of issue positions over another,"[11] and that the consequence of electoral outcomes is that "the public severely limits the options of leaders at the time policy is made."[12] In short, the central feature of this approach to elections—that elections allow the public to influence or control future policy decisions—seems to have been realized!

Despite the vigor with which the proponents of the prospective-policy-choice approach have made their case, there are many reasons that we should not accept their view of the electoral process completely. In fact, in previous chapters we have considered an extensive body of evidence that suggests that in many ways contemporary campaign communication is inconsistent with this approach.

The first dubious assertion of the prospective-policy-choice approach concerns the nature of candidate communication in general and of post-1960 presidential candidate rhetoric in particular. In contrast to the specific, clear, distinctive, and prevalent policy-oriented rhetoric thought to be typical by the proponents of this approach, we found that a large portion of candidate rhetoric has nothing to do with future policy choices or deals with such choices in only the vaguest and most ambiguous way. Although there is always some revelation of fairly specific policy preferences by presidential candidates, we found that this constitutes a small portion of presidential rhetoric and that there was no evidence for an increase in the specificity or distinctiveness of rhetoric over time. We did find that presidential debates are an unusually good forum for forcing candidates to reveal specific, future policy preferences; but there were no such debates in the 1964, 1968, or 1972 presidential campaigns. Also, there is good evidence that what we found to be true of the candidate appeals in presidential spot ads and debate appearances is also true for campaign speeches,[13] and that nonpresidential candidate rhetoric is no more likely to contain specific policy positions than presidential rhetoric is.[14]

We have also seen that modern communication techniques have, with increasing efficiency, permitted candidates to use electoral appeals that are shared by the intended audience and to communicate these to selective audiences. Public opinion polling allows candidates to pretest the impact of rhetorical choices; direct mail, spot ads, and telephone banks allow candidates to segment the public into specialized audiences for the purpose of delivering tailor-made messages. These techniques allow candidates to preserve more control over the appeals that are made and probably permit candidates to avoid making the kind of policy-related appeal that the prospective-policy-choice approach requires.

Not only is candidate communication less consistent with the prospective-policy-choice approach than is often asserted, but the content of campaign news coverage also raises serious doubts about the accuracy of any approach to elections that focuses primarily on policy-oriented information. We have seen that journalists are either unable or unwilling to force candidates to reveal specific policy preferences and that most news stories do not communicate candidate policy preferences to the public. Horse-race coverage dominates campaign news, "issues" more typically arise from campaign activities or blunders than from programmatic concerns, objectivity prevents journalists from explicitly contrasting the policy proposals of candidates, and covering the campaign by accompanying candidates from pseudoevent to pseudoevent delimits the type of story that can be written about a campaign. Furthermore, there is some evidence that campaign news coverage has become less policy-oriented over time. Changes in the duration and visibility of the presidential nomination campaign may have resulted in dispersing a given amount of substantive news coverage across increased time and space; and the development of the modern mode of campaigning (extensive travel, series of pseudoevents, enforced distance between candidate and press) represents a recent added barrier to programmatic news coverage. In summary, the policy-oriented component of news coverage is not as prevalent as the prospective-policy-choice approach suggests, and it may have actually shrunk in recent years.

Given the nature of candidate rhetoric and campaign news coverage, it is not at all clear that election campaigns have the educative effect asserted by the prospective-policy-choice approach. True, citizens do learn some things during an election campaign, and some of this learning involves the formation and adjustment of perceptions regarding the policy preferences of candidates. It is also clear, however, that much of what is learned is not policy-oriented (perceptions of the likely outcome and impressions of candidate attributes, for example) and that citizens have ample opportunity to project their own preferences onto their favored candidates and to rationalize their preferences and those of their favored candidates into agreement. As a result, there may be significant agreement among a citizen's own policy preferences, the citizen's perceptions of the candidates' policy preferences, and the citizen's evaluation of competing candidacies; but the agreement may have been reached through a process other than the selection-of-a-candidate-*because*-of-policy-proximity model suggested by the prospective-policy-choice approach. Furthermore, most of the evidence arguing that citizen perceptions regarding candidate policy preferences have become more accurate during election campaigns has been based on selected presidential election campaigns. Given the paucity of news coverage of non-presidential campaigns, it is difficult to see how such an educative process could possibly take place in any arena other than the presidential one.

Finally, it is not altogether clear that policy preferences have the robust impact on voter choices that the prospective-policy-choice approach suggests. Although a complete review of the voting-behavior literature would take us too far afield, it may simply be said here that the *most* that has ever been demonstrated or claimed is that policy-related attitudes (some of which do not involve future-oriented policy comparisons) exert an impact on voters' electoral choices that is roughly comparable to that of party identification and of evaluations of candidate attributes. Although it is difficult to devise an agreed-on measure of just how important each of these three attitudes (party, policy, and candidate) is in shaping electoral choices, it is clear that a substantial amount of voter choice may *not* be understood on prospective-policy-choice grounds. The proportion of electoral choices that may be explained on policy grounds may have been larger in some recent presidential elections, but it is difficult to tell whether this is part of a durable or general trend. It is more likely that the extent of policy-related voting is itself dependent on the ideological distance between the candidates and the visibility of their policy alternatives. In fact, given my previous comments on candidate rhetoric and campaign news coverage, it would be surprising if the prevalence of prospective-policy voting were undergoing an enduring, secular increase. Similarly, given the nature of nonpresidential rhetoric and campaign news coverage, there is no reason to expect comparable levels of issue voting at nonpresidential levels. Instead, there is abundant evidence that voting for congressional candidates is based on a much lower information base than is the case in presidential elections, and that it has much less policy-oriented significance than presidential voting does.[15]

In short, campaign communication and voting behavior are largely, though not entirely, inconsistent with the prospective-policy-choice approach. Although this approach may remain a valuable normative goal and may be a view of elections that has potent implications for various electoral reforms, it is not an approach that is compelling because of its empirical accuracy. This suggests that we ought to turn to some other plausible, but less commonly held, approaches to the study of election campaigns.

THE RETROSPECTIVE-POLICY-SATISFACTION APPROACH

A second policy-oriented approach to elections argues that although public policies are an important consideration in election campaigns, the policies debated are as often as not past rather than future policies, and the standard of evaluation voters use is likely to be a more global assessment of satisfaction with *past* policy *performance* than agreement with *future* policy *proposals*. This approach also makes a number of empirical claims about the behavior of candidates, journalists, and voters.[16]

First, this approach observes that candidates devote a significant portion of their campaign rhetoric to placing blame and claiming credit for previous policy decisions and political conditions. This discourse may not necessarily contain any indication of what a candidate would have done differently or of what the candidate would propose doing in the future, nor is the discourse necessarily careful about holding incumbent officeholders or parties responsible only for policy decisions or consequences over which they had some control or could have had some influence. In turn, this discourse asks voters to determine whether or not they are generally satisfied with recent public policy and political conditions.

In times of war, economic depression, or civil unrest, "the reality of bad times speaks largely for itself, and the job of the challenger is simply to draw attention to it, to fasten the blame securely on the incumbents, and to promise that things will be better under his administration."[17] In less anxious or critical times, challengers attempt to raise the salience of social or economic conditions or problems that are worrisome and to convince the electorate that the incumbents have been unduly inattentive to or unsuccessful in dealing with such problems. Incumbents, on the other hand, combat such rhetoric with evidence of previous policy accomplishments or improved conditions of some sort, also without necessarily being too careful about what they take credit for. The rhetoric of both incumbents and challengers is designed to persuade the public that in a general way "things are going well" or "things are going poorly" or "it's not my fault that things have gone poorly." In this approach the identification of particular policy options is less important than the formation of an overall evaluation of previous policy decisions and current social conditions.

Second, this approach holds that the main contribution news coverage makes to civic education and electoral outcomes is to provide between-election surveillance of public policy decisions and policy implementation and to familiarize the electorate with policy consequences not readily experienced. Campaign news coverage is also important for the transmission of candidate criticisms of past policy decisions and current conditions and for the ongoing process of policy evaluation by the citizenry. News coverage, however, is less important for how it informs the public about the future policy proposals of competing candidates than for the way in which it gives the public an information base prior to the campaign. This information base may then be used by the public to evaluate the conflicting attempts by candidates to take credit and place blame for policy successes and failures.

Third, although this approach holds that the basis on which voters make electoral choices is policy-oriented, as it was in the first approach, the pertinent policy orientation is backward- rather than forward-looking. That is, the public is thought to select a candidate on the basis of its general level of satisfaction with policy decisions or outcomes already experienced, rather than that of policy promises for the future. The focal point of this evaluation is the incumbent party or candidate, and the nature of the evaluation made by the voter is whether to stick with or turn out the incumbent:

> As voters mark their ballots they may have in their minds impressions of the last TV political spectacular of the campaign, but, more important, they have in their minds recollections of their experiences of the past four years. Those memories may be happy ones or they may be memories of dissatisfaction with what government has done or has left undone.
>
> The impact of events from the inauguration of an Administration to the onset of the next presidential campaign may affect far more voters than the fireworks of the campaign itself. Governments must act or not act, and action or inaction may convert supporters into opponents or opponents into supporters.[18]

This type of policy-related choice is thought to be more within the reach of the U.S. electorate because it requires citizens to form a general impression of their acceptance of or satisfaction with recent policies rather than a precise measure of the distance between their own policy preferences and the policy proposals of two or more candidates. As two electoral scholars have argued, this type of evaluation is much more easily done:

> Voters aren't sure of their policy preferences because they don't know, and can't easily find out, just what the effects of alternative policies would be. But they do know their basic goals and values, and can rather easily in their daily lives get some information about whether times are good or bad in terms of these values.[19]

Again,

> The prospects for the future may generally tend less to engage the voter or to govern his actions. Those prospects tend to be hazy, uncertain, problematic. Voters may respond most assuredly to what they have seen, heard, experienced. Forecasts, promises, predicted disaster, or pie in the sky may be less moving.[20]

Given the formation of this type of policy-related attitude, the decision rule to be followed by the voter is straightforward: "reward the incumbents if they have done well, and punish them if they have done badly."[21]

Finally, this approach argues that elections represent a referendum of sorts on the behavior of incumbents and incumbent administrations rather than an indication of future policy preferences. Voters are thought to punish incumbents for policy failures and reward incumbents for policy successes.[22] Any mandate conferred by a particular electoral outcome, therefore, is simply a general statement of preference for the status quo or for change, rather than a more specific mandate for particular policy initiatives.

To what extent is campaign communication and voter behavior consistent with the retrospective-policy-satisfaction approach? First, it is clear from our discussion of candidate communication that criticizing previous policy decisions and raising unsolved public problems or conditions *are* prevalent forms of campaign rhetoric. In fact, we saw that *policy salience* appeals, in which a policy issue or social condition is simply raised, are as common a message in televised spot ads as is the revelation of a specific policy position. If one also considers the expression of a vague policy position, which is frequently done with reference to some past policy failure, as also at least partly consistent with the retrospective-policy-satisfaction approach, then it is clear that most candidate rhetoric in both spot ads and debates is consistent with this approach. In fact, one analyst of candidate appeals has singled out television spot ads as being one form of campaign communication that is "poorly suited for complicated discussions of policy, but . . . highly effective at damning past performance."[23] In addition, campaign rhetoric in general, "while occasionally inspiring, is rarely very enlightening. It seldom goes beyond superficial promises and accusations. Furthermore, talk about goals or performance provides only weak and unreliable hints about which policies will be pursued."[24] This suggests that candidate rhetoric is much more consistent with the retrospective-policy-satisfaction than with the prospective-policy-choice approach.

Second, although the behavior of news organizations between elections was not within the purview of our discussion here, even an unsystematic perusal of U.S. journalism reveals that much of interelection news coverage brings policy decisions and the consequences of policy actions to light and, in the case of particularly visible and serious policy failure, devotes a considerable amount of attention to such issues. This is not to say that all unsolved social problems and governmental policy consequences are given extensive or regular coverage in U.S. news journals. The ability of governments to obscure and disguise policy failures is considerable, and the willingness of journalists to devote attention to social conditions, problems, and policy consequences is limited. Nonetheless, daily journalism does keep ongoing tabs on enough of the more important policy conditions—inflation rates, interest rates, unemployment rates, educational test scores, crime rates, industry productivity, product safety, environmental quality, foreign events—to permit members of the public to supplement their personal experience with an acquaintance with other information useful for forming an impression of overall policy satisfaction. In fact, most of the news stories that have dominated U.S. journalism in the past two decades—the civil rights movement, urban unrest, the Vietnam War, the environmental movement, crime, Watergate, the energy crisis, nuclear power and weaponry, U.S.-Soviet relations, and the Middle East—have provided citizens with potent and accessible bases on which to form global policy-satisfaction opinions. In other words, U.S. journalism provides the U.S. public with a much richer information base on which to make retrospective-policy-satisfaction than prospective-policy-choice decisions.

Campaign news coverage also contributes to retrospective policy judgments by transmitting and juxtaposing competing candidate claims regarding policy successes and failures. Journalism shows a general preference for he said–he responded–he said exchanges, thus making campaign arguments between candidates over who should be held responsible for what a fairly prevalent type of news story. Such conflicts are seldom resolved, of course, but they probably do provoke the public to form an impression in their own minds of who to blame or give credit for which policy decisions and social conditions.

Given the pervasiveness of U.S. journalism and the relevance of personal experience for opinions regarding policy satisfaction, it is plausible that the public has little or no difficulty forming perceptions of overall policy satisfaction and of who should be held responsible for such perceptions. Unlike the prospective-policy-choice approach, which requires the public to perceive candidate policy positions accurately and match them up with their own policy preferences, the retrospective-policy-satisfaction approach only requires the public to decide how satisfied they have been with previous policy decisions (or indecisions), and the consequences thereof, and to decide who should be credited with or blamed for previous policy successes and failures. In fact, it could be argued that the public would satisfy the requirements of this approach even if it "knew little about the causes of bliss or misfortune, and simply attributed everything to incumbents."[25]

Although there is considerable evidence that public attitudes do not measure up to the requirements of the prospective-policy-choice approach, public opinion is more consistent with the provisions of the retrospective-policy-satisfaction approach. It is certainly not difficult to get citizens to reveal whether they think they, their family, and their country are better or worse off now than at some time in the past; nor is it difficult to get citizens to reveal what they think the most serious political problems of the day are, how incumbents are handling their jobs, and which party or candidate they think will best solve current problems. On the other hand, it must also be admitted that although it is plausible that people are the best judges of their own policy satisfaction, it is unclear how accurate citizen perceptions of policy successes and failures are and how reasonable the apportionment of responsibility or blame for policy failures is. Politicians often attempt to persuade the public that a problem is more serious than it "really" is (for example, John Kennedy's missile gap issue in 1960 and Richard Nixon's more hyperbolic claims about political dissent and crime in 1968 and 1972); they also disagree on whom the public should blame for current, unresolved problems (such as the early 1980s debate between a Republican president and Democratic House of Representatives over whom to hold responsible for soaring unemployment rates). At this point, and until more relevant evidence is accumulated on this topic, the safest conclusion seems to be that public opinion is more consistent with the retrospective than the prospective policy approach, but that there are a number of inconsistencies between public opinion and the retrospective view as well.

Finally, there is some evidence that voters do cast their ballots guided in part by past policy performance and current policy satisfaction. This evidence consists of findings at both the presidential and congressional levels, and with both aggregate and individual-level data, that there is a relationship between policy satisfaction and candidate choices.

V. O. Key was the first analyst of presidential voting returns to argue that the electorate was making a retrospective policy evaluation with their votes. Key analyzed the attitudes of voters who switched party ballots between presidential elections and of new voters in a given presidential election and found that electoral choices in the 1936, 1940, 1944, 1948, 1952, and 1956 (but not 1960) elections

> reflect the electorate in its great, and perhaps principal, role as an appraiser of past events, past performance, and past actions. It judges retrospectively; it commands prospectively only insofar as it expresses either approval or disapproval of that which has happened before. Voters may reject what they have known; or they may approve what they have known. They are not likely to be attracted in great numbers by promises of the novel or unknown. Once innovation has occurred they may embrace it, even though they would have, earlier, hesitated to venture forth to welcome it.[26]

More recently, Benjamin Page and Edward Tufte have demonstrated that in 1968, 1972, and 1976 there were strong relationships between individual evaluations of the incumbent president's general job performance and presidential voting, and between discontent with a particular domestic or foreign policy or dissatisfaction with one's financial situation, and voting against presidential incumbents.[27] Furthermore, in the presidential elections since 1948 there have been very strong relationships between economic conditions (as measured by change in real disposable income) and the presidential vote for the incumbent presidential party.[28] Presumably the reason for this relationship is that voters punish incumbent presidential candidates when economic times are tough (or at least getting worse): "Despite all the short-run 'noise' in presidential contests, the extent of prosperity prevailing in the election year remains a regular and significant determinant of the vote won by the nominee of the in-party."[29]

At the congressional level there has been a persistent relationship over time between short-term changes in economic conditions (again measured in terms of the change in real disposable income), overall satisfaction with the job performance of incumbent presidents, and the amount the aggregate midterm congressional vote deviates from the normal two-party split.[30] Midterm congressional elections may be viewed as "a referendum on the performance of the president and his administration's management of the economy."[31]

There is much evidence, then, for the retrospective-policy-satisfaction approach. The campaign rhetoric of candidates is largely consistent with it, the content of interelection news coverage supports it, the expectations the approach has of public opinion are reasonable and within reach, and many voters in many different elections have shown signs of policy-satisfaction-related voting. In fact, the behavior of both candidates and the populace suggests that of the two policy-oriented approaches considered here, the one that is backward-looking is the more empirically compelling one:

> . . . candidates may accentuate predispositions to vote on the basis of past performance by talking so insistently about whether things are going well or poorly, while inhibiting policy voting through the ambiguity and similarity of their policy stands . . . we have [also] suggested that voters may in any case prefer to judge on the basis of the past, and that—in the face of information costs—it is rational for them to do so.[32]

THE SELECTION-OF-A-BENEVOLENT-LEADER APPROACH

Both of the approaches to elections we have considered so far focus on the public policy content and consequences of campaigns and elections. Yet it is clear that elections also involve *nonprogrammatic* competition between two or more *human beings* for the support and loyalty of the population. This nonprogrammatic competition involves attempts to convince the populace that the personal attributes of a candidate make him or her a "fit leader." Viewed in this way, elections become one of a number of processes by which human societies select leaders to make authoritative decisions. As is often the case in other forms of leadership selection—such as combat—this process may elevate the personal, nonprogrammatic attributes of the potential leader to a more central position than the consideration of policy decisions, conditions, or proposals.

When elections are seen as an exercise in *leadership* rather than *policy* selection, our attention is directed toward the nonpolicy aspects of electoral communication and behavior. This perspective requires us to consider instead the desirable leadership attributes in cultures like our own, and to study the ways in which these attributes are presented, contrasted, and emphasized. More specifically, the approach to elections as selection of a benevolent leader reminds us of a number of features of campaign communication that we have discussed in previous chapters.

First, this benevolent-leader approach asserts that a fair amount of the campaign communication of both candidates and journalists focuses on the nonprogrammatic personal characteristics of candidates for public office. This recognizes that a candidate represents not only past and future policy decisions, but also a personality and character to which other people respond. Communication regarding these personal characteristics, both verbal and nonverbal, is thought to be prevalent both before and during an election campaign. In fact, even communication involving policy alternatives may really be concerned with the creation of impressions about a candidate's personality; hence public policies become simply one of many vehicles through which such impressions may be created.

Second, this approach assumes that citizens are willing and able to form perceptions concerning the nonprogrammatic attributes and character traits of candidates. This is partly because information regarding these characteristics is so readily available (unlike information concerning prospective policy preferences) and partly because judging the character of another human being is something we do frequently and know something about. The perceptions that citizens form in this way may not be particularly rich or accurate—we often speak of a citizen's *image* or *impression* of a candidate—but they are thought to be part of the natural process of responding to human communication and choosing between prospective leaders.

Third, this approach argues that the evaluation of the character traits or personalities of candidates is an important determinant of the citizen's candidate choice and vote. In this view, voter images or impressions of the personality or character of candidates help voters decide for whom to vote; candidates capable of creating the most positive personal impression are more likely to achieve electoral success.

Finally, the benevolent-leader approach to elections argues that the meaning of the election is not to be found in any programmatic preferences (either past or future) indicated by the citizenry, but rather in the conferral of approval on an officeholder who begins his or her tenure with a measure of support and legitimacy. The victorious candidate is more likely to embody culturally desirable leadership traits and to have been the most successful at creating a reassuring or comforting personal impression than to represent any sort of aggregate preference or mandate for specific policy choices. In fact, in this view, an electoral victory grants to the benevolent leader considerable policy latitude within which to maneuver, experiment, and bargain. In other words, this perspective does not view elections as a process by which the citizenry controls or influences public policy, except in the most inadvertent or indirect way. It is, however, a process by which human societies select an attractive, comforting focus of attention possessing, initially, a measure of legitimacy and support.

There is considerable evidence in support of this benevolent-leader approach to election campaigns. First, we have seen that candidate communication contains frequent references to the nonprogrammatic personal attributes of candidates. At the presidential level, both campaign rhetoric in general and political spot ads in particular contain frequent explicit attempts to create favorable, personal, nonprogrammatic impressions. If we had also considered the more implicit, nonverbal types of candidate appeals—including, for example, the use of props, settings, and camera angles to create impressions—we might well have found that *the* single most prevalent type of presidential campaign appeal is an attempt to communicate an image of a benevolent leader.[33]

At the congressional level, incumbent members of the U.S. House also "present themselves" to their constituents in such a way as to leave favorable personal impressions with the constituency. Congressmen believe that their prospects for reelection depend more on how they are perceived as a person than on the public policy positions they have taken. Toward this end, legislators attempt "to convey their qualifications, their sense of identification and their sense of empathy" to their district.[34] This communication is seldom rich with policy discussions or proposals, although policy issues may be used as a vehicle for creating positive personal impressions.

Although it is clear that candidate communication emphasizes the attributes suggested by the benevolent-leader approach, the evidence is a good deal more mixed concerning the contribution of campaign news coverage to such a view of campaigns and elections. One gets the impression from reading journalistic accounts of campaigns that journalists are deeply involved in trying to discern what kind of person—in a psychological sense—they are covering and in trying to communicate this knowledge in a way that does not violate journalistic norms.[35] Careful analyses of daily news coverage, however, have come to differing conclusions about the extent to which information about the personal attributes of candidates finds its way into daily campaign coverage. We saw earlier that two studies of daily news coverage of the 1972 and 1976 presidential campaigns found that coverage of candidates' personal and leadership qualifications was extremely sparse in both years. Television network news coverage of candidate leadership/personal qualifications *totaled* from five to fifteen minutes for each candidate on each network for the entire fall campaign in 1972, constituting about 1 percent of the news time available during this period; and coverage of the personal and leadership characteristics of presidential candidates amounted to less than 12 percent of the 1976 campaign news coverage in television network news, daily metropolitan newspapers, and weekly opinion magazines.[36]

Other research, however, directly contradicts this conclusion. A study of newspaper coverage in the 1968, 1972, and 1976 presidential campaigns found that "the media discuss the qualifications of the candidates more amply than campaign events and issues," and more than one analyst has commented on the news media's tendency to make *implicit* comments about a candidate's personality and character by using stereotypes to portray the candidate's daily activities.[37] At this point, then, the contribution that journalistic accounts of election campaigns make to the selection of a benevolent leader is uncertain.

Despite the uncertainty regarding the nature of candidate coverage provided by campaign news coverage, there is considerable evidence that voters do evaluate candidates as people rather than (or in addition to) bundles of issue preferences. Citizen perceptions or images of candidates are more often personal than programmatic and consist more of stylistic impressions than of ideological ones.[38] The major exception to this finding involves incumbent presidents. Given the public's experience with the visible policy decisions made by incumbent presidents, citizen perceptions of incumbent presidents tend to be more political and programmatic than they are for other political candidates.[39] In general, however, people tend to form personal impressions of candidates in a way similar to how they respond to any human being who attempts to persuade them to do something.

Third, there is also clear evidence that these personal impressions of candidates show a strong relationship to electoral choices. We saw in the previous chapter that it is difficult to disentangle the effects of party identification, policy preferences, and candidate attributes on the vote. This is partly because it is difficult to devise a precise measure of each attitude that is not contaminated with one or more of the other attitudes (measures of personal attributes have been particularly prone to this problem) and partly because of the relationships among the attitudes that result from projection, selective perception, and rationalization. Research into the presidential voting behavior of the U.S. electorate since 1952, however, suggests that "perceptions of candidates' personalities have an enormous effect on the outcome of elections,"[40] with some evidence that, of the political attitudes most immediately related to presidential voting, perceptions of candidate attributes are increasingly the most important.[41] At the presidential level a number of character traits—such as strength, warmth, competence, and trustworthiness—are continuously at the center of both candidate rhetoric and citizen behavior; other personal traits, such as activity (vigor), religion, and geographical origins, appear and disappear in different contexts.[42] Similarly, at the congressional level, Richard Fenno has pointed out that constituents may well want things other than policy agreement—for example, assurances of access and trustworthiness—from their legislators.[43]

In sum, both the nature of campaign information and the public's reaction to that information suggest that the benevolent-leader approach is largely consistent with the available evidence. Unlike the first two approaches, however, this approach accords very little intended policymaking significance to election campaigns and electoral outcomes. In fact, if this is an accurate approach to the understanding of contemporary election campaigns, the normative consequences could be quite troubling:

> Even if . . . the electoral process casts up a paragon of benevolent leadership every time, we would still have to ask whether it is not a debasement of language to call this democracy. It has about it a flavor of citizen abdication, of giving up on instrumental benefits of government and settling for the symbolism of a father figure or a dignified elected monarch.
>
> In isolation, certainly, the selection of a benevolent leader is a weak sort

of democracy. "Rule by the people" must concern substance as well as style, and the connections between presidential personality and policy and performance, while significant, are not sufficient to dictate in detail what government does. *Only in conjunction with other processes* of democratic control does the selection of an appropriate presidential personality take on normative importance [emphasis added].[44]

THE ELECTIONS-AS-RITUAL APPROACH

The three approaches to election campaigns discussed so far differ in many significant ways regarding the meaning of electoral communication and electoral outcomes. All three, however, share a common assumption that elections are useful for or serve the interests of the general citizenry. A fourth approach to election campaigns does not share this assumption but argues instead that elections serve the interests of political elites by preserving social stability, keeping the citizenry misinformed, and channeling political participation into a routine, nonthreatening, and impotent form. This approach, here called the *ritualistic* approach, clearly looks at electoral behavior in a fundamentally different way.

The elections-as-ritual approach holds that elites shape public opinion through the communication of myths and cultural values such as "free enterprise, honesty, industry, bravery, tolerance, perseverance, and individualism."[45] These myths strike a responsive—but noncognitive—chord in the mass citizenry, and are capable of stimulating political controversy as individuals differ over which myth to apply to which circumstance. Communication of these myths tends to be dramatic and filled with imagery or symbols, and its imprecision permits multiple interpretations on the part of the citizenry. The myths themselves are selected from a rigid cultural consensus concerning the limits of acceptable debate and rhetoric, and they stimulate recognition and response from the deepest levels of our consciousness. Election campaigns, in this view, are a ritual in which mythical representations are transmitted to and reinforced among the populace: "Rituals use dramatic themes and actions to attract attention, simplify problems, emphasize particular principles, and structure the responses of participants."[46]

One way in which these myths are transmitted to the populace is through the electoral appeals made by candidates. Although many observers have criticized what they see as the emptiness of candidate rhetoric, this type of rhetoric may be seen as the essence of any political ritual. According to this view the symbolism, drama, ambiguity, and nonspecificity of candidate communication are what is typical of and meaningful about candidate appeals, since this rhetoric reveals what elections are *not* about and serves to *delimit* public understanding. Furthermore, the ritualists tend to be critical of researchers (usually policy-oriented ones) who criticize candidate communication and suggest ways in which elections could be reformed to increase the substance, rationality, or clarity of candidate appeals. These reformist sentiments, they say, miss the inevitability of the nature of political communication in any ritual, and contribute to the mythical view of the policymaking capabilities of elections by suggesting that they could be reformed.

To the ritualist, then, it is not the policy-oriented communication of candidates that is significant, or even the discussions of past performances or personal qualities. Rather, it is the articulation of certain culturally agreed-on values or world views. Furthermore, the ritualist considers the variations in candidate appeals that are typically studied to be epiphenomena. Instead, it is the similarity of the myths and symbols used by *all* candidates that is of most consequence.

This approach also does not consider election campaigns to be opportunities for public education or enlightenment. The populace may learn something about a candidate during a campaign, and may even reject what they perceive to be untrue (for example, George McGovern's 1972 guaranteed-minimum-income plan); but the learning that takes place will be noncognitive and shallow, and will depend on how familiar the mythical context of the stimulus is rather than on a cognitive understanding of the stimulus itself. In general, the ritualist sees far more consensus than conflict, and agreement than disagreement, in an election campaign, and feels that the net result is to reinforce rather than challenge consensually held values and attitudes: "most campaign speeches consist of the exchange of clichés among people who agree with each other. The talk, therefore, serves to dull the critical faculties rather than to arouse them."[47] To say that the citizenry learns something during an election campaign, according to the ritualists, is really to observe that the citizenry recognizes, recalls, and applies myth-themes and world views that it has encountered many times before.

Finally, elections, to the ritualist, do not represent opportunities for popular control over or popular influence on public policy. That is simply part of the mythology of elections. Instead, it is primarily elites who benefit from elections through the legitimation of their positions and the delimiting of popular influence. The significance of elections is to be found in their ability to "limit the possibilities for political change, broad interest representation, or effective political action . . . while organizing support for the government and reinforcing particular images of polity and society."[48] Nonelites benefit primarily only from the symbolic reassurance that elections provide:

In short, the standard view of elections as policy processes ignores the functions of campaign practices in the context of the election ritual. As a result, it is easy to overlook the possibility that the public opinion expressed in response to campaign issues has less to do with making policy than with reducing social tensions and reinforcing enduring images of the political order.[49]

This view of elections is not often encountered in contemporary U.S. society, and it is difficult to evaluate it with the empirical evidence at hand. Very little research has been done that sheds any light at all on the symbolic nature of candidate communication or the process by which the public recognizes and applies myth-themes during election campaigns. One provocative analysis of candidate communication, however, has identified four different mythical appeals that are commonly made by candidates.[50]

Macromyths are appeals that attempt to associate a candidate with myths about the origin and destiny of the nation. Many of these appeals refer to the founding; to the notion of the United States having some unique, divinely ordained destiny; to patriotic figures and events; and to consensually held political values. According to this view, Richard Nixon in 1972 attempted to tap a materialist mythology by emphasizing individual effort, work, self-reliance, competition, and the goodness of wealth and success; his opponent, George McGovern, emphasized a moralist myth consisting of Christian duty to our fellow human, equality and democracy, reform, and morality. A particularly good example of this sort of appeal was Ronald Reagan's use of potent imagery concerning the religious-ordained destiny of the United States in his acceptance speech at the 1980 Republican convention:

Can we doubt that only a Divine Providence placed this land, this island of freedom, here as a refuge for all those people in the world who yearn to breathe freely: Jews and Christians enduring persecution behind the Iron Curtain, the boat people of Southeast Asia, of Cuba and Haiti, the victims of drought and famine in Africa, the freedom fighters of Afghanistan and our own countrymen held in savage captivity.

I'll confess that I've been a little afraid to suggest what I'm going to suggest—I'm more afraid not to—that we begin our crusade joined together in a moment of silent prayer. . . . God bless America.[51]

Myths of *us and them* attempt to tap long-term identities, loyalties, and identifications. The most common of these in election campaigns is the use of partisan appeals, although many candidates also attempt to appeal to people's group identities. We saw in Chapter 2 that group appeals are a prevalent type of campaign appeal, although explicit partisan appeals are becoming decreasingly visible.

Primal myths typically involve our desires for success—such as for love, power, security, and popularity—and our fears of failure—such as worries about safety, financial ruin, and the loss of freedom. Candidates often attempt to convince the public that their election, or their opponent's defeat, will lead to personal gratification and satisfaction in some significant way. A typical tactic is for candidates to imply that their opponent's election will lead to economic collapse and/or international disgrace. As we saw in Chapter 2, a large proportion of candidate communication involves such vague goals as adequate medical care, peace through strength, elimination of waste, bureaucratic efficiency, and reform of a "disgraceful" tax system. Such a list of goals does seem to conform to the appeals here characterized as primal myths.

Finally, *hero myths* attempt to demonstrate that candidates possess the traits of a political hero. Although this type of appeal is similar to what we discussed previously in the benevolent-leader approach, the point here is that it is not just individual traits that are communicated, but more holistic images or *personas*. Thus Jimmy Carter's advertising recalled a "Waltons" image of self-reliance, an extended family, rugged individualism, and pastoral tranquillity that transcends individual personality traits; and the association of John Kennedy's administration with "Camelot" nicely demonstrates the tightness of the connection between a president and a mythical persona.

It is clear that a large proportion of candidate communication is consistent with the ritualist's focus on mythology and drama. The articulation of consensually held political goals, the attempt to transform candidates into political heroes, and the use of symbolic props and settings (such as the Statue of Liberty) are all consistent with the type of communication held to be important by this approach. As two analysts have concluded:

> . . . campaign flackdom has become remarkably sophisticated in the exploitation of myths. Many of the messages constructed are directed at people's emotions, tugging at deeply held myths about their country, political values, and prejudices. Flacks also create fantasy worlds for people, allowing potential voters to be transported into the drama presented.[52]

Although it is clear that much candidate communication is mythical in nature, what is much less clear is whether candidate communication and campaign news coverage are *completely* devoid of substantive information and whether the campaign truly has an insignificant educative effect on the citizenry. Candidates, after all, do reveal some fairly specific policy preferences, particularly in debate appearances; and public perceptions of the policy preferences of candidates are somewhat responsive to the clarity of campaign news coverage and candidate policy positions.

At present, the elections-as-ritual approach is useful primarily because it forces us to reconsider our commonly held assumptions about elections. Future research should illuminate the extent to which campaign communication emphasizes consensually held but empty symbols, takes place within a narrow range of programmatic disagreement, legitimizes the positions of political authorities, and defuses more violent political behavior. Until then it is difficult to assess empirically the central assertions of this approach.

Conclusion

Table 9–1 summarizes the characterization of campaign communication and voting behavior in each of the four approaches to elections discussed here. The empirical evidence regarding campaign communication and the public's response to that communication would seem to be more consistent with the retrospective-policy-satisfaction and selection-of-a-benevolent-leader approaches than with the other two. Candidate appeals and daily campaign news stories are filled with the type of information emphasized by these approaches, and citizen perceptions and candidate choices depend on this information flow. This means that elections may best be understood as processes by which the electorate reveals global feelings of policy satisfaction or dissatisfaction, indicates a preference for change or continuity of a general sort, and selects as a focus of attention political leaders who possess reassuring and comforting personalities.

In contrast, campaign communication and the behavior of the electorate are less consistent with the prospective-policy-choice perspective (and the dearth of evidence makes it difficult to tell how accurate the elections-as-ritual view is). Neither candidate appeals, campaign news coverage, nor citizen interest and capabilities convincingly support this approach. Consequently, it is difficult to see how electoral outcomes could possibly confer specific, future-oriented policy mandates on victorious candidates. The attractiveness of this approach, then, must be accounted for on other than empirical grounds. Perhaps because this approach to elections conforms the closest to the standard civic-education justification for elections, there is a special interest in protecting its status.

This does not mean that election campaigns and electoral outcomes have no policy significance. The fact that one set of officials rather than another is selected means that the outcome may well make a considerable difference. Throughout our nation's history there have been times in which the policy preferences of competing sets of candidates have differed significantly and the selection of one party or candidate over another had an important programmatic effect. Surely it mattered, after all, whether Taft or Bryan was selected in 1896, whether Hoover or Roosevelt won in 1932, whether Johnson or Goldwater was elected in 1964, and in 1980 whether Ronald Reagan and a host of Republican senators or Jimmy Carter and a group of Democratic senators were

TABLE 9–1   Campaign Communication and Perspectives on Elections

	Prospective Policy Choice	Retrospective Policy Satisfaction	Selection of Benevolent Leader	Elections-as-Ritual
The types of appeals made by candidates	Visible, clear, specific, contrasting indications of future policy proposals, preferences	Criticism of social conditions, policy decisions of incumbents; promises to do better; conflict over blame-placing, credit-taking	Presentation of self; personality traits, character, style, performance	Use of myths; vague, symbolic, dramatic appeals; importance of nonverbal cues, e.g. props and setting
The information provided by campaign news coverage	Transmission of policy preferences of candidates; attempt to highlight policy differences/disagreements	Interelection surveillance of policy decisions, social trends/conditions; intraelection coverage of debate over blame-placing and credit-taking	Inferences about the personality, character, style, and performance of candidates	Fairly passive transmission of myth-themes used by candidates; use of prevailing stereotypes, "portrayals" to guide and shape coverage

The perceptions formed by the citizenry during the campaign	Accurate perceptions of candidate policy preferences, particularly when campaign communication is advantageous; ideological consistency, constraint	Global evaluation of policy satisfaction; decision regarding whom to blame/credit for what; recognition of social conditions/problems	Images or impressions of the personality, stylistic traits of candidates	Recognition of familiar mythologies; noncognitive response to candidates; reinforcement of cultural consensus; reassurance
The attitudes leading to candidate choices	Policy proximity (comparative distance between voter and candidates, weighted by salience of issue), discounted by processes of projection, persuasion, rationalization	Reward incumbents if satisfied; punish incumbents if unsatisfied; perhaps greater inclination to punish than reward; some possibility of holding parties responsible	Candidate selected who is more reassuring; fits ideal image of candidate/office	Choice between competing mythologies; rejection of unfamiliar myth-themes
The consequences of electoral choices	"Mandates" empowering victors to vigorously pursue articulated policy preferences	Decision for general policy continuity or change depending on fate of incumbent and/or incumbent's party	Victor begins tenure with measure of legitimacy, support; able to exercise considerable policy discretion	Increased efficacy on part of participants; social stability; channeling of dissent into non-threatening mode; legitimacy of office-holders and institutions; perpetuation of status quo

elected. The argument here, however, has been that because of the nature of campaign communication, these policy consequences are often *inadvertent* rather than intended by the electorate, or are at most intended only insofar as the electorate reveals a general tolerance for change.

Whether or not the retrospective-policy-satisfaction and benevolent-leader approaches to elections provide a large enough role for the citizenry and a strong enough avenue for constraining public officials to advance self-government is a provocative and complex question. Whether any other type of campaign communication and electoral process in our cultural, economic, and political environment is *possible* is also a perplexing but worthwhile query. At this point, however, it appears that the campaign communication that characterizes the contemporary electoral process does more to entertain than enlighten, to reassure than challenge, and to disorient than empower the U.S. public. Although this campaign communication may be functional for all involved, meaningful public choice—and hence self-government—would seem to be less than it might be.

Notes

1. Philip E. Converse, "Information Flow and the Stability of Partisan Attitudes," in Angus Campbell, Philip E. Converse, Warren E. Miller, and Donald E. Stokes, eds., *Elections and the Political Order* (New York: Wiley 1966); Edward C. Dreyer, "Media Use and Electoral Choices: Some Political Consequences of Information Exposure," *Public Opinion Quarterly* 35 (Winter 1971–1972): 544–553; A. Cohen, "Attention to the Mass Media among Straight and Split Ticket Voters: A Research Note," *Human Communication Research* 2 (1975): 75–78; T. Macaluso, "Political Information, Party Identification and Voting Defection," *Public Opinion Quarterly* 41 (1977): 255–260; Cliff Zukin, "A Reconsideration of the Effects of Information on Partisan Stability," *Public Opinion Quarterly* 41 (1977): 244–254; and Richard A. Joslyn, "The Impact of Campaign Spot Advertising on Voting Defections," *Human Communication Research* 7, no. 4 (1981): 347–360.

2. Paul H. Weaver, "The New Journalism and the Old—Thoughts after Watergate," *The Public Interest* 35 (Spring 1974): 67–88; Michael J. Robinson, "Public Affairs Television and the Growth of Political Malaise: The Case of 'The Selling of the Pentagon,'" *American Political Science Review* 70 (June 1976): 409–432.

3. For a concise summary of this approach, see Robert Weissberg, *Public Opinion and Popular Government* (Englewood Cliffs, N.J.: Prentice-Hall, 1976), pp. 170–172.

4. John O. Field and Ronald E. Anderson, "Ideology in the Public's Conceptualization of the 1964 Presidential Election," *Public Opinion Quarterly* 33 (1969): 380; and John C. Pierce, "Party Identification and the Changing Role of Ideology in American Politics," *Midwest Journal of Political Science* 14 (1970): 33.

5. Philip E. Converse, Warren E. Miller, Jerrold G. Rusk, and Arthur C. Wolfe, "Continuity and Change in American Politics: Parties and Issues in the 1968 Election," *American Political Science Review* 63 (1969): 1097.

6. James A. Stimson, "Belief Systems: Constraint, Complexity, and the 1972 Election," *American Journal of Political Science* 19 (1975): 396.

7. Arthur H. Miller, Warren E. Miller, Alden S. Raine, and Thad A. Brown, "A Majority Party in Disarray: Policy Polarization in the 1972 Election," *American Political Science Review* 70 (1976): 754.

8. Norman H. Nie, Sidney Verba, and John R. Petrocik, *The Changing American Voter* (Cambridge, Mass.: Harvard University Press, 1976), p. 151, 163, 173, 192.

9. Gerald Pomper, "From Confusion to Clarity: Issues and American Voters, 1956–1968," *American Political Science Review* 66 (June 1972): 426.

10. Miller et al., "A Majority Party," p. 771.

11. Pomper, "From Confusion," p. 426.

12. Richard W. Boyd, "Popular Control of Public Policy: A Normal Vote Analysis of the 1968 Election," *American Political Science Review* 66 (June 1972): 429.

13. Benjamin I. Page, *Choices and Echoes in Presidential Elections* (Chicago: University of Chicago Press, 1978).

14. Richard A. Joslyn, "The Content of Political Spot Ads," *Journalism Quarterly* 57, no. 1 (Spring 1980): 92–98.

15. Barbara Hinckley, *Congressional Elections* (Washington, D.C.: Congressional Quarterly Press, 1981), Chap. 2; and Gary Jacobson, *The Politics of Congressional Elections* (Boston: Little, Brown, 1983), Chap. 5.

16. For an insightful discussion of this approach, see Morris P. Fiorina, *Retrospective Voting in American National Elections* (New Haven: Yale University Press, 1981).

17. Page, *Choices and Echoes*, p. 194.

18. V. O. Key, Jr., *The Responsible Electorate* (New York: Vintage Books, 1966), p. 9.

19. Page, *Choices and Echoes*, p. 194.

20. Key, *The Responsible Electorate*, p. 52.

21. Page, *Choices and Echoes*, p. 221.

22. Some proponents of this approach argue that "negative voting"—that is, voting to punish the incumbent—is more prevalent than voting to reward an incumbent. Policy satisfaction is more likely to lead to complacency and failure to vote, whereas policy dissatisfaction is more likely to lead to the motivation necessary for paying the costs associated with voting. For example, see Sam Kernell, "Presidential Popularity and Negative Voting: An Alternative Explanation of the Mid-Term Congressional Decline of the President's Party," *American Political Science Review* 71 (March 1977): 44–66.

23. Page, *Choices and Echoes*, p. 202.

24. Ibid., p. 220.

25. Ibid., p. 222.

26. Key, *The Responsible Electorate*, p. 61.

27. Page, *Choices and Echoes*, pp. 223–227; and Edward Tufte, *Political Control of the Economy* (Princeton, N.J.: Princeton University Press, 1978), pp. 127–134. See also the evidence cited in Fiorina, *Retrospective Voting.*

28. Tufte, *Political Control*, pp. 120–123.

29. Ibid., p. 123.

30. Ibid., p. 106–119.

31. Ibid., p. 115.

32. Page, *Choices and Echoes*, p. 229.

33. Ibid., Chap. 8; Joslyn, "The Impact."

34. Richard Fenno, *Home Style: House Members in Their Districts* (Boston: Little, Brown, 1978), p. 134. See also David Mayhew, *Congress: The Electoral Connection* (New Haven: Yale University Press, 1974), for a discussion of how members of Congress, ever mindful of their reelection prospects, communicate with their constituents.

35. Timothy Crouse, *The Boys on the Bus* (New York: Ballantine, 1972); and Elizabeth Drew, *Portrait of an Election* (New York: Simon and Schuster, 1981).

36. Thomas E. Patterson and Robert D. McClure, *The Unseeing Eye* (New York: G. P. Putnam's Sons, 1976), Chap. 1; and Thomas E. Patterson, *The Mass Media Election* (New York: Praeger, 1980) Chap. 3.

37. Doris Graber, *Mass Media and American Politics* (Washington, D.C.: Congressional Quarterly Press, 1980), pp. 169–177 (the quote is on p. 169); Edwin Diamond, *Good News, Bad News* (Cambridge, Mass.: MIT Press, 1978), Chap. 2; and Michael Robinson, "A Statesman Is a Dead Politician: Candidate Images on Network News," in Elie Abel, ed., *What's News* (San Francisco: Institute for Contemporary Studies, 1981).

38. Graber, *Mass Media*, pp. 183–185; Patterson, *Mass Media Election*, Chap. 12; and Dan Nimmo and Robert L. Savage, *Candidates and Their Images* (Pacific Palisades, Calif.: Goodyear, 1976), Chap. 3.

39. Patterson, *Mass Media Election*, pp. 134–135.

40. Page, *Choices and Echoes*, p. 261.

41. For evidence on this point, see Donald E. Stokes, "Some Dynamic Elements of Contests for the Presidency," *American Political Science Review* 60 (March 1966): 19–28; and Mark A. Schulman and Gerald M. Pomper, "Variability in Electoral Behavior," *American Journal of Political Science* 19 (February 1975): 1–18. Much of this literature is summarized in Herbert Asher, *Presidential Elections and American Politics* (Homewood, Ill.: Dorsey, 1980), Chaps. 5, 8; and in Nimmo and Savage, *Candidates*, Chap. 8.

42. Page, *Choices and Echoes*, Chap. 8; Graber, *Mass Media*, pp. 169–171; Nimmo and Savage, *Candidates*, Chap. 3, 8. V. O. Key, who was so concerned with demonstrating the policy-oriented nature of electoral behavior, admitted that the 1960 presidential campaign consisted of "fluffy and foggy political stimuli" from two candidates who were in "agreement on many basic propositions," and that the outcome turned largely on nonprogrammatic impressions. See Key, *The Responsible Electorate*, p. 113.

43. Fenno, *Home Style*.

44. Page, *Choices and Echoes*, p. 265.

45. W. Lance Bennett, "Culture, Communication and Political Control," Paper presented to the American Political Science Association, Washington, D.C., 1980, p. 3.

46. W. Lance Bennett, *Public Opinion in American Politics* (New York: Harcourt, Brace, Jovanovich, 1980), p. 386.

47. Murray Edelman, *The Symbolic Uses of Politics* (Urbana: University of Illinois press, 1964), pp. 17–18.

48. Bennett, "Culture," pp. 19–20.

49. Bennett, *Public Opinion*, p. 390.

50. The subsequent discussion relies heavily on Dan Nimmo and James E. Combs, *Subliminal Politics* (Englewood Cliffs, N.J.: Prentice-Hall, 1980), pp. 107–116.

51. *1980 Congressional Quarterly Almanac*, p. 39-B.

52. Nimmo and Combs, *Subliminal Politics*, p. 116.

Bibliography

Abramowitz, Alan I. "The Impact of a Presidential Debate on Voter Rationality." *American Journal of Political Science* 22, 3 (August 1978): 680–690.
———. "A Comparison of Voting for U.S. Senator and Representative in 1978." *American Political Science Review* 74, 3 (September 1980): 633–640.
Abramson, Paul R., and Aldrich, John H. "The Decline of Electoral Participation in America." *American Political Science Review* 76, 3 (September 1982): 502–521.
Adams, William C., and Smith, Dennis J. "Effects of Telephone Canvassing on Turnout and Preferences: A Field Experiment." *Public Opinion Quarterly* 44, 3 (Fall 1980): 389–395.
Agranoff, Robert. *The New Style in Election Campaigns.* Boston: Holbrook Press, 1976.
Aldrich, John H. *Before the Convention.* Chicago: University of Chicago Press, 1980.
———. "A Dynamic Model of Presidential Nomination Campaigns." *American Political Science Review* 74, 3 (September 1980): 651–669.
Alexander, Herbert E. *Financing Politics.* Washington, D.C.: Congressional Quarterly Press, 1976.
———. *Financing Politics,* 2nd ed. Washington, D.C.: Congressional Quarterly Press, 1980.
Asher, Herbert. *Presidential Elections and American Politics.* Homewood, Ill.: Dorsey, 1980.
Atkin, Charles, and Heald, Garry. "Effects of Political Advertising." *Public Opinion Quarterly* 40, 2 (Summer 1976): 216–228.
Atkin, Charles; Bowen, Lawrence; Nayman, Oguz B.; and Sheinkopf, Kenneth G. "Quality versus Quantity in Televised Political Ads." *Public Opinion Quarterly* 37 (Summer 1973): 209–224.
Barber, James David, ed. *Race for the Presidency: The Media and the Nominating Process.* Englewood Cliffs, N.J.: Prentice-Hall, 1978.
Becker, Jules, and Fuchs, Douglas A. "How Two Major California Dailies Covered Reagan vs. Brown." *Journalism Quarterly* 44 (Winter 1967): 645–653.
Becker, Lee B., and McCombs, Maxwell E. "The Role of the Press in Determining Voter Reactions to Presidential Primaries." *Human Communication Research* 4, 4 (Summer 1978): 301–307.
Bennett, W. Lance. "Culture, Communication and Political Control." Annual meeting of the American Political Science Association, 1980.
———. *Public Opinion in American Politics.* New York: Harcourt, Brace, Jovanovich, 1980.
Berelson, Bernard; Lazarsfeld, Paul; and McPhee, William. *Voting.* Chicago: University of Chicago Press, 1954.

Bishop, George F.; Meadow, Robert G.; and Jackson-Beeck, Marilyn, eds. *The Presidential Debates*. New York: Praeger, 1980.

Bishop, Robert L., and Brown, Robert L. "Michigan Newspaper Bias in the 1966 Campaign." *Journalism Quarterly* 45 (Summer 1968): 337–338, 375.

Black, Jerome H. "The Multicandidate Calculus of Voting: Application to Canadian Federal Elections." *American Journal of Political Science* 22, 3 (August 1978): 609–638.

Blume, Norman, and Lyons, Schley. "The Monopoly Newspaper in a Local Newspaper Election: The Toledo Blade." *Journalism Quarterly* 45 (Summer 1968): 286–292.

Booth, Alan. "Recall of News Items." *Public Opinion Quarterly* 34 (Winter 1970–1971): 604–610.

Boyd, Richard W. "Popular Control of Public Policy: A Normal Vote Analysis of the 1968 Election." *American Political Science Review* 66, 2 (June 1972): 429–449.

Broder, David S. "Political Reporters in Presidential Politics." In James J. Lengle and Byron E. Shafer, eds., *Presidential Politics*. New York: St. Martin's, 1980.

Cain, Bruce E. "Strategic Voting in Britain." *American Journal of Political Science* 22, 3 (August 1978): 639–655.

Campbell, Angus; Converse, Philip E.; Miller, Warren E.; and Stokes, Donald E. *The American Voter*. New York: Wiley, 1960.

Clor, Harry M., ed. *Mass Media and American Democracy*. Chicago: Rand McNally, 1974.

Cohen, A. "Attention to the Mass Media among Straight and Split Ticket Voters: A Research Note." *Human Communication Research* 2 (1975): 75–78.

Congressional Quarterly Almanac. "Political Consultants: Mixed Results in 1970 Elections." Washington, D.C.: Congressional Quarterly Press, 1970, p. 1098.

Congressional Quarterly Weekly Report. "Campaign Management Grows into National Industry." Washington, D.C.: Congressional Quarterly Press, 1968, pp. 707–714.

———. "Campaign Consultants: Pushing Sincerity in 1974." Washington, D.C.: Congressional Quarterly Press, 1974, pp. 1105–1108.

Converse, Philip E. "Information Flow and the Stability of Partisan Attitudes." In Angus Campbell, Philip E. Converse, Warren E. Miller, and Donald E. Stokes, eds., *Elections and the Political Order*. New York: Wiley, 1966.

———. "Public Opinion and Voting Behavior." In Fred I. Greenstein and Nelson W. Polsby, eds., *Handbook of Political Science; Nongovernmental Politics*, Vol. 4. Reading, Mass.: Addison-Wesley, 1975.

Converse, Philip E.; Miller, Warren E.; Rusk, Jerrold G.; and Wolfe, Arthur C. "Continuity and Change in American Politics: Parties and Issues in the 1968 Election." *American Political Science Review* 63, 4 (December 1969): 1083–1105.

Crotty, William J., and Jacobson, Gary C. *American Parties in Decline*. Boston: Little, Brown, 1980.

Crouse, Timothy. *The Boys on the Bus*. New York: Ballantine Books, 1974.

Diamond, Edwin. *Good News, Bad News*. Cambridge, Mass.: MIT Press, 1978.

Dollar Politics. Washington, D.C.: Congressional Quarterly Press, 1982.

Drew, Elizabeth. *Portrait of an Election*. New York: Simon and Schuster, 1981.

Dreyer, Edward C. "Media Use and Electoral Choices: Some Political Consequences of Information Exposure." *Public Opinion Quarterly* 35, 4 (Winter 1971–1972): 544–553.

Dunn, Delmer D. *Financing Presidential Campaigns.* Washington, D.C.: Brookings Institution, 1972.

Edelman, Murray. *The Symbolic Uses of Politics.* Urbana: University of Illinois Press, 1964.

Ellsworth, John W. "Rationality and Campaigning: A Content Analysis of the 1960 Presidential Campaign Debates." *Western Political Quarterly* 18 (December 1965): 794–802.

Epstein, Edwin J. *News From Nowhere.* New York: Random House, 1973.

Epstein, Laurily K., and Strom, Gerald. "Election Night Projections and West Coast Turnout." *American Politics Quarterly* 9, 4 (October 1981): 479–491.

Erbring, Lutz. "Media Monitoring and Public Opinion Change in 1980." Annual meeting of the American Political Science Association, 1981.

Erbring, Lutz; Goldenberg, Edie N.; and Miller, Arthur H. "Front-Page News and Real-World Cues: A New Look at Agenda-Setting by the Media." *American Journal of Political Science* 24, 1 (February 1980): 16–49.

Erikson, Robert S. "The Influence of Newspaper Endorsements in Presidential Elections: The Case of 1964." *American Journal of Political Science* 20, 2 (May 1976): 207–233.

Erikson, Robert S.; Luttbeg, Norman R.; and Tedin, Kent L. *American Public Opinion.* New York: Wiley, 1980.

Evans, Susan H., and Clarke, Peter. "Press Coverage and Competition for House Seats: Another Incumbent Edge." Annual meeting of the American Political Science Association, 1981.

Eyal, Chaim H.; Winter, J. P.; and DeGeorge, W. F. "The Concept of Time Frame in Agenda-Setting." In G. Cleveland Wilhoit and Maxwell McCombs, eds., *Mass Communication Review Yearbook,* Vol. II. Beverly Hills, Calif.: Sage Publications, 1981.

"Face Off." *Public Opinion* 3, 6 (December–January 1981): 2–12, 63–64.

Fenno, Richard. *Home Style: House Members in Their Districts.* Boston: Little, Brown, 1978.

Field, John O., and Anderson, Ronald E. "Ideology in the Public's Conceptualization of the 1964 Presidential Election." *Public Opinion Quarterly* 33, 3 (Fall 1969: 380–398.

Fiorina, Morris P. *Retrospective Voting in American National Elections.* New Haven: Yale University Press, 1981.

Flanigan, William H., and Zingale, Nancy H. *Political Behavior of the American Electorate.* Boston: Allyn and Bacon, 1979.

Foley, John; Britton, Dennis A.; and Everett, Eugene B., Jr., eds. *Nominating a President: The Process and the Press.* New York: Praeger, 1980.

Frank, Robert Shelby. *Message Dimensions of Television News.* Lexington, Mass.: Lexington Books, 1973.

Fuchs, Douglas A. "Election-Day Radio-TV and Western Voting." *Public Opinion Quarterly* 30 (Summer 1966): 226–236.

Gans, Herbert. *Deciding What's News.* New York: Pantheon, 1979.

Ginsberg, Benjamin. *The Consequences of Consent: Elections, Citizen Control and Popular Acquiescence.* Reading, Mass.: Addison-Wesley, 1982.

Glaser, William A. "Television and Voting Turnout." *Public Opinion Quarterly* 29 (Spring 1965): 71–86.

Goldenberg, Edie N., and Traugott, Michael W. "Campaign Effects on Voting Behavior in the 1978 Congressional Elections." Annual meeting of the American Political Science Association, 1979.

Graber, Doris. *Mass Media and American Politics.* Washington, D.C.: Congressional Quarterly Press, 1980.

Greenfield, Jeff. *The Real Campaign.* New York: Summit Books, 1982.

Hadley, Arthur. *The Invisible Primary.* Englewood Cliffs, N.J.: Prentice-Hall, 1976.

Hinckley, Barbara. "The American Voter in Congressional Elections." *American Political Science Review* 74, 3 (September 1980): 641–650.

——. *Congressional Elections.* Washington, D.C.: Congressional Quarterly Press, 1981.

Hofstetter, Richard. *Bias in the News.* Columbus: Ohio State University Press, 1976.

Hooper, Michael. "Party and Newspaper Endorsement as Predictors of Voter Choice." *Journalism Quarterly* 46 (Summer 1969): 302–305.

Hyman, Herbert H. and Sheatsley, Paul B. "Some Reasons Why Information Campaigns Fail." *Public Opinion Quarterly* 11 (Fall 1947): 413–423.

Jacobson, Gary. "The Effects of Campaign Spending in Congressional Elections." *American Political Science Review* 72 (June 1978): 469–491.

——. *Money in Congressional Elections.* New Haven: Yale University Press, 1980.

——. *The Politics of Congressional Elections.* Boston: Little, Brown, 1983.

Johannes, John R., and McAdams, John C. "The Congressional Incumbency Effect: Is It Casework, Policy Compatibility, or Something Else? An Examination of the 1978 Election." *American Journal of Political Science* 25, 3 (August 1981): 512–542.

Joslyn, Richard. "The Content of Political Spot Ads." *Journalism Quarterly* 57, 1 (Spring 1980): 92–98.

——. "Manifestations of Elazar's Political Subcultures: State Public Opinion and the Content of Political Campaign Advertising." *Publius* 10, 2 (Spring 1980): 37–58.

——. "The Impact of Campaign Spot Advertising on Voting Defections." *Human Communication Research* 7, 4 (1981): 347–360.

Katz, Elihu, and Lazarsfeld, Paul F. *Personal Influence.* New York: Free Press, 1955.

Keeter, Scott, and Zukin, Cliff. "The 1980 Presidential Election: Tracking Citizens' Opinions and Preference." Annual meeting of the Midwest Political Science Association, 1981.

Kernell, Sam. "Presidential Popularity and Negative Voting: An Alternative Explanation of the Mid-Term Congressional Decline of the President's Party." *American Political Science Review* 71 (March 1977): 44–66.

Key, V. O., Jr. *The Responsible Electorate.* New York: Vintage Books, 1966.

Klapper, Joseph T. *The Effects of Mass Communications.* New York: Free Press, 1960.

Kraus, Sidney, ed. *The Great Debates.* Gloucester, Mass.: Peter Smith, 1968.

——. *The Great Debates, Ford-Carter, 1976.* Bloomington: Indiana University Press, 1979.

Lang, Kurt, and Lang, Gladys Engel. *Politics and Television*. Chicago: Quadrangle Books, 1968.

Lazarsfeld, Paul; Berelson, Bernard; and Gaudet, Hazel. *The People's Choice*. New York: Columbia University Press, 1948.

Lemann, Nicholas. "Barney Frank's Mother and 500 Postmen." *Harper's* 266 (April 1983): 31–37.

Lower, Elmer W. "Is Television Undermining Our Elections?" *TV Guide* January 17, 1981.

Macaluso, Theodore F. "Political Information, Party Identification and Voting Defection." *Public Opinion Quarterly* 41, 2 (Summer 1977): 255–260.

Mann, Thomas E., and Wolfinger, Raymond E. "Candidates and Parties in Congressional Elections." *American Political Science Review* 74, 3 (September 1980): 617–632.

Mannheim, Jarol B. *The Politics Within*. New York: Longmans, 1982.

Markus, Gregory B. "Political Attitudes During an Election Year: A Report on the 1980 N.E.S. Panel Study." *American Political Science Review* 76, 3 (September 1982): 538–560.

Markus, Gregory B., and Converse, Philip E. "A Dynamic Simultaneous Equation Model of Electoral Choice." *American Political Science Review* 73, 4 (December 1979): 1055–1070.

May, Ernest R., and Fraser, Janet, eds. *Campaign '72: The Managers Speak*. Cambridge, Mass.: Harvard University Press, 1973.

Mayhew, David. *Congress: The Electoral Connection*. New Haven: Yale University Press, 1974.

McCombs, Maxwell E., and Shaw, Donald L. "The Agenda-Setting Function of Mass Media." *Public Opinion Quarterly* 36 (Summer 1972): 176–187.

McGinniss, Joe. *The Selling of the President, 1968*. New York: Trident Press, 1969.

McLeod, Jack M., and Becker, Lee B. "The Uses and Gratifications Approach." In Dan D. Nimmo and Keith R. Sanders, eds., *Handbook of Political Communication*. Beverly Hills, Calif.: Sage Publications, 1981.

McLeod, Jack M.; Becker, Lee B.; and Byrnes, James E. "Another Look at the Agenda-Setting Function of the Press." *Communication Research* 1 (April 1974): 134–165.

Mendelsohn, Harold. "Election-Day Broadcasts and Terminal Voting Decisions." *Public Opinion Quarterly* 30 (Summer 1966): 212–225.

Miller, Arthur H., and Mackuen, Michael. "Learning about the Candidates: The 1976 Presidential Debates." *Public Opinion Quarterly* 43, 3 (Fall 1979): 326–346.

Miller, Arthur H., and Miller, Warren E. "Ideology in the 1972 Election: Myth or Reality." *American Political Science Review* 70 (September 1976): 832–849.

Miller, Arthur H.; Miller, Warren E.; Raine, Alden S.; and Brown, Thad A. "A Majority Party in Disarray: Policy Polarization in the 1972 Election." *American Political Science Review* 70, 3 (September 1976): 753–778.

Miller, Arthur H., and Wattenberg, Martin P. "Policy and Performance Voting in the 1980 Election." Annual meeting of the American Political Science Association, 1981.

Miller, Roy E., and Richey, William M. "The Effects of a Campaign Brochure 'Drop' in a County-Level Race for State's Attorney." Annual meeting of the International Communication Association, 1980.

Miller, Warren E., and Shanks, J. Merrill. "Policy Directions and Presidential Leadership: Alternative Interpretations of the 1980 Presidential Election."

Mueller, John E. "Choosing among 103 Candidates." *Public Opinion Quarterly* 34 (Fall 1970): 395–402.

Mulder, Ronald. "The Effects of Televised Political Ads in the 1975 Chicago Mayoral Election." *Journalism Quarterly* 56 (Summer 1979): 336–340.

Mullen, James J. "How Candidates for the Senate Use Newspaper Advertising." *Journalism Quarterly* 40 (Autumn 1963): 532–538.

———. "Newspaper Advertising in the Kennedy-Nixon Campaign." *Journalism Quarterly* 4 (Winter 1963): 3–11.

———. "Newspaper Advertising in the Johnson-Goldwater Campaign." *Journalism Quarterly* 45 (Summer 1968): 219–225.

Neuman, W. Russell. "Patterns of Recall among Television News Viewers." *Public Opinion Quarterly* 40 (Spring 1976): 115–123.

Nie, Norman H.; Verba, Sidney; and Petrocik, John R. *The Changing American Voter.* Cambridge, Mass.: Harvard University Press, 1976.

Niemi, Richard G., and Riker, William H. "The Choice of Voting Systems." *Scientific American* 234 (June 1976): 21–27.

Nimmo, Dan, and Combs, James E. *Subliminal Politics.* Englewood Cliffs, N.J.: Prentice-Hall, 1980.

———. *Mediated Political Realities.* New York: Longmans, 1983.

Nimmo, Dan, and Savage, Robert L. *Candidates and Their Images.* Pacific Palisades, Calif.: Goodyear, 1976.

O'Keefe, Garrett J., and Atwood, L. Erwin. "Communication and Election Campaigns." In Dan D. Nimmo and Keith R. Sanders, eds., *Handbook of Political Communication.* Beverly Hills, Calif.: Sage Publications, 1981.

Page, Benjamin I. *Choices and Echoes in Presidential Elections.* Chicago: University of Chicago Press, 1978.

Page, Benjamin I., and Jones, Calvin C. "Reciprocal Effects of Policy Preferences, Party Loyalties and the Vote." *American Political Science Review* 73, 4 (December 1979): 1071–1089.

Paletz, David L., and Entman, Robert M. *Media, Power, Politics.* New York: Free Press, 1981.

Patterson, Thomas E. "Press Coverage and Candidate Success in Presidential Primaries: The 1976 Democratic Race." Annual meeting of the American Political Science Association, 1977.

———. *The Mass Media Election.* New York: Praeger, 1980.

Patterson, Thomas E., and McClure, Robert D. *Political Advertising: Voter Reaction to Televised Political Commercials.* Princeton, N.J.: Citizen's Research Foundation, 1973.

———. "Political Advertising on Television: Spot Commercials in the 1972 Presidential Election." *Maxwell Review* 9, 2 (Spring 1973): 57–69.

———. "Political Advertising: Voter Reaction." Annual meeting of the American Association for Public Opinion Research, 1973.

———. *The Unseeing Eye.* New York: G. P. Putnam's Sons, 1976.

Pierce, John C. "Party Identification and the Changing Role of Ideology in American Politics." *Midwest Journal of Political Science* 14, 1 (February 1970): 25–42.

Pomper, Gerald. "From Confusion to Clarity: Issues and American Voters, 1956–1968." *American Political Science Review* 66, 2 (June 1972): 415–428.

Popkin, Samuel; Gorman, John W.; Phillips, Charles; and Smith, Jeffrey A. "Comment: What Have You Done for Me Lately? Toward an Investment Theory of Voting." *American Political Science Review* 70, 3 (September 1976): 779–805.

Repass, David E. "Comment: Political Methodologies in Disarray; Some Alternative Interpretations of the 1972 Election." *American Political Science Review* 70, 3 (September 1976): 814–831.

Robinson, John P. "Perceived Media Bias and the 1968 Vote: Can the Media Affect Behavior After All?" *Journalism Quarterly* 49 (Summer 1972): 239–246.

———. "The Press as King Maker: What Surveys from Last Five Campaigns Show." *Journalism Quarterly* 51 (Winter 1974): 587–594.

Robinson, Michael J. "TV's Newest Program: The Presidential Nominations Game." *Public Opinion* 1, 2 (May–June 1978): 41–46.

———. "A Statesman Is a Dead Politician: Candidate Images on Network News." In Elie Abel, ed., *What's News.* San Francisco: Institute for Contemporary Studies, 1981.

Robinson, Michael J., and Zukin, Clifford. "Television and the Wallace Vote." *Journal of Communication* 26 (Spring 1976): 79–83.

Roll, Charles W., and Cantril, Albert H. *Polls: Their Use and Misuse in Politics.* Cabin John, Md.: Seven Locks Press, 1980.

Roshco, Bernard. *Newsmaking.* Chicago: University of Chicago Press, 1975.

Sabato, Larry J. *The Rise of Political Consultants.* New York: Basic Books, 1981.

Schram, Martin. *Running for President 1976: The Carter Campaign.* New York: Stein and Day, 1977.

Schramm, Wilbur, and Carter, Richard F. "Effectiveness of a Political Telethon." *Public Opinion Quarterly* 23 (Spring 1959): 121–127.

Schudson, Michael. *Discovering the News: A Social History of American Newspapers.* New York: Basic Books, 1978.

Schulman, Mark A., and Pomper, Gerald M. "Variability in Electoral Behavior." *American Journal of Political Science* 19 (February 1975): 1–18.

Sears, David O., and Freedman, Jonathan L. "Selective Exposure to Information: A Critical Review." *Public Opinion Quarterly* 31 (Summer 1967): 194–213.

Shaffer, Stephen D. "Multivariate Explanation of Decreasing Turnout in Presidential Elections, 1960–1976." *American Journal of Political Science* 25, 1 (February 1981): 68–95.

Shanks, J. Merrill, and Palmquist, Bradley. "Changing Determinants of Candidate Preferences: Design Issues in Studying Electoral Behavior before and after the Major Party Conventions." Annual meeting of the American Political Science Association, 1982.

Shaw, Donald L., and McCombs, Maxwell E. *The Emergence of American Political Issues: The Agenda-Setting Function of the Press* (St. Paul: West, 1977).

Sherrod, Drury R. "Selective Perception of Political Candidates." *Public Opinion Quarterly* 35 (Winter 1971–1972): 554–562.

Simon, Herbert A., and Stern, Frederick. "The Effect of Television upon Voting Behavior in the 1952 Presidential Election." *American Political Science Review* 49, 2 (June 1955): 470–477.

Smith, Robert R. "Mythic Elements in Television News." *Journal of Communication* 29, 1 (Winter 1979): 75–82.

Spero, Robert. *The Duping of the American Voter: Dishonesty and Deception in Presidential Television Advertising.* New York: Lippincott/Crowell, 1980.

Stevenson, Robert L.; Eisinger, Richard A.; Feinberg, Barry M.; and Kotok, Alan B. "Untwisting *The News Twisters*: A Replication of Efron's Study." *Journalism Quarterly* 50, 2 (Summer 1973): 211–219.

Stimson, James A. "Belief Systems: Constraint, Complexity, and the 1972 Election." *American Journal of Political Science* 19, 3 (August 1975): 393–417.

Stokes, Donald E. "Some Dynamic Elements of Contests for the Presidency." *American Political Science Review* 60 (March 1966): 19–28.

Swerdlow, Joel. "The Decline of the Boys on the Bus." *Washington Journalism Review* (January–February 1981): 15–19.

Tuchman, Sam, and Coffin, Thomas E. "The Influence of Election Night Television Broadcasts in a Close Election." *Public Opinion Quarterly* 35 (Fall 1971): 305–326.

Tufte, Edward. *Political Control of the Economy.* Princeton, N.J.: Princeton University Press, 1978.

Weaver, David H.; Graber, Doris A.; McCombs, Maxwell E.; and Eyal, Chaim H. *Media Agenda-Setting in a Presidential Election.* New York: Praeger, 1981.

Weaver, Paul H. "The New Journalism and the Old: Thoughts after Watergate." *The Public Interest* 35 (Spring 1974): 67–88.

———. "Captives of Melodrama." *The New York Times Magazine*, August 29, 1976, 6, 48, 50–51, 54, 56–57.

Weissberg, Robert. *Public Opinion and Popular Government.* Englewood Cliffs, N.J.: Prentice-Hall, 1976.

Wheeler, Michael. *Lies, Damn Lies, and Statistics.* New York: Norton, 1976.

White, Theodore. *America in Search of Itself.* New York: Harper and Row, 1982.

Winter, James P. "Media-Public Agenda-Setting for Five Issues, 1948–1976." Annual meeting of the Midwest Political Science Association, 1981.

Wolfinger, Raymond, and Linguiti, Peter. "Tuning In and Tuning Out." *Public Opinion* 4, 1 (February–March 1981): 56–60.

Wolfinger, Raymond, and Rosenstone, Steven J. *Who Votes.* New Haven: Yale University Press, 1980.

Zukin, Cliff. "A Reconsideration of the Effects of Information on Partisan Stability." *Public Opinion Quarterly* 41, 2 (Summer 1977): 244–254.

Index